# MANUAL FOR THE PREPARATION OF INDUSTRIAL FEASIBILITY STUDIES

*Newly revised and expanded edition*

W. Behrens     P. M. Hawranek

UNITED NATIONS INDUSTRIAL DEVELOPMENT ORGANIZATION
Vienna, 1991

ID/372

UNIDO PUBLICATION
Sales No. E.91.III.E.18
ISBN 92-1-106269-1

# Foreword

The *Manual for the Preparation of Industrial Feasibility Studies* was first published by UNIDO in 1978. It was designed to provide developing countries with a tool for improving the quality of investment proposals, and to contribute to the standardization of industrial feasibility studies, which had often been found to be both incomplete and ill-prepared. UNIDO efforts to achieve those objectives have since met with a positive response in many countries, developing and developed alike. The approach promoted by UNIDO for the preparation of feasibility studies has been adopted by government ministries, banks, investment promotion agencies, universities and other institutions of higher learning, as well as by consulting firms and investors. Many institutions and firms have also cooperated with UNIDO in improving their investment decision-making capability through the application or promulgation of advanced project preparation and appraisal methodologies.

Over the past decade, UNIDO has observed a remarkable qualitative improvement in feasibility studies, an increasing number of which have led to appreciable investment in developing countries. At the same time, however, it noted that various adverse factors impeded industrial development in most developing countries. In an endeavour to overcome those constraints, the General Conference of UNIDO identified priority areas for UNIDO action in the current decade, the main emphasis being on human resource development, development and transfer of technology, industrial rehabilitation, small- and medium-scale industries and environment and energy.

This new and extensively revised edition of the *Manual* focuses primarily on a strategic approach to investment. It devotes particular attention to environmental impact assessment, technology transfer, marketing and human resources, as well as the mobilization of funds. The *Manual* should be used in conjunction with other UNIDO publications on economic analysis and with the UNIDO Computer Model for Feasibility Analysis and Reporting (COMFAR). I hope that the second edition will once again attract the interest of all those concerned with improving the industrial development process in developing countries and prove to be of continued practical value to an ever broader range of users.

D. L. Siazon, Jr.
*Director-General*

# Acknowledgement

Special acknowledgement is due to the Federal Ministry of Economic Cooperation of Germany for its generous financial support, without which this second edition would not have become reality.

# Preface

The publication of this revised and expanded second edition of the *Manual for the Preparation of Industrial Feasibility Studies* is the result of the long and dedicated efforts of all those involved in this production. The revision of the text required a careful analysis of voluminous correspondence and comments from readers before a decision could be made on its scope and contents. The complexities of drafting the final version were increased by the inclusion of new subject-matter based on contributions by selected experts.

In its conception, organization and scope, this *Manual* is due to the close collaboration of its principal authors, Werner Behrens and Peter M. Hawranek, of the UNIDO Division of Industrial Operations Support, who drafted the bulk of the text and shared overall responsibility for its final preparation. In carrying out this task, they received valuable assistance and advice from numerous UNIDO consultants and staff. The authors are particularly grateful to UNIDO consultants for the contributions described below.

The introduction of the concept of strategic orientation was proposed by H. R. Arm, who drafted the analysis of this concept presented in part one, section B, and who also made a valuable contribution to the contents and restructuring of part two, chapter III, which covers market analysis and the marketing concept. R. Irvine revised the annexes covering demand forecasting techniques, sampling principles and field surveys, and helped with the revision of chapter III. The analysis of maintenance and replacement requirements, as well as various revisions in the treatment of organization, personnel training and implementation planning, were drafted by B. Knauer, who also checked the whole manuscript from the point of view of the practical application of the *Manual* by engineers. Rana K. D. B. Singh, who had already contributed to the first edition, drafted the revision of chapter VI, which deals with engineering and technology. Increasing concern about the environmental impact of industrial projects has led to the expansion of chapter IV, which now covers location, site and evironment. Valuable material, including information on the practical application of environmental impact assessment, was provided by R. Schoenstein, G. Schoerner and D. Sussman. The text of chapters IV, V and VIII was reviewed by B. Andersson, and that of chapter X by J. Bendeković and G. Eckstein.

Although this *Manual* is based on the first edition, as well as on contributions by consultants, responsibility for the final text remains that of the authors, who hope that readers will find this revised and expanded *Manual* as useful for their work as the first edition published over 10 years ago.

# Explanatory notes

References to dollars ($) are to United States dollars, unless otherwise stated.

In tables:

Totals may not add precisely because of rounding.

A hyphen indicates that the item is not applicable.

An em dash (—) indicates that the amount is nil or negligible.

Two dots (..) indicate that data are not available or are not separately listed.

The following abbreviations are used in this publication:

| | |
|---|---|
| c.i.f. | cost, insurance, freight |
| COMFAR | Computer Model for Feasibility Analysis and Reporting |
| FAO | Food and Agriculture Organization of the United Nations |
| ILO | International Labour Organisation |
| INTIB | Industrial and Technological Information Bank |
| IRR | internal rate of return |
| NCU | national currency unit |
| NPV | net present value |
| NPVR | net-present-value ratio |
| UNDP | United Nations Development Programme |
| UNEP | United Nations Environment Programme |

# CONTENTS

## Annexes

## Tables

## Figures

## Check-lists and worksheets

## Schedules

# Introduction

Since its first publication in 1978, the *Manual for the Preparation of Industrial Feasibility Studies* has demonstrated the usefulness of its methodological approach by having been translated into 18 languages and applied throughout the world, with 11 reprints of the English edition alone, and four of the French.[1] In recent years many developing countries have standardized their project planning in line with the UNIDO approach. Consulting firms, industrial enterprises, banks and investment promotion agencies in developed countries have also introduced the UNIDO procedure or have adapted it to their own requirements.

Many new problems have emerged during the 1980s. In particular, there has been a great change in the general economic situation, with high foreign debts, low raw-material prices and a widespread shortage of foreign exchange making it difficult for developing countries to secure fresh investment resources. In addition, major projects completed in the 1970s very often failed to generate the cash flow necessary to service the debt and finance new investment in expansion, modernization, rehabilitation and other projects. A shortage of international capital and foreign exchange earnings, combined with a low level of national savings, have created a need for more efficient project planning and for project design with a strategic orientation, on the basis of an integrated financial and economic analysis.

UNIDO has had more than 10 years to accumulate wide experience in applying the *Manual* in the preparation of a vast number of feasibility studies carried out under its technical cooperation programme. The *Manual* is also used in UNIDO institution-building and training programmes. The successful identification, formulation, preparation, appraisal and promotion of industrial investment projects rests to a large extent on the availability of national institutions capable of performing such tasks. The UNIDO technical cooperation programme, which focuses mainly on the establishment and strengthening of consulting firms, investment promotion agencies, project appraisal units in development finance institutions and industrial development centres, contributes to the upgrading of national capabilities of developing countries in the preparation of pre-investment studies and the appraisal of investment projects. This activity has expanded considerably and led to the creation of an inter-university cooperation network, with members from developing and developed countries, using UNIDO manuals and guidelines on pre-investment studies as student textbooks and conducting joint training programmes and research.

---

[1] After its publication in English, UNIDO provided translations of the *Manual* into Arabic, Chinese, French, Russian and Spanish. Users of the *Manual* prepared translations into Czech, Dari, Farsi, German, Greek, Hungarian, Japanese, Laotian, Polish, Portuguese, Serbo-Croatian, Turkish and Vietnamese.

1

Practitioners working in the pre-investment field all over the world provided UNIDO with many valuable suggestions on how to adapt the *Manual* to the needs of contemporary investment consultancy. Its close dialogue with readers and its own experience thus led to the preparation on the present revised edition of the *Manual*.

The following new topics feature prominently: the strategic orientation of business planning as a basis for the preparation of investment projects; and the inclusion of environmental impact assessment in the selection of the project location, sites and technologies. The market chapter has been completely rewritten to reflect the increasing importance of the development of proper marketing concepts for the feasibility of investments. Several chapters of the original text were recast and a case-study was added to produce a coherent whole and achieve even wider utilization for the *Manual* in training activities. The use of computers for financial and economic analysis has become commonplace. The working forms and schedules originally designed for manual computations have therefore been adapted to reflect that change and made fully compatible with the third generation of the UNIDO Computer Model for Feasibility Analysis and Reporting (COMFAR).[2]

The *Manual* consists of three parts. The first deals with categories and basic aspects of pre-investment studies. Part two—the main part—covers the different chapters of the feasibility study, and part three contains additional supporting material, including a case-study and descriptions of techniques used for the assessment and projection of data.

New in part one is the introduction of the concept of strategic orientation of business planning as a useful instrument for the preparation of pre-investment studies. The different phases of the investment project cycle are outlined and their interlinkages described, as well as the stages of the pre-investment phase and the activities that should be carried out simultaneously, such as investment promotion and planning of both investment financing and project implementation. Part one also shows that the *Manual* applies not only to the establishment of new industrial plants, but also to the rehabilitation and expansion of existing factories. It closes with a brief introduction to the institutional infrastructure for pre-investment studies and the use of electronic data processing in the pre-investment phase.

Part two constitutes the core of the *Manual* and its outline corresponds to the framework of a feasibility study. It includes a number of important changes as compared with the first edition. Those changes are described below.

Chapter III was almost entirely rewritten and is now entitled "Market Analysis and Marketing Concept". It is conceived in a much broader way and presents marketing research as a basic tool for defining the marketing concept to be adopted by the project. It concludes with the determination of the sales programme and the forecast of sales revenues. The design of the production programme and of the plant capacity is now covered in chapter VI.

Chapter IV, "Raw Materials and Supplies", deals with the classification and specification of input requirements, contrasting them with supplies available.

---

[2]COMFAR is the property of UNIDO and protected by copyright 1982, 1984, 1985, 1988 and 1990.

2

Chapter V, "Location, Site and Environment", has been considerably revised with the addition of a new part dealing with the environmental impact of industrial investment projects on the choice of location and site. Check-lists and worksheets for the classification of different types of environmental impact are provided in the appendix to chapter V. The coverage of environmental aspects is extended throughout the *Manual*.

Chapter VI, "Engineering and Technology", now begins with the determination of the production programme and the plant capacity which in the earlier version were covered in chapter III. It is the task of the engineering team to design the functional and physical layout required for the industrial plant to meet production goals. This edition highlights the fact that project engineering is concerned not only with engineering design, the computation of investment expenditures and the determination, for the operational phase, of human and material inputs, including their costs, but also with a wide range of interrelated activities such as the choice, acquisition and transfer of technology, which have to be carefully planned, assessed and coordinated.

In chapter VII, "Organization and Overhead Costs", the question of organizational design received particular attention, whereas in chapter VIII, "Human Resources", more emphasis is placed on the need, already at the project planning stage, to identify training requirements and to estimate ensuing costs during the investment and operational phases. In chapter IX, "Implementation Planning and Budgeting", the stages of project implementation planning are presented in a coherent manner in order to facilitate the projection of the implementation budget and the outflow of capital expenditures during the construction period.

Chapter X, "Financial Analysis and Investment Appraisal", has been restructured and expanded. After a discussion of the objectives and scope of financial analysis, the basic criteria for investment and financing decisions are introduced. Those criteria concern the role of private and public interests, the impact of pricing of project inputs and outputs, the planning horizon and the problems relating to risks and decisions in conditions of uncertainty. The structure of investment, production and marketing costs is analysed, taking into account the reliability of data and the need to identify critical variables as a precondition for the appraisal of investment projects by investors and financing institutions. Basic investment appraisal methods, including the computation of the discounted cash flow (internal rate of return, net present value) and conventional ratios, as well as the interpretation of figures, are discussed in detail, with investment being defined[3] as a long-term commitment of economic resources with the objective of producing and obtaining net gains in the future, and with the transformation of financial resources (that is, liquidity) into productive assets being viewed as the main aspect of that commitment. After consideration of project financing and various aspects of risk and uncertainty (sensitivity, break-even and probability analysis), chapter X closes with a brief review of the objectives of economic analysis and a bibliography of publications recommended for use in practical work.

To ensure clarity and facilitate its practical use, each chapter in the second part of the *Manual* is presented in four parts, as follows: chapter review; detailed examination of the subject, starting with basic principles and the

---

[3]See part two, chap. X, sect. A.

definition of terms used, then continuing with the preparation of the corresponding chapter of the feasibility study; bibliography; and check-lists, working forms and schedules.

The detailed text given in each chapter is intended to acquaint the reader with the conceptual problems to be faced in completing the study. These texts have as much detail as is possible in a manual dealing with the many multidisciplinary problems of a feasibility study. The bibliographies point the way to further study of individual issues raised in the *Manual*.

This format allows a stage-by-stage analysis of the various study components, with the sets of figures generated for each component gradually converging to the most important totals. This method also allows any single component of the entire study to be dealt with separately, within the overall logic of the study. The format was designed in this way because the true evaluation of an investment proposal can only be done correctly if data are collected properly during the preparatory stage.

Each chapter of the *Manual* contains several pro-forma schedules suitable for data collection.[4] The schedules are designed in such a way as to correspond to the timing requirements of cash-flow analysis. Furthermore, the schedules are sequential and can ultimately provide an accounting of all the major inflows and outflows of funds needed for financial evaluation and planning.

For a number of reasons the *Manual* does not address problems related to economic evaluation. First of all, the subject would require too much space for appropriate coverage. Secondly, when preparing an investment proposal, an investor or promoter is normally not very much concerned with the costs and benefits the projects may represent for the economy as a whole. Interest is focused on commercial considerations, that is, the rate of return to be expected from the investment involved, taking into account the prevailing market prices to be obtained for the products and to be paid for material inputs, utilities, labour, machinery and equipment and the like.

Another important reason why economic evaluation is not a part of this *Manual* is that various publications[5] cover the subject at great length, paying particular attention to socio-economic factors having an impact on project choice. Only in the final chapter of this *Manual* is the value of subjecting any major profitable investment proposals to economic evaluation emphasized in order to promote an awareness of the significance of economic evaluation among private and public investors.

The preparation of a feasibility study is a task which, if it is to be done well, requires inputs from many professional disciplines for the various

---

[4]The schedules in the first edition were designed basically with manual computations in mind. Since then the use of personal computers has spread rapidly, and commercial as well as user-developed programmes are now used for discounting, the computation of debt-service schedules etc. With the development of computer applications in project analysis the scope and quality of financial analysis has been increased considerably. The schedules were therefore redesigned to better reflect this development, and also to correspond with the UNIDO COMFAR software of the third generation, to be released with the publication of this *Manual*. The figures shown in the schedules contained in the appendix to chapter X are based on the data given in the example case presented in annex I to this *Manual*.

[5]In particular, *Guidelines for Project Evaluation* (United Nations publication, Sales No. 72.II.B.11), *Guide to Practical Project Appraisal* (United Nations publication, Sales No. E.78.II.B.3) and *Manual for Evaluation of Industrial Projects* (United Nations publication, Sales No. E.80.II.B.2).

components of the study, the most important of which are as follows: market analysis and marketing; location, site and environment; engineering and technology; and financial analysis. The intended audience of this *Manual* therefore includes market and financial analysts, economists, engineers and social scientists. Having such a wide readership, the *Manual* can deal with each of the above-mentioned topics only in the depth required to present the concepts and methodologies needed for the preparation of a feasibility study. Each of the topics referred to could be the subject of separate publications. As a compromise in this regard, a comprehensive bibliography is provided at the end of each chapter in part two of the *Manual*.

# PART ONE

# Pre-investment studies and the investment project cycle

## A.  Investment project cycle and types of pre-investment studies

The development of an industrial investment project from the stage of the initial idea until the plant is in operation can be shown in the form of a cycle comprising three distinct phases, the pre-investment, the investment and the operational phases. Each of these three phases is divisible into stages, some of which constitute important consultancy, engineering and industrial activities. As the objective of this *Manual* is to explore the problems encountered in carrying out the various studies required during the pre-investment phase, only a brief summary will be given of the investment and operational phases in order to show the interrelationship between all three.

Several parallel activities take place within the pre-investment phase and even overlap into the suceeding investment phase. Thus, once an opportunity study has produced fairly dependable indications of a viable project, investment promotion and implementation planning are initiated, leaving the main effort, however, to the final investment appraisal and the investment phase (figure I). To reduce wastage of scarce resources, a clear comprehension of the sequence of events is required when developing an investment proposal from the conceptual stage by way of active promotional efforts to the operational stage. It is also important to understand the role to be played by the different actors, such as investors, promotional agencies, commercial banks, development finance institutions, suppliers of equipment, export credit insurance agencies and consulting firms.

All phases of the project cycle lend themselves to important consultancy and engineering work to be carried out by the above-mentioned actors. Increasing importance should, however, be attached to the pre-investment phase as a central point of attention, because the success or failure of an industrial project ultimately depends on the marketing, technical, financial and economic findings and their interpretation, especially in the feasibility study. The costs involved should not constitute an obstacle to an adequate examination and appraisal of a project in the pre-investment phase, as such a process might save considerable costs, including those relating to misdirected investment, after start-up of the enterprise.[6]

### 1.  The pre-investment phase

The pre-investment phase (figure I) comprises several stages: identification of investment opportunities (opportunity studies); analysis of project alternatives and preliminary project selection as well as project preparation[7] (prefeasibility and feasibility studies); and project appraisal and investment

---

[6]Werner Behrens, "Investitionsberatung", in *Handwörterbuch. Export und Internationale Beratung* (Stuttgart, C. E. Poeschel, 1989), p. 1002.

[7]Sometimes also referred to as project formulation.

**Figure I. Pre-investment, investment and operating phases of the project cycle**

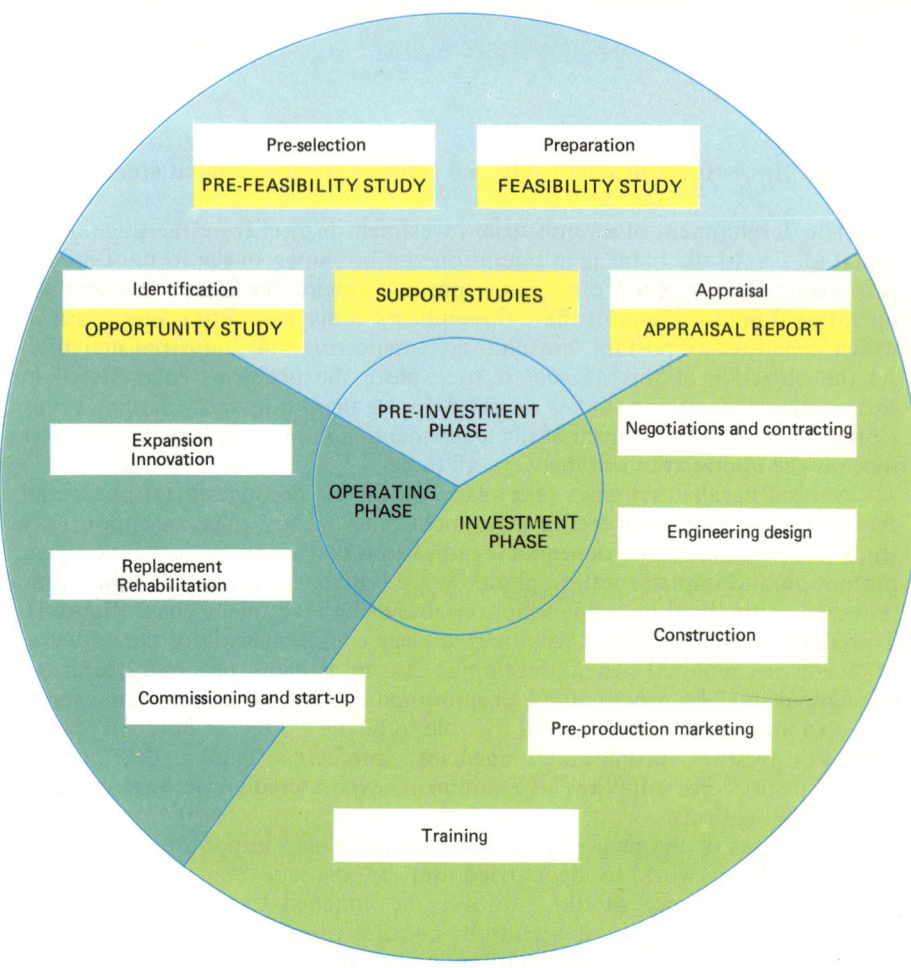

decisions (appraisal report). Support or functional studies are also a part of the project preparation stage and are usually conducted separately, for later incorporation in a pre-feasibility study or feasibility study, as appropriate. The development of a project through several stages also facilitates investment promotion and provides a better basis for project decisions and implementation by making the process more transparent.

While it is easier to grasp the scope of an opportunity study, it is not an easy task to differentiate between a pre-feasibility and a feasibility study in view of the frequently inaccurate use of these terms. In this *Manual*, therefore, definitions are made general enough to be widely accepted and applied in developing countries.

The division of the pre-investment phase into stages avoids proceeding directly from the project idea to the final feasibility study without examining the project idea step by step or being able to present alternative solutions. This also cuts out many superfluous feasibility studies that would presumably have little chance of reaching the investment phase. And finally it ensures that the project appraisal to be made by national or international financing institutions becomes an easier task when based on well-prepared studies. All too often project appraisal actually amounts to project preparation, given the low quality of the feasibility study submitted.

## Opportunity studies

The identification of investment opportunities is the starting-point in a series of investment-related activities (figure I). It may eventually even be the beginning of the mobilization of investment funds. Potential investors, private or public, from developing and developed countries are interested in obtaining information on newly identified viable investment opportunities. To generate this information, the sector and the enterprise approach to investment project identification will have to be taken. Both approaches have two dimensions. At the sector level, it will require an analysis of the overall investment potential in developing countries and the general interest of developed countries in investing abroad, that is, in developing countries. At the enterprise level, it will necessitate the identification of specific investment requirements of individual project promoters in both developing and developed countries.

The sector approach to the identification of investment potential in developing countries is often associated with the compilation of area, industrial sector and resource-based studies and the preparation of *industrial master plans*. Analysing developed-country interest in investment in developing countries requires a review of the current economic situation in developing countries, including a study of the structural problems faced by their manufacturing sector. The micro-economic approach is mainly concerned with a review of the investment ideas of industrialists, investment promotion offices and financial institutions in both developing and developed countries.

The main instrument used to quantify the parameters, information and data required to develop a project idea into a proposal is the opportunity study, which should analyse the following:

- Natural resources with potential for processing and manufacture, such as timber for wood-based industries
- The existing agricultural pattern that serves as a basis for agro-based industries
- Future demand for certain consumer goods that have growth potential as a result of increased population or purchasing power or for newly developed goods such as synthetic fabrics or domestic electrical products
- Imports, in order to identify areas for import substitution
- Environmental impact
- Manufacturing sectors successful in other countries with similar economic background and levels of development, capital, labour and natural resources
- Possible interlinkage with other industries, indigenous or transnational
- Possible extension of existing lines of manufacture by backward or forward integration, linking, for example, a downstream petrochemical

industry with a refinery, or an electric-arc steel plant with a steel rolling-mill

- Possibilities for diversification, for example, from a petrochemical complex into the pharmaceutical industry
- Possible expansion of existing industrial capacity to attain economies of scale
- The general investment climate
- Industrial policies
- Availability and cost of production factors
- Export possibilities

Opportunity studies are rather sketchy in nature and rely more on aggregate estimates than on detailed analysis. Cost data are usually taken from comparable existing projects and not from quotations of sources such as equipment suppliers. Depending on the prevailing conditions under investigation, either general opportunity studies (sector approach) or specific project opportunity studies (enterprise approach), or both, have to be undertaken.

*General opportunity studies*

General opportunity studies (annex II) may be divided into the following three categories:

- Area studies designed to identify opportunities in a given area such as an administrative province, a backward region or the hinterland of a port
- Industry studies designed to identify opportunities in a delimited industrial branch such as building materials or food processing
- Resource-based studies designed to reveal opportunities based on the utilization of natural, agricultural or industrial products such as forest-based industries, downstream petrochemical industries and metal-working industries

*Specific project opportunity studies*

Specific project opportunity studies should follow the initial identification of general investment opportunities in the form of products with potential for domestic manufacture, and an investment profile should be circulated to potential investors. Although in many developing countries a governmental investment promotion agency or a chamber of commerce and industry may perform such work, it is most often undertaken by the prospective investor or an entrepreneurial group.

A specific project opportunity study, which is more common than a general opportunity study, may be defined as the transformation of a project idea into a broad investment proposition. As the objective is to stimulate investor response, a specific project opportunity study must include certain basic information; the mere listing of products that may have potential for domestic manufacture is not sufficient. While such a list—derived from general economic indicators such as past imports, growing consumer demand or from one of the general opportunity studies relating to areas, sectors or resources—

can serve as a starting-point, it is necessary, first, to be selective as to the products so identified, and secondly, to incorporate data relating to each product so that a potential investor, either domestic or foreign, can consider whether the possibilities are attractive enough to proceed to the next stage of project preparation. Such data can be supplemented with information on basic policies and procedures that may be relevant to the production of the particular product. A broad investment profile would then emerge that would be adequate for the purpose of stimulating investor response.

The information conveyed in a project opportunity study should not involve any substantial costs in its preparation, as it is intended primarily to highlight the principal investment aspects of a possible industrial proposition. The purpose of such a study is to arrive at a quick and inexpensive determination of the salient facts of an investment possibility. Where a project opportunity study is undertaken by a national or international investment promotion or financing agency to develop entrepreneurial interest, the pre-feasibility study has to be carried out as and when entrepreneurial response is forthcoming.

## Pre-feasibility studies

The project idea must be elaborated in a more detailed study. However, formulation of a feasibility study that enables a definite decision to be made on the project is a costly and time-consuming task. Therefore, before assigning larger funds for such a study, a further assessment of the project idea might be made in a pre-feasibility study (annex III), the principal objectives of which are to determine whether:

- All possible project alternatives have been examined;
- The project concept justifies a detailed analysis by a feasibility study;
- Any aspects of the project are critical to its feasibility and necessitate in-depth investigation through functional or support studies such as market surveys, laboratory tests or pilot-plants tests;
- The project idea, on the basis of the available information, should be considered either non-viable or attractive enough for a particular investor or investor group;
- The environmental situation at the planned site and the potential impact of the projected production process are in line with national standards.

A pre-feasibility study should be viewed as an intermediate stage between a project opportunity study and a detailed feasibility study, the difference being in the degree of detail of the information obtained and the intensity with which project alternatives are discussed.[8] The structure of a pre-feasibility study (annex III) should be the same as that of a detailed feasibility study.

A detailed review of available alternatives must take place at the stage of the pre-feasibility study, since it would be too costly and time-consuming to have this done at the feasibility study stage. In particular, the review should cover the various alternatives identified in the following main fields (components) of the study:

- Project or corporate strategies and scope of project

---

[8]An outline of the types of decisions to be taken during different pre-investment stages is presented in annex IV to this *Manual*.

- Market and marketing concept
- Raw materials and factory supplies
- Location, site and environment
- Engineering and technology
- Organization and overhead costs
- Human resources, in particular managerial (entrepreneurial) staff, labour costs and training requirements and costs
- Project implementation schedule and budgeting

The financial and economic impact of each of the above-mentioned factors should be assessed. Occasionally, a well-prepared and comprehensive opportunity study may justify bypassing the pre-feasibility study stage. Such cases should be confined to investors who have complete knowledge of the project conditions. A pre-feasibility study is, however, conducted if the economics of the project are doubtful. Short cuts may be used to determine minor components of investment and production costs but not to determine major cost items. The latter must be computed on the basis of reliable primary sources.

## Support (functional) studies

Support or functional studies (figure I) cover specific aspects of an investment project, and are required as prerequisites for, or in support of, pre-feasibility and feasibility studies, particularly large-scale investment proposals. Examples of such studies are as follows:

- Market studies of the products to be manufactured, including demand projections in the market to be served together with anticipated market penetration;
- Raw material and factory supply studies, covering current and projected availability of raw materials and inputs basic to the project, and the current and projected price trends of such materials and inputs;
- Laboratory and pilot-plant tests, which are carried out to the extent necessary to determine the suitability of particular raw materials or products;
- Location studies, particularly for potential projects where transport costs would constitute a major determinant;
- Environmental impact assessment, which covers current environmental conditions in the area surrounding the envisaged site (current emissions and potential long-range transport of pollutants), possible low-emission technologies or environmental protection technologies, alternative sites, the use of alternative raw materials and auxiliary materials. An environmental impact analysis will have to be carried out particularly for projects involving, for example, chemical plants, paper and cellulose mills, petroleum refineries, the iron and steel industry, and nuclear, thermal and hydropower plants;
- Economies-of-scale studies, which are generally conducted as a part of technology selection studies. These are separately commissioned when

several technologies and market sizes are involved, but the problems are confined to economies of scale and do not extend to the intricacies of technology. The principal task of such studies is to assess the size of plant that would be most economic after considering alternative technologies, investment costs, production costs and prices. Several plant capacities are analysed and the broad characteristics of the project developed, including a computation of results for each capacity;

- Equipment selection studies, which are required when large plants with numerous divisions are involved and the sources of supplies and the costs are widely divergent. The ordering of equipment, including preparation of and invitations for bids, their evaluation, contracting and deliveries, is usually carried out during the investment or implementation phase. When very large investments are involved, the structure and economics of the project depend heavily on the type of equipment, its price and production costs; even the operational efficiency of the project is a direct function of the selected equipment.

The contents of a support study vary, depending on its type and the nature of the projects. However, as it relates to a vital aspect of the project, the conclusions should be clear enough to give direction to the subsequent stage of project preparation. In most cases, the results of a support study, when undertaken either before or together with a feasibility study, form an integral part of the latter and lessen its burden and cost.

When a basic input may be a decisive factor in determining the viability of a project, then a support study is carried out before commissioning a pre-feasibility or a feasibility study. When detailed work required for a specific output is too involved to be undertaken as part of the feasibility study, a support study is commissioned separately but simultaneously with a pre-feasibility or a feasibility study. A support study is undertaken after completion of a feasibility study when it is discovered in the course of the study that it would be safer to identify a particular aspect of the project in much greater detail, although the preliminary evaluation as part of the decision-making process may commence earlier.

### Feasibility studies

A feasibility study should provide all data necessary for an investment decision (figure I). The commercial, technical, financial, economic and environmental prerequisites for an investment project should therefore be defined and critically examined on the basis of alternative solutions already reviewed in the pre-feasibility study. The result of these efforts is then a project whose background conditions and aims have been clearly defined in terms of its central objective and possible marketing strategies, the possible market shares that can be achieved, the corresponding production capacities, the plant location, existing raw materials, appropriate technology and mechanical equipment and, if required, an environmental impact assessment. The financial part of the study covers the scope of the investment, including the net working capital, the production and marketing costs, sales revenues and the return on capital invested.

Final estimates on investment and production costs and the subsequent calculations of financial and economic profitability are only meaningful if the scope of the project is defined unequivocally in order not to omit any essential part and its related cost. The scope should be defined in drawings and schedules that should then serve as a supporting structure during further project work.

There is no uniform approach or pattern to cover all industrial projects of whatever type, size or category. Moreover, the emphasis on, and consideration of, different components varies from project to project. For most industrial projects, however, the broad format described in this *Manual* is of general application—bearing in mind that the larger the project the more complex will be the information required.

Although feasibility studies are similar in content to pre-feasibility studies, the industrial investment project must be worked out with the greatest accuracy in an iterative optimization process, with feedback and interlinkages, including the identification of all commercial, technical and entrepreneurial risks. Should weak points be revealed initially and the profitability of the project prove inadequate, then sensitive parameters such as the size of the market, the production programme or the mechanical equipment selected should be examined more closely, and better alternatives should be looked for, in order to improve the feasibility of the project. All of the assumptions made, data used and solutions selected in a feasibility study should be described and justified in order to make the project more comprehensible to the promoter or investor in his evaluation of the study. If a project is not viable despite a review of all alternatives, that fact should be stated and the reasons given. In other words, even a feasibility study that does not lead to an investment recommendation is of great value as it prevents the misallocation of scarce capital.

The term "feasibility study" is often misunderstood and deliberately misused by suppliers of equipment or technology. Frequently, an outline of a project primarily oriented to the supply of equipment or the choice of a particular technology is called a feasibility study, although it is rather a technical or support study, not covering all feasibility aspects, as required for an unbiased project appraisal. Sometimes production or sales estimates are based on conditions observed in a developed country and bear little relation to those in a developing country. As these studies are unrelated or ill-adapted to the local business environment, they can be misleading and result in the misallocation of resources, as has often occurred in developing countries. A feasibility study must be related to available production factors and local market and production conditions, and this requires an analysis that has to be translated into costs, income and net gains.

A feasibility study should be carried out only if the necessary financing facilities, as determined by the studies, can be identified with a fair degree of accuracy. There would be little sense in a feasibility study without the reliable assurance that, in the event of positive study findings, funds could be made available. For that reason, possible project financing must be considered as early as the feasibility study stage, because financing conditions have a direct effect on total costs and thus on the financial feasibility of the project.

*Appraisal report*

When a feasibility study is completed the various parties involved in the project will carry out their own appraisal of the investment project in accordance with their individual objectives and evaluation of expected risks, costs and gains. Large investment and development finance institutions have formalized project appraisal procedures and usually prepare an appraisal report. This is the reason why project appraisal should be considered an independent stage of the pre-investment phase (figure I), marked by the final investment and financing decisions taken by the project promoters.

The better the quality of the feasibility study, the easier will be the appraisal work. Until this point is reached, considerable amounts of time and funds may already have been expended since the initiation of the project idea (figure II). The appraisal report will prove whether these pre-production expenditures were well spent. Project appraisal as carried out by financial institutions concentrates on the health of the company to be financed, the returns obtained by equity holders and the protection of its creditors. The techniques applied to appraise projects in line with these criteria centre around technical, commercial, market, managerial, organizational, financial and possibly also economic aspects. The findings of this type of appraisal enter into the appraisal report.

Since this *Manual* is designed also to facilitate project appraisal work, it is sufficient to draw attention to the relevant chapters of part two, where the appraisal aspects are dealt with. In particular, chapter X shows how to project cash flow tables, income statements and balance sheets and how the working capital requirements and the financing and debt-servicing plans of an enterprise are developed. Each project proposal is subjected to detailed sensitivity analysis in order to take care of multiple adjustments of input and output factors. Risk analysis may likewise be applied in order to appraise the uncertainties attached to project data and alternatives.

Appraisal reports as a rule deal not only with the project but also with the industries in which it will be carried out and its implications for the economy as

## Figure II.   Project promotion and capital expenditures

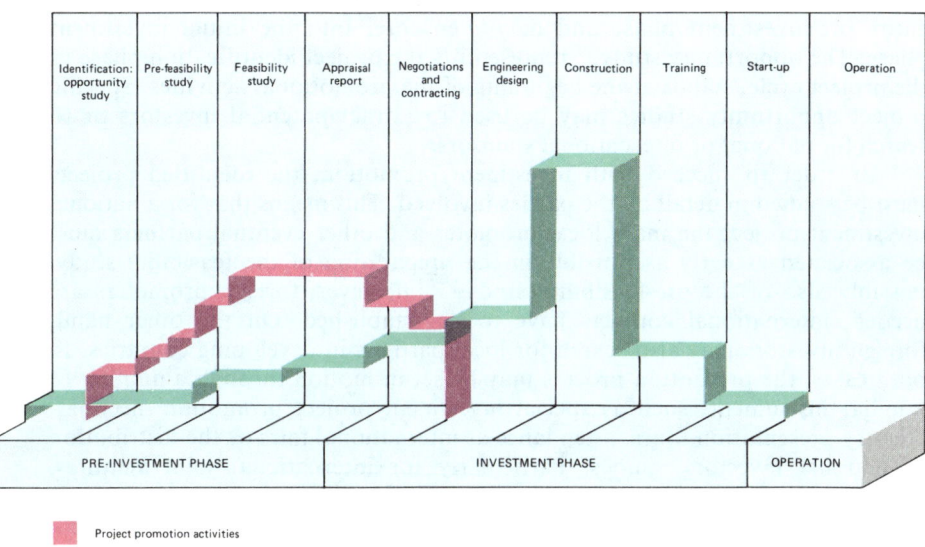

| Identification: opportunity study | Pre-feasibility study | Feasibility study | Appraisal report | Negotiations and contracting | Engineering design | Construction | Training | Start-up | Operation |

PRE-INVESTMENT PHASE           INVESTMENT PHASE           OPERATION

■ Project promotion activities

■ Pre-production capital expenditures

17

a whole. Thus, if a car manufacturing plant is to be appraised, the report will also review the relationship of the plant to its feeder industry, the transport sector, the availability of highways and the energy supply. For large-scale projects, appraisal reports will require field missions to verify the data collected[9] and to review all those factors of a project that are conditioned by its business environment, location and markets and the availability of resources.

*Promotion of industrial investment projects*

The investment project promotion process extends over the entire pre-investment phase and may even enter into the investment phase proper (figure II). It embraces a number of related activities such as the identification of potential sponsors, negotiations and establishment of cooperation agreements for the entire investment project or for limited areas of concern (export marketing, transfer of managerial or technical know-how, critical supplies etc.) as well as determining potential sources of finance. To be successful, investment promotion also requires the conscientious collaboration of all parties concerned.

The success of investment promotion is largely dependent on the business environment (prevailing investment climate), development objectives, industrial development policies or strategies, the institutional infrastructure,[10] and the mechanisms adopted by decision makers. Government development objectives and investment promotion policies need to be clearly defined, especially the role that national private and foreign investors may play. Foreign participation is usually sought to supply technical, managerial and marketing know-how, and is rarely limited to loan or equity financing. The particular combination of foreign inputs required varies naturally with the type of project and from country to country. Another important factor is the "right" balance between the public and the private sector. Whereas in many developing countries the public sector played a dominant role up to the mid-1980s, its role is now being reduced, leaving more room to the private sector.

As shown in figure II, the investment promotion process extends over the entire pre-investment phase and may even enter into the initial investment phase. The opportunity study,[11] representing the project identification phase of the project cycle, stands at the beginning of the promotional activities. Specific project opportunity studies may be used to attract potential investors or to search for national or international sponsors.

In order to succeed with investment promotion, the identified projects must be studied in detail by the parties involved. This means that for a national investment project the main local promoter and other eventual partners must be associated as early as possible in the preparation of the feasibility study, possibly also of the pre-feasibility study. If, however, foreign promoters are needed, international contacts have to be established. On the other hand, foreign investors may also search for local partners in developing countries. In both cases, the promotion process may be set in motion through a number of familiar instruments such as special investment project promotion meetings, country presentation tours, attendance at international fairs or the distribution of national investors' guides. Particularly for international joint ventures,

---

[9]Sources of data must always be quoted. See also part one, sect. B (3).

[10]See also part one, sect. E.

[11]See also part one, sect. A (1).

attention must be given to the joint conduct of feasibility studies by all parties concerned, so as to ensure that the joint investment decision is based on the results of a study agreed upon by everybody. The costs of the study are usually shared by all parties.

Figure II shows also the distribution of capital expenditures during the various stages of project development and promotion. The capital expenditures continue to increase and reach a peak in the construction stage, while the promotional activities usually peak during the preparation of the feasibility study and the appraisal of the project.

As far as financing is concerned, investment in most developing countries still depends on foreign funds, mainly because of their relatively low saving capacity. Promotion of investment financing, however, has become very difficult with the unhealthy accumulation of foreign debt—the debt crisis—in many developing countries. Well-prepared project feasibility studies are undoubtedly required to promote projects and find the necessary finance.

It has already been noted that sufficient institutional support is required for the successful promotion of investment projects. In almost all developing as well as many developed countries, specialized national investment promotion and development agencies were set up for this purpose. The main objectives of such agencies are not only to identify investment opportunities and to prepare opportunity studies, but, more important, to find suitable national and foreign partners interested in investing in such ventures. On the international level UNIDO operates an Industrial Promotion Programme comprising the following three main elements: the System of Consultations as an international forum to initiate contacts between international, regional and non-governmental institutions and to identify investment opportunities and cooperation projects; the Development and Transfer of Technology Programme for assisting developing countries in the acquisition of technology, know-how and negotiation capability; and the Industrial Investment Programme, with offices in a number of industrialized countries.[12]

## 2. The investment phase

The investment or implementation phase (figure I) of a project provides wide scope for consultancy and engineering work, first and foremost in the field of project management. The investment phase can be divided into the following stages:[13]

- Establishing the legal, financial and organizational basis for the implementation of the project
- Technology acquisition and transfer, including basic engineering
- Detailed engineering design and contracting, including tendering, evaluation of bids and negotiations
- Acquisition of land, construction work and installation

---

[12]UNIDO operates Investment Promotion Services at Cologne, Milan, Paris, Seoul, Tokyo, Vienna, Warsaw, Washington, D.C., and Zurich, and Industrial Cooperation Offices at Beijing and Moscow, which promote the flow of investment to developing countries.

[13]Most of these topics have been covered in UNIDO publications listed in the bibliography to part one of this *Manual*.

- Pre-production marketing, including the securing of supplies and setting up the administration of the firm
- Recruitment and training of personnel
- Plant commissioning and start-up

Detailed engineering design comprises preparatory work for site preparation, the final selection of technology and equipment, the whole range of construction planning and time-scheduling of factory construction, as well as the preparation of flow charts, scale drawings and a wide variety of layouts.

During the stage of tendering and evaluation of bids it is specially important to receive comprehensive tenders for goods and services for the project from a sufficiently large number of national and international suppliers of proven efficiency and with good delivery capacity. Negotiations and contracting are concerned with the legal obligations arising from the acquisition of technology, the construction of buildings, the purchase and installation of machinery and equipment, and financing. This stage covers the signing of contracts between the investor or entrepreneur, on the one hand, and the financing institutions, consultants, architects and suppliers of raw materials and required inputs, on the other. During negotiations developing countries in particular are confronted with great problems that necessitate cooperation with experienced consultancy firms. But even the selection of suitable consultancy firms is often difficult and is based on appropriate expert knowledge and on trust.

The construction stage involves site preparation, construction of buildings and other civil works, together with the erection and installation of equipment in accordance with proper programming and scheduling.

The personnel recruitment and training stage, which should proceed simultaneously with the construction stage, may prove very crucial for the expected growth of productivity and efficiency in plant operations. Of particular relevance is the timely initiation of marketing arrangements to prepare the market for the new products (pre-production marketing) and secure critical supplies (supply marketing).

Plant commissioning and start-up is usually a brief but technically critical span in project implementation. It links the preceding construction phase and the following operational (production) phase. The success achieved at this point demonstrates the effectiveness of implementation planning and the execution of the project, and is a portent of the future performance of the project.

Good project planning and efficient project management must ensure that the necessary action for setting up a factory, such as construction, delivery and assembly of the equipment, recruitment and training of the operating personnel and the delivery of all production inputs, is taken in good time before the projected start-up. Any delay or gaps in the planning of one of the above-mentioned stages would have a negative effect on the successful implementation of the project, especially during the start-up phase. In order to avoid this, effective, balanced organization of the various activities is necessary, and can be achieved only by careful scheduling. Various methods have been developed for this purpose, for instance, the critical path method (CPM) and the project evaluation and review technique (PERT). Whatever methods are chosen, it is important to review the original timetable regularly in the course of project implementation, to detect any discrepancies that may have occurred during construction work and to take into account their effects on costs. Therefore, all critical work tasks that can serve as valuable guidelines in revising the timetable should be described in the feasibility study.

A continuous comparison of the forecasts made in the feasibility study with the actual investment and production cost data accruing during the investment phase is required in order to monitor and control the resultant changes in the overall profitability of the project, which may in turn require adjustments in the short-term loan and equity financing of the investment project.

In summary, it is to be noted that in the pre-investment phase, the quality and dependability of the project are more important than the time factor, while in the investment phase, the time factor is more critical in order to keep the project within the forecasts made in the feasibility study. It is therefore conceptually wrong when investors, complaining about the costly and time-consuming project preparation process, try to short-circuit the stages of project preparation and analysis, moving directly from project identification to the application for a loan. Industrial investment usually involves long-term financial commitments, and the time used to study all strategic market, locational, technical, managerial, organizational and financial project alternatives, so as to find the optimal solution, usually pays for itself many times.[14]

### 3. The operational phase

The problems of the operational phase (figure I) need to be considered from both a short- and a long-term viewpoint. The short-term view relates to the initial period after commencement of production when a number of problems may arise concerning such matters as the application of production techniques, operation of equipment or inadequate labour productivity owing to a lack of qualified staff and labour. Most of these problems have their origin in the implementation phase. The long-term view relates to chosen strategies and the associated production and marketing costs as well as sales revenues. These have a direct relationship with the projections made at the pre-investment phase. If such strategies and projections prove faulty, any remedial measures will not only be difficult but may prove highly expensive.

The above outline of the investment and operational phases of an industrial project is undoubtedly an oversimplification for many projects, and, in fact, certain other aspects may be revealed that have even greater short- or long-term impacts. The wide range of issues that needs to be covered during these phases highlights the complexities of the pre-investment phase which constitutes the base for the subsequent phases. The adequacy of a pre-investment study and analysis largely determines the ultimate success or failure of an industrial activity, provided there are no serious deficiencies at the implementation and operational phases. If the pre-investment study is based on flawed or inadequate information and assumptions, the techno-economic rectification of the project will be very difficult, however well it may have been executed and operated.

Rehabilitation and expansion projects are discussed below in section C.

---

[14]See W. C. Baum, *The Project Cycle, Finance and Development* (Washington, D.C., World Bank, 1978).

# B. Basic aspects of pre-investment studies

## 1. Strategic orientation

Strategic orientation of business planning is not wholly new. As a formalized concept and methodology, however, it is relatively new, and has become an increasingly attractive and useful instrument of modern management. One of the reasons for this development is that management instruments are needed in a rapidly changing business world to cope with the risks associated with management decisions. Investment decisions are critical for the success and even the survival of an enterprise when the relative volume of financial commitments is significant.

### Characteristics of strategic orientation

The strategic orientation of business planning may be best characterized by the approaches outlined below.

#### Doing the right things: the search for the right investment

In a time of dramatic and increasing economic, technological, ecological and political change, survival and success in the business world depends more than ever on making the right decisions. An investment decision is one of the most critical business initiatives to be undertaken by entrepreneurs or managers, because investments bind financial resources for a relatively long period despite expectations of continuing change. But how can the right investment be identified? From the business point of view, any investment that can economically achieve its basic objectives over its lifetime can be considered the right investment. It is important to understand that the basic objectives of investment projects are not the maximization of output value or the minimization of input costs, or the technical efficiency of the project or profit maximization, but the optimal combination of all these technical and economic aspects, which should be the aim of long-term business planning. Management orientation towards the optimal combination implies that the principal objective of risk minimization should in general govern the development of a proper strategy in an unstable environment. How can managers or investors determine the best course of action? The concept of strategic orientation requires planners and decision makers to understand what is behind the process of change, and to identify and develop those skills essential for survival in a competitive environment.

#### Understanding change

Any enterprise or investment project should be understood as an integral part of a socio-economic and ecological system. A relationship of interdependence exists between the system and the enterprise. Although the characteristics, in particular the objectives and requirements, of the project depend on the system, which is superior to the enterprise, the project itself will also have a certain impact on the system. This superior system is usually referred to as the overall corporate or investment environment, which consists of two interrelated environments, the socio-economic and the natural (or ecological), as reflected in figure III.

**Figure III.  The firm and its environment**

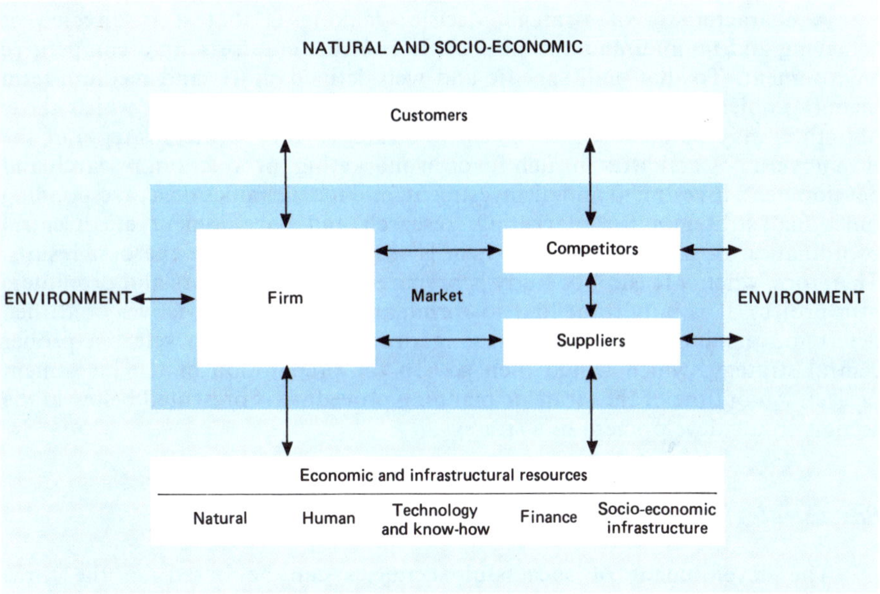

NATURAL AND SOCIO-ECONOMIC

| | | |
|---|---|---|
| | Customers | |
| ENVIRONMENT | Firm    Market    Competitors    Suppliers | ENVIRONMENT |
| | Economic and infrastructural resources | |

| Natural | Human | Technology and know-how | Finance | Socio-economic infrastructure |
|---|---|---|---|---|

*Note:* This diagram has been simplified by excluding the international dimension.

Within the overall corporate investment environment the firm or the investment project under study can be seen as an economic and social entity placed as a mediator between consumers and resources. As part of this environment it operates within a competitive market, competing with other producers for resources (suppliers) and consumers. The interdependence between enterprise and environment has two consequences: first, the enterprise must adapt to environmental change when and where required; and secondly, it should try to influence or control such change. Investment projects should, therefore, be designed to cope with future environmental change. Hence, it is not sufficient for a feasibility study to assess the current environment, it must also analyse and understand the active forces behind the process of change. For this purpose, potentially important or critical environmental factors must be determined and monitored prior to an investment decision.

*Development of skills*

In order to survive in a competitive environment an enterprise needs certain core skills that set it apart from competitors, because such skills enable the enterprise to gain competitive advantages and, in the long run, to achieve better results than its competitors. Firms should develop and maintain core skills centred on product design, reduced production costs, control of distribution channels, short lead times etc. The feasibility study should try to identify core skills that competitors will find difficult to imitate; that utilize existing and future market forces in the best possible way; and that secure long-term business success.

23

## Importance and utility of a strategy

A characteristic of strategic decision-making is that it is directed at achieving and maintaining optimal positions of the enterprise in a competitive environment. To that end, specific and well-defined short- and medium-term planning objectives can be determined, as well as the means by which those objectives may be achieved. The central strategy[15] (corporate strategy) of the firm governs its activities in such fields as marketing, production, research and development, investment and disinvestment, and it determines the corresponding functional strategies for marketing, research and development etc. Central coordination of all activities of a firm is required to achieve the best results. Therefore, when a feasibility study is prepared for the investors and promoters of a project, it is important first to formulate its general objectives, and then determine the immediate objectives, in order to be able to select a proper central strategy, which would then govern the preparation of the investment project. An outline of the strategic planning procedure is presented below in the section on the development of a strategy.

## Basic strategic principles

The development of successful strategies can be based on the three generally accepted principles outlined below, which remain valid irrespective of the type of industry and the type or size of a project.

### Concentration of forces

The concentration of forces is presumably the most important principle of strategic planning. In investment planning it means that projects are planned to avoid weaknesses as far as possible, and to develop the forces needed to concentrate on possible success areas. Forces may be concentrated on selected product-market combinations and the development of essential skills, as well as the provision of the necessary financial, personnel, material and managerial resources. A successful strategy is characterized by a careful reconciliation of objectives and means. When objectives are set too high, the enterprise may run short of resources before those objectives are reached. If targets are too low, however, the full potential of the enterprise will not be activated and utilized, resulting in a failure to reach the best possible competitive position.

### Risk balance

Each strategy entails risks that should be identified in the feasibility study. Identifying risks makes it possible to determine how to manage and minimize those risks. If this is not considered feasible, the decision to invest should not be taken. Risk balance means that resources are not completely concentrated on one strategy, and that the project design requires a sound balance between the various risks, including those relating to the market, supply, technology and political matters.

---

[15]When a new enterprise is to be founded, the basic project objective is identical to the corporate objective, and so are the strategies to achieve that objective. Where expansion, modernization or rehabilitation projects are concerned, the basic project objective and strategy depend on the higher corporate objectives and strategies.

*Cooperation*

It is often very costly and time-consuming to build up all the means or skills required to implement project objectives. By identifying and establishing cooperation with others through a coalition strategy, each party could benefit considerably. There are various forms of cooperation ranging from loose agreements to partnerships, joint ventures, holdings and the acquisition or merger of enterprises. The feasibility study should analyse the possibilities and potential advantages of such cooperation.

## Developing a strategy

The development of the project strategy as well as of functional strategies is a central responsibility of project management and cannot be delegated to staff. Strategies should, however, be systematically developed through team-work, with the early involvement of the line functions responsible for implementation. In pre-investment studies, the development of any strategy should be organized in accordance with the steps outlined in the strategic planning procedure presented below.

1. Formulation of the general objectives of the investment project

   • What is the leading idea (project vision)?

   • What are the options and preferences with regard to the basic strategic principles?

2. Determination of the immediate project objectives (chapter III)

   • What products and services are to be offered?

   • On which markets?

   • What market position and growth rates are to be achieved?

   • What are the objectives for the functional units of the enterprise (marketing, production, supply, finance, personnel management and organization)?

   • What profit or risk policy is to be observed?

   • What cooperation, mergers or acquisition policy is to be observed?

3. Choosing the project strategy

   • What basic strategy best suits the objectives (geographical area, market share, cost leadership etc.)?

   • What is the scope of the project?

   • What are the (critical) main resources and inputs required?

   • What is the location?

4. Determining the functional objectives and strategies

   • Marketing objectives, strategies and operation (marketing concept, chapter III; see also check-list below)

   • Supply (materials and inputs) objectives and strategies (supply marketing, chapter IV)

- Production objectives and strategies (chapter VI)
- Technology (research and development) objectives and strategies (chapter VI)
- Finance objectives and strategies (chapter X)
- Human resources, social relations (chapter VIII)

5. Development of the right (competitive) mix of functional objectives and strategies (see also figure IV presented below)

6. Planning of strategy implementation
   - Planning and optimal combination of resources required (chapter IX)

7. Checking and adaptation of the strategy during implementation and operation

**Figure IV. Coordination and harmonization of the functional strategies**

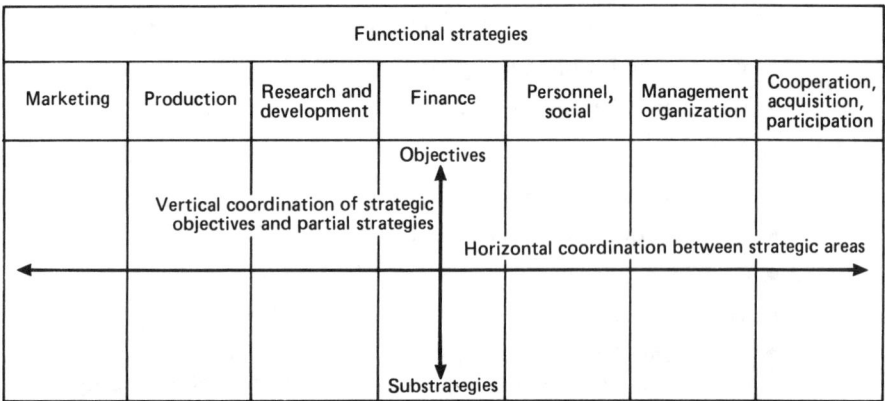

*Check-list of functional objectives and strategies*

| Strategies | Strategic objectives | Substrategies |
|---|---|---|
| Marketing | Markets | Market performance |
|  | Products | Price |
|  | Marketing and productivity | Market treatment |
|  |  | Distribution |
| Production and supplies | Production | Production methods |
|  | Productivity | Location |
|  | Supplies | Automation |
|  |  | Investment |
|  |  | Suppliers, resources, stocks, inventories |
| Research and development | Research and development | Internal and external development |
|  |  | Patents and licensing |

26

| Strategies | Strategic objectives | Substrategies |
| --- | --- | --- |
| Financing | Profits<br>Liquidity<br>Safety | Financing<br>Profits<br>Efficiency<br>Liquidity<br>Risk and safety |
| Personnel | Staff-and-worker-oriented<br>   objectives<br>External social objectives | Employment, recruitment<br>Training<br>Salary and wages<br>Social services and health<br>External social strategies |
| Management and<br>organization | Management<br>Organization | Management systems<br>Management means<br>Management methods<br>Organization<br>Information<br>Participation |
| Participation,<br>acquisition<br>and cooperation | Participation<br>Acquisition<br>Cooperation | Acquisition<br>Cooperation<br>Coalition |

The structure of part two of this *Manual* corresponds in principle to the steps necessary to develop strategies, although the process of development, like the preparation of the complete feasibility study, is not strictly sequential but iterative, as indicated by the use of bidirectional pointers in figure V.

**Figure V.   Interrelationship between the components of the feasibility study**

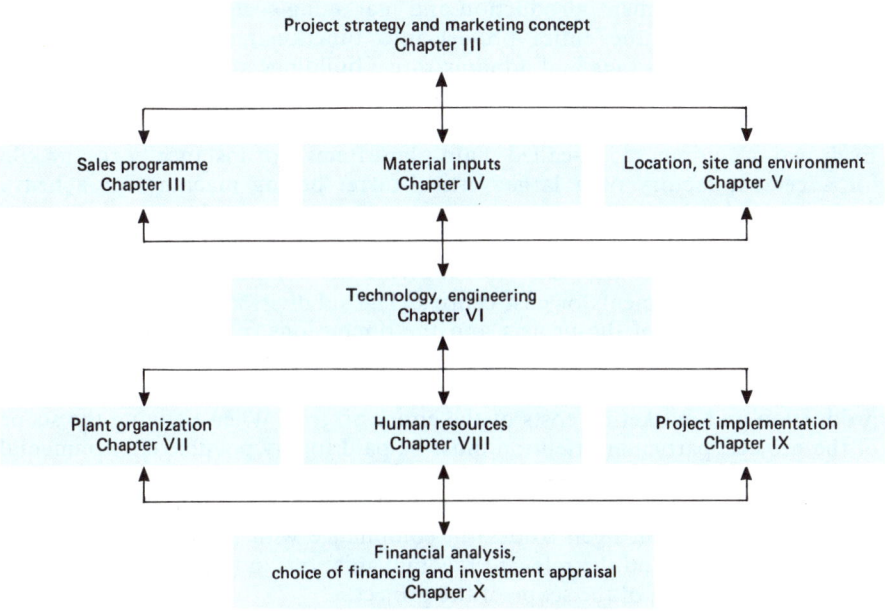

Whether a new enterprise is planned or a large and significant investment is intended in an existing firm, in each case the optimal long-term position of the project should be analysed and determined in the feasibility study. The determination of the central objective of the project and the development and selection of the project strategy is described in detail in part two, chapter III. It is important to note that the project strategy determines the production volume, the resources and technology required and the location of the project. Figure V shows the interrelationship between the main subjects to be covered by any pre-investment study.

## 2. Scope of the project

The scope of the project must be clearly understood in order to be able to prepare reliable forecasts on investment, production and marketing costs. As industrial projects frequently extend beyond the boundaries of the production plant site, it is necessary to define the battery limits of the project, and to include cost computations, estimates and projections related to the supply of inputs, the delivery of outputs and ancillary investments. The "scope of the project" should therefore embrace: all activities scheduled to take place at the plant site; the auxiliary operations relating to production, extraction, sewage and the treatment of pollutants; off-site transport and storage of inputs and outputs (including final products, by-products, wastes and emissions); and off-site ancillary activities such as housing schemes and educational, training and recreational facilities, to the extent required to achieve the project objectives.

The main reason for this arrangement is to force the project planner to look at the material and product flow not only during the processing stage but also during the preceding and succeeding stages. In addition, it can be decided whether storage and off-site transport of inputs and outputs and the corresponding investments are to be provided by the project or by such third parties as the supplier of inputs or the distributors of the final products.

To better understand the structure of the project and to facilitate the calculation of investment, production and marketing costs, the project planner should next divide the entire project into functional components such as production sheds, storage and administrative buildings and auxiliary facilities, including water, gas, electricity and telephone networks, internal connecting roads, quality control systems, laboratories, maintenance units and workshops. Even major equipment, so-called main plant items (for instance, a rotary kiln for a cement factory or a large vertical-turret boring machine for a heavy engineering plant) may be regarded as components.

To facilitate the calculation of investment, production and marketing costs, it may often be necessary to subdivide the components since they may cover several departments or cost centres. The subdivision should be based on the physical layout of the project and the dimensions of its components. The computation of project costs can be further facilitated by treating the components as "subprojects", the sum of which will yield the investment, production and marketing costs of the entire project. When defining the scope of the project, particular attention must be paid to any possible environmental implications. Thus, clean-waste technologies (such as closed-circuit processes) and environmental protection technologies (for example, in filters and systems for the removal of nitrogen oxides) in compliance with the regulations of the country concerned and the relevant recommendations in force world-wide may require the extension of the scope of the project.

## 3. Data for pre-investment studies

Although investment, production and marketing costs should be identified or estimated as precisely as possible, the costs and time involved in obtaining such data are not always justified, and it may therefore be necessary for the project team to rely on assumptions. When this is the case, it should be so stated in the study.[16]

Investment cost estimates, which may be ranked according to their accuracy and the costs and time required to obtain them, are made by the following means:[17]

- Calling for tenders based on specifications and bills of quantities. This is the most accurate but also the most expensive and time-consuming method;

- Using prices from similar projects to calculate costs based on specifications and bills of quantities;

- Using the unit cost parameters derived from comparable operational projects, measured, for example, in cost per cubic metre of enclosed space or cost per square metre of built-up area;

- Estimating the totals for groups of equipment or functional project parts based on the costs of comparable, existing projects. The degree of accuracy decreases, and the chance of omitting essential project parts increases, with the increase of coverage of the lump sums.

Investment cost estimates based on cost parameters and on lump sums should be adjusted, taking into account, among other things:

- Annual inflation rates; changes in foreign exchange rates

- Differences in local conditions, such as the climate, which may cause additional costs for air conditioning

- Different laws and regulations, for instance, on safety

- Accessibility of the construction site

- Possible errors resulting from lack of reliable data, preliminary project design, methodological deficiencies, physical contingencies for miscellaneous items etc.

The reliability of production cost estimates depends on the availability of data on materials, personnel and overheads. The latter are difficult to estimate, particularly at the opportunity and pre-feasibility study stages.

Quotations for material and labour costs can be obtained locally or, in the case of imports, through tenders from suppliers abroad. The prevailing labour legislation, the skills of local labour etc. have to be accounted for in estimating labour costs. When estimating input requirements the following parameters should be considered: marketing concept; production programme; work programme (number of shifts, working days per year etc.); type of technology and equipment; skills of labour and staff; quality of material inputs; and environmental protection requirements.

---

[16]The sources of data must always be quoted in a pre-investment study to allow later checking of their reliability (whether assessed or assumed) and updating. Copyrights etc. must also be observed.

[17]See also part two, chap. VI, sect. H.

Important data sources for pre-investment studies are reference data published by specialized data banks, industrial associations, equipment manufacturers, development banks and international organizations. They have to be used carefully, taking into account their date of collection, the plant size and possible economies of scale, the country of origin and applied technical and economic conversion factors. As location, site and civil engineering data are frequently collected in the field, it is recommended that the sources or groups of related data be identified in order to verify or complete them. The date of collection, the person or team in charge of the collection, and the samples and methods used should be specified. If laboratory tests or pilot plant processing were required, they should be described briefly and the results communicated.

### 4. Selection and verification of alternatives

The preparation of a feasibility study is often made difficult by the number of available alternatives (regarding the choice of technology, equipment, capacity, location, financing etc.) and the assumptions on which the decision-making process has to be based. As a rule, the available alternatives should already have been reviewed and preselected at the stage of the pre-feasibility study. Sometimes, however, it may be necessary at the feasibility study stage to determine the detailed costs and revenues for a limited number of alternatives, as in the case of two or three possible locations, or two production programmes with different appropriate technologies. A detailed justification of the selection of any particular alternative should be given, together with a description of the methods and formulas used in the selection process.

### 5. Accounting terminology and related matters

In financial analysis, it is important to distinguish between the flow of cash and balance-sheet entries.

#### Expenditures and costs

Expenditures represent an outflow of cash within a given period. Costs are not related to an outflow of funds during a certain period, but represent the total expenditures required to produce a certain product or service. A distinction has to be made between investment, production and marketing expenditures (representing the real cash outflow) and costs (required for calculating the net income).

#### Revenue and income

The term revenue—also called sales revenue or sales—is used in this *Manual* to represent an inflow of cash, thus being the opposite of expenditures. The term income is used in connection with the profit and loss account or net income statement. Income is generally defined as the remuneration received, for example, from sales of products or for services. After deducting the related (direct and indirect) costs and direct taxes, the net income or net profit is obtained. The terms revenue and gross income are often used synonymously, and for the purposes of financial analysis it is usually assumed that the income shown in the net income statement equals the cash inflow arising from selling the produce.[18] The term income, however, would also include interest received or any extraordinary income (such as proceeds from the sale of assets). For the purpose of financial analysis, only that income which arises from the productive use of the investment should be considered.

The difference between costs and expenditures as well as between revenue and income becomes clearer if the expenditures and the utilization of values (as in the case of raw material costs) for a product within a specified period (for example, one year) are compared. With regard to raw materials, the difference lies between the purchase and processing that occur at different times or that overlap; with regard to equipment, the difference between expenditures and costs is taken care of by depreciating the investment expenditures within a certain period (determined mainly by tax laws[19]) in order to apportion investment costs through annual depreciation charges in accordance with the utilization of the equipment, that is, the fixed assets. The application of the terms is described below.

For financial calculations (involving, for example, project financing and liquidity) the terms expenditures and sales revenue or income from operations should be used. The same applies to cash-flow analysis and related discounting methods (internal-rate-of-return (IRR) and net-present-value (NPV) methods). Depreciation charges, however, are a part of the annual costs,[20] but not of the expenditures in the same year, as the entire sum of investment was already entered as a cash outflow at the time the investment took place. The term costs should be used only in the context of accounting, when calculating unit costs or costs of products sold. When calculating the internal rate of return or the present value, a simplification is frequently introduced regarding expenditures and revenues, as well as costs and income, assuming that the difference between annual revenues and expenditures is on average the same as annual net profits (income less costs) plus annual depreciation charges. However, this simplification is applicable only if there are no significant changes in the stock of fixed and current assets.

*Total investment costs*

As already mentioned in connection with the scope of the project, investment[21] costs for land and site preparation, pre-production expenditures and working capital concern the entire project and do not have to be calculated

---

[18]The annual sales revenue, or the cash received in one year, corresponds to the income from sales, plus accounts receivable from the previous year, less accounts receivable from the current year. Apart from the first year of production or the case of a considerable change in the accounts receivable, the assumption that previous-year receivables equal current-year receivables is sufficiently accurate for the purpose of a feasibility study.

[19]In some cases, tax law does not determine depreciation for reporting to stockholders.

[20]Annual depreciation charges do have an impact on the cash outflow related to the payment of corporate or income taxes (see part two, chap. X, sect. E).

[21]The term investment is defined in part two, chap. X, sect. A.

separately according to project components. On the other hand, investment costs for technology, equipment and civil works should be computed according to project components and cost centres.

Investment cost items are dealt with in part two of this *Manual* as follows:

| Subject | Chapter |
|---|---|
| *Fixed investment* | |
| Land and site preparation | V and VI |
| Technology (lump sum and initial payments) | VI |
| Equipment | |
|     Production | VI |
|     Auxiliary | VI |
|     Costs for environmental protection technology, waste disposal, internal infrastructural services | V and VI |
|     Spare parts, wear- and tear-parts, tools | VI |
| Civil works | |
|     Site preparation and development | V and VI |
|     Buildings | VI |
|     Outdoor works | VI |
|     Engineering and design costs (unless included in equipment) | VI |
|     Incorporated fixed assets (intangibles) | VI and IX |
|     Project design costs (engineering etc.) (unless included above groups) | |
|     Transport, handling costs and charges | |
|     Insurance | |
|     Duties, taxes | |
| Pre-production expenditures | |
|     Cost of previous studies | II |
|     Preliminary and capital issue, legal costs etc. | IX and X |
|     Project and site management | IX |
|     Pre-production marketing costs | III |
|     Pre-production implementation costs | IX |
|     Personnel recruitment, training, administration and overheads | VII and IX |
|     Trial runs, start-up and commissioning | IX |
|     Interests on loan, accrued during construction | X |
| *Working capital* | X |
| *Total investment: costs* | X |

## Total costs of products sold

The total costs of products sold are composed of the following two different types of costs: total production or manufacturing costs (dealt with in chapter VI); and marketing costs (dealt with in chapter III), also referred to as costs of sales and distribution.

## Production costs

Production cost estimates should be based on the requirements of the feasible normal capacity that is achievable under normal working conditions, taking into account the capacity of installed equipment and technical conditions of the plant, such as normal stoppages, down time, holidays, maintenance, tool changes, desired shift patterns and indivisibilities of major machines as well as possible rejects. The feasible normal capacity is the number of units produced during one year under the above conditions.

Conversely, the nominal capacity is the technically feasible capacity, which frequently corresponds to the installed capacity as guaranteed by the supplier of the plant. A higher capacity—nominal maximum capacity—may be achieved, but this would entail overtime, excessive consumption of factory supplies, utilities, spare parts and wear-and-tear parts, as well as disproportionate production cost increases.

Production and marketing cost items are dealt with in part two of this *Manual*, as follows:

| *Subject* | *Chapter* |
|---|---|
| A.  Factory costs | |
| Material inputs (usually direct variable costs), in particular raw materials and factory supplies | IV |
| Human resource costs (wages, salaries, mostly direct costs, either fixed or variable, depending on type) | VIII |
| Products rejected or returned | III and VI |
| Effluent and waste treatment, environmental protection costs | V and VI |
| | |
| B.  Factory overheads (direct and indirect fixed costs of production) | |
| Services (supervision, quality control, indoor climate control, internal transport, consulting engineers etc.) | VI and VII |
| Royalties (fixed and variable costs) | VI |
| Rents, leasing fees for production buildings, machinery and equipment (fixed or variable costs) | VI |
| Research and development costs | VI and VII |
| Product storage costs (direct and indirect costs) | VI and VII |
| | |
| C.  Administrative overheads (usually indirect, basically fixed costs) | |
| Salaries, wages (management, administrative staff etc.) | VII and VIII |
| Office supplies, materials | VII |
| Rents, leasing fees for office buildings and equipment | VI and VII |
| Services (communications, transports etc.) | VI, VII and VIII |
| | |
| D.  Operating costs $(A + B + C)$ | X |
| | |
| E.  Depreciation costs (usually indirect fixed costs) | VI and X |
| | |
| F.  Cost of financing | X |
| | |
| G.  Production costs $(D + E + F)$ | X |
| | |
| H.  Marketing costs | III and X |
| Direct marketing costs | III |
| Packaging, storage | |
| Costs of sales (sales force, commissions, discounts, returned products, royalties etc.) | |

| Subject | Chapter |
|---|---|
| Promotional costs (advertisements, samples etc.) | |
| Distribution costs (transport, interim storage, insurance etc.) | |
| Indirect marketing costs | III |
|   Overhead costs of the marketing department (personnel, communications, materials and services, marketing research, general promotional activities etc.) | |
| I.  Total costs of products sold ($G + H$) | X |

## Schedules

Each chapter contains several schedules for the calculation of investment, production and marketing costs. In general, it will be necessary to disaggregate the project into its components and cost centres in order to arrive at the investment and costs of the product to be sold. For such cases, summary sheets are provided to sum up all cost items. The schedules and summary sheets provide the basis for the schedules in chapter X, in which total initial investment, production and marketing costs are summed up and projected with a view to evaluating the viability of the project. Figure VI shows the flow of data and the linkage of schedules.

## Local currency and foreign exchange

In most developing countries the financing of investment in new industrial projects requires local and foreign currency. Funds in local, mostly non-convertible, currency are required for local purchases, and foreign, mostly convertible, currency is required for imports of goods and foreign services. Most of the non-convertible currencies have suffered from higher inflation than most of the convertible currencies. Moreover, since many foreign investors and bankers are less familiar with fluctuations in the value of the numerous non-convertible currencies, they prefer to read and analyse financial data and projections expressed in an international currency such as the United States dollar.

When financial institutions indicate an interest in financing part of a new venture, their regulations concerning the selection of the currency to be used for presenting financial data in feasibility studies should be taken into account. In practice, this means that all local costs (mainly in non-convertible currency) will have to be converted into an agreed international (freely convertible) currency. Moreover, for national cost-benefit analysis it is necessary to distinguish in a pre-investment study between local and foreign currency requirements.

## Contingencies and inflation

Two types of contingencies, physical and financial, are usually encountered when planning an investment project. Physical contingencies are related to the probable margin of reliability of sales forecasts, engineering design and plant layout, production materials and services. As it may not be possible in the

34

**Figure VI. Information flow chart for the preparation of industrial feasibility studies**

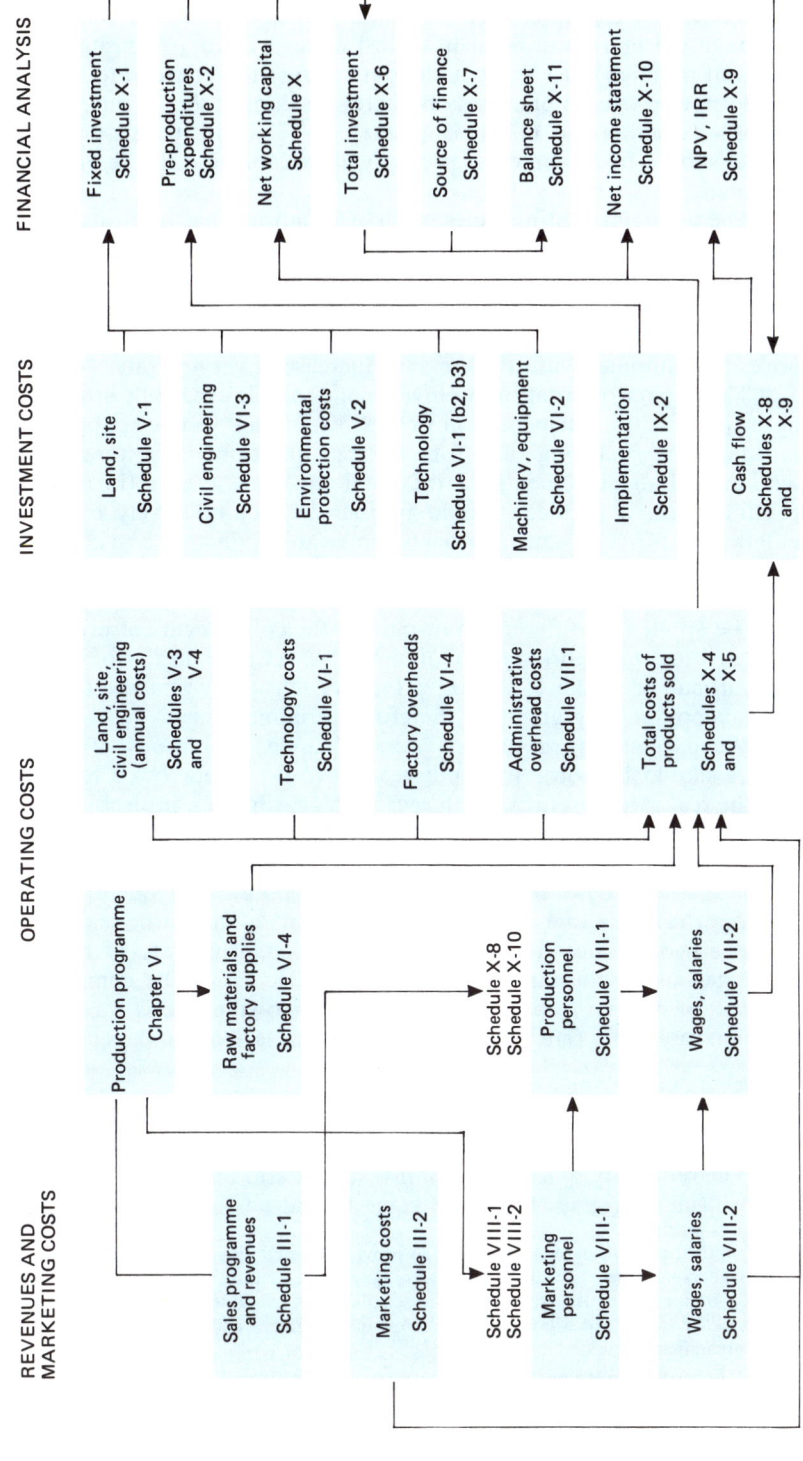

pre-investment phase to determine precisely the amount of raw materials, factory supplies etc., the discrepancy is compensated by adding a certain percentage (for example, between 5 and 10 per cent) to the physical volumes. Although the margin of error in the estimates will vary from item to item, the common practice is to apply a standard across-the-board rate. This approach should not be overemphasized, as there is a danger that it might be used as a means of evening out mistakes. Therefore, all main items of the investment project should be estimated as precisely as possible and the degree of reliability indicated.[22]

The financial contingencies (such as inflation) that occur during the life of a project may have a much stronger bearing on its financial viability than the physical contingencies, since they influence the amount of fixed investments, working capital, production and marketing costs and sales. It is very difficult to estimate the impact of inflation on these five items, as sales, wages, salaries, prices for equipment, utilities etc. may increase at varying rates.

The impact of inflation on investment costs is especially strong in the case of projects with implementation periods extending over several years. In order to adjust the financing plan for expected inflation, the estimated annual or semi-annual disbursements of the total investment cost (including physical contingencies, if applied) should be increased cumulatively by an estimated inflation factor. The same approach applies to production costs.[23]

To summarize, it is recommended that, provided inflation would have a significant impact on the outcome of the feasibility analysis, different inflation rates be applied to different countries for the components of production costs, fixed investments, working capital and sales. As the margins of error are wide, it is difficult to make valid projections. A sensitivity analysis (see chapter X) using computer programmes is therefore recommended.

When reviewing a project proposal under conditions of inflation, two factors should be borne in mind: gearing (ratio of borrowed to owner funds) and the real rate of return. With regard to gearing, if a project is financed by a mixture of equity and loans, the equity holder gains by inflation. If a fixed-term loan has to be paid back, it is easier with inflation since the real cost of the loan declines. It may be observed, therefore, that inflation frequently encourages a disproportionately high rate of loan financing. As far as the real rate of return is concerned, it should be noted that if the internal rate of return (IRR) is calculated using constant prices, then the IRR should be compared with the real cost of money, in other words, if the borrowing rate is $X$ per cent and the inflation rate $Y$ per cent, the real cost of capital is $X$ minus $Y$ per cent.

*Reliability of cost estimates*

The reliability of estimates of investment and production costs increases as the project progresses from one stage to the next. The following percentage

---

[22]In the first edition of this *Manual*, no provision for contingencies was made in the schedules. Many readers and users of COMFAR have suggested the inclusion of contingencies, which may be specially important if use is made of the schedules or computer software for opportunity and pre-feasibility studies, in which cases the scope of investment and outline of the project is usually rather preliminary.

[23]The recommended practice is to use current (inflated) prices for the construction phase, and constant prices for the operational phase, when computing the discounted cash flows for the investment project. The current prices are applied for financial planning, especially in the case of significant inflation rates. For a detailed discussion, see part two, chap. X.

**Figure VII.    Reliability of different types of pre-investment studies**

Reliability

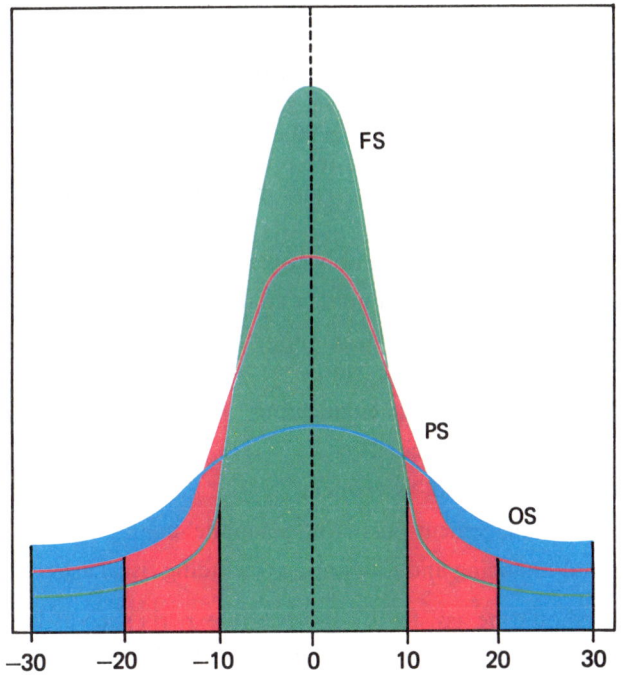

Margin of error (percentage)

Key:  FS = Feasibility study
      PS = Pre-feasibility study
      OS = Opportunity study

   *Note:* The area covered under each curve between the reliability
margins (expressed in percentage deviation) indicates the approximate
probability of the final implementation budget falling within the confidence limits of the estimates.

ranges of reliability (see figure VII) can be considered acceptable for each of the
stages:

| | |
|---|---|
| Opportunity study | ± 30 per cent |
| Pre-feasibility study | ± 20 per cent |
| Feasibility study | ± 10 per cent |

   The above percentages may differ from project to project and according to
the applied method of cost estimates.[24] They are not to be used for an
upgrading from one stage to the next, for instance by adding 30 per cent to the
estimated costs of the opportunity study without checking all relevant facts and
ascertaining their impact on the project and on costs.

—————————
   [24]See also part two, chap. VI, sect. H.

## 6.  Implementation of studies

### The project team

It is advisable to have a feasibility study conducted by a team of experts, although frequently, because of such constraints as paucity of funds and non-availability of expertise at the right level and time, only small expert teams may be available. As a general rule, the members of the team should be selected to cover the major substantive fields of the project. Depending on the conditions, type and scope of a project, the team members should ideally cover the following areas:

- Industrial economics (preferably covered by the team leader)
- Marketing (dealt with by a market analyst or marketing expert)
- Process engineering and technology (covered by a specialist in the related industry)
- Mechanical and industrial engineering
- Civil engineering (if needed)
- Environmental impact assessment
- Industrial management (including personnel management)
- Industrial financing and accounting (including fiscal aspects)

The team should be assisted by short-term experts such as land surveyors, soil experts, laboratory technicians and sociologists, as required. The team leader's responsibility, besides his or her role as a specialist, is to plan, organize, direct and supervise all activities of the team until the study is finalized.

Ideally, the project promoters should actively participate in the preparation of the study. In many cases the project is initiated by the promoter, who frequently has also made the opportunity study and can therefore be considered a major source of information on the background and history of the project. During the preparation of the study many decisions (for example, on marketing and production programmes and the selection of alternatives) are to be taken by the promoters.

### Cost and financing of studies

There are no established norms governing the costs of pre-investment studies. These depend on such factors as the magnitude and nature of the project, the type, scope and depth of the pre-investment study, the agencies commissioning and undertaking the study, and the time and effort required to collect and assess the necessary information. The practice is to relate the costs of studies to the estimated number of man-months required.[25] Costs should be calculated in each individual case to cover salaries, travel, living allowances, drawings, mapping, writing, printing as well as office overheads.

---

[25]As a rule of thumb, a specific project opportunity study should normally not require more than 2 to 3 man-months; a pre-feasibility study would require between 6 and 12 man-months of work, and a feasibility study would need an input of a minimum of 12-15 man-months. These figures are applicable for most industrial investment projects of up to $10 million to $15 million.

As costs are a vital determinant of various types of pre-investment studies, it is preferable to indicate the order of magnitude of the costs if such studies are undertaken by outside agencies. Costs of pre-investment studies expressed in percentages of investment costs are approximately as follows:

- 0.2-1.0 per cent for an opportunity study
- 0.25-1.5 per cent for a pre-feasibility study
- 1.0-3.0 per cent for a feasibility study for small to medium-sized industrial projects
- 0.2-1.0 per cent in the case of large industries or large projects with sophisticated technology or difficult markets

The above percentage figures must be treated with caution, as a rough guide. The actual fees charged by a consulting engineering firm may vary considerably because of such variables as:

- The experience of the consultant
- The scope of work to be covered
- The complexity of the industry concerned, process plants with a number of variables requiring greater engineering inputs than relatively straight-forward operations
- Cost conditions in the country of the consultant
- Competition between consultants and the condition of their order books, with the possibility of lower fees being quoted when business is lean
- The interest of the consultant in further work on the project, which could prompt him to submit a low bid for establishing business relations
- The technical competence of the client in negotiating with the consultant and in providing strong support that could facilitate the task of the consultant and also lower consultancy costs

The cost of feasibility studies may be financed as follows: by the investor; jointly by the investor and a partner; and out of technical cooperation grants extended through bilateral or international programmes involving such bodies as the United Nations Development Programme (UNDP) and UNIDO. Different types of funding facilities have been set up for this purpose at bilateral and multilateral levels (for example, the International Finance Corporation, UNIDO and UNDP). Their modalities range from a 100 per cent grant to various forms of co-financing between project promoter and funding agency. Also revolving funds are in operation. Experience shows that pre-investment studies funded under cofinancing arrangements have better chances of leading to investment follow-up.

## C. Rehabilitation and expansion projects

Relatively easy money stimulated a large amount of investment activity in developing countries during the 1970s. The investment decisions taken during this period resulted in the implementation of a large number of projects that still do not operate satisfactorily. In some cases the easy availability of funds, coming from excess foreign-exchange earnings of the oil-exporting countries and being recycled through the international banking system into developing countries, gave these countries a sufficient reason to invest. The preparation of feasibility studies, adequately analysing the technical, financial and socio-economic feasibility of investment proposals, was often not even requested by the international community because the actors involved in the investment process had very different interests.

## 1. Rehabilitation studies

Today, many developing and developed countries are undergoing extensive restructuring at the enterprise, industrial-sector, regional and national levels. The World Bank Group, United Nations bodies and bilateral assistance organizations in cooperation with the national Governments concerned have initiated large-scale restructuring programmes at both the national economic and enterprise levels.

During this process rehabilitation measures at the enterprise or plant level have gained increasing importance. More and more ailing factories are subjected to complete technical, commercial, financial and economic reviews in order to increase the efficiency of their operations and their profitability and to maintain them as independent entities, as well as to decide on their amalgamation with other plants or even their complete shut-down. In addition, the debt crisis forces many development and commercial banks to study their portfolios of money-losing industrial investment projects with a view to rehabilitating them, swapping their equity holdings for debts accumulated, or writing off the investments altogether.

Whatever the reasons for launching the rehabilitation process, it requires the following carefully planned stages:

- *Pre-diagnostic stage.* Industrial enterprises needing to be rehabilitated should be identified during the pre-diagnostic stage, in which a survey is made of the economy and industrial sector or branch, to identify the potential candidate enterprises and to choose the enterprises to be rehabilitated;

- *Diagnostic stage.* The second stage is the diagnostic stage, in which weaknesses are determined and the potential for as well as the means of rehabilitation are identified. The main task at this stage is to work out detailed medium- and long-term plans for the rehabilitation of the entire enterprise and the corresponding units, respectively. The diagnostic stage would need to cover each aspect of the operation of the enterprise, including management, energy utilization, environment, marketing, technology and equipment. In this context, rehabilitation feasibility studies are to be implemented. Depending on the local capacity to undertake restructuring and rehabilitation analysis, this work will be done by local or international consulting firms;

- *Short-term rehabilitation measures.* During this stage short-term reorganization and restructuring measures may be carried out (in the areas, for example, of financial management, inventory control, quality control or preventive maintenance) which do not yet require major capital investment;

- *Appraisal of projects and fund-raising.* Once the diagnostic analysis is completed, the project needs to be evaluated and approved by the investors. If loan financing is required, the proposal would have to be appraised by a financing institution. Partners may be needed for the implementation of larger rehabilitation projects, and in such cases promotional measures (for instance, an investors forum) would be necessary to assist the countries in soliciting financial support for planned restructuring activities;

- *Rehabilitation.* The fourth stage concludes the process with rehabilitation proper, which could cover a wide gamut of activities such as technical and technological overhauling, investment or divestment, further training in all aspects of rehabilitation, introduction of preventive maintenance and quality control, improvement of financial and general management, advice on sectoral strategy and planning.

Rehabilitation is sometimes a very costly operation. It involves in most cases additional investment outlays in order to increase the performance of the existing equipment, train staff, make complementary investment (in infrastructure, for example), hire expatriate consultants for the phase of rehabilitation itself, and operate the plant better in the long run.

Figure VIII identifies and illustrates the tasks to be undertaken in order to restructure a plant.

The result of the restructuring process has to be carefully studied before a decision on rehabilitation is made. A comprehensive feasibility study on rehabilitation (rehabilitation study) has to be prepared. This study should examine the scope and the cost of the work to be done as compared with the expected benefits over the project lifetime. Positive results from the study provide an indication of whether to go ahead with the rehabilitation or abandon the idea. As indicated above, one of the reasons for many failures of plants in the past was the lack of properly prepared feasibility studies. Plant rehabilitation not backed by a feasibility study is again a gamble, where an investor and financial institutions risk a lot with unknown chances of success. Contrary to the case of new investments, plant owners and their banks do not shy away from the high cost of rehabilitation studies, since they are aware that an efficient rehabilitation may be the last alternative to bankruptcy and the only possibility to regain outstanding debts.

A team of experts is needed to prepare a rehabilitation study. Its composition depends on the complexity of the work to be done, but basically the team should be composed of a management and financial analyst (team leader), an industrial economist, a marketing specialist, an organization specialist, a process specialist (industrial engineer), and eventually specialized short-term consultants (on the environment, sociology etc.) to join the team depending on the specific nature of the project.

Only teamwork can guarantee good coordination of work done by consultants and a comprehensive final conclusion indicating whether to carry on rehabilitation or to abandon the project. The conclusions of individual consultants, although valuable, are often contradictory, and the coordination work is costly and not always sufficient to guarantee the full consistency of the rehabilitation study.

**Figure VIII.   The phases of rehabilitation projects**

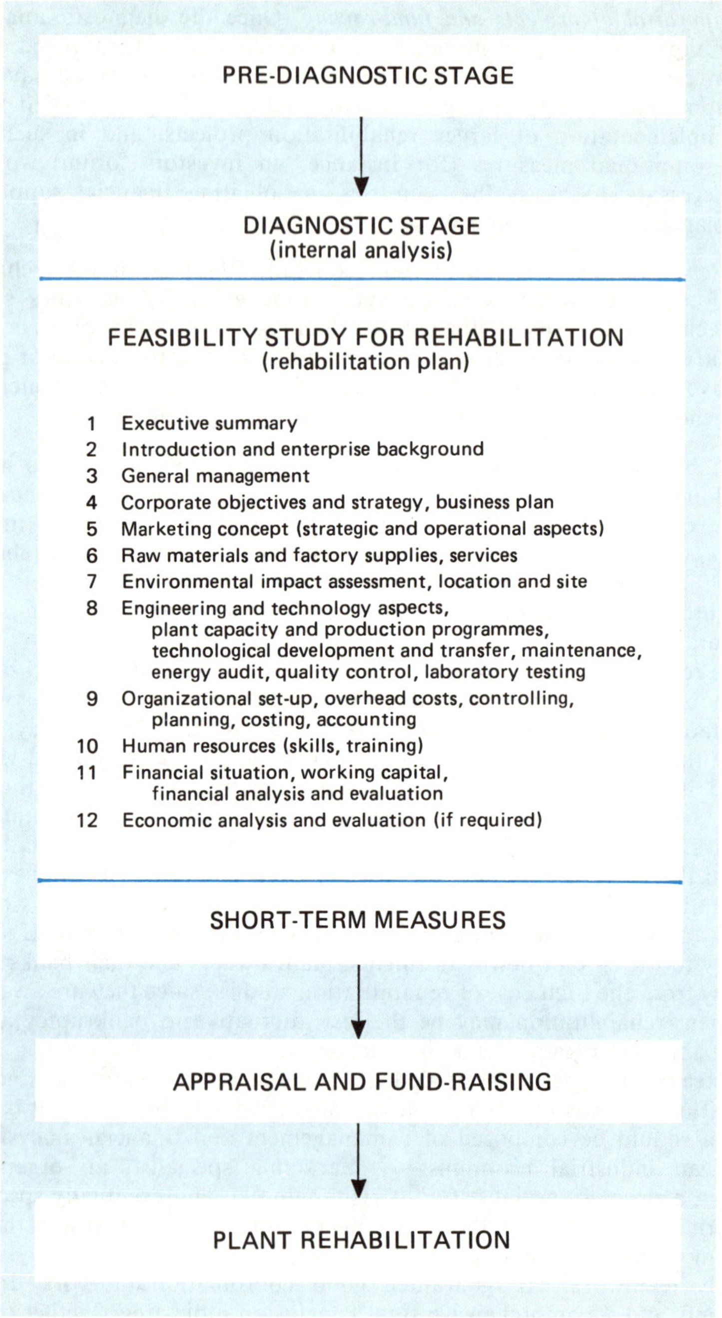

PRE-DIAGNOSTIC STAGE

DIAGNOSTIC STAGE
(internal analysis)

FEASIBILITY STUDY FOR REHABILITATION
(rehabilitation plan)

1   Executive summary
2   Introduction and enterprise background
3   General management
4   Corporate objectives and strategy, business plan
5   Marketing concept (strategic and operational aspects)
6   Raw materials and factory supplies, services
7   Environmental impact assessment, location and site
8   Engineering and technology aspects,
       plant capacity and production programmes,
       technological development and transfer, maintenance,
       energy audit, quality control, laboratory testing
9   Organizational set-up, overhead costs, controlling,
       planning, costing, accounting
10  Human resources (skills, training)
11  Financial situation, working capital,
       financial analysis and evaluation
12  Economic analysis and evaluation (if required)

SHORT-TERM MEASURES

APPRAISAL AND FUND-RAISING

PLANT REHABILITATION

## Structure of rehabilitation studies

The structure of a feasibility study for a new investment and of a rehabilitation study should be the same. It should indicate whether the project is feasible or not, and consequently whether it is worthwhile to carry out the rehabilitation works. However, different parts of the study might be worked out in a more detailed way, depending on the critical issues identified during the preliminary screening of the plant to be rehabilitated. As compared with new investment projects (greenfield-site project), a rehabilitation study may be more difficult to carry out because of various constraints, such as the given location of the plant, existing equipment or the employees on board. Although the contents of a feasibility study will be described in detail in part two of this *Manual*, the structure and contents of a rehabilitation study will be briefly described at this point, highlighting the relationships between studies for new investment and rehabilitation projects.

### General management

A major subject to be covered in a rehabilitation study is the existing structure and performance of the general management of the firm. By applying, in principle, the concepts referred to in the section on corporate or internal analysis,[26] the strengths and weaknesses of the top and middle management should be assessed, and recommendations drawn up, in cooperation with the key personnel of the firm, on how to improve the management structures and performance.

### Corporate analysis, market analysis and marketing concept

One of the main reasons for plant rehabilitation is the insufficient utilization of installed capacities. Its dimensions are usually excessive in relation to the size of the market segment that could possibly be covered by the plant.[27] A corporate (internal) analysis should be made, using check-list III-6. The basic project objectives and corporate strategies should be analysed *vis-à-vis* the current business environment, and a forecast of the short- and medium-term changes, such as market trends for critical outputs, has to be made. A new marketing strategy and a product analysis may lead to a redefinition of the production programme. Old products that have reached the last stage of the product cycle will have to be replaced by a new generation of products. Costs of marketing and product promotion are to be estimated. As with new investment, this part of the rehabilitation study is the most difficult.

### Raw material and factory supplies

Failure to achieve the project objectives economically may be due to problems with the raw materials and supplies required for a smooth operation. This could be because of quality or delivery problems and price increases. Once the reasons have been determined, possible strategies should be identified to overcome the deficiencies.

---

[26]See part two, chap. III, sect. B.

[27]The combination of production programme, capacity and the technology chosen often did not fit the business environment and conditions of a competitive market even when the initial investment was made, or the firm has not been able to adjust production to a changing business environment (see part one, sect. A, and part two, chap. III).

### Location, site and environment

The given site of a plant normally limits the flexibility of the study team. Heavily polluting industries may in extreme cases have to be relocated or even closed.

### Engineering and technology

The subjects to be studied include plant design, production planning, quality control, energy and equipment efficiency, including recommendations for installing new and scrapping old equipment within the framework of the physical rehabilitation programme, safety and environmental protection, as well as design of a new maintenance and spare-parts programme. The rehabilitation study may be limited to only one subject, such as an energy audit or quality control study.

### Plant organization and overhead costs

A frequent reason for rehabilitation is the lack of qualified local personnel. Other important reasons for inefficiency in plant operation are inappropriate organizational structures and the resulting high overhead costs. Frequently, plants undergoing rehabilitation lack well-functioning accounting and management information systems capable of producing reliable data for financial planning and cost control relating, in particular, to overhead costs. A review of the effectiveness of accounting practices and procedures may reveal the need for organizational adjustments and restructuring.

### Human resources

The main focus will be on staffing and training. Plants are frequently overstaffed because of governmental labour regulations. The findings of the rehabilitation study have to be presented to management in special seminars, and skill levels may need upgrading in order give effect to the recommendations of the rehabilitation programme.

### Project implementation

In cases where projects never came on stream, the reasons might have to be found in improper implementation planning, causing cost overruns, faulty construction etc. Such problems often arise from insufficient project preparation, as reflected in the choice of technology, engineering design, errors in data assessment and over-optimistic forecasts, as well as from an incomplete assessment of the resources required and available. Identifying the causes would help to determine possible rehabilitation measures.

### Financial evaluation

Directly linked to organizational matters is the analysis of the present financial structure and performance. Balance sheets, income statements, sources and the use of funds, debts, equity, working capital requirements and cash flow management are to be studied. The financial merits of the rehabilitation programme have to be highlighted, paying particular attention to the provision of sufficient working capital, the main cause of liquidity bottlenecks faced by ailing plants. Once the rehabilitation study has been completed and an action plan is designed, the physical rehabilitation of the plant will be initiated and implemented. Close monitoring of the result should guarantee that the provisions and forecasts made in the action plan are measured and achieved.

## 2. Expansion studies

This *Manual* is concerned with new industrial projects, but it may equally be applied to the expansion of existing production plants to determine the feasibility of, for example:

- An increase in the quantitative output of products and by-products without changing the range of products
- A change in the production programme by adding new products of the same line
- A combination of the foregoing

The quantitative expansion may be achieved by the following means:

- Introduction of shift work
- Raising the capacity of the weakest sections of a production line in order to increase its total capacity
- Upgrading the technology or increasing the capacity of entire production lines

The introduction of new products may lead to the installation of new production lines within the existing plant or, depending on their scale, to the erection of new production facilities at a separate location. Such expansion should, however, be treated as a new project. The procedure for the preparation of a feasibility study for expansion projects of the same product line is analogous to that given in the *Manual*, taking into account the determinant factors of the existing enterprise.

In order to formulate a comprehensive project proposal, the data of the expansion project must be synchronized and consolidated with those of the existing plant. Depending on the size of the expansion project, it should be clear whether the existing internal organizational structure and supporting facilities (such as utilities, administration and sales department) will be sufficient or need adjustments, or whether the expansion proposal should allow for a new structure that will absorb all existing ones. The extreme case may even be the selection of a new location.

The financial impact of an expansion may be expressed in terms of the marginal costs and benefits, as well as by comparing the overall economic implications of undertaking the expansion project with those of not doing so.

A list of data to be collected on an existing enterprise is provided in annex V. In order to facilitate the integration of the data into the feasibility study, the check-list is structured in the same way as the feasibility study.

## D. Role of institutions, consultancy services and information systems

### 1. Institutional infrastructure and consultancy

All those involved in the investment process must be interested in ensuring that adequate facilities are available to them for investment consultancy in both developing and developed countries. In that context, it should be taken into account, particularly in developing countries, that to a large extent consultancy services must still be obtained from abroad. It is therefore the task of technical cooperation, particularly on the part of international organizations, to strengthen or even establish a national consultancy capacity,[28] with special emphasis on investment.

### National investment promotion and development agencies

In most developing countries, development agencies have been established in the past with the primary task of identifying investment projects, formulating them in project profiles or opportunity studies, and seeking prospective promoters in the country and abroad. In the search for projects, they use, *inter alia*, area studies as well as market, industry and resource-based project studies. In many countries, however, such agencies also offer consultancy services for the preparation of pre-investment studies, covering technical, financial and economic aspects of project proposals. In that context, both pre-feasibility and feasibility studies are used as investment consultancy tools. With the growth of investment activities, many of these agencies have also started with the supervision of projects during the investment phase. In many cases, as development reaches higher stages, such agencies have developed into national consultancy firms with their own areas of specialization.

UNIDO in particular has actively cooperated in the past in setting up such development agencies in Africa and Asia. Technical cooperation projects have laid the foundation for efficient investment promotion and development agencies in Congo, Ethiopia, Malaysia, Nepal, Saudi Arabia, Senegal, Sri Lanka and United Republic of Tanzania.

### National financing agencies

Investment consultancy is also offered by the national development banks and commercial banks that take part in project financing. The focal point of consultancy by commercial banks is still the study of projects with material collateral. Only in the rarest cases are investment studies worked out as described in this *Manual*.

Commercial banks investigate investment projects as a rule from the point of view of their bankability. The creditworthiness of the customer and examination by the bank of the collateral offered are in general more important to the bank, which basically aims at risk minimization through securities, than taking on the task of analysing and appraising investment projects as an active

---

[28]See Werner Behrens, "Investitionsberatung", in *Handwörterbuch. Export und Internationale Beratung* (Stuttgart, C. E. Poeschel, 1989), p. 1002.

contribution to investment consultancy (through risk identification, evaluation and control). Such services would reduce the risk for the commercial banks and their customers, since the clarity of the projects would increase as a result, and uncertainty would thus be reduced. In recent years, commercial banks have therefore mainly financed working capital and, to a lesser extent, fixed capital investment, so that they have neglected a large field for business and industrial development.

Development banks, on the other hand, have emerged actively as investment consultants. In this role, they not only evaluate the bankability of projects, but also frequently prepare investment and profitability calculations for those of their customers who cannot perform such tasks. Only through even closer cooperation[29] between development and commercial banks will it be possible in future to counterbalance the narrower approach of the commercial banks and bring into play the greater project specialization of the development banks as an up-to-date form of investment consultancy.

## National consulting firms

Building up efficient consulting firms is of great importance to developing countries. Precisely in the field of investment consultancy it is important to have available national capacity so that there is less dependence on services from abroad. Good progress has been made in Latin America and Asia, where many competitive consulting firms have emerged that also work internationally. There are still great gaps in Africa. In some countries such as Algeria, Ethiopia, Kenya, Nigeria and the United Republic of Tanzania, there are already a few state and private consulting firms that have for a considerable time been able to make pre-investment studies of all kinds, and that participate actively in investment consultancy in the widest sense, rendering services in project management, engineering, construction supervision etc. In other countries, national consulting firms have also been set up, but owing to the lack of suitable management and other staff, as well as because of inadequate experience, they are not yet able to provide internationally acceptable investment consultancy services. Great scope exists for long-term international technical cooperation in the establishment of efficient consulting firms. The target groups are not only the development agencies and consulting firms, but also national and subregional development banks. The purpose of these activities is to standardize the pre-feasibility and feasibility studies to be carried out in the context of investment consultancy, and to improve their quality to such an extent that they meet an international standard.

## International organizations

Industrial investment consultancy has long been one of the traditional tasks of international organizations such as the United Nations, a number of its specialized agencies, including UNIDO, the Food and Agriculture Organization of the United Nations (FAO) and the International Labour Organisation

---

[29]Commercial banks have become interested in cofinancing projects adopted by development finance institutions such as the World Bank Group and various regional and national development banks.

(ILO), as well as the World Bank. All of these organizations provide the consultancy services required, either themselves, through their own staff, or by using the services of national and international consulting firms and consultants.

## International consulting firms and consultants

Investment consultancy during the pre-investment and investment phases is provided mainly by firms and individual consultants. However, universities, research institutes and international organizations are also working in this field. The number of institutions competing internationally for work in developed and developing countries is very large. The selection of the most suitable consultants is a difficult task, especially for investors from developing countries. Cooperation with consulting firms is also not simple, because appreciation of what a feasibility study is and how it should be used as an investment consultancy tool often varies widely.

The use of international consulting firms and consultants in investment consultancy comprises the preparation of pre-feasibility and feasibility studies, the training of management staff in this field, assistance in building up and expanding national consulting firms and investment promotion agencies etc. The experience and the know-how gained in that context exercise a decisive influence on the competitiveness of consulting firms. Not only must the high quality of consultancy be guaranteed, it must also be possible to purchase it at a price that has emerged as a result of international competition. As far as developing countries are concerned, difficulties often arise in the selection of firms and individual consultants, but they can be overcome, for example, by using the services of international organizations as neutral intermediaries.

Unfortunately, the quality of the studies delivered by consulting firms often leaves much to be desired, since the firms come from a wide variety of socio-economic systems and the focal points of the studies are often wrongly chosen. As experience shows, the requirements stated in the so-called terms of reference for feasibility studies are often too vague and incomplete, which is later reflected in the studies delivered. This deficiency is not surprising, as knowledge of the requirements of modern feasibility studies, precisely among medium-sized entrepreneurs, is not always up-to-date. Only through cooperation between the customer and the consultant in drafting the terms of reference, in an atmosphere of trust, which will, moreover, serve as the basis for determining the fee to be charged, can this difficulty be overcome. The UNIDO proposal to use standardized terms of reference is finding wider and wider acceptance in developing and developed countries.

## Equipment suppliers

Many developing countries are confronted with the problem that they must often make investment decisions on the basis of feasibility studies that sometimes even have to be prepared free of charge by equipment suppliers. This procedure is difficult to prevent, since no third party who could indicate the dangers of this type of investment consultancy is involved in direct contacts between investors and suppliers of equipment. The negative experience of African developing countries in particular indicates that studies prepared by suppliers are very often only expanded bids or "sales aids", and are offered in many countries simultaneously, with only slight alterations specific to the country in question. In many cases this procedure has led to misdirected investment and to the creation of excess capacity—cases now up for rehabilitation.

Investment consultancy on the part of equipment suppliers also has the disadvantage that no genuine alternatives for the selection of the technology and machines are discussed in such project proposals (which rarely meet with the minimum requirements for an unbiased feasibility study). In conducting pre-feasibility studies, investors or promoters may obtain alternative project proposals[30] worked out by several suppliers for one and the same project. In such cases, the proposals should be prepared under the same terms of reference to ensure that the studies are comparable. It should be further noted that many equipment suppliers, even from developed countries, still have too little experience of feasibility studies.

## 2. Electronic data processing

The amount of information required by decision makers during the different phases of the project cycle increases with the scope and complexity of investment projects. Data must be assessed and analysed for reliability, and the required projections (extrapolations) must be prepared and justified by the supporting data. It is also necessary to draw up project alternatives at the early opportunity or pre-feasibility stage, and to select the most promising alternative for which a more detailed feasibility study must be prepared. Under the constraint of limited human and financial resources, electronic data processing clearly has a significant contribution to make to improving the quality of pre-investment studies and subsequent investment and financing decisions.

### Role of personal computers

During the 1980s microcomputers, or personal computers as they are now usually called, have developed from small programmable desk calculators into very powerful machines that have the same or an even higher performance capacity, at only 1 per cent or less of the cost of the much bigger mainframe computer generation used in the 1970s. The personal computers currently available to users would, however, be of relatively little use without the many types of application software that have been developed at the same time. Apart from word processing for report writing and programmes for technical design, the application software described below plays an important role in project preparation and evaluation.

### Information systems

The purpose of information systems is to allow retrieval of selected information previously stored in the system or data bank. A data bank contains data in an organized and well-structured format, and the user of the system can

---

[30]The proposals would usually focus on technical or technological matters. It is therefore essential in such cases to ensure that the other critical aspects are also considered, as described in this *Manual*.

retrieve information, in other words, data defined by certain conditions. For example, the user may ask for a list of the total investment costs of all textile manufacturing projects prepared after 1982, or for data relating to investment projects implemented in a certain country between 1976 and 1985 with initial investment costs of over $5 million etc. When designing a data bank the following considerations are of utmost importance: objectives and volume of information; data bank structure; user interface (query language); data exchange with other systems (compatibility); and data bank maintenance. Project data banks can facilitate both the preparation and the evaluation of feasibility studies.

### Expert support systems

The main objective of expert support systems is to assist the user in the analysis of information. Like a modern user-friendly interface guiding the user in the operation of application software on a personal computer, an expert support system would be expected to guide the user through the logically necessary steps involved in data entries, computations and analysis. For example, when an industrial economist "tells" the system that he or she wants to produce a break-even analysis, the expert support system would "ask" for all data required to be entered. If reference data are available in a connected data bank, the system could also check whether the entered data are within a predefined margin. If this is not the case, the user would receive a warning message informing him that an entry might be wrong. Similarly, the system could compare the results, for example the break-even conditions, with reference data of similar and comparable projects.

### Statistical analysis systems

Statistical analysis systems often form part of an integrated software tool and allow the analysis of data series using statistical methods. Typical applications are time-series analyses for trend extrapolation, reliability tests and probability analysis.

### Simulation models

For the analysis of the feasibility of investment projects it is important to have an answer to the following question: what is the impact of a change of project parameters? Simulation models used for feasibility studies include market models, production models and financial statements such as projected balance sheets and net income statements. With a cash-flow model it is possible, for example, to calculate changes in the net present value or internal rate of return as a function of varying sales prices.

### Decision models

While simulation models help decision makers by showing how the feasibility of an investment would probably be affected by a change of the scenario, decision models help to determine which project alternative is preferable under certain conditions or constraints. Projects not fulfilling those conditions would be rejected.

## UNIDO software for project preparation and appraisal

Soon after the publication of the first edition of this *Manual*, UNIDO decided to develop COMFAR,[31] a software system that has evolved since 1982 from a model for financial analysis at the enterprise level into a complex system for financial and economic analysis of investment projects. This UNIDO software supports the preparation, appraisal and evaluation of pre-investment studies. Being available in the official languages of UNIDO as well as a number of other languages, it has been well accepted by development planning and financing institutions, consulting companies, banks and training institutions in most of the Member States of the United Nations.

COMFAR is basically a standardized simulation model for financial and economic analysis, directing the user through the physical operation of the personal computer on which COMFAR is installed and guiding him also in the entry of data and the computation of statements and various financial and economic indicators and ratios as required for project analysis. The new COMFAR generation, developed in conjunction with this second edition of the *Manual*, allows the exchange of data with spreadsheet and data-bank software available from leading software producers. With the new method of, on the one hand, guiding the user through the data entry system by requesting exactly the input required for the computation of the system output as predefined by the user, and, on the other hand, assisting with the analysis of the data by allowing a comparison with key data from similar investment projects previously stored in a COMFAR DataBank, the third generation of this UNIDO-developed computer software can be expected to contribute further to the improvement of financial and economic analysis and appraisal of investment projects.

The schedules contained in chapters III to X of part two of this *Manual* have a format compatible with COMFAR, although the UNIDO software incorporates many additional features permitting, for example, entries in different currencies and the preparation of economic cost-benefit analysis following different methodologies.

### Bibliography

Amachree, S.M.O. Investment appraisal in developing countries. Aldershot, Avebury, 1988.

Gittinger, J. P. Economic analysis of agricultural projects. 2. and rev.ed. Baltimore, Maryland, Johns Hopkins, 1982.

Gourdain Mitsotaki, A. Public development finance corporations; their role in the new forms of investment in developing countries. Paris, Organisation for Economic Cooperation and Development, 1986.

Handbook of development economics. Amsterdam, North Holland, 1989. 2 v.

Handwörterbuch. Export und Internationale Beratung. Stuttgart, C. E. Poeschel, 1989.

Hofmann, M. *and* K. Schedl, Hrsg. Entwicklungsmanagement: Beiträge zu einer neuen Dimension im internationalen Management. Berlin, Duncker und Humblot 1982.

---

[31]The UNIDO Computer Model for Feasibility Analysis and Reporting. User licences may be obtained from the UNIDO Department of Industrial Operations, Feasibility Studies Branch.

Mennes, L.B.M. Investment planning for economic cooperation among developing countries. Rotterdam, Erasmus Universiteit Rotterdam, Centrum voor Ontwikkelings-programmering, 1985.

Organisation for Economic Cooperation and Development. Development Centre. Manual of industrial project analysis in developing countries, v. 1. Rev.ed. Paris, 1972.

Sen, A. Resources, values and development. Oxford, Blackwell, 1984.

United Nations. Guide to practical project appraisal; social benefit/cost analysis in developing countries. [Prepared by John R. Hansen]
Sales no.: 78.II.B.3.

_____ Guidelines for project evaluation. [Prepared by P. Dasgupta, S. Marglin and A. Sen]
Sales no.: 72.II.B.11.

_____ Manual for evaluation of industrial projects. Prepared jointly by the United Nations Industrial Development Organization and the Industrial Development Centre for Arab States. (ID/244)
Sales no.: E.80.II.B.2.

_____ Manual on the establishment of industrial joint-venture agreements in developing countries. (ID/68)
Sales no.: 71.II.B.23.

PART TWO

# The feasibility study

# I. Executive summary

A feasibility study should arrive at definitive conclusions on all the basic aspects of a project after consideration of various alternatives. These conclusions and any recommendations made with regard to decisions or actions required from parties involved in the project would have to be explained and supported by compelling evidence. For convenience of presentation, the feasibility study should begin with a brief executive summary outlining the project data (assessed and assumed) and the conclusions and recommendations, which would then be covered in detail in the body of the study; any supporting material (statistics, results of market surveys, detailed technical descriptions and equipment lists, plant layouts etc.), however, should be presented in a separate annex to the study. The executive summary should concentrate on and cover all critical aspects of the study, such as the following: the degree of reliability of data on the business environment; project input and output; the margin of error (uncertainty, risk) in forecasts of market, supply and technological trends; and project design.

The executive summary should have the same structure as the body of the feasibility study, and cover—but must not be limited to—the following areas:

*Summary of the project background and history* (chapter II)

- Name and address of project promoter
- Project background
- Project (corporate) objective and outline of the proposed basic project strategy, including geographical area and market share (domestic, export), cost leadership, differentiation, market niche
- Project location: orientation towards the market or towards resources (raw materials)
- Economic and industrial policies supporting the project

*Summary of market analysis and marketing concept* (chapter III)

- Summarize results of marketing research: business environment, target market and market segmentation (consumer and product groups), channels of distribution, competition, life cycles (sector, product)
- List annual data on demand (quantities, prices) and supplies (past, current and future demand and supplies)
- Explain and justify the marketing strategies for achieving the project objectives and outline the marketing concept
- Indicate projected marketing costs, elements of the projected sales programme and revenues (quantities, prices, market share etc.)

- Describe impacts on: raw materials and supplies, location, the environment, the production programme, plant capacity and technology etc.

*Raw materials and supplies* (chapter IV)

- Describe general availability of:
  Raw materials
  Processed industrial materials and components
  Factory supplies
  Spare parts
  Supplies for social and external needs
- List annual supply requirements of material inputs
- Summarize availability of critical inputs and possible strategies (supply marketing)

*Location, site and environment* (chapter V)

- Identify and describe location and plant site selected, including:
  Ecological and environmental impact
  Socio-economic policies, incentives and constraints
  Infrastructural conditions and environment
- Summarize critical aspects and justify choice of location and site
- Outline significant costs relating to location and site

*Engineering and technology* (chapter VI)

- Outline of production programme and plant capacity
- Describe and justify the technology selected, reviewing its availability and possible significant advantages or disadvantages, as well as the life cycle, transfer (absorption) of technology, training, risk control, costs, legal aspects etc.
- Describe the layout and scope of the project
- Summarize main plant items (equipment etc.), their availability and costs
- Describe required major civil engineering works

*Organization and overhead costs* (chapter VII)

- Describe basic organizational design and management and measures required

*Human resources* (chapter VIII)

- Describe the socio-economic and cultural environment as related to significant project requirements, as well as human resources availability, recruitment and training needs, and the reasons for the employment of foreign experts, to the extent required for the project

- Indicate key persons (skills required) and total employment (numbers and costs)

*Project implementation schedule* (chapter IX)

- Indicate duration of plant erection and installation

- Indicate duration of production start-up and running-in period

- Identify actions critical for timely implementation

*Financial analysis and investment appraisal* (chapter X)

- Summary of criteria governing investment appraisal

- Total investment costs
  Major investment data, showing local and foreign components
    Land and site preparation
    Structures and civil engineering works
    Plant machinery and equipment
    Auxiliary and service plant equipment
    Incorporated fixed assets
    Pre-production expenditures and capital costs
    Net working capital requirements

- Total costs of products sold
    Operating costs
    Depreciation charges
    Marketing costs
    Finance costs

- Project financing
    Source of finance
    Impact of cost of financing and dept service on project proposal
    Public policy on financing

- Investment appraisal: key data
    Discounted cash flow (internal rate of return, net present value)
    Pay-off period
    Yield generated on total capital invested and on equity capital
    Yield for parties involved, as in joint venture projects
    Significant financial and economic impact on the national
      economy and environmental implications

- Aspects of uncertainty, including critical variables, risks and possible strategies and means of risk management, probable future scenarios and possible impact on the financial feasibility of the investment project

- National economic evaluation

- Conclusions
    Major advantages of the project
    Major drawbacks of the projects
    Chances of implementing the project

# Bibliography

United Nations. Extracts of industrial feasibility studies, v.1. Industrial planning and
programming series, No. 7. (ID/SER.E/7)
Sales no.: 73.II.B.4.

See also the bibliographies provided for the individual chapters.

# II. Project background and basic idea

To ensure the success of the feasibility study, it must be clearly understood how the project idea fits into the framework of general economic conditions and industrial development of the country concerned. The project should be described in detail and the sponsors identified, together with a presentation of the reasons for their interest in the project.

*Description of the project idea*

- List the major project parameters that served as the guiding principles during the preparation of the study
- Project (corporate) objectives and description and analysis of proposed basic project strategy,[32] including:
    Geographical area and market share (domestic, export)
    Cost leadership
    Differentiation
    Market niche
- Project location: market- or resource- (raw material) oriented etc.
- Product and product mix, plant capacity and location, implementation schedule
- Economic and industrial policies supporting the project
- Outline economic, industrial, financial, social, and other related policies
- Show different geographical levels, such as international, regional, national, areal and local
- Highlight the economic, sectoral and subsectoral project coverage

*Project promoter or initiator*

- Names and addresses
- Financial possibilities
- Role within the project
- Other relevant information

*Project history*

- Historical development of the project (dates of essential events in project history)

---

[32]See part one, sect. A, and part two, chap. III.

- Studies and investigations already performed (titles, authors, completion dates, ordering parties)
- Conclusions arrived at and decisions taken on the basis of former studies, and investigations for further use within the current study

*Feasibility study*
- Author, title
- Ordering party

*Cost of preparatory studies and related investigations*[33]
- Pre-investment studies
- Opportunity studies
- Pre-feasibility studies
- Feasibility study
- Partial studies, support studies
- Experts, consultant and engineering fees
- Preparatory investigations, such as:
    Land surveys
    Quantity surveys (quantification of building materials)
    Quality (laboratory) tests
    Other investigations and tests
- For calculation use schedule II and insert total in schedules X-2 and X-6.

---

[33]Provided they form part of the pre-production project expenses (schedule X-2) covered by the project and not by third parties.

## Schedule II. Costs of pre-investment studies and preparatory investigations
### (insert in schedule X-2)

Project:
Date:
Source:

Currency:                    Units:

| Item description | Costs of foreign components | Costs of local components | Total costs | Year |
|---|---|---|---|---|
| Pre-investment studies<br>...<br>...<br>... | | | | |
| Total costs, pre-investment studies | | | | |
| Preparatory investigations<br>...<br>...<br>... | | | | |
| Total costs, preparatory investigations | | | | |
| Grand total | | | | |

# III.  Market analysis and marketing concept

The basic objective of any industrial investment project is to benefit either from the utilization of available resources or from the satisfaction of existing or potential demand for the output of the project. As already discussed in part one, a project may also serve certain corporate strategies, such as strengthening the market position of a company or securing future supplies of necessary resources. However, for all investment projects, including those with the primary objective of resource utilization, market analysis is the key activity for determining the scope of an investment, the possible production programmes, the technology required and often also the choice of a location. As the preparation of a feasibility study is not a linear but an iterative process, market analysts must have an understanding of the quantity and quality of the products and by-products involved, and of possible alternatives with regard to the economic size, as determined by input availability and requirements, as well as by technological and locational constraints.

Once the present effective demand for the envisaged project output, the characteristics of the corresponding markets (unsatisfied demand, competition, imports, exports etc.) and possible marketing concepts have been determined, the desired production programme, including the required material inputs, technology and human resources, as well as suitable locations, can be defined. The demand or market analysis must be carefully structured and planned in order to obtain the required information within the time and cost limits, and to determine the possible marketing and production strategies required to reach the basic or corporate objectives. Planning of marketing research requires an understanding of the marketing system, the determination of the objectives and scope of the research, and proper structuring of the market to be analysed.

In this chapter the analyst will be guided through market analysis and the elaboration of a marketing concept, including the definition of a sales programme, the projection of revenues and marketing costs. Ideally the marketing experts should communicate and cooperate with the other members of the feasibility study team from the very beginning of the work, so as to avoid isolated marketing or engineering solutions that could prove to be financially unsound.

## A.  Marketing

The term marketing can be best explained as a market orientation of management with regard to business decisions. Market orientation of investment and finance decisions would therefore imply that feasibility studies need to incorporate the design of a marketing concept, which should be based on proper marketing research. Marketing can be characterized by the following four elements: business philosophy; marketing research; marketing instruments; and marketing plan and budget.

*Business philosophy.* Marketing is above all a business philosophy that does not focus on products or production, but puts the problems, needs and desires of existing or potential consumer groups at the centre of the business activities of the firm. This requires that decision makers at all levels and in all functional areas of the enterprise will have to orient their thinking towards the market.

*Marketing research.* Well-planned and systematic market and market-related research is a precondition for market-oriented decision-making. On the basis of information obtained about the potential market as well as the human, production and financial resources available for the project, marketing strategies are to be developed to ensure the achievement of the project objectives. It is important to note that market orientation of project preparation is not limited to sales markets of the enterprise. It is also necessary to analyse the supply markets and design a concept for securing the required project inputs. The aspects of supply marketing are dealt with in chapter IV, but the methodology for analysing both markets follows the same basic concept.

*Marketing instruments.* The successful implementation of marketing strategies requires shaping and influencing the market in a well-planned manner, using the necessary combination or mix of marketing instruments.

*Marketing plan and budget.* To achieve the marketing objectives it is necessary to determine the required measures or means and to prepare a plan of action on the basis of the findings of marketing research and using the marketing tools available. The corresponding marketing costs are summarized in the marketing budget, which is required for the evaluation of the project and for controlling its operation and performance after implementation.

The basic structure of this chapter and the integration of the marketing concept within the project strategy are shown in figure IX below. The pyramid shows how the planning process becomes more and more specific and detailed from the top (strategies) to the bottom (means and actions). It should be noted that the final marketing concept of the project can be developed only when the market data are assessed and scrutinized systematically, as described in the following sections. Only then will it be possible to minimize the risks related to uncertain future developments.

## Project strategy

A project strategy, as explained in part one of this *Manual*, is a set of objectives and principles defined for a project with a view to determining the allocation of resources over a period of time representing the planning horizon chosen for the project. The determination of project objectives and principles is important for the feasibility study, and is also the starting-point for the work described below.

The project strategy is central to both the preparation and the evaluation of an investment project, and to the design of a proper marketing concept. It also has a determining impact on the choice of location, technical plant parameters (production capacity, choice of technology etc.) and resource

**Figure IX. Marketing research and preparation of a marketing concept**

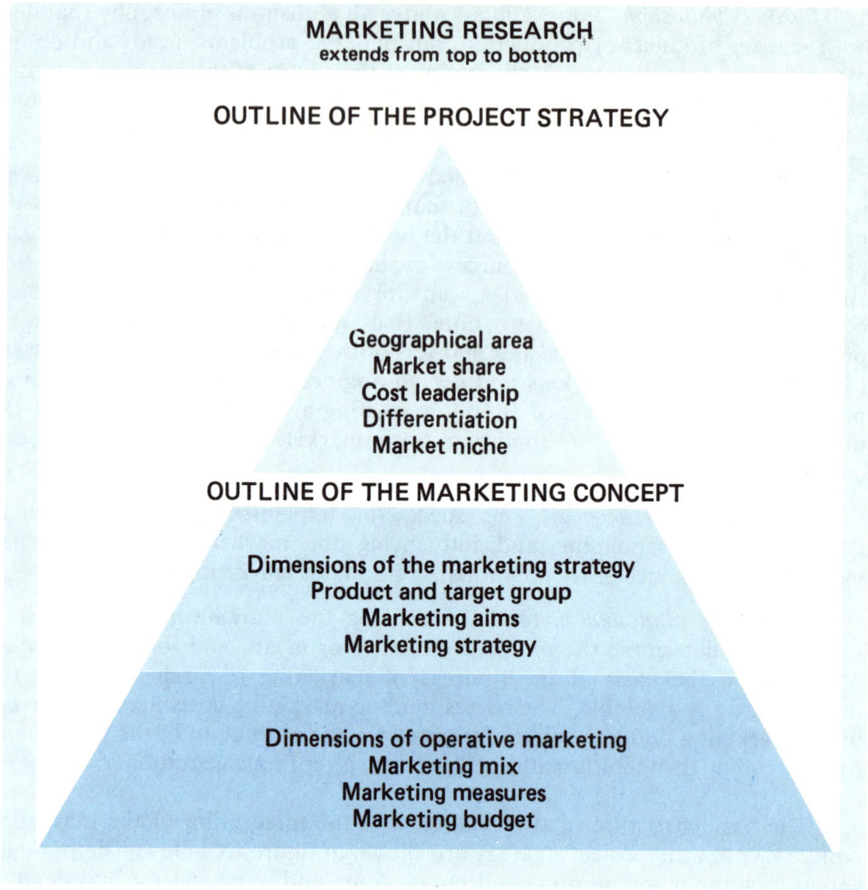

MARKETING RESEARCH
extends from top to bottom

OUTLINE OF THE PROJECT STRATEGY

Geographical area
Market share
Cost leadership
Differentiation
Market niche

OUTLINE OF THE MARKETING CONCEPT

Dimensions of the marketing strategy
Product and target group
Marketing aims
Marketing strategy

Dimensions of operative marketing
Marketing mix
Marketing measures
Marketing budget

requirements. The formulation of a project idea should include a description of a preliminary project strategy, such as achieving a production cost advantage over competitors, or penetrating an international capital goods market by co-operating with a foreign partner, or specializing in the manufacture of a high-quality product. One of the tasks of marketing research will be to examine a preliminary project strategy from the marketing point of view, and to identify alternative strategies.

### Marketing concept

The marketing concept comprises the marketing strategy and the operative measures required to implement the project strategy and reach the project or corporate objectives. When a project strategy has been defined, a suitable marketing concept can be designed in accordance with the phases described below.

## Strategic dimensions of marketing

The principal question is as follows: which marketing strategy is suitable to achieve the marketing targets within the conditions defined by the project strategy? The elaboration of the marketing strategy requires long-term orientation of project planning as well as long-term operation in the market after the project has become operational (the opposite concept being that of ad hoc reactions based on daily business). The marketing strategy to be considered involves the following dimensions: identification of target groups and of the products likely to win their favour; and determination of competition policies, that is, whether a low-price strategy or a differentiation strategy should be pursued to defeat competitors.

## Operative dimensions of marketing

*The marketing mix.* A distinction is usually drawn between four marketing tools, the combination known as the marketing mix. Figure X lists the activities related to four components, namely product, price, promotion and place.[34]

The four components are also referred to as submixes of the marketing mix. In this case, for example, it is possible to speak of a product mix, a distribution mix, a communications mix, and a price mix.

---

[34]The "four Ps" of Philip Kotler.

### Figure X. The marketing mix

PRODUCT
Scope of product mix
Depth of product mix
Quality
Design
Packaging
Maintenance
Service
Warranty service
Possibility of returning a purchase

PRICE
Price positioning
Rebates and conditions of payment
Financing conditions

PROMOTION
Advertising
Public relations
Personal sale
Sales promotion
Brand policy

PLACE
Channels of distribution
Distribution density
Lead time
Stock
Transport

*Source:* As proposed by Philip Kotler.

*Marketing measures and the marketing budget.* For the feasibility study it is necessary to determine the marketing activities and to prepare a time schedule indicating the starting-point and duration of those activities which are essential for the project. The objective of marketing activities planning is to determine the means and resources required, and to coordinate and control pre-production marketing as well as marketing during the operational phase of the project. The marketing activities plan is therefore the main precondition for the projection of both marketing costs and sales revenue (sales volume and prices), which are discussed later in this chapter.

## B. Marketing research

For the development of the project strategy and the marketing concept, careful marketing research, that is, a concise and systematic assessment of information on the market and market environment, is essential. It is the task of marketing research to obtain, analyse and interpret this information, and to provide the basis for decisions of a strategic or marketing nature. Marketing research consists mainly in the analysis of demand (end-use and trading) and competition, customer behaviour and consumer needs, competitive products and marketing instruments, taking into account the interdependencies between the individual subjects themselves, their relation to the market as a whole, and the impact of social, ecological and economic factors.

The scope of marketing research required for a feasibility study is determined by the need to select and justify a project strategy (and alternatives) and the development of a corresponding marketing concept. The research work proceeds step by step, in line with the planning process, as reflected in figure IX. Logically, the quality of all subsequent decisions depends on the quality of data assessment. Any errors made in the research phase would result in wrong marketing concepts, and may place the whole project in jeopardy.

### The marketing system

Before starting with marketing research and the subsequent design of a marketing concept, it is necessary to have an understanding of the functions of marketing, the marketing tools, and who and what determines the characteristics of the market that the project is supposed to enter. Enterprises cannot act independently and autonomously in a market and within an economy or socio-economic system. There are interdependencies between competitors and partners as well as relations between producers and customers. For both activities, the market analysis and the design of a marketing concept, an understanding is needed of these interconnections between producers and end-users—which may be interpreted as a marketing system—and of the instruments or tools available to enterprises to achieve their sales targets.

The choice of the marketing tools for a product is not only influenced by the customers, but depends on the objectives and activities of all market participants. These objectives and activities are interdependent in so far as each participant, before determining the optimal strategies and marketing mix, has to consider what the other participants are doing or planning. Figure XI shows the structure of the system of relations between manufacturers, sales agents and consumers.

**Figure XI. Marketing research and the marketing system**

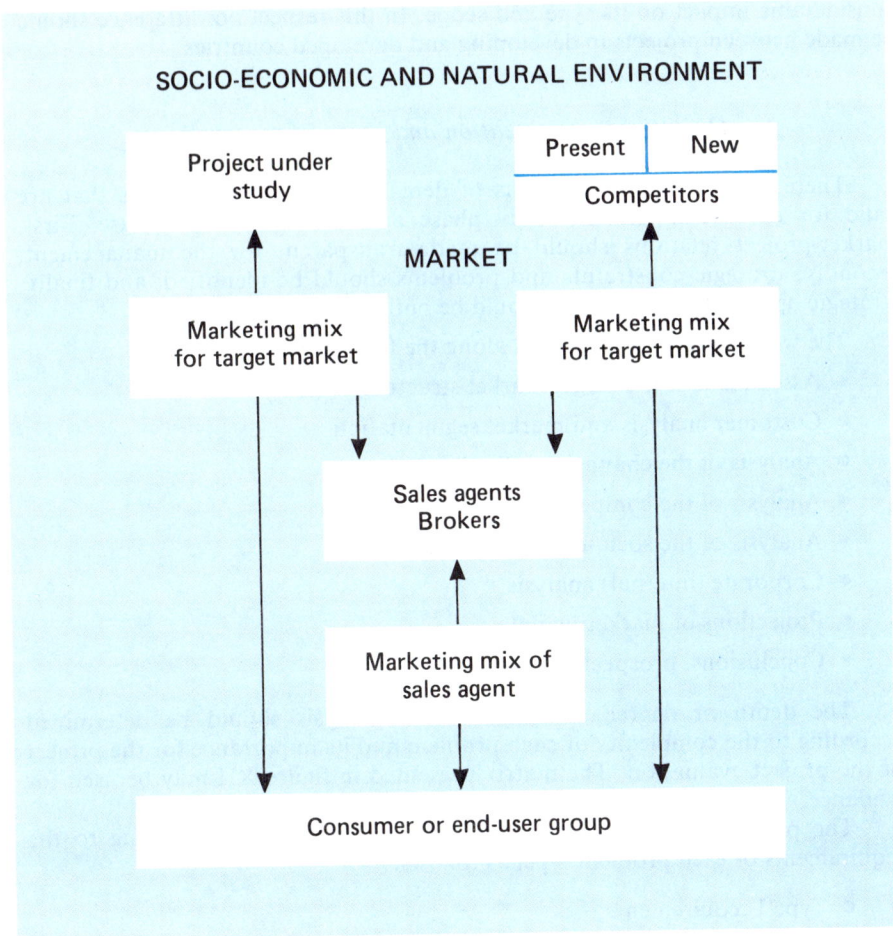

A systems approach to marketing, as shown in figure XI, facilitates the understanding of interdependencies between market participants and their activities. The elements of this system are enterprises and organizations as well as single persons playing a specific role in the market exchange process. For example, there could be a competitor with a high-price policy; another competitor could have a low-price policy and a correspondingly low-quality product; there may be wholesalers or retailers offering special customer services; and, last but not least, there are consumers with different levels of purchasing power.

The relations between market participants (the elements of the system) relevant for marketing research are primarily represented by the activities of the participants, such as the exchange of goods and services, payments and the use of marketing instruments *vis-à-vis* traders and consumers. During the pre-investment phase of a project, marketing research usually concentrates on market analysis (basically the analysis of supply and demand). Often the marketing instruments are insufficiently or not at all considered in the research work, although assessment of the marketing mix of the main competitors and the determination of a marketing mix suitable for the project could have a considerable impact on its type and scope. In this respect no difference should be made between projects in developing and developed countries.

### Objectives, organization and scope of research

There are three principal aims of demand and market analysis that are valid for the pre-investment study phase and the operational phase. First, market-project relations should be made transparent for the management; secondly, strategic constraints and problems should be identified; and finally, strategic options for the project should be outlined.

The work should be organized along the following lines:

- Assessment of the target market structure
- Customer analysis and market segmentation
- Analysis of the channels of distribution
- Analysis of the competition
- Analysis of the socio-economic environment
- Corporate (internal) analysis
- Projections of marketing data
- Conclusions, prospects and risks

The depth or degree of detail of the analysis should be determined according to the complexity of each problem and its importance for the project or the project evaluation. The matrix presented in figure XII may be used for guidance.

The problem classification matrix may be interpreted according to the requirements of each problem type, as follows:

- Type I requirements

    A very precise and comprehensive analysis

    A thorough market and competition analysis

    A detailed consideration of further strategic options

    Gradual refining of functional strategies (marketing, production etc.), with checking or justification of underlying critical assumptions

- Type II requirements

    A thorough analysis of problems

    A rough consideration of the most important strategic alternatives

    A gradual refining of critical functional strategies

- Type III requirements

    An assessment and description of the problems relating to the project

    Drafting of a concept without explicitly elaborating alternative options

68

**Figure XII.   Problem classification**

| Importance for the project / Novelty or complexity of the problem | High | Medium | Low |
|---|---|---|---|
| High | I | I | II |
| Medium | I | II | III |
| Low | II | III | IV |

Source: Based on R. Kühn.

- Type IV requirements

    A simple assessment of the project conditions

    Preparation of a concept based on the most important or critical aspects only

A feasibility study would by definition fall under type I, although not all problem areas of the study would finally be in this category. For example, some problem areas in the market analysis may have little importance for the project and be of medium or low complexity. As a general rule, pre-feasibility studies would be of type II, and opportunity studies of type III or IV.

### Data assessment

There are basically two options for obtaining the required data, and in most cases both options are combined. Whereas overall quantitative estimates are based entirely or mainly upon results of *desk research,*[35] more detailed quantitative findings and those of a qualitative nature emerge typically from the other principal form of market research, the *field survey.*[36] Overlapping between these two means of data assessment occurs because, when assessing market size and characteristics, written sources will quite commonly have to be supplemented by interviewing, tests and observations. Interviewing of carefully selected key persons is an efficient way to extract the necessary market know-how. No field survey should be undertaken before the full potential of desk research has been exhausted. All relevant written material from within and outside the enterprise should be collected and then analysed, in order to minimize, on the one hand, the various financial costs incurred in field surveys, and, on the other, the possibility of straining the tolerance of respondents by undue consumption of time at interviews. Sampling principles are explained in annex G, while annex H deals with the details of field surveys.

---

[35]Desk research is the assessment of existing information contained, for example, in statistics and reports that were originally collected or prepared for other purposes.

[36]A field survey is the assessment of information directly by interviews, tests and observations.

Two types of market information can be distinguished, namely general market data and specific data for a particular market segment (consumer group, product or product group). Most marketing studies include data on the following:

- General economic indicators relating to product demand, such as population level and growth rate, per capita income and consumption, gross domestic product per capita and annual growth rate, and income distribution

- Government policies, practices and legislation, to the extent directly related to consumption, production, imports and exports of the products in question, standards, restrictions, duties, taxes, as well as subsidies or incentives, credit control and foreign exchange regulations

- Present level of domestic production, by volume and value, including production intended for internal consumption and not placed on the market

- Present level of imports, by volume and value (c.i.f. and local costs)

- Production and imports of substitutes and near-substitutes

- Critical inputs (see also chapter IV) and complementary products

- Production targets determined in national economic plans, where applicable for products in question, substitutes and complementary products

- Present level of exports, by volume and value (f.o.b.)

- Behavioural patterns, such as consumer habits and responses, individual and collective, and trade practices

The specific demand and market data for a particular market segment should be identified and its availability for the feasibility study ascertained. The range of the data, however, depends on the nature of the product and the type and degree of market research that it may involve (see figure XII). It is not practicable to make any classification or prescribe any guidelines in this regard. In one case, past production figures may be decisive; in another, they may be misleading. The same holds true for data on imports, past consumption and prices. The determinants in each case should be considered, since in most developing countries free market forces are hardly operative, and varying controls can result in considerable distortion of data. The demand for a product may have been suppressed by market imperfections such as mono-polistic or oligopolistic competition and trade policies involving high import tariffs, which would not be payable on domestic products. Artificially high domestic prices may be imposed on certain products whose imports are severely restricted, but the pattern of demand, and consequently of product pricing, would change materially once the product became available in large quantities.

It is, however, necessary to identify the specific demand and market data required for a particular product, the extent to which such data are available and could be utilized in the feasibility study, or the alternative data on which the conclusions of the study have to be based. Sources of information have to be identified and located in each case. Considerable information may be available from official published data, including statistical handbooks, census reports and resource, area or sectoral opportunity studies conducted by governmental agencies, institutions or associations such as chambers of commerce. Such data are seldom complete or broken down for the purpose of marketing research, and may serve rather as a starting-point for the work. In developing countries it is common for data to be available on general economic indicators but inadequate or not readily available on existing production figures. In some developing countries such information is considered confidential as far as production in particular industries is concerned. Import data, for example, may not always be accessible and up-to-date, and in many cases a number of items are lumped together and disaggregation may be difficult, if not impossible. Should recent statistics on imports be unavailable from one Government, a picture may in some instances be deduced from the export statistics of others. Desk research is normally decisive in establishing the quantitative parameters, and recourse to all conceivable written sources, including special government statistical compilations, is often necessary.

The period to be covered by a demand and market study varies. In one case, data over 10 years may be barely adequate because of abnormal fluctuations during the period; in another, it may not be possible to cover a period of more than three or four consecutive years. Figures for a single recent year may be exceptional in some way, and should not be used as a basis for projections.

### Assessment of the target market structure

In accordance with the proposed organization of marketing research, the first step of demand and market analysis is to determine the target market of the project and to describe and analyse the structure of this market. The clear identification of the market and the qualitative analysis of the market structure are fundamental to concise market research. It is important to assess and describe all significant relations between the elements of the marketing system (see figure XI), that is, the structure of the industry (suppliers, types of enterprises, organization of the industry or branch), customer profiles, patterns of employment and competition and structure of distribution. Examples of standard forms for this analysis are shown in the appendix to chapter III (check-lists III-1 and III-2).

### Customer analysis and market segmentation

After the assessment of the market structure, the customers and their needs and behaviour must be identified. The following aspects should be analysed:

- What is bought on the market?
- Why is it bought? What is the purchasing motive?
- Who are the buyers, the purchasing decision makers and persons participating in the decision?
- When is it bought (decision-making process, purchasing practices such as seasonal purchases)?
- How much is bought (purchasing quantity and frequency)?
- Where is the purchase made?

The above questions must be studied carefully before the marketing mix is designed. Different markets have different characteristics as regards customer behaviour. There is normally a difference between consumer-goods markets and capital-goods markets.

*Consumer-goods markets* show the following characteristics:

- The customer has complex needs that he or she is often only partially aware of;
- The performance offered has not only a functional, but also an emotional significance to the customer;
- There is often no real decision-making process, but rather brand-oriented, routine or impulse buying;
- Customer opinion is highly important.

*Capital-goods markets* show the following characteristics:

- The items purchased are intended for further use in a production process;
- Customer needs are most frequently based on a clearly defined purpose;
- There is often a complicated decision-making process within organizations with many internal opinion leaders;
- The customer often has a deep or expert knowledge of the product;
- There is a relatively long period of time between the first customer contact and the conclusion of the contract.

## Market segmentation

A market analysis can be made for either the market as a whole or each market segment separately. It is advisable, however, to divide the market into certain segments, on the basis of differentiated customer behaviour. Market segmentation is, moreover, a central prerequisite for efficient use of the marketing tools.

A market segment has to meet three requirements:

- Customer behaviour within the segment has to be as uniform as possible;
- The segment has to be clearly distinct from others;
- The size of the segment has to be big enough to ensure that a differentiated market treatment by the enterprise would pay off.

Segmentation can be based on the following factors:

- Geographical or linguistic criteria, such as nationality, region, urban or rural predominance etc.;
- Socio-demographic criteria for individuals (age, sex, income, education, profession, size of household etc.) or enterprises (corporate size, industrial branch etc.);
- Psychological criteria (innovativeness of customers, purpose, status etc.).

*Market analysis*

In general, the first step is the preparation of a detailed estimate of the actual market volume (for example, current sales in a certain market or market segment) and the market potential, or maximum possible demand of the total market (see figure XIII). The second step is to project the development of the future market volume, dealt with below in the section on the projection of marketing data. This is the basis for the question of the actual or envisaged market share of the enterprise. The targeted market share provides the basis for the projection of sales quantities, and therefore for the production programme, plant capacity and derived requirements for materials and inputs, labour, investment etc., as shown elsewhere in this *Manual*.

Market segmentation and market analysis are highly interrelated, and should therefore always be linked and not carried out separately.

**Figure XIII.   Market volume and market share**

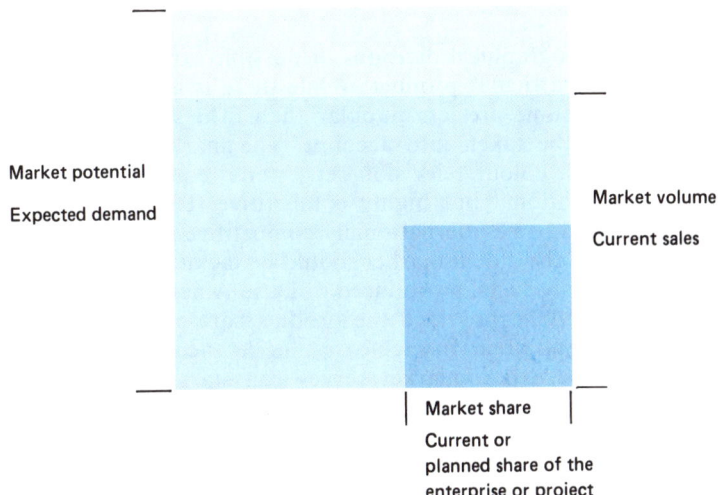

*Export markets*

The possibility of extending the market to other countries should be explored for most projects of any size, as export sales have to be taken into consideration in determining plant capacity. It may be possible, through expansion of plant capacity, to cater to a much larger market than that of the home country. Though a project may be conceived primarily as an import-substitution measure, it may nevertheless have export capability either immediately on commencement of production, or within a reasonable period during which productive skills can be developed in order to be able to offer a product meeting international quality standards at a competitive price. For example, a petrochemical or fertilizer plant can enter export markets much easier after commencement of operations, but the export of heavy electrical equipment may take some years until plant capability is adequately established and products are fully tested. In all such cases, export capability needs to be

73

assessed, and the determination of possible export markets is therefore an essential feature of demand forecasts.

International competition is furthered especially through economies of scale, for example, in production or marketing, through comparative locational advantages, the development of international cooperation, access to technologies etc. On the other hand, international marketing may be hampered by high shipping and warehouse costs, sensitivity to terms of delivery, different national product requirements and trade barriers, such as import restrictions, foreign exchange control and stringent industrial standards.

For products that developing countries are contemplating, or have just started, manufacturing—and these would be the majority of goods and services from developing countries—the starting-point should be an analysis of past imports into the home country, the unit cost of such imports, the exporting countries and the characteristics of the imported product. Such information is necessary, even from the viewpoint of domestic production, to test the competitiveness of the product.[37]

First, the price and quality of the product in the international market should be determined, which is not difficult. When related to export incentives and facilities provided by the home country, the pricing factors can be identified.

Secondly, the geographical divisions of possible exports should be defined in the context of a particular product. While there is an international market for most products, some are less popular than others, and various obvious constraints have to be taken into account. The market for such consumer products as cameras, colour television sets, stereo equipment and electronic calculators is international but highly competitive. However, if a proposed product is considered to be internationally competitive in terms of quality and technological inputs, the global market should be tackled step by step. There is no reason why such products, if produced in Latin America, should not be able to enter markets in Asia, provided the products are competitive in terms of technology, quality and price. In such cases, no detailed survey of all countries is necessary, and the export market survey can start with certain principal markets to be penetrated initially and gradually extended to other countries as plant capacity is expanded to meet increased market demand.

The feasibility study should therefore deal with the following questions:

- Will the enterprise gain strategic advantages by operating more internationally?

- What advantages will it gain in particular (example: economies of scale in production)?

- To what degree and in which fields does international competition pose a threat to the project?

---

[37]Except for small projects designed solely for local markets, there is a close relationship and interaction between the domestic and foreign manufacture of a product. Domestic products are frequently in competition with imported products except in countries imposing severe import controls. But even in the latter case, the price, quality and delivery of equivalent imported products has a considerable impact on the price and quality of domestic products. In some countries, a direct relationship is established in the matter of pricing, and domestically manufactured products have to sell at a certain percentage (approximately 20-25 per cent) below equivalent imported products. Even in the case of public sector projects, it is attempted to relate product pricing to the pricing of comparable imported products.

74

- What will be the future extent of the advantage of the enterprise operating on a geographically limited field?

The possibility of extending the market to other countries should be explored for most projects. After delineation of the geographical division of possible export markets on the basis of reasonable projections as to the degree of penetration, a special market survey may need to be undertaken in selected countries. The scope of such a survey would vary depending on the degree of export orientation contemplated for the project.

The factors governing export markets tend to be more complex than those governing domestic markets. While the techniques of estimating and forecasting are basically the same, they need to be considered in a selective way by analysing certain countries. The scope of such a survey varies according to the degree of export orientation contemplated for the project. Thus, export surveys could range from projections of past imports in an external market with general projections for the future to a detailed demand forecast in any particular external market using the forecasting techniques described later (see annex VI to this *Manual*). This should, however, be undertaken rarely, and only when the export prospects of a particular product justify such an expensive course.

For customer analysis and market segmentation see check-lists III-1, III-2 and especially III-3 in the appendix to chapter III.

## *Analysis of the channels of distribution*

Sales or distribution channels are the chain connecting producers and end-users. This mediation function is usually performed by specialized enterprises, agencies or representatives, using their own marketing instruments. In addition, these channels are also lines of information between manufacturers and consumers. Either separately or in combination, the three main routes to the end-customer are as follows: through wholesalers to retailers; through retailers only; directly to consumers. The choice of distribution channels should be based on the results of the market research.

### *Distribution through wholesalers*

This channel performs a particularly valuable function where many different articles are involved, and when distribution must be made to many small retail outlets. The advantages of this distribution channel are as follows:

- The wholesaler often accepts large commodity consignments to hold in stock or inventory;
- The wholesaler reaches a majority of the small shopkeepers;
- The transport problems of the manufacturer, invoicing and credit control are comparatively simple;
- Relatively few salespersons are needed by the manufacturer.

### *Distribution through retailers*

Distribution may be unrestrictive or selective, the former being feasible for some branded articles such as cigarettes, which are bought by a very wide variety of consumers at frequent intervals, and for certain unbranded items which are similarly purchased. Selective distribution is suitable for products of high quality, branded and advertised nationally or regionally, and which may require skilled installation with after-sales service; some consumer durables are likely to be distributed thus. The advantages of selective distribution are, among other things, that the producer is closer to the consumers, and that there exists a closer relationship between manufacturer and retailer.

### Distribution directly to consumers

Direct sale is the usual channel for industrial products and capital goods, for which it is ordinarily most cost-effective, although the appointment of distributors can be necessary in certain industries. Manufacturers' agents may be appointed by an existing or emergent manufacturing enterprise, by a larger one entering distant markets or within a restricted market. Such agents can be responsible for distribution but not usually for warehousing; they order from the factory as they sell, earning a commission. In an export territory the importer will carry out the functions of a manufacturer's agent, and others such as customs clearance, but the importer buys the goods for resale.

If the manufacturer takes over all distributive functions, there may be resulting advantages of closer control of relations with, and better service to, users. Other direct sales channels are house-to-house selling and mail orders.

As reflected in figure XI, the sales agent services as a channel through which the producers can reach the consumer. The project marketing measures have to support the marketing mix of the sales agents, whose interests, mainly in packaging and promotion, have to be taken into account from the very beginning.

### Analysis of the competitors

Assessing the project situation must also take into account the intentions of competitors. In analysing the competitors it is essential to focus on important individual competitors or on groups displaying similar behaviour. The questions raised in figure XIV must be confronted.

In a second step the analysis will have to be further elaborated, giving special attention to the following questions:

- How do the competitors use their marketing tools?
- Which target groups (segments) do they work on and how extensively?
- In which segments have they special strengths and where are their weaknesses?

Check-list III-4 in the appendix to chapter III shows the most important information to be identified in the analysis of the competitors.

### Analysis of the socio-economic environment

The market research should include an analysis of the industrial subsector concerned, as well as an assessment and analysis of the relevant economic and social environment of the project. The subsector analysis should provide an

**Figure XIV. Assessing the profile of possible reactions of competitors**

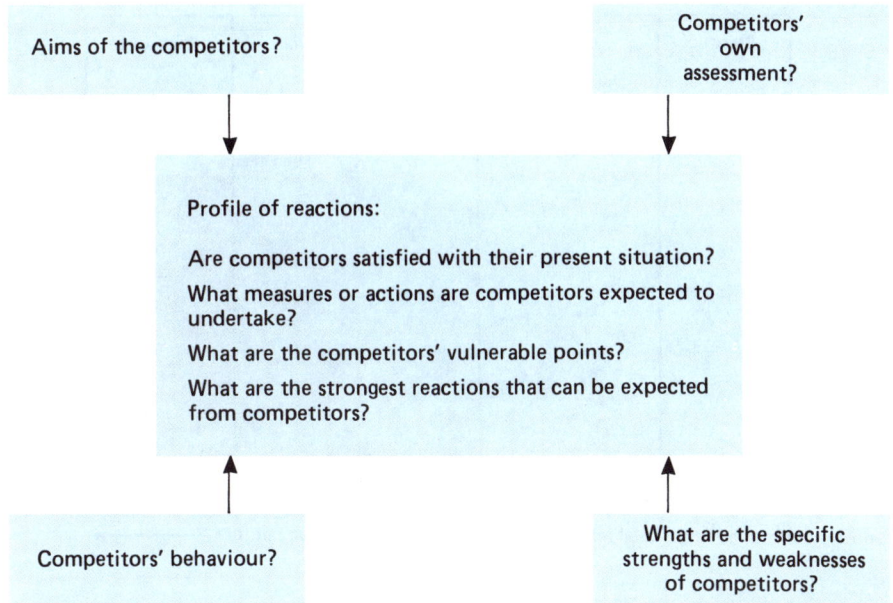

answer to the following main question: what are the key success factors in a competitive environment, and what significant opportunities and risks are sector-specific? The analysis should in principle concentrate on the life cycle of the subsector, its profitability and the wider socio-economic environment of which the industrial subsector is a part.

*Life cycle of a subsector*

The life cycle of a subsector[38] is of special importance. Figure XV shows the various phases of the cycle.

The subsector in which a project is planned may be in any of the typical phases of its life cycle. The following are examples of subsectors in different phases: solar energy (start-up); electronics components (growth); cars and food (maturity or saturation); and shipbuilding (shrinkage). The phases in the life cycle of a subsector may differ, however, depending on whether it is viewed in the context of the world economy or the economy of a single country. The exact definition of the relevant market aimed at by the project is therefore a vital element of the assessment.

Identifying the phase of the life cycle is important because it also implies conclusions as regards the present and future development of the market potential, the market volume and the market share. In order to be successful in competition, different strategies will have to be applied for each individual phase of the life cycle.

---

[38]A subsector comprises a group of enterprises manufacturing products that could almost replace each other. It should be noted that because of technological innovations, for example, an industry in the maturity phase may become a subsector in the growing phase again.

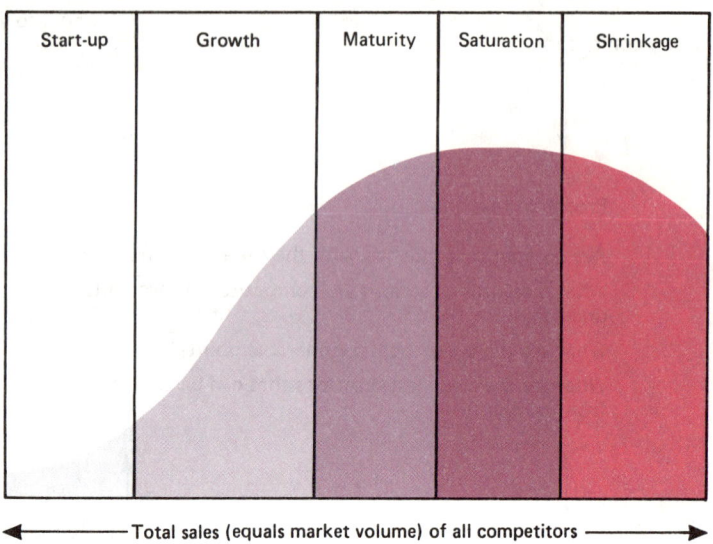

**Figure XV.    The life cycle of a subsector**

Market volume

| Start-up | Growth | Maturity | Saturation | Shrinkage |

◄──────── Total sales (equals market volume) of all competitors ────────►

*Profitability of the subsector*

The higher the intensity (strength) of competition in a subsector, the greater the pressure on the (operational) margin of the sellers. The intensity of competition, as reflected in figure XVI, is basically expressed by the height of entry and exit barriers, the phase in the subsector life cycle, the pressure through substitute products, and the negotiating power of the buyers and suppliers.

**Figure XVI.    Intensity of competition**

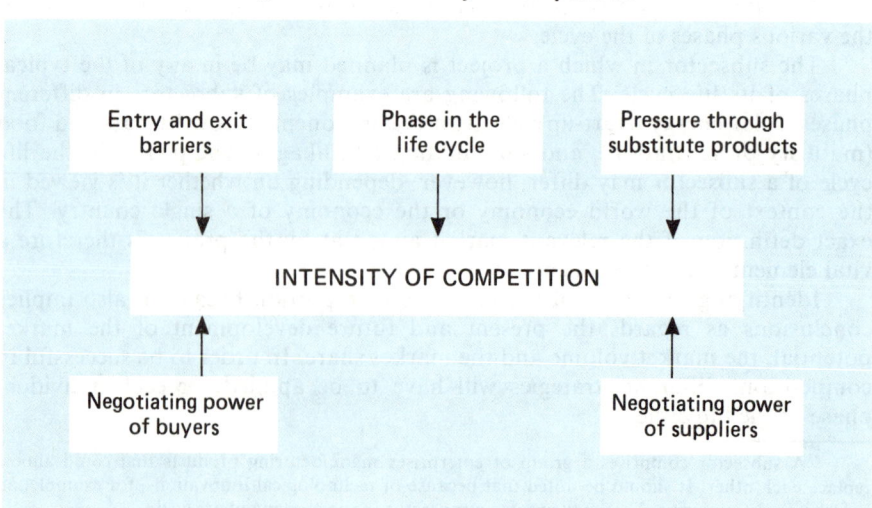

| Entry and exit barriers | Phase in the life cycle | Pressure through substitute products |

INTENSITY OF COMPETITION

| Negotiating power of buyers | | Negotiating power of suppliers |

*Height of entry and exit barriers.* Entry barriers prevent new competitors from entering the subsector. The risk of other competitors entering the market mainly depends on the reaction by established competitors and the height of entry barriers. Entry barriers include experience and size of the established firms, strong existing customer relations, franchises, legal protective barriers, high investment etc.

High exit barriers also intensify competition in a subsector and tend to reduce prices and margins. Exit barriers exist when:

- Capacity utilization should be as high as possible owing to high fixed expenditure;
- It is difficult to lay off employees;
- Political considerations have to be made.

*Phase in the life cycle.* The intensity of competition among existing competitors is highest when many firms compete for slowly growing, stagnating or even shrinking sales.

*Pressure through substitute products.* In a broader sense, many subsectors are competing with industries in which substitutes are manufactured. For the buyer, substitutes fulfil the same function as the original products. These functions are often met by means of a different technology. The more flexible the buyers, the higher the pressure on margins in an individual subsector.

*Negotiating power of the buyers and suppliers.* The possession of substantial negotiating power by the buyers and suppliers is another cause for smaller margins. The negotiating power of the buyers and suppliers mainly depends on the importance of an individual firm for the buyers. The pressure on margins is increased in particular when a choice of buyers and suppliers is lacking or limited.

### Analysis of the wider socio-economic environment

The objective of the analysis of the wider socio-economic environment is to determine social and socio-economic aspects relevant to the preparation and evaluation of the project strategy and marketing concept. Such aspects may reflect the society and its culture, social and economic policies, and related regulations, customs and habits. They are relevant to the extent that they have an impact on project opportunities and risks. Check-list III-5 in the appendix to chapter III gives an idea of aspects to be explored by the analysis of the wider socio-economic environment.

### Corporate or internal analysis

The internal analysis usually applies only for investment projects of existing enterprises, as in the case of expansion, rehabilitation and modernization projects. As a general rule, this analysis has to refer to all corporate areas. Thus marketing, production, research and development, finance, personnel, management and organization have to be taken into account.

The following questions must be answered first, in order to determine proper project strategies:

- Which aims and strategies does the enterprise currently pursue?
- What strengths and weaknesses does the enterprise have?
- With regard to strengths and weaknesses of the enterprise, which are the current core skills?

A check-list and form (III-6) for the analysis of an existing enterprise is given in the appendix to chapter III.

### Projecting marketing data

The projection of future developments is, perhaps, the most significant and certainly the most complex element of marketing research, as it is the critical factor for determining both the scope of the project and the resources required. Essentially, such projections need to cover quantitative and qualitative data concerning supply and demand in the markets, the market shares envisaged, the competitive situation etc., as previously described. The basis for quantitative methods is always a thorough understanding of how a certain subsector is developing, and all figures produced with statistical methods should always be interpreted with regard to any possible reasons or causes underlying a trend. No forecast method can substitute for a wrong or incomplete understanding of market and subsector characteristics and trends.

Where a particular product is to be manufactured in a country for the first time and a system of licensing and import controls is operating, consumer reactions and the possibility of product substitution would be the determining factors. For instance, market penetration of the first synthetic fibres produced in a country would depend on the substitution of such fabrics for natural fibres. As successive units are established, however, the competitive element would be the principal determining factor and price considerations would be dominant, although other aspects, such as quality and brand names, could also have some impact.

The various forecasting techniques are described briefly in annex F, to facilitate the selection of those methods which are the most suitable for the preparation as well as for the evaluation of feasibility studies. The following techniques may be used for demand forecasting:

- The trend (extrapolation) method
- The consumption-level method (including income and price elasticities of demand)
- The end-use (consumption coefficient) method
- The leading indicator method
- Regression models

Whatever method or combination of methods is used, forecasts necessarily involve various assumptions and probabilities. Some factors relating to demand are not apparent, and full account cannot be given of them. Unpredictable events, such as the energy crisis of the 1970s, can cause an enormous change in input costs, indirectly altering effective demand for many products. Some of the uncertainties are as follows: the rate of increase of national and per capita incomes; perceptible changes in the structure of family budgets; the discovery of new sources of raw materials for the subject industry; emergence of a substitute; technological developments inside or outside the subject industry or in the production of inputs; inflationary price rises or price declines; the discovery of new applications for a product; changes in import quotas or tariff rates; emergence of industrial cooperation among neighbouring countries; and the emergence or disappearance of a dominant competitor.

### Conclusions, opportunities and risks

At this stage, after having summarized all results obtained so far by the marketing research, the market opportunities that can make the project feasible, as well as the market risks endangering it, can be summed up. These potential opportunities and risks, which are the critical variables of the project or its alternatives, provide the bases for the following development of the project strategy and marketing concept, as well as for any decision concerning the final choice of the scope of the project, human and material resources, location, engineering and technology, management, organization, and the financial evaluation and appraisal of the investment project.

## C. Outline of the project strategy

After the introduction of marketing and its dimensions for the management of enterprises in general and for feasibility studies in particular, the scope and structure of marketing research have been described. The preparation of a marketing concept for an investment project requires, as shown in figure IX, that a project strategy has been determined beforehand. For this purpose it is necessary to differentiate between objectives and strategies. The objectives indicate the direction of the investment project (for example, import substitution, utilization of national resources, earning of foreign exchange), while a strategy defines the means and activities required to reach the project objectives (for example, cost leadership, differentiation, market niche). The main steps for defining the project strategy and corresponding marketing concept are shown in figure XVII.

Assessment of the situation and analysing the initial position are the first steps required for the determination of a project strategy. This includes, but is not limited to, demand and market analysis. In the case of expansion or rehabilitation projects, for example, the internal analysis of strengths and weaknesses would be as essential for the preparation of a feasibility study as the market analysis. A check-list for the internal analysis (III-6) is shown in the appendix to chapter III.

The purpose of determining a project strategy is to identify and reflect systematically the basic strategic problems of a project. Usually the significance of such problems varies from project to project, and it is essential for the preparation and appraisal of a project to identify such critical elements and analyse them carefully. For example, a project applying well-known basic technology in a market that is in the maturity stage of the life cycle may have to focus especially on problems concerning distribution channels and how to gain any advantages over existing competitors. The objective of penetrating

**Figure XVII. Outline of the project strategy and marketing concept**

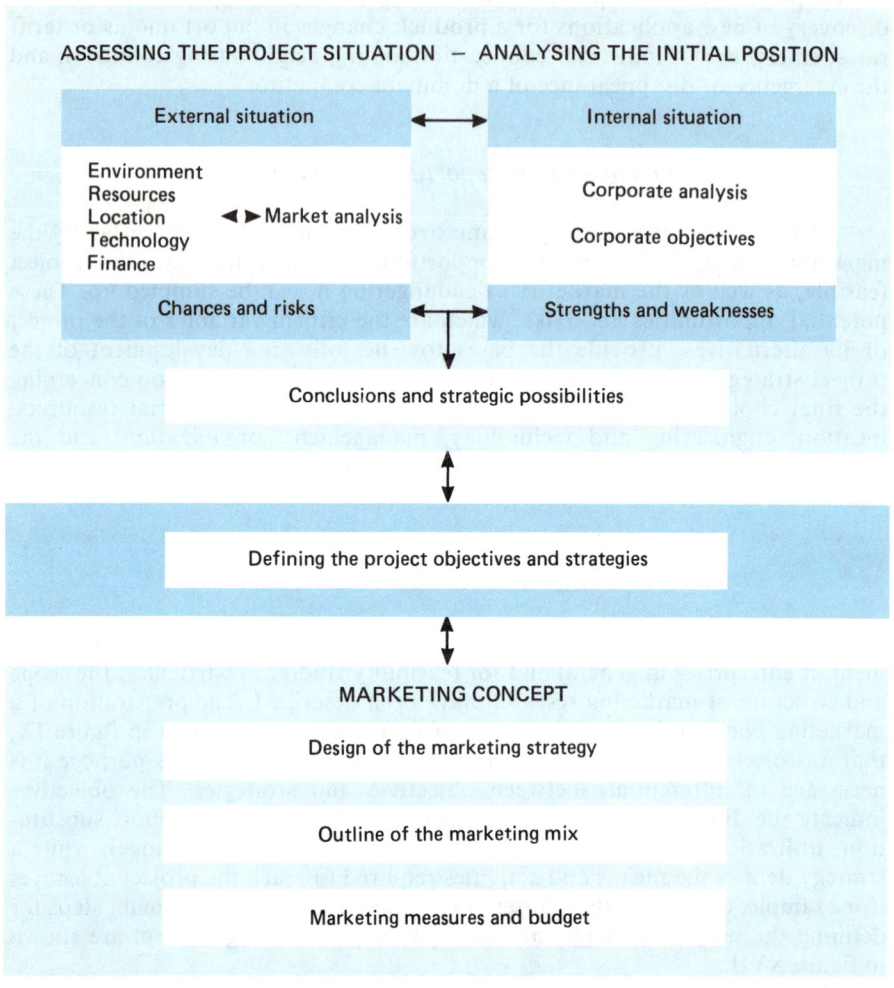

ASSESSING THE PROJECT SITUATION — ANALYSING THE INITIAL POSITION

External situation

Environment
Resources
Location ◄ ►Market analysis
Technology
Finance

Internal situation

Corporate analysis

Corporate objectives

Chances and risks

Strengths and weaknesses

Conclusions and strategic possibilities

Defining the project objectives and strategies

MARKETING CONCEPT

Design of the marketing strategy

Outline of the marketing mix

Marketing measures and budget

international markets for capital goods, for example, could require cooperation in research, and product or technology development might become a central question for the determination of a project strategy. When developing a project strategy, special emphasis should be given to the following four elements by which it can be determined: the targeted geographical area; the market share; product-market relations; and competition and market development.

*Geographical area of the strategy*

In order to identify a realistic competitive position, an enterprise needs to determine its relevant market (current and potential future customers) and, in particular, its geographical area of operations. For example, the market for consumer goods such as cameras, television sets and electronic calculators is international and highly competitive, and the fact that international competition is increasing is of central importance for the development of a project strategy. Since there are relatively few industries where new international enterprises are established, it is possible and also essential to make a careful analysis of all the forces acting in the direction of either international (global) or national (geographically limited) competition. Types of project strategies with regard to geographical areas or markets are reflected in figure XVIII.

On the basis of the assessment of the project situation, the feasibility study should consider different strategic alternatives with regard to the geographical limitations of its business field. These alternatives should be defined for particular products and with a view to a locally or regionally limited market, a national market or a multinational market (for example, exports to different countries or to a few selected countries). In the last case, export can start with certain principal markets to be penetrated initially and then gradually extended to other markets.

**Figure XVIII. Types of geographical project strategy**

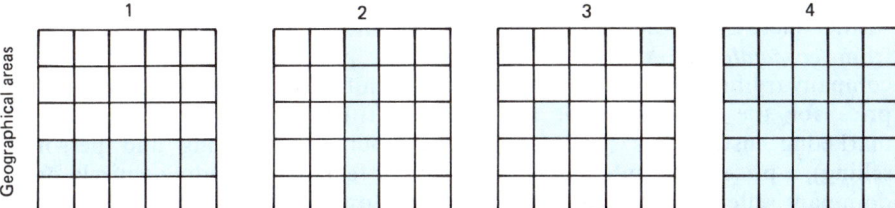

Product and customer segments

Key:  1  Example of a geographically limited local or regional market on which all segments are dealt with.
2  Example of a selected segment (a product group) that is dealt with on all national and international markets.
3  Selected segments are dealt with in selected geographical areas.
4  All segments are promoted in all geographical areas. In the extreme case this would mean world-wide competition involving all product segments or aimed at all customer segments. This strategy would require enterprises with a very strong financial potential.

## Market share and basic strategies

Another element of the project strategy is the target position to be achieved in the market. For an investment project it is necessary to define the long-term market position or market share that it is aiming at in a certain market or market segment. In general, the profitability varies with the market share, as shown in figure XIX below.

A small market share may be highly profitable as a result of focusing on a limited number of products or customers, comparatively simple market concept or low overheads. As the sales volume and thus the market share increases, there is a rise in the overall investment, production and marketing costs. It may, however, not always be possible to benefit immediately from a corresponding decrease in unit costs, in other words, the marginal sales values

## Figure XIX. Profitability and market share

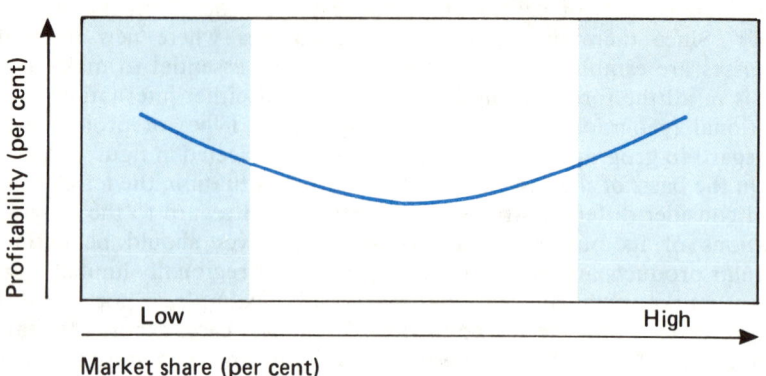

may be lower than the *marginal cost of a production* increase (for a certain production capacity and technology). Profitability is therefore reduced. A further increase in the market share would then make it possible to benefit from *economies of scale,* and consequently profitably would improve. A company trying to extend its market share even further may pay a considerable price for the acquisition of additional territory or the excessive use of marketing instruments (such as price discounts, advertising and personal selling), a price that could extend to customer fears of depending entirely on a dominant seller. Profitability may then turn down again. However, since each market has its individual characteristics, the feasibility study should analyse each profitability and market-share relationship very carefully. Figure XX shows three types of (generic) project strategy with regard to the envisaged market share.

## Figure XX. Basic strategic options

|  | Singularity from customers' point of view | Low costs relative to competitors |
|---|---|---|
| Subsector covered | Differentiation strategy | Cost leadership strategy |
| Limitation to market segments | Focus on main points Niche strategy | |

*Source:* Based on M. E. Porter, *Competitive Strategy: Techniques for Analyzing Industries and Competitors* (New York, Free Press, 1980), chap. 2.

## Strategy of cost leadership

Achieving and maintaining lower costs than those incurred by competitors is central to the entire strategy. The cost advantage attributable to the learning and experience curve[39] provides protection against competition because competitors incurring higher costs tend to disappear first. In order to achieve cost leadership, it is often necessary to have a considerable market share or other important advantages such as access to low-cost raw materials.

The assets usually required for a cost leadership strategy are as follows:

- High investment capacity, that is, access to capital
- Process innovations and improvements
- Thorough supervision of labour force
- Products designed for easy manufacturing
- Low-cost distribution system

## Differentiation strategy

The differentiation strategy aims at differentiating the products or services of a firm in such a way as to create something that is considered unique in the industry. Differentiation protects against competition in that it binds the buyers to the brand or the firm and thus reduces price sensitivity. The assets usually required for a differentiation strategy are as follows:

- Powerful marketing potential
- Strenghs in research and development
- Customer groups with higher purchasing power
- Parts of the product line
- Tradition in the industry
- Cooperation with supply and distribution channels

## Emphasis on main points (niche strategy)

The niche strategy is based on the fact that focusing on a strictly confined aim is more efficient than operating in a broad field of competition. Emphasis may be placed on a limited group of buyers, parts of the product line or a geographically limited area. The skills usually required result from the strategic objective emphasized. They cannot be defined in general.

In order to achieve a concentration of forces, it is usually necessary to opt for one of the three generic types of strategy. This always implies a certain position in the market (market-share) and a preliminary determination of the price level. A cost leadership strategy will aim at low sales prices in the market for a certain product. A differentiation strategy will aim at a middle range or relatively high level of sales prices. A high price level can only be achieved with

---

[39]The experience curve includes the empirically proven fact that total unit costs are reduced by 20 to 30 per cent whenever the cumulative quantity of a product manufactured and sold is doubled.

the strategy of niches, because the market segment for a high price is relatively small, and an enterprise would not focus on that segment and at the same time aim at a high plant capacity (that is, economies of scale).

### Product-market relations and basic strategies

The selected product-market relation determines the strategic dimensions of the marketing concept (discussed in section D of this chapter), and a product-market orientation is also fundamental to the determination of a project strategy. Four basically different types of marketing strategy are reflected in figure XXI.

*Market penetration strategy.* The enterprise, operating on a specific market, aims at intensifying its market efforts. The main means are advertising and selling, and the focus is on existing products. A variation of an existing product is called a "relaunch". Another tool of the market penetration strategy is the "unbundling" of existing products into unbundled components.

*Market development strategy.* With existing products the enterprise aims at new geographical areas, new customer segments, increasing sales through new distribution channels etc.

*Product development strategy.* The enterprise aims at developing its products and finding new solutions for future customers.

*Diversification.* The enterprise aims at succeeding on new markets with new products.

**Figure XXI.  Product-market relation**

| MARKET | PRODUCT | |
|--------|---------|---|
|        | Old | New |
| Old | Market penetration | Product development |
| New | Market development | Diversification |

*Source:* Based on H. I. Ansoff, "Strategies for diversification", *Harvard Business Review*, September-October 1957, pp. 113-124.

### Competition and market expansion strategy

Any increase of the market share can arise either from a gain at the expense of competitors, if the total market volume is stable or decreasing, or from an expanding market. Figure XXII shows the characteristics of the two corresponding strategies, which are related to the project strategy, on the one hand, and determine the marketing concept, on the other.

*Competition strategy.* A competition strategy must describe how market shares are to be won from competitors. This strategy may be chosen when it is

**Figure XXII.   Competition and market expansion strategy**

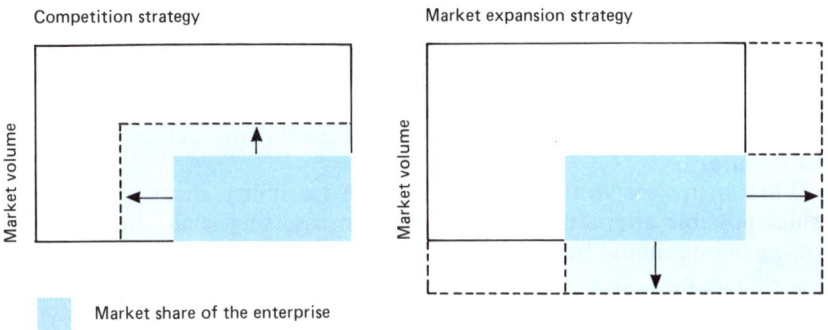

Competition strategy

Market expansion strategy

Market volume

Market volume

Market share of the enterprise

not advisable to plan for an enlargement of the total market volume, which would be the case, for example, when the market has reached saturation or maturity. Existing enterprises, if they had adopted a market development strategy, should then return to a competition strategy. It is interesting to note that often the company with the largest market share is the last to change its strategy.

*Market expansion strategy.* A market development strategy implies that the means of the marketing mix of an enterprise are primarily geared towards the creation of a new market or the enlargement of the existing market volume. It would generally imply a change of habits (utilization or consumption habits, norms etc.). The principal idea of this strategy is to obtain a leading position *vis-à-vis* competitors already during the first phase of the development of a new market.

## *Determination of the project strategy*

When the project strategy is being determined, the following problems should be addressed:

- What is the geographical area in which the project will operate?
- What basic strategy should be chosen: cost leadership, differentiation or market niche?
- What market position (market share) is aimed at, and how much time is required to reach the target?
- Which product-market relation should be the basis for the marketing concept (see figure XXI)?
- What will be the product range (products, price level)?
- Which target group of customers will be focused on?
- Which strategy will be chosen: competition or market expansion?
- What core skills are required for success in respect of actual or potential competitors?
- Will the project develop the market position exclusively by its own means or are there possibilities for cooperation?

The three basic conceptional questions to be analysed for the determination of the project strategy are interrelated. The starting-point for developing the outline of the project strategy is in any case the definition and segmentation of the market. The Ansoff-matrix (figure XXIII) indicates the product range and helps to determine the production programme. Porter's concept of strategic alternatives helps to identify the market position for the project and to determine the plant capacity, indicating the necessary production potential and infrastructure.

When a project strategy is selected, the feasibility study should always consider possible alternative strategies. When assessing such alternatives, the following points should be considered:

- To what extent do the strategic alternatives fulfil the original aims of the feasibility study (improving the situation for basic food items etc.)?

- What is the financial impact of the alternatives (profitability, return on investment)?

- What risks are linked with each alternative (political, ecological, financial etc.)?

**Figure XXIII. Basic elements for the determination of a project strategy**

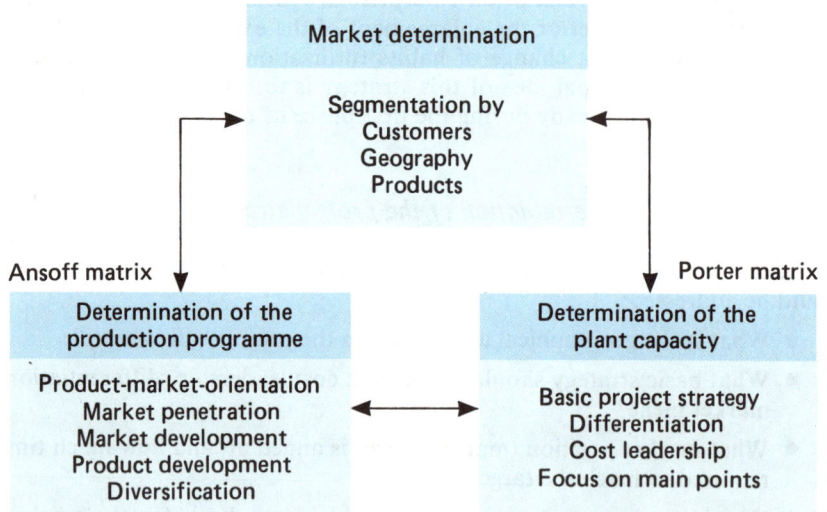

### D. Outline of the marketing concept

The marketing concept for the project comprises the specific marketing strategies (focus on target market and customer needs), measures and means (coordinated marketing) required to achieve the project objectives in a chosen market. This marketing concept is developed within the framework of the project strategy determined in accordance with the findings of marketing research. The marketing concept includes the following two dimensions that should be considered when developing a marketing concept (see figure IX):

- A strategic dimension covering long-term marketing management (product target-groups, marketing aims and strategies)
- An operative dimension controlling short-term use of individual marketing tools, marketing measures and the budget

### Strategic dimensions of the marketing concept

### Determination of the product target-groups

The determination of the product target-groups is fundamental to the preparation of the marketing concept, because the decision in favour of certain product target-groups determines not only the relationship between project and market, but also the engineering design and choice of technology. The assessment of the relationship between types of products and customer groups is illustrated in the product-target-group matrix shown in figure XXIV.

Besides preliminary estimates of the costs involved in market penetration and working in the market, the following factors are of particular interest and

**Figure XXIV. Assessment of product-target-group fields**

| Target groups / Product types | Customers | | | |
|---|---|---|---|---|
| | Prestige-oriented | Aesthetics-oriented | Technology-oriented | Price-oriented |
| Plastic watches | − | − | + | + + + |
| Designer watches | + + + | + + + | + | − |
| Sports watches (timers, waterproof) | − | ? | + + | ? |
| Watches with extras (moon phases, alarm etc.) | + + | ? | + + + | − |

Key:  + + +  Very important product-market field
      + +    Important product-market field
      +      Product-market field should not be neglected
      −      Negligible product-market field
      ?      Unknown, importance depends on product details

should be identified for each target group (see also check-list III-1 in the appendix to chapter III):

- Market structure and potential market volume
- Consumer needs and criteria for purchasing decisions
- Competition
- Market price level
- Product requirements
- Existing core skills or new skills

## Determination of the marketing objectives

Marketing objectives comprise sales objectives as well as the desired position in the product and target-group fields. To determine the sales objectives for any of the individual product and target-group fields, the following corporate objectives should be considered:

- Turnover
- Market share
- Image
- Profit

It is important to avoid unrealistic targets and uncritical extrapolations. The position of the products in the product and target-group fields can be determined in relation either to competitors or to end-users. To provide a basis for the determination of marketing objectives and strategies, information on the following is required:

- Strengths and weaknesses of the competitors
- Own weaknesses and strengths
- Specific needs of the end-user
- Image of the enterprise
- Cost outline

## Determination of the marketing strategy

In the feasibility study alternative marketing strategies should be assessed. It is important to understand that the strategy selected will have an impact on the project parameters (scope and type of project, choice of technology and location etc.), and must therefore be related to the project strategy (see figures XXI, XXII and XXIII).

### (a) Competition strategy

This strategy aims at gaining market shares from competitors. When a market has reached saturation or its growth limit, it is usually advisable to determine a competitive strategy. As mentioned before, the firms with the greatest market shares in general change to a competitive strategy later than the

90

smaller ones. The following competitive strategies can be distinguished: aggressive price strategy (with, for example, dumping prices); imitation strategy (for example, with the objective of benefiting from the main competitor's marketing efforts); and profile strategy (focusing not on price competition but on quality, extra performance and brand name). The profile strategy corresponds to the differentiation or niche strategy.

### (b)  Market expansion strategy

The marketing mix can be geared to the creation of new markets (new customer groups, demand expansion) or to demand intensification (more consumption by existing consumer groups). This strategy would be typical for growing markets (early phase in the life cycle). Before choosing this strategy, the following aspects should be considered: the current phase of the subsector life cycle; the possibilities of influencing the market; the structure of production costs *vis-à-vis* the competitors, whether the sales price is an important purchasing criterion; and whether there are any possibilities for building up a special image.

### Operative dimensions of the marketing concept

### Determination of the marketing mix

The combination of the marketing instruments must be determined with regard to the customers or end-users, as well as the distribution channels. Product, price, promotion and distribution—the components of the marketing mix—must be seen as interdependent marketing tools, which are to be combined in an optimal way so as to achieve the marketing objectives. Essential for the determination of the marketing mix is the understanding of the interrelations existing in each market between the market participants (customers, competitors, traders), as already reflected in figure XI. For the design of the marketing mix it is also important to consider the nature of competition and any likely consumer and competitor responses. The optimal combination or marketing mix would be determined by the market characteristics, on the one hand, and the selected marketing strategy, on the other. The basic cost leadership strategy, for example, requires a combination of marketing tools, entirely different from those necessary in the case of differentiation strategies, and would have to be designed totally differently for the same market, price, product quality, maintenance services, lead time etc.

### (a)  Product and product policy

An investment project is only financially feasible when the project output has a value for the consumers, in other words, when the product can be sold on the market. The feasibility study will have to analyse the present market situation and determine the elements of the product mix already described in this chapter (see discussion of operative dimensions of marketing in section A of this chapter).

In the feasibility study it should be investigated whether the project better concentrates on a single product or a range of different products, and whether such product or products should be manufactured in one variety or in different sizes, colours, qualities etc. (scope and depth of the product mix). The product mix should be designed to meet the needs and preferences of the customers. It may be necessary to design prototypes and test them on the market before deciding on the final sales and production programme.

Although national product standards and regulations may be an obstacle for producers, compliance with such conditions can be turned into a promotional advantage, especially if international acceptance of a product can be achieved. The functional and engineering design, although an important criterion for the success of a product, is not the only one; the "eye appeal" of a product and the packaging may also be important.

After-sales services may be necessary for the acceptance of a product. Such services may extend from the supply of simple wear-and-tear parts to the provision of extensive maintenance and repair services, possibly requiring considerable inventories in the production plant or in different locations. The nature and costs of after-sales facilities and services should be determined in the feasibility study, if a significant impact on costs and revenues is likely.

The determination of the characteristics of products and the outline of a product policy are the basis for the production programme and plant capacity, the engineering design, the projection of investment, production and marketing costs, as well as the evaluation of the market risks against possible marketing strategies.

### (b) Price and price policy

The determination of product price levels is part of both the basic project strategy and the long-term marketing strategy. Relatively low-quality products usually need a low-price strategy, while a high-price strategy would require a higher performance level in terms of product quality, design, warranties, brand names (image) and services[40].

For the determination of sales prices, the internal production and marketing costs, customer reactions to different prices (price elasticity) and the price policies of competitors must be considered. In this context, it should be noted that prices would have to be appropriate for different consumer segments (price differentiation). Other factors to be assessed when determining the price policy for a product are as follows:

- The margins wholesalers and retailers require to include a product in their sales programme (as sortment) and to promote it;

- Any existing public price controls (for example, price regulations are often found for agricultural products);

- Any generally accepted (and expected) discount policy. If certain discounts are usual in a country, they have to be considered for the price calculation. Discounts are given during an introduction period, for purchasing of larger quantities, to important customers etc. Discounts are a useful price policy when market prices are well established;

- The importance of delivery and payment conditions. For example, who usually bears the costs of delivery (extra packaging, costs of mailing or

---

[40]The selected price strategy would have to correspond with the marketing strategy, as described earlier (see discussion of the determination of the marketing strategy in section D of this chapter).

forwarding, insurances etc.), and what are the usual payment conditions (advance payment, supplier credit, leasing, barter or compensation purchase etc.).

Products may have to be priced below the total costs for certain periods,[41] not only because of possibly excessive initial production and marketing costs (start-up period), but also because such lower prices would facilitate entry into the market and help to achieve a high utilization of installed production capacities in the beginning. In the case of new products, a particular market may have to be developed through initially low prices, for example, because of the existence of a lower-priced substitute, or a competitive market. In all these cases where sales prices would not satisfactorily cover the cost of products sold, such pricing policies must, however, be limited to a specific period, and any losses accumulating during this period must be compensated for by corresponding future cash surpluses.

The marketing strategy must take into account any possible reactions of competitors selling the same or similar products. A main competitor may be in a position to reduce sales prices, to protect its market share against a newcomer. In such a situation current prices would not be an adequate basis for the projection of sales revenues.

After the above characterization of price policy as a marketing instrument, it is obvious that price policy is not limited to the relationship between the volume and price of sales but plays a central role in the marketing mix. The market analysis, as part of the feasibility study, should assess the present market situation, compare it with possible future trends, and indicate which pricing strategies would be feasible.

### (c) Promotion

Promotional measures will be required by the investment project, first for entering the market with the new product, and, secondly, to stay in the market and reach the long-term objectives of the project. The feasibility study should identify the promotional measures required to reach the projected sales volume and estimate the costs of these measures. The following promotional tools can be distinguished:

- Advertising to stimulate or create a demand has made mass production possible for many consumer goods. Practically all advertising is commissioned through specialized agencies, which design the advertisement and select proper media;

- Public relations, although concerned, like advertising, with opinion and image aspects, is more involved with how to reach and influence key persons in relevant positions in, for example, public institutions and the media;

- Personal sales or face-to-face selling has traditionally been regarded as a very effective way of increasing the sale of most goods. Selling by phone and mailing to potential and actual customers are variations of personal sales. Costs of salesmen (usually a part of the remuneration is fixed and another variable) should be in accordance with the kind of product;

---

[41] For direct costing see discussion of unit costs of production in chap. X, sect. C.

- Sales promotion or merchandising is an instrument to support especially the retailers. Display at the point of sale, start-up events for a new product, free samples, presentation at fairs etc. are typical examples of this marketing procedure;

- Brand policy is an important instrument of the promotional mix. An enterprise has to decide whether to aim at developing a brand name for a product, or at selling "no-name" products. This decision is usually central in the case of consumer goods. Consumers, for example, expect a brand to be of a certain quality, to be available in almost every shopping area and principally everywhere at the same price. Establishing a brand name is usually very cost-intensive, which could have a significant impact on the feasibility of a project during its initial operational phase. However, this policy could also, in the long term, result in a very effective differentiation *vis-à-vis* competitors.

The detailed promotional mix will most probably be determined during project implementation. However, a preliminary budget estimate for the pre-production marketing should be included in the feasibility study, and to the extent significant for financial planning.

### (d)  Sales and channels of distribution

Distribution through wholesalers to retailers, through retailers or directly to consumers (end-users) are the main distribution channels used by producers to reach the end-users. They have been analysed in section B of this chapter. The main task of distribution is to get the products from the manufacturers to the consumers, that is, to the place where and at the time when the goods are needed. The physical distribution, that is, the logistical aspects, therefore deserve special attention when determining the distribution mix. The most important elements of the marketing mix are the terms of delivery (delivery time, means of transport, optimization of transport routes, establishment of depots), the control of the stock (ability to fulfil orders, optimization of inventory turn over, organization of inventory control and dispatch), and the protection of goods during transport.

The choice of a distribution channel has a significant impact on the profitability of the project. When determining ex-factory prices, it is important to identify the margins needed for the wholesalers and retailers to include the products in their sales programme.

### Determination of marketing measures

The final step in marketing planning is concerned with the preparation of a schedule or plan of action and the projection of the marketing budget. The schedule should outline all measures that are important for the success of the project. It should also help to orient and define the detailed marketing plan later during project implementation.

If a project is critical from the marketing point of view, an assessment of probable stumbling-blocks is recommended, together with an analysis of the project sensitivity to such contingencies. The analysis should not be limited to risk computation applying statistical measures, but should also identify the proper means of avoiding or minimizing their impact.

# Determination of the marketing concept

The steps necessary for determining a marketing concept are listed in figure XXV.

**Figure XXV.  Development of a marketing concept**

| Steps | Information required |
|---|---|
| 1.  Defining the product-target-group fields<br>   Define the product types per target group | Market volume and market potential<br>Competitive situation<br>Price level of the market<br>Marketing skills, existing and to be developed<br>Existing market structure |
| 2.  Defining the marketing objectives (aims)<br>   What sales objectives are realistic for each product-target field<br>   What position in the product-target fields should be reached | Strengths and weaknesses of competitors<br>Own weaknesses and existing or achievable strengths<br>Specific needs of product users |
| 3.  Defining the marketing strategy in case of a market expansion strategy<br>   Demand expansion<br>   Demand intensification<br>   In case of a competition strategy<br>   Aggressive price strategy<br>   Imitation strategy<br>   Profile strategy | Position in the life cycle of the subsector<br>Possibilities of influencing the market cost structure in comparison with competitors<br>Importance of the price as a purchasing criterion |
| 4.  Defining the marketing mix (operative marketing)<br>   Defining the end-user mix<br>   if sales agents are used<br>   Defining the channels mix | |
| 5.  Defining the marketing measures and budget<br>   Define the measures corresponding to the individual marketing tools<br>   Establish the projection of sales<br>   Establish the projection of marketing costs | Detailed measures required to achieve the objectives of the marketing mix<br>Estimate of marketing costs<br>Estimate of sales revenues |

## E.   Marketing costs and revenues

The projection of marketing costs comprises all cost components resulting from the marketing activities described in this chapter. Depending on the scope of the study and the depth of the analysis, the marketing costs may be projected for each product separately or for a group of products. For a detailed analysis, it is usually necessary to determine the direct variable and direct fixed unit costs for each cost or profit centre, as well as the indirect marketing costs (marketing overhead costs). The costs may be structured in line with the check-list shown in schedule 3-2 in the appendix to this chapter.

## Projection of sales revenues

The projection of sales revenues is essentially an extension of marketing research, on the basis of which a project is developed also in terms of specific sales volumes during different periods after the project goes into production. Estimating sales revenues, however, is an iterative process that should also take into account the optimal plant capacity, appropriate technology, a technically feasible production programme and alternative marketing strategies. The final determination of sales revenues may therefore only be possible once technology and plant capacity are more clearly known. The project planner has consequently to feed the technological concept into the sales and marketing programme in order to harmonize both and to outline the production programme. Without such a cycle of feedbacks, it would not be possible to cope with the complex matter of project planning. The period covered by such projections depends on the nature and type of the product. It should be between 15 and 20 years for a machinery product and a reasonable estimate of demand and sales growth and production costs has to be assumed. For products having a short life-span, such as certain pharmaceuticals, the period can be limited to 5 to 10 years. The forecasts of annual sales in terms of quantity or volume and the anticipated income from sales should be projected as outlined in schedule III-1.

*Sales tax.* Since sales taxes (for instance, value added tax and turnover tax) are usually not a cost item for a project, sales revenues should be shown net of sales tax. However, if an economic analysis is intended, the sales tax, like all other taxes and duties, must be included in the feasibility study. In this case, it may be convenient to show both gross sales and sales net of tax.

## Production programme

After having determined the required sales programme, a feasibility study should define the detailed production programme. A production programme should indicate the levels of output to be achieved during specified periods, and, from this viewpoint, should be directly related to the specific sales forecasts. To plan such a programme the various production stages should be considered in detail, in terms of both production activities and timing. Within the overall plant capacity, there can be various levels of production activity during different stages, such levels being determined by various factors in different projects. It would be prudent to recognize that full production may not be practicable for most projects during the initial production operations. Owing to various technological, production and commercial difficulties, most projects experience initial problems that can take the form of only a gradual growth of sales and market penetration, on the one hand, and a wide range of production problems, on the other, such as the adjustment of feedstocks, labour and equipment to the technology selected. Even if full production were to be achieved in the first year, marketing and sales might prove a bottleneck.

The determination of the production programme and design of the plant capacity are dealt with in chapter VI, section A.

## Bibliography

Ansoff, H. I. Strategic management. London, Macmillan, 1979.

Behrens, K. Chr. Handbuch der Marktforschung. Wiesbaden, Betriebswirtschaftlicher Verlag Gabler, 1977.

Bernsen, J. Design: the problem comes first. Copenhagen, 1986.

Bonoma, Th. V. *and* B. P. Shapiro. Segmenting the industrial market. Massachusetts, Lexington Books, 1983.

Corey, E. R. Industrial marketing: cases and concepts. 3. ed. Englewood Cliffs, New Jersey, Prentice-Hall, 1983.

Crimp, M. The marketing research process. Hemel Hempstead, United Kingdom, Prentice-Hall, 1985.

Hart, N. A. *and others.* Marketing of industrial products. Maidenhead, United Kingdom, McGraw, 1984.

Kinnear, Th. C. *and* Taylor, J. R. Marketing research: an applied approach. Singapore, McGraw, 1987.

Kotler, Ph. Marketing management: analysis, planning, implementation and control. 6. ed. Englewood Cliffs, New Jersey, Prentice-Hall, 1988.

———— The new competition. New York, Prentice-Hall, 1985.

Leavitt, Th. The marketing imagination. New York, 1983.

Parsons, R. Statistical analysis: a decision-making approach. New York, Harper and Row, 1974.

Porter, M. E. Competitive advantage: creating and sustaining superior performance. New York, Collier Mac., 1985.

———— Competitive strategy: techniques for analyzing industries and competitors. New York, Free Press, 1980.

Rothschild, E. E. Product development management. Melbourne, Australia, T. Wilson, 1987.

Turnbull, P. W. *and* M. T. Cunningham. International marketing and purchasing; a survey among marketing and purchasing executives in five European countries. London, Macmillan, 1981.

Urban, G. L. *and* J. R. Hauser. Design and marketing of new products. Englewood Cliffs, New Jersey, Prentice-Hall, 1980.

# Appendix

## CHECK-LISTS, WORKSHEETS AND SCHEDULES

*III-1.  Definition of the market and analysis of the market structure*

| |
|---|
| Project/alternative: |
| Market definition (product groups, regions): |
| Structure of the target market (see check-list III-2 and figure X), with description of the interrelationships within the system, the action of the parties etc.: |

*III-2.  Analysis of the marketing system*

| | |
|---|---|
| Branch structure | Name of suppliers of goods and services<br>Heterogeneity of suppliers<br>Types of enterprises offering products (services)<br>Organization of the branch (associations etc.) |
| Customer structure | Names of customers<br>Types of customers |
| Employment and competition | Utilization of capacities installed<br>Action against competitors |
| Principal means of competition | Quality<br>Product assortment<br>Advertising<br>Pricing<br>Terms of delivery |
| Structure of distribution | Geographical distribution<br>Channels of distribution |

## III-3.  Analysis of market characteristics

Quantitative data

Market volume
Position in the market life cycle
Saturation of the market
Growth rates (absolute values and percentage per annum)
Partial markets
Stability of demand

Qualitative data

Structure of customer needs
Purchasing motives
Purchasing process, attitudes in relation to information
Intensity and strength of competition


## III-4.  Analysis of the competitors

General information about the competitor

Competitor's position

Total sales
Sales in most important segments
Total market share
Market shares in most important segments

Total marketing expenditures

First step of the analysis

What are the aims of the competitors?
How do the competitors behave?
How do the competitors assess their own situation?
What are the strengths and weaknesses of the competitors?

Second step of the analysis (main strengths and weaknesses of the competitors)

| | Assessment relative to own company | | | |
|---|---|---|---|---|
| | Worse | Equal | Better | Notes |
| **Product** | | | | |
| Scope of product mix | | | | |
| Depth of product mix | | | | |
| Quality | | | | |
| Design | | | | |
| Packaging | | | | |
| Maintenance/services | | | | |
| Warranty services | | | | |
| Possibility of return | | | | |
| **Price** | | | | |
| Price positioning | | | | |
| Rebates and discounts | | | | |
| Conditions of payment | | | | |
| Conditions of financing | | | | |

| | Assessment relative to own company | | | |
|---|---|---|---|---|
| | Worse | Equal | Better | Notes |
| Promotion | | | | |
|   Advertising | | | | |
|   Personal sale | | | | |
|   Sales promotion | | | | |
|   Brand policy | | | | |
|   Public relations | | | | |
| | | | | |
| Place | | | | |
|   Channels of distribution | | | | |
|   Distribution density | | | | |
|   Lead time | | | | |
|   Stocks, transport | | | | |

## III-5.   Analysis of the environment

Ecology

  Available energies
  Petrol
  Gas
  Electricity
  Coal
  Other sources

Available raw materials

Environmental protection plans

  Development of environmental consciousness
  Pollution
  Environmental protection laws and regulations

Recycling

  Availability of recycled materials
  Recycling costs

Technology

  Production technology
  Trends in technology development
  Innovation potential
  Automation and process control

Innovations in production materials

  Trends in the development of product technology (hardware, software)
  Innovation potential

Technology substitution

  Possible innovations
  Cost development

Recycling technology

Economy

  Trends in revenue development in the project country

Development of international trade

Exchange of goods
Economic integration
Protectionism

Trends in the development of the balance of payments and the foreign exchange rate
Inflation
Development of the capital market
Development of the employment situation
Expected investments trends
Fluctuations in the economic development cycles

Frequency
Intensity

Development of the economic sector concerned with the project

Social development

Demographic development in the project country

In general
Development of important population groups
Migrations

Cultural, socio-psychological aspects

Attitudes towards work
Propensity to save
Leisure-time behaviour
Attitudes towards the economy
Attitudes towards automation
Attitudes towards materials utilized
Attitudes towards products offered

Politics and law

General policy trends

East—West
North—South
General risks of local or international conflicts
Position in the market for raw material supplies

Trends in the relationship between political parties in the country concerned
Trends in economic policies
Trends in social legislation and labour laws
Importance and influence of unions
Degree of freedom of enterprises to decide and act

*III-6.  Corporate (internal) analysis*

|  | *Strengths* | *Weaknesses* | *Conclusions* |
|---|---|---|---|
| Marketing<br>  Market performance<br>  Price performance<br>  Promotion<br>  Distribution<br>  ... |  |  |  |

|  | Strengths | Weaknesses | Conclusions |
|---|---|---|---|
| **Production**<br>Facilities<br>Capacities<br>Productivity<br>Availability of supplies<br>... | | | |
| **Research and development**<br>Activities<br>Know-how<br>Patents, franchises<br>... | | | |
| **Finance**<br>Capital volume and structure<br>Reserves<br>Financing potential<br>Working capital<br>Liquidity<br>Capital turnover<br>Investment intensity<br>Return on investment<br>... | | | |
| **Personnel**<br>Employee qualifications<br>Human relations<br>Social benefits<br>... | | | |
| **Management and organization**<br>Information<br>Planning and control<br>Clear organizational development<br>... | | | |

*Note:* This check-list highlights some of the most important areas generally subject to internal analysis. As it is impossible to establish an even fairly complete listing, "tailor-made" questionnaires must be prepared through practical internal analysis for each individual case and with the help of specialized literature.

## Schedule III-1. Projected sales programme
*(insert in schedules X-8, X-9 and X-10)*

Project:
Date:
Source:

| Product/cost centre:<br><br>Code: | Market: | | Currency:<br><br>Units: | | | |
|---|---|---|---|---|---|---|
| | Local sales | | | Exports | | | Total revenues |
| Year | Units sold | Price | Revenues | Units sold | Price | Revenues | |
| | | | | | | | |

## Schedule III-2. Estimate of total marketing costs
## (direct/indirect costs of sales and distribution)
### (insert in schedule III-3)

Project:
Date:
Source:

[  ]  Direct costs
[  ]  Indirect costs

| Product/cost centre:<br><br>Code: | Market:<br><br>(local, export) | | Currency:<br><br>Units: | |
|---|---|---|---|---|
| | Cost projections for year: | | | |
| | *Local costs* | | *Foreign costs* | |
| *Cost item* | *Variable per unit* | *Fixed per period* | *Variable per unit* | *Fixed per period* |
| | | | | |
| Total unit costs | | | | |
| Total units per period | | | | |
| Total costs per period | | | | |
| Total marketing costs | | | | |

*Note* : Units of products sold are defined in schedule III-1 for each product. The grand total for each profit centre may be computed using the same forms. However, data may also be introduced directly into the data input file of the UNIDO COMFAR system.

## Schedule III-3. Projection of total marketing costs
### (insert in schedules X-3, X-8, X-9 and X-10)

Project:
Date:
Source:

| Product/cost centre: Code: | Market: | Currency: Units: | |
|---|---|---|---|
| | Total local costs | | | Total foreign costs | | | Grand total |
| Year | Variable | Fixed | Total | Variable | Fixed | Total | |
| | | | | | | | |

Note : Units of products sold are defined in schedule III-1 for each product. The grand total for each profit centre may be computed using the same forms. However, data may also be introduced directly into the data input file of the UNIDO COMFAR system.

# IV.  Raw materials and supplies

The different materials and inputs required for the operation of the plant are identified and described in this chapter, and their availability and supply, as well as the method of estimating the resulting operating costs, are analysed and described. The cost estimates are summarized in schedule IV-1, and the totals are carried forward to the total production cost table (schedule X-3) described in chapter X.

There is a close relationship between the definition of input requirements and other aspects of project formulation, such as the definition of plant capacity, location and selection of technology and equipment, as these inevitably interact with one another. The selection of raw materials and supplies depends primarily on the technical requirements of the project and the analysis of supply markets. Important determinants for the selection of raw materials and factory supplies are environmental factors such as resource depletion and pollution concerns, as well as criteria related to project strategies, for example, the minimization of supply risks and of the cost of material inputs.

In order to keep the cost of feasibility studies at a reasonable level, key aspects are to be identified and analysed in terms of requirements, availability, costs and risks, which may be significant for the feasibility of a project. The approach taken in this *Manual* is first to classify the raw materials and supplies, then to specify the requirements, check their availability and estimate their costs.

## A.  Classification of raw materials and supplies

### Raw materials (unprocessed and semi-processed)

#### Agricultural products

If the basic material is an agricultural product, first the quality of the product must be identified. The assessment of the quantities currently and potentially available may become a cardinal feature in most pre-investment studies involving the use of agricultural products. In food-processing industries, only the marketable surpluses of agricultural produce should be viewed as basic raw materials, that is, the residue remaining after the quantities required for consumption and sowing by producers have been subtracted from the total crop. In the case of commercial crops, the marketable surplus is the total production minus sowing requirements.

If the project involves large quantities, the production of the agricultural input may have to be increased. This may require the extension of the area under cultivation and often the introduction of another crop. In the case of sugar cane, for example, it would be necessary to increase the area under cane cultivation within the same region, since cane cannot be transported over long distances without involving prohibitive transport costs, loss of sucrose content or both.

In order to estimate the supplies and availability of agricultural products, it may be necessary to collect data on past crops and their distribution by market segment, that is, by geographical area or end-use. Storage and transport costs often assume major significance and should be assessed. In some cases, machinery and methods of collection have also to be studied. For paper plants, the felling and collection of the raw material from the forests may need detailed analysis.

Projects based on agricultural produce to be grown in the future may call for actual cultivation on experimental farms under varied conditions. The produce has then to be tested in laboratories and, if necessary, in pilot plants. The laboratory facilities for pilot plants may not be available within developing countries. The samples, scientifically selected, may have to be sent to other countries where such facilities exist. A project should not be based on an entirely new crop to be grown in the area, unless pilot plant tests based on actual produce from the area have established the validity and viability of the raw material for the project in question.

### Livestock and forest products

In most cases of livestock produce and forest resources, specific surveys are called for to establish the viability of an industrial project. The general data may be obtained from official sources and from local authorities, but these are sufficient only for opportunity studies. For feasibility studies, a more dependable and precise database is required and this can be obtained only by specific surveys, even though these tend to be expensive.

### Marine products

With regard to marine-based raw materials, the major problem is to assess the potential of availability, the yields and the cost of collection. The facilities required for marine operations have often to be provided for in the industrial project. Availability of marine products may not only depend on ecological factors, but also on national policies and bilateral or multilateral agreements. Particularly when fishing quotas are not limited by official quantity-related licences, the danger of overfishing must be considered, especially with more fish processing industries entering the scene.

### Mineral products

For minerals (metallic and non-metallic including clays), detailed information on the proposed exploitable deposits is essential, and an industrial feasibility study of a project can only be legitimately based on proven reserves. The study should give details, unless the reserves are known to be very extensive, of the viability of opencast or underground mining, the location, size, depth and quality of deposits, and the composition of the ore with other elements, that is, the impurities and the need for beneficiation. Mineral products differ widely in their physical and chemical composition. Products from any two locations would rarely be uniform, and the processing of each type may involve distinctly divergent methods and equipment. It is frequently necessary to obtain a detailed analysis of physical, chemical and other properties of the subject ores to be processed and the results ought to be incorporated in the feasibility report. Analysis and tests of most mineral products for identification of their physical, chemical and other properties can be organized in most developing countries. Frequently, however, pilot plant tests may be required, in which case no risks should be taken by using short cuts, and samples should be sent to laboratories or research facilities in countries where these exist.

## Processed industrial materials and components

Processed industrial materials and goods constitute an expanding category of basic inputs for various industries in developing countries. Such inputs can be generally classified under base metals, semi-processed materials relating to a wide variety of industries in different sectors, and manufactured parts, components and subassemblies for assembly-type industries, including a number of durable consumer goods and the engineering goods industry. In all these cases, it is necessary to define requirements, availability and costs in some detail, to ensure that the specifications in the case of the two latter categories suit the production programme envisaged for the project.

In the case of base metals, availability and prices during any particular period depend on sometimes unstable international markets. The substitutability of such metals should therefore be examined, for example, the replacement of copper by aluminium in the case of electrical power lines, if these are available at lower costs. Where such substitution is not technically feasible, however, pricing of project outputs would have to be adjusted to fluctuations in the cost of metals. While the availability of imported base metals at defined international prices is usually not a problem, if there are no foreign exchange constraints, unexpected price increases could have a severe financial impact on the project.

In the case of process intermediates, particularly for the chemical and petrochemical industries, careful analysis is necessary of their availability from external sources and the cost, and of the implications of domestic manufacture of such inputs. Since backward linkages for the production of such basic inputs involve large capital outlays, these have to be considered independently and are not usually related to the manufacture of the final product. Thus, polyester fibre production has to be based on caprolactum, which would either have to be imported or produced in another plant. In some countries the manufacture of basic petrochemicals is restricted to the public sector, and this factor has also to be taken into consideration in assessing the date at which they would be domestically available and the likely pricing.

In assembly-type industries, ranging from durable consumer goods to heavy plant and machinery, the basic input, apart from steel, is a large conglomeration of parts, components and subassemblies. While similar considerations prevail in respect of domestic and imported inputs, a different emphasis is given by the fact that the nature of the input may be changed by a project through higher backward linkages. Thus, a plant that produces diesel engines can start either with a foundry and go on to the final product, with outside supplies being limited to electrical parts, or have a high degree of bought-out parts and components, limiting itself primarily to the final assembly operation. The feasibility study should determine which alternative is chosen and why. This aspect is essential in the determination of plant capacity and is dealt with in chapter VI.

## Factory supplies

### Auxiliary materials and utilities

Apart from basic raw materials and processed industrial materials and components, all manufacturing projects require various auxiliary materials and utilities, usually subsumed as factory supplies. It is not always easy to distinguish between auxiliary materials, such as chemicals, additives, packaging materials, paints and varnishes, and factory supplies, such as maintenance materials, oils, grease and cleaning materials, since these terms are often used interchangeably. However, the requirements of such auxiliary materials and supplies should be accounted for in the feasibility study. The current consumption of wear-and-tear parts as well as of tools should also be projected.

A detailed assessment of the utilities required (electricity, water, steam, compressed air, fuel, effluent disposal) can only be made after analysis and selection of location, technology and plant capacity, but a general assessment of these is a necessary part of the input study. Input studies frequently do not allow for, and even the overall feasibility study tends to underestimate, the utilities required, often resulting in miscalculation of investment and production costs. An estimate of utilities consumption is essential for identifying the existing sources of supply and any bottlenecks and shortages that exist or are likely to develop, so that appropriate measures can be taken to provide for either internal or external additional supplies in good time. Such identification is particularly important since it may materially affect the investments to be made in the form of buildings, machinery and equipment and other installations, if such major utilities are in short supply in the plant and need to be provided internally.

*Electricity.* An analysis of the energy situation must specify the requirements and the sources, availability and costs of supply of electric power. The maximum power demand, the connected load, peak-load and possible stand-by requirements, as well as the daily and annual consumption both by shift and in total, must therefore be estimated in a feasibility study. Industrial projects with high-energy requirements at sites where electric energy can only be supplied by obsolete high-polluting power plants, such as thermal power plants, may have to be rejected for environmental reasons.

*Fuel.* When using large quantities of solid and liquid combustion materials, all the relevant environmental protection technologies will have to be integrated in the planning and calculation of a project. Consequently, the price of energy inputs will have to be increased by the costs of disposal measures (filters, desulphurization etc.). Given the world-wide carbon dioxide pollution and the probably resulting increase in global temperatures (the so-called greenhouse effect), the growing use of coal favoured by the exploitation of huge coal mines is liable to reach a critical point. This problem can only be solved through enhancing the net efficiency factor of the industrial plants concerned, achieving less energy consumption for the same output.

*Water.* A general estimate should be made of water requirements (taking into account recycling arrangements) for the production process, auxiliary purposes (cooling, heating and boiling, rinsing, transport facilities, grading, steam generation) and general purposes, so that these can be considered in locational decisions, at which stage the cost can be specifically defined. Especially in the case of production processes with substantial water requirements at locations with shortages in water supply, so-called closed-circuit processes should be promoted. The quality of intake water should be tested in order to avoid problems such as the damaging of pipes and pumps by aggressive substances.

*Packaging materials, containers, crates.* All types of containers and packaging materials serve in principle the following two purposes: physically holding and protecting a product (semi-finished or finished) stored by the producer, distributor or consumer; and achieving the marketing objectives defined in the marketing concept (see chapter III), such as the functional design of bottles and boxes in line with the objectives of product design and promotional functions of packaging. The costs of the materials may be considerable in relation to the production costs of the product sold; for example, goods produced for export may need special protective packaging if transported by ship. Goods with a highly visible product image (brand policy) may require costly packaging to be competitive in the local or foreign market. The feasibility study should not only identify needs for the various types of packaging material, but also assess the timely availability of the necessary quantities, the qualities required and available, as well as the corresponding costs.

*Other supplies.* The input study should determine the broad requirements for various fuels and identify sources of supply and unit costs. Similarly, general requirements for other utilities such as steam, compressed air, air-conditioning and effluent disposal should also be identified, so that they can be analysed in the course of selection of location.

### Recycled waste

The issue of waste disposal is assuming increasing importance in developing countries, depending on the type of production process. Today the issue of waste disposal has become so controversial in developed countries that specific new production plants can only be erected provided extremely sophisticated recycling methods are used, since the dumping of specific types of waste is no longer possible. Waste combustion, especially combustion of high-risk waste, is technically feasible, provided adequate measures are taken and the appropriate technologies applied. However, such measures sometimes fail because of resistance from the population in the surroundings, or for economic reasons.

The disposal of effluents is technically feasible, provided the appropriate installations have been selected. Investments, however, can reach enormous dimensions, not only in absolute figures, but also in relation to the total investment costs. Today the most critical sectors in this regard are the chemical and nuclear industries.

## Spare parts

In spite of regular maintenance, all machinery and equipment will finally break down after a certain lifetime. Various spare parts will be required to keep a plant in operation. The importance of correctly identifying essential spare parts, the quantities required and available suppliers cannot be overemphasized, because interruption of production owing to lack of essential spare parts is often the reason for project failure. Spare parts comprise numerous small items, but also major components and parts for the equipment in question. The list of spare parts required is determined as part of the engineering design, as described in chapter VI. Usually the initial investment includes spare parts for the first one or two years of plant operation under the heading of the initial net working capital (current assets). The consumption of spare parts during plant operation is a part of the annual production costs, as described in chapter X.

## Supplies for social and external needs

Some projects will require provision of materials and inputs that are not directly related to the production. A remote location, or some other reason, might require the project (or the company) to provide and pay for foodstuffs, medicine, clothing, education and training materials etc. for the employees and perhaps also their families.

Sometimes it may be necessary for the investing company to take responsibility for maintenance of external infrastructure. This might be the case if the plant depends on external infrastructure and the public does not allocate adequate resources to maintain it. Maintenance of roads might require sand, shingle or asphalt. Maintenance of railways might require shingle, anti-corrosive agents, paint etc. for the track and rolling-stock.

## B.   Specification of requirements

In order to estimate the requirements of materials and supplies during the future operation of the plant, such requirements should be identified, analysed and specified in the feasibility study, both quantitatively and qualitatively. In carrying out this work, consideration must be given to a number of socio-economic, financial and technical factors that could have a strong influence on the types, quantities and qualities of the project inputs, in particular the following:

- *Socio-economic factors:* social and cultural environment, socio-economic infrastructure (social and economic policies and regulations, infra-structural services, transport and communications system etc.)

- *Commercial and financial (business) factors:* project size, skill and pro-ductivity of the labour force, market demands regarding product quality, product mix, competition for materials, supplies and services etc.

- *Technical factors:* type of industry, technology and production process, type of machinery and equipment, production capacity and estimated production etc.

The specification of raw materials and factory supplies, as required for the envisaged production technologies, is the basis for the assessment and analysis of the availability of the project inputs. Normally these specifications will be based on a preliminary project design, and only when the detailed specifications of the inputs available are known, the final engineering design of the project can be prepared. However, it is very important to consider during this stage of project design that there exists not only a relationship between material input and engineering design, but also an interdependence with the market and marketing concept, locational aspects and the availability of human resources. For example, a change of the characteristics of raw materials may also result in a change of the product range (for example, by-products) and quality, which may require a revision of the marketing concept, or even of the project strategy (different market segments, concentration on a market niche etc.[42]). Therefore, the determination of raw material input and factory supplies can be carried out in steps only, and it might be unwise to choose a technology or equipment that is too sophisticated in relation to the quality of materials and inputs and the experience and skill of the labour force.

### *Project characteristics and material inputs*

For a given type of industry the envisaged technology can be capital- or labour-intensive, computerized or mechanized, complex or fairly simple. Machinery and equipment can likewise be of different types and sizes, manually or automatically operated and controlled, mechanized or electronic, driven by electricity or steam. Alternative production processes are sometimes feasible, but may have different prerequisites with regard to project strategies, marketing concepts or resource requirements.

The nominal and *feasible plant capacity* will have to be defined on the basis of varying supply conditions. Any significant dependencies on raw materials and factory supplies of the product mix and production target will have to be identified, and should be analysed, *inter alia*, in view of market potential expected sales, transport facilities and the production capacity. The feasible capacity and projected production level will depend not only on engineering factors as discussed above (technology, machinery and equipment, process), but also on the number of shifts and products, the numbers and skills of the labour force, marketing strategies, management and availability of external infrastructure. This rather complex list of interdependencies clearly illustrates the need for all conditions, prerequisites and assumptions to be identified and presented as a starting-point and basis for further analytical work on, for example, requirements of materials and inputs.

A useful means of facilitating a better understanding of the project design is to draw up flow sheets. *A process flow sheet* should identify vital sections of

---

[42]See chap. III.

the process and illustrate how production proceeds via those sections. The purpose is to present main activities rather than to go into details.[43]

Flow sheets for materials and inputs as well as material and energy balance or a diagram indicating the quantitative flows, should also be prepared. These sheets should indicate how and when different items enter various sections of the process. Sections outside the manufacturing process itself should also be included, in particular supply of different inputs, transport of materials and inputs, storage, packaging of finished goods, storage and transport of products, and emissions from different sections should be identified.

Each section of a process flow sheet can be analysed in more detail in separate section diagrams. Machinery, equipment and other facilities are to be specified in such diagrams, which should include the type of machinery, capacity, technical standards etc. Together with other project specifications described earlier, this information would provide an adequate basis for the task of analysing and specifying requirements of raw materials and factory supplies. A most important though often neglected aspect has to be remembered, namely the consequences that quality demands on the final products may have for the requirements of material inputs. These demands should be carefully identified and analysed and treated as a guiding principle when selecting technology, machinery and equipment, as well as the types and qualities of materials and inputs.

### Requirements of raw materials and factory supplies

The requirements of raw materials and factory supplies can be expressed in different ways that supplement each other. The overall objective should be to describe and analyse features and characteristics in such a way that a good understanding of what the project requires, is developed. This will form the basis for the supply programme and the subsequent cost estimates. The specification of requirements described below might form a useful check-list.

*User demands.* Users of the produced finished goods have expectations and demands that will have consequences not only for the choice of technology, machinery and equipment, but also for the materials and inputs used. It is therefore helpful to identify and describe such demands and try to analyse the effects on input requirements.

*Quantities required.* In order to allow greater flexibility in the conduct of the study (for example, sensitivity analysis of variations in assumptions and input data), the quantities required can be expressed in the following terms:

- Units produced (for example, items, tonnes, cubic metres), applicable to raw materials, intermediates, components, auxiliary materials etc.

---

[43]For example, a flow sheet for a mining and enrichment plant can consist of the following sections: mining—internal transport—crushing—grinding—flotation—dewatering—disposal of tailings. For cane-sugar manufacturing the flow sheet may show: cultivating—harvesting—transport—crushing/milling—clarification (heating, precipitation, filtration)—boiling/evaporation/crystallization—separation—washing—drying—packaging. In the case of a cement-manufacturing process, it may consist of: quarrying—transport—crushing—grinding—blending of raw materials—preparation of fuel (drying or pulverization)—burning in kilns—cement-grinding—packaging.

- Section of the production process, applicable to raw materials, intermediates, components, factory supplies (auxiliary materials, utilities), spare parts etc.
- Machine or labour hours, applicable to factory supplies, spare parts etc.
- Employees, applicable to foodstuffs, medicine and other social costs

*Qualitative properties.* The type of analysis required to identify the characteristics of materials and inputs depends on the nature of the inputs and their usage in the particular project. An analysis may have to cover various features and characteristics such as the following:

- Physical properties: size, dimension, form (plate, rod etc.), density, viscosity, porosity, state (gaseous, liquid, solid), and melting and boiling points
- Mechanical properties: formability, machinability, tensility, compressive and shearing strength, elasticity, stiffness, fatigue resistance, hardness and annealing qualities
- Chemical properties: form (emulsion, suspension), composition, purity (hardness of water etc.), oxidizing and reducing potentials, flammability and self-extinguishing properties
- Electrical and magnetic properties: magnetization, resistance, conductance and dielectric constants

There may be inadequate or no experience in the use of a particular material input. In such a case, where a body of experience has to be accumulated, pilot plant and other tests may be necessary.

## C. Availability and supply

The sources and the constant availability of basic production materials are crucial to the determination of the technical and economic viability as well as the size of most industrial projects. In many industries, the selection of technology, process equipment and the product mix depend largely on the specifications of the basic materials, while in others the potential quantities available determine the size of the project. The prices at which such materials are available is a determinant of the commercial and financial viability of most industrial projects. In fact, a number of projects are conceived either to exploit available raw materials or to utilize basic materials that become available from other production processes.

A feasibility study must show how the materials and inputs required will be provided. General availability, data about materials, potential users and supply sources and programmes will have to be analysed and described. The interdependencies between project design, material and input requirements and supply of these items should be considered. This means that machinery, equipment, production process, capacity etc. may have to be revised if inputs with the specified characteristics and quantities cannot be provided as required.

At the initial stage of the study the quantities of basic material inputs that may be required should be assessed principally for the purpose of determining availability and sources for immediate and long-term needs. A final assessment of input requirements can be made only after the plant capacity as well as the technology and equipment to be used are defined.

If a basic input is available within a country, its location and the area of supplies, whether concentrated or dispersed, should be determined. The alternative uses likely to be made of such materials, and the consequent impact on availability, should be assessed for the project in question. For example, natural gas may be available in a remote area where it is economic to use it for the generation of electricity in the absence of other demands. However, if the gas is piped to major consumption centres or if the area is opened up through better communications, it would be in much greater demand for other products such as fertilizers and petrochemicals, and it may then not be economic to use it for power generation.

The question of transportability and transport costs should be carefully analysed. The distance over which basic material inputs have to be transported and the available and potential means of transport should be defined together with possible bottlenecks.

When the basic material has to be imported, either in whole or in part, the implications of such imports should be fully assessed. First, the sources of imported inputs have to be determined. Certain materials such as intermediates and commonly used products (springs, bearings etc.) are available from external sources whose access, however, may be greatly restricted in certain cases. Foreign-exchange restrictions may allow for imports only from particular currency areas or restrictive clauses in technology supply agreements may bind licensees to obtain basic inputs, particularly parts, components and other intermediate products, from licensors. Subsidiaries and affiliates of foreign-controlled companies tend to purchase such materials only from their parent companies. In many cases, there may be a lack of knowledge of alternative external sources of basic inputs, especially of intermediate and manufactured inputs.

Secondly, the uncertainty that may relate to imported inputs should be stated. There have been cases where projects have been set up in developing countries based on imported raw materials from particular sources that have then ceased to produce the material in question. Such cases primarily relate to processed materials and manufactured parts and components.

Thirdly, the implications of domestic production of a basic material that was being imported should be analysed. In most developing countries, such production is accompanied by import control and user industries have to adjust to domestic supplies of basic materials. This may involve adjustments to the quality, specifications and price of such materials. While these changes cannot be anticipated in any great detail, it should be recognized that when a project is based on imported basic materials, external and internal forces can affect availability, and they should at least be identified and the general implications highlighted.


*Input alternatives*

In many projects different raw materials can be used for the same production. When this is the case, the raw materials must be analysed to determine which is most suitable, taking all relevant factors into consideration. If alternative materials are easily available, the problem is one of economics of the process and technology rather than of feedstock selection, although the feed material is still a basic issue. If alternative materials are used, the discussion should also include an assessment of the environmental impact of each material.

## D.  Supply marketing and supply programme

An enterprise acts as a buyer on supply markets when purchasing required raw materials and factory supplies. In this respect, the comments made in sub-chapter 3.2 about marketing of the products manufactured apply also to purchasing of material input. For example, relations with the suppliers will have to be established and developed, with bargaining power playing a possible key role, especially when capital goods are purchased or in the case of long-term supply contracts. Supply marketing must be planned for the initial purchases for a plant erection but also for the continuous operation of a plant.

### Supply marketing

The objectives of supply marketing are basically cost minimization, risk minimization (reliability of supplies) and the cultivation of relations with supplier.

### Cost minimization

Input costs can be reduced, *inter alia*, by selecting appropriate suppliers and by choosing a proper volume and frequency of the orders. Any cost minimization opportunity not identified and considered during the feasibility study phase is difficult to make up later during plant operation. This could have then a significant impact on the financial feasibility of the project by reducing the net cash flows and net profits generated. Supply marketing is therefore a vital factor for success.

### Risk minimization and reliability of supplies

Reliability as regards quantities, qualities, deadlines and prices is significant for the entire manufacturing process. Late deliveries, lack of quality or poor maintenance services may have serious consequences for the entire manu-facturing process. These risks must therefore also be considered in the purchasing strategy to ensure that supplies are in accordance with the production requirements.

### Cultivating relations with the supplier

Purchases should be focused not only on acceptable prices, but also on establishing smooth and productive relations with the supplier. In the long run, it can be very advantageous to establish a relationship of mutual trust.

Supply marketing should be designed to reinforce the bargaining position of a project or enterprise. Purchasing prices and conditions largely depend on the bargaining power of the project and its management. Both short- and long-term considerations should prevail. To select a supplier with favourable purchasing prices may seem tempting, but if the supplier is unable to carry out sufficient repair and maintenance work when a plant is in operation, the selection could easily prove very unfavourable in the long run.

As in the case of product marketing, the systematic observation and analysis of supply markets is of central importance. Supply marketing must be carried out all the more intensely in the following cases:

- The higher the share of a product in the total purchase volume. In this case, 20 per cent of the total number of goods supplied usually represents 80 per cent of the total purchased value (the 80-20 rule). Therefore, any increase in the price of one of the goods in the 20 per cent group may have severe consequences for the profitability of the total project;

- The higher the risk of having additional processing costs or production failures (losses, damage, return of products sold etc.) because of delivery constraints or lack of quality.

In this context, it is essential to identify possible supply alternatives. Purchases may be carried out as follows:

- Directly by the individual enterprise

- Through agents, purchasing on their own account or on behalf of an enterprise

- Through purchasing cooperatives formed by a number of enterprises

In order to achieve the objectives of supply marketing it is necessary to build up maximum bargaining power and to select suppliers carefully. These requirements should be considered when identifying potential suppliers in the feasibility study.

Building up maximum bargaining power means optimizing between the following two extremes:

- Too many suppliers, with a wide distribution of risk but a lack of bargaining power (small quantity discounts and limited support provided by suppliers)

- Too few suppliers, with substantial bargaining power but high supplier risk (large quantity discounts, possibly high reorganization costs, development of technical dependence)

Suppliers should be identified and the input quantities to be purchased from each should be determined in the study, taking into account:

- Price competitiveness (including stock, transport and insurance costs)

- Extras (conditions of payment, warranty terms, just-in-time deliveries, repair and spare parts service, customized packaging etc.)

- Expected supplier compliance with quality requirements

- Risk to further in-house processing in case of a deviation from specified quality requirements

- Expected stability of supplier relations

- Reorganization cost incurred through a later change of supplier

- Possibility of purchasing directly from manufacturers or wholesalers

## Supply programme

The overall purpose of the outline of a supply programme in the feasibility study is to show how supplies of materials and inputs will be secured. Evidence should be presented to justify the assumptions and suggestions. Cost estimates should be based on the supply programme presented. A supply programme should deal with the following:

- Identification of supplying sources and suppliers
- Agreements and regulations
- Quantities and qualities
- Consignments
- Means of transport
- Storage
- Risk assessment

In the identification of a particular key supplier, consideration should be given to its geographic location, ownership, main activities, financial strength and profitability, production capacity, output over the last years, key customers and business experience with the type of products and the country concerned. Some suppliers may, for instance, have a long history but still be inexperienced in certain fields of production, in making business with certain parts of the world or in making long-term commitments. An estimate of the level of priority that the supplier may be expected to give the contract in question is usually informative. Where the order represents a high proportion of production, the supplier may be expected to fulfil orders with more dedication, but the supply may, on the other hand, be more sensitive to production problems in such a case.

The types of agreement suggested and possibly already prepared, such as long-term contracts and licence agreements, should be presented. Letters of intent regarding supply contracts and obligations should be referred to, and the general terms of suggested agreements, such as period of validity, payment terms, currency conditions and guarantees, outlined. The feasibility study should indicate, for instance, whether it is common practice to pay in advance when placing orders or receiving consignments. Such information is essential for the later calculation of working capital requirements.

Import policies and regulations, including application procedures for obtaining import licences, validity periods, permits to acquire or use foreign currency, possible tax exemptions and duty-free imports, the existence of import restrictions etc., should be described, and their consequences for the project analysed.

The qualities and quantities that can be supplied from various sources should be indicated. This means that a comparison with the specified input requirements must be made, taking into account not only quality, but also environmental and health aspects, physical and chemical properties etc.

Means of transport for key materials and inputs, by air, water, road or rail, should be identified in the study. The availability, capacity, reliability and technical condition of the facilities must be analysed. For example, an existing railway line does not necessarily mean that reliable transport can be arranged. The railway company may be badly managed, lack required spare parts and maintenance materials, have a limited rolling stock, suffer from ageing and deteriorating facilities etc. On the other hand, railway facilities may be in good physical condition and professionally managed, but suffer from high capacity utilization and bottlenecks.

The study should consequently not only identify existing means of transport, but also analyse their condition, describe how they can be used and suggest measures to be taken by the company concerned in order to obtain some confidence in the level of reliability and capacity. One recommendation would be to establish preferential agreements with transport companies. Alternative means of transport could also be used or project-owned facilities, such as a fleet of lorries, built up for stand-by purposes.

Loading, unloading and storage facilities should be analysed in a similar way. Congested and inefficient port facilities and reloading bottlenecks are common problems in many countries. In addition to an analysis of technical conditions, organizational and management matters and administrative routines should be examined in the study. It may well be that technical facilities are adequate, but customs clearance and administrative routines are bureaucratic and time-consuming.

Storage facilities are usually required at the plant, but may also be needed at ports, railway stations or other places. The study should indicate the capacity of such facilities, describe their utilization, and present estimated quantities to be stored on the basis of anticipated production levels and deliveries of materials and inputs.

An attempt should be made in the feasibility study to identify and assess risks and uncertainties in the supply programme presented. This may lead to certain modifications in the project design (such as the addition of stand-by facilities and extra storage capacity and the use of alternative suppliers and means of transport), but can also serve to alert users of the feasibility study to potential risks. A distinction should be made between external and internal project risk factors, including failure of suppliers to meet their obligations, delayed consignments, supply shortages, quality defects, transport breakdowns, utility malfunctions, strikes, climate variations, changed import regulations and shortages of foreign exchange for imports.

## E. Costs of raw materials and supplies

### Unit costs

Not only the availability but also the unit cost of basic materials and factory supplies have to be analysed in detail, as this is a critical factor for determining project economies. In the case of domestic materials, current prices have to be viewed in the context of past trends and future projections of the elasticity of supply. The lower the elasticity, the higher the price as related to growing demand for a particular material. For domestic inputs the costs of alternative means of transport should also be considered. For imported material inputs, c.i.f. prices (including costs, insurance and freight) should invariably be adopted together with clearing charges (including loading and unloading), port charges, tariffs, local insurance and taxes, and costs of internal transport to the plant. The prices of imported inputs generally fluctuate less, except when:

● International markets are rather volatile;

- Monopolistic or oligopolistic conditions prevail;
- Supplies are linked contractually to a particular source, as between a foreign subsidiary and its parent firm or between a licensee and licensor;
- There is governmental action by way of tariffs or duties or major changes therein.

The impact of the domestic manufacture of a material that is a basic input for an industrial project may be significant. In most cases, domestic production costs and consequently prices of such inputs are higher than prices of imported inputs, particularly during initial production years. This can have substantial effects on production costs of user industries. The extent to which consequent price adjustments in the final product would affect demand for the product should be assessed.

*Annual costs*

Estimates of annual operating costs for materials and supplies are to be made and inserted in schedule IV-1. The price basis for the estimates (price level, quotations from suppliers, world market prices, comparisons with similar inputs in other projects etc.) should be stated in order to enable the reader to check their reliability.

The price mechanism should be explained. Some prices may be fixed or related to an international index for a certain contract period. Others may be subject to a predetermined rate of escalation or be renegotiated every year. Some items may be expected to experience a more rapid price escalation than others. For critical inputs the feasibility study should also determine key factors affecting prices, state whether a monopolistic or oligopolistic situation exists, identify possibilities for obtaining preferential prices and specify government or other administrative price controls.

Cost estimates are to be divided into foreign and local currency components. The currencies most likely to be used and the exchange rates applied for the cost estimates should be identified. This will enable the impact of exchange rate variations to be determined later by sensitivity analysis.

It should be made clear whether the cost estimates refer to a hypothetical level of production at full capacity utilization during the operation phase, or to the first year (or some other year) of operation according to the time schedule for project implementation. In the latter case, possible price escalation should be considered and related to a realistic judgement of the feasible capacity utilization. A distinction should be made between materials and inputs purchased and those actually used or consumed in that particular year, the difference being stocked.

Some costs vary with the production level of the plant in question, while others are more or less fixed. For example, the normal tariff for electricity is divided into an annual fixed fee and a consumption fee per kilowatt-hour. Taking into account expected variations in the production level of the proposed plant, it is advisable to divide cost items into variable and fixed costs.[44]

As explained above in the section on unit costs, the feasibility study should clearly indicate the cost items included in the estimates and the price basis (for

---

[44]The subjects of variable and fixed costs and of direct and indirect costs are dealt with in chapter X.

example, c.i.f. prices for imported materials) used in each case. Clearing charges (including loading and unloading), port charges of different kinds, customs duties, local taxes, local insurance and costs of transport to the plant site are to be identified and included in the feasibility study.

The costs of materials and supplies used or kept in stock are specified in schedule IV-1. The schedule, which can be expanded to allow for the relevant number of items, should present cost estimates related to a certain production level. Cost estimates for materials and inputs can be expressed either as the cost per unit produced or in terms of a certain production level, for example 100,000 units per year. The latter alternative can also be expressed as full capacity utilization, which is equivalent to a certain production level. In either case, it will be possible to carry out a sensitivity analysis of different levels of production and of capacity utilization in the financial calculations. The report should also identify the unit costs applied.

The following information should be presented in schedule IV-1:

- Type of material and input;
- Unit of measurement (barrels, tonnes, cubic metres etc.);
- Number of input units consumed per unit produced;
- Estimated cost per input unit;
- Estimated cost per unit produced;
- Estimated cost per unit produced divided into direct (predominantly variable) and indirect (predominantly) fixed cost components;
- Direct cost per unit produced divided into foreign and local currency components (although expressed in one common currency);
- Indirect cost per unit produced divided into foreign and local currency components.

When calculating indirect costs, the amounts resulting from environmental protection and pollution control measures should be established per unit of production or per accounting period, whichever is appropriate. In order to arrive at the total operating costs by product as well as the total costs per year, the estimated costs per unit are multiplied by the total number of units to be produced.

Schedule IV-2 is used to project the costs over the production period. The totals per main input category are recorded in this schedule, and the grand totals for direct and overhead costs (factory and administrative overheads) are then inserted in schedule X-3.

## Overhead costs of supplies

When estimating material and input requirements by project components, the project planner has to plan not only at the level of production cost centres, but also at the level of service, administration and sales cost centres. A check-list of the usually encountered cost centres of the latter type is provided in chapter VII. Once the material overhead costs are computed, and if no computerized model is used, the totals may be directly transferred to schedule X-3, in chapter X.

# Bibliography

Crompton, H. K. Supplies and materials management; a textbook for purchasing and supply. 2. ed. Plymouth, Devon, MacDonald and Evans, 1979.

Henzel, Friedrich. Die industrieinternen Marktprobleme: Beschaffung, Lagerhaltung, Absatz. Berlin, Duncker und Humblot, 1973.

Lee, L. *and* D. Dobler. Purchasing and material management. New York, McGraw-Hill, 1971.

Tersine, R. I. Principles of inventory and materials management. 3. ed. Amsterdam, North-Holland, 1988.

United Nations. A guide to industrial purchasing. (ID/82)
Sales no.: 72.II.B.19.

_____ UNIDO guides to information sources.

| | |
|---|---|
| No. 1/Rev.1 (ID/163) | Meat-processing industry |
| No. 3 (ID/226) | Leather and leather products industry |
| No. 5/Rev.1 (ID/192) | Foundry industry |
| No. 6/Rev.1 (ID/256) | Industrial quality control |
| No. 7 (ID/197) | Vegetable oil processing industry |
| No. 8 (ID/270) | Agricultural implements and machinery industry |
| No. 10 (ID/280) | Pesticides industry |
| No. 13 (ID/131) | Animal feed industry |
| No. 14 (ID/135) | Printing and graphics industry |
| No. 15 (ID/136) | Non-alcoholic beverage industry |
| No. 16 (ID/138) | Glass industry |
| No. 17 (ID/143) | Ceramics industry |
| No. 19 (ID/158) | Canning industry |
| No. 21 (ID/164) | Fertilizer industry |
| No. 22 (ID/168) | Machine tool industry |
| No. 23 (ID/177) | Dairy product manufacturing industry |
| No. 24 (ID/181) | Soap and detergent industry |
| No. 25 (ID/190) | Beer and wine industry |
| No. 26 (ID/191) | Iron and steel industry |
| No. 27 (ID/194) | Packaging industry |
| No. 28 (ID/198) | Coffee, cocoa, tea and spices industry |
| No. 29 (ID/199) | Petrochemical industry |
| No. 30 (ID/210) | Non-conventional sources of energy |
| No. 31 (ID/214) | Woodworking machinery |
| No. 32 (ID/225) | Electronics industry |
| No. 34 (ID/230) | Natural and synthetic rubber industry |
| No. 35 (ID/234) | Utilization of agricultural residues for the production of panels, pulp and paper |
| No. 36 (ID/236) | Industrial maintenance and repair |
| No. 37 (ID/241) | Industrial training |
| No. 38 (ID/267) | Essential oils |
| No. 39 (ID/268) | Flour milling and the bakery products industry |
| No. 40 (ID/283) | Grain processing and storage |

## Schedule IV-1. Estimate of costs of
## raw materials and supplies
### (insert in schedule IV-2)

Project:
Date:
Source:

| Product/cost centre:<br><br>Code: | First year of production: | | | | Currency:<br><br>Units: | |
|---|---|---|---|---|---|---|
| | Cost projections for year: | | | | | |
| Cost item | F<br>L | Quantity | Unit | Costs per unit | Total costs | Variable share of total (%) |
| | | | | | | |
| | | | | | | |
| Total unit costs, local | | | | | | |
| Total unit costs, foreign | | | | | | |
| Total units per period | | | | | | |
| Total costs per period, local | | | | | | |
| Total costs per period, foreign | | | | | | |
| Total costs of raw materials and supplies | | | | | | |

F = foreign        L = local

## Schedule IV-2. Estimate of costs of raw materials and supplies
### (insert in schedule IV-3)

Project:
Date:
Source:

| Product/cost centre: Code: | First year of production: | | Currency: Units: | |
|---|---|---|---|---|
| | Cost projections for year: | | | |
| Cost item | Local costs | | Foreign costs | |
| | Variable per unit | Fixed per period | Variable per unit | Fixed per period |
| | | | | |
| Total unit costs | | | | |
| Total units per period | | | | |
| Total costs per period | | | | |
| Total costs, materials and supplies | | | | |

*Note* : Units of products sold are defined in schedule III-1 for each product. The grand total for each profit centre may be computed using the same forms. However, data may also be introduced directly into the data input file of the UNIDO COMFAR system.

## Schedule IV-3. Projection of total costs of raw materials and supplies
*(insert in schedule X-3)*

Project:
Date:
Source:

| Product/cost centre:<br><br>Code: | | | First year of sales: | | | Currency:<br><br>Units: | | |
|---|---|---|---|---|---|---|---|---|
| | Total local costs | | | Total foreign costs | | | Grand total | |
| Year | Variable | Fixed | Total | Variable | Fixed | Total | | |
| | | | | | | | | |

# V. Location, site and environment

Following the assessment of demand and the definition of basic project strategies with regard to the sales and production programmes, plant capacity and input requirements, a feasibility study should determine the location and site suitable for an industrial project. Location and site are often used synonymously but must be distinguished. The choice of location should be made from a fairly wide geographical area, within which several alternative sites can be considered. An appropriate location could extend over a considerable area, such as along a river bank or a 15-kilometre radius around an urban area in a particular geographical district. Within a recommended location one or more specific project sites should be identified and assessed in detail. For each project alternative the environmental impact of erecting and operating the industrial plant should be assessed. In many countries, regulations also require the preparation of an environmental impact assessment in order to obtain the permits for the erection and operation of industrial plants. In case of industrial complexes with a significant impact on the environment, the socio-economic and ecological consequences have to be studied carefully in detail, and their evaluation should be instrumental in making the final decision not only on the choice of site, but also on the scope of the project and the selection of technology.

While the traditional approach to industrial location focused on the proximity of raw materials and markets, mainly with a view to minimizing transport costs, the integrated feasibility study proposed in this *Manual* requires the consideration not only of technical and commercial or financial factors, but also of the social and environmental impact a project might have. Consequently, the relative weight of, and interaction between, these factors as well as the relevant public policies must also be considered in the location and siting of industrial investment projects.

The main criteria or key requirements for selecting proper locations and sites should always be identified at an early stage of the study. The qualitative analysis of these key requirements would then allow the assessment of a number of potential locations and sites, and the rejection of those not fulfilling the key requirements. The remaining alternatives are then subject to a more in-depth qualitative and quantitative analysis of technical and financial criteria, including social, environmental and economic aspects of location and site selection.

Each project has specific requirements which, if met, would produce certain external impacts. Those more important or critical for the project should be assessed and studied carefully, and the fact that some requirements or impacts are easier to quantify should not lead to the mistake of underestimating the importance of qualitative aspects.

## A. Location analysis

Location analysis has to identify locations suitable for the industrial project under consideration. A project can potentially be located in a number of alternative regions, and the choice of location should be made from a fairly wide geographical area within which several alternative sites may have to be considered. The feasibility study should also indicate on what grounds alternative locations have been identified, and give reasons for leaving out other locations that were suitable but not selected.

The choice of location is not always based on a systematic step-by-step analysis and assessment of a gradually reduced number of possible locations, ending up with the optimum solution. A location may sometimes be suggested at an early stage by the project promoters. However, the methodology of analysing such a suggestion is the same, and the location in question will still have to fulfil the key requirements identified as essential or critical for a feasible and viable implementation and operation of the project.[45]

The impacts and requirements to be identified may be classified as follows:

- Natural environment, geophysical conditions and project requirements
- Ecological impact of the project, environmental impact assessment
- Socio-economic policies, incentives and restrictions and government plans and policies
- Infrastructural services, conditions and requirements, such as the existing industrial infrastructure, the economic and social infrastructure, the institutional framework, urbanization and literacy

The *strategic orientation* of the choice of suitable locations requires an assessment of, *inter alia*, market and marketing aspects, the availability of critical project inputs such as raw materials and factory supplies, technical project requirements, the type of industry, technology and process, characteristics and products or outputs, size of the plant, organizational requirements and management structure. The study should not go into unnecessary details but rather aim at an understanding of the background to and relevance of the aspects identified. Since the key aspects vary from industry to industry, project analysts will have to use their professional skill to identify those key criteria which are relevant for each specific project.

The identification of key requirements helps to reduce the number of potential locations and sites at an early stage. An analysis of key aspects is basically made in qualitative terms and does not enter into any financial calculations. The primary task at this stage is rather to sort out unrealistic and less attractive alternatives than to make a correct ranking.

## B. The natural environment

*Climatic conditions.* Climate can be an important locational factor. Apart from the direct impact on project costs of such factors as dehumidification, air-conditioning, refrigeration or special drainage, the environmental effects

---

[45]The requirements that a project would have to fulfil are dealt with in the section on environmental impact assessment later in this chapter.

127

may be significant. Information should be collected on temperature, rainfall, flooding, dust, fumes and other factors for different locations. A check-list on local conditions is provided at the end of this chapter.

Climatic conditions are relevant in different ways, depending on the type of project. Agro-industrial projects may experience fluctuating quantities and qualities of raw materials owing to extreme weather conditions. Means of transport may become less reliable in the case of heavy snow or rainfall, causing interrupted supplies of perishable products to distant markets. Transport and construction works are usually more complicated and expensive under extreme conditions, which may be a critical factor in projects with heavy transport and large construction works.

A project may also be dependent on climatic conditions in an indirect way. The construction, operation and management of the plant may be less efficient or more expensive if an inadequately skilled labour force is reluctant to work in areas with extreme climatic conditions. This aspect is particularly important for personnel in key positions (top management, administrative staff, skilled labour) and in scarce supply.

Climatic conditions can be specified in terms of air temperature, humidity, sunshine hours, winds, precipitation, hurricane risk etc. Each of these can be specified in greater detail, such as maximum, minimum and average temperatures on an average day, in particular months or over a period of 10 years. There is sometimes a tendency to overdo this description. The study should instead concentrate on the identification and analysis of climatic factors that can be expected to be of vital importance for the feasibility of the project in question.

Geodesic aspects are in general more relevant for the selection of suitable sites. These include soil conditions, subsoil water levels and a number of special site hazards, such as earthquakes and susceptibility to flooding, all of which extend over greater areas.

*Ecological requirements.* Some projects may not have a negative environmental impact themselves, but rather be sensitive to such effects. An agro-industrial project clearly depends on the use of raw materials that have not been degraded by contaminated water and soil. A project using huge volumes of process water with strict quality requirements will suffer if nearby industries use a river as a recipient of waste water. Management and labour may be reluctant to work in a factory located in a polluted area with health risks.

## C.  Environmental impact assessment

The feasibility study should include a thorough and realistic analysis of the environmental impact of industrial investment projects. This impact is often of crucial importance for the socio-economic, financial and technical feasibility of a project.[46] The site and environmental impact analysis will cover the impact of

---

[46]For example, some effluents may be totally unacceptable and require purification and treatment facilities. Others may be tolerable in certain conditions based on such factors as climate, geology and distance to urban centres. The technological project layout will indicate whether a particular environmental impact is to be expected. Some projects may use materials and inputs that involve the risk of spontaneous ignition or explosion, or perhaps toxicological risks. Other projects may generate flue gases, fumes, waste water, waste materials, tailings, noise etc., which affect the environment negatively. Contamination of groundwater and surface water, air and soil would have an impact on the natural environment, on plants, trees, animals and people. Some emissions may even affect houses and metal products, for instance as a result of acid precipitation.

the project and its alternatives (in terms of size, technology etc.) on the surrounding area, including its population, flora and fauna. This analysis should be integrative and interdisciplinary, assessing the overall impact while taking into account the synergetic effects of interlinked systems.

Environmental impact assessment is designed to develop an understanding of the environmental consequences of a newly planned or existing project and of any project-related activities. These consequences and the beneficial or adverse effects of such human activities on the environment are assessed and evaluated from a technical, financial and socio-economic point of view, to the extent that they are significant for the project implementation decision. A project may impinge upon the human habitat directly or indirectly. An ecological perspective regards the human habitat in terms of the complex network of interactions with the natural, cultural and socio-economic environment.

Environmental impact assessment is part of the project planning process. Through statute or practice it is an integral part of feasibility analysis. Environmental benefits or costs of a project are usually externalities or side-effects that affect the society in whole or in part. As such they are appropriately assessed in a socio-economic context at the local level, as well as the superior regional and national levels, if required and as determined by the geo-political dimensions of the impact. In a comprehensive socio-economic evaluation of the feasibility of a project, environmental effects on the quality of life are considered along with other criteria to decide if the overall effect of the project is positive, or to determine what modifications may be necessary to achieve a positive evaluation. Some economically quantifiable environmental impacts are also included along with other economic factors in the cost-benefit appraisal of the project.

Environmental effects are measured both qualitatively and quantitatively. As the various environmental parameters are often incommensurate, a multi-objective evaluation, or optimization, may be required. In such an evaluation, deviations from the desired condition are weighted either systematically or subjectively for each factor or combination of factors to arrive at an assessment of the overall impact. In some cases cost-benefit analysis supplements qualitative assessments of environmental factors that are not readily quantifiable. Techniques have been developed for deriving monetized valuations of impacts that may or may not be directly linked to markets. While these techniques were originally developed to assess the economic impact of environmental regulations, they can also be used to make an economic evaluation of environmental changes in the absence of any regulations. A further description of some of these techniques is given below.

In countries where the analysis of environmental impacts is already required by law, the usual procedure is for the promoters of the project to prepare an extensive environmental impact statement[47] that must be submitted to the authorities for examination and clearance. This statement can also be a part of the feasibility study. However, it should be drawn up in such a way that it can be put forward as a separate paper when the project is submitted for

---

[47]The format and contents of environmental impact statements is not uniform and varies depending on the regulations of a country. The concept adopted in this *Manual* follows to some extent the terminology and concept established in the United States of America.

approval. Where such legal provisions for environmental protection do not yet exist, an environmental impact assessment should be made in the interests of the investor, in particular when the intention is to apply for international financing, since many of the international development finance institutions already require assessment of the environmental impact of industrial investment projects. Whenever possible, the basic data for such assessments should include all the documentation currently available on the project, in particular test results and calculations from university institutes, regional and urban data collection units or networks, documents from central statistics institutes, statistics issued by United Nations bodies and other organizations.

In many cases it may well be particularly difficult to obtain sufficiently precise data on specific regional areas. If such data are required for the appraisal of the project, however, the assessment of the necessary information may be rather costly and time-consuming.

In principle, environmental impacts should be assessed on the basis of legal regulations and emission standards and guidelines established in the country where the project is located. In countries where no or only vague regulations and standards are defined, it may be advisable to anticipate a future tightening of environmental impact control measures, especially in the case of long-term projects. A growing consciousness and concern for environmental problems and ecological consequences have in fact become noticeable world-wide, and is strongly supported by international development and financing organizations, with the establishment of environmental protection institutions in each of the countries concerned in order to define and enforce corresponding environmental protection standards and policies. Therefore, trends anticipated in the industry life cycles should also be considered in investment planning especially for industries with high potential environmental impacts. If trends are properly considered during the project planning stage, unexpected costs for later plant adaptations, conversions, rehabilitations or even the shut-down of operations can be avoided or minimized. In countries where environmental protection standards and guidelines are not yet defined, standards published by United Nations organizations, such as the Food and Agriculture Organization of the United Nations, the United Nations Environment Programme (UNEP), the World Health Organization and the World Meteorological Organization, or other international, regional or national institutions, may by used as reference for environmental impact assessment, when performed within feasibility studies.

*Environmental conflicts*

Some projects may have environmental impacts that will obviously rule out certain locations, if serious or irreparable pollution and damages are to be avoided. Environmental conflicts might also lead to compensation claims, substantial costs for purification and equipment, and possibly a risk that the plant will have to be closed down. The potential risks related to the location of projects with negative environmental impacts are usually so great that these aspects must be seriously considered in the feasibility study, including potential conflicts with existing and future neighbouring industries, urban settlements and other elements, which should be identified and analysed in so far as they may affect the investment decision.

## Objectives of environmental impact assessment

The general objective of environmental impact assessment in project analysis is to ensure that development projects are environmentally sound. This implies that the effects of the project over its projected life do not unacceptably degrade the environment, and that no residual effects are anticipated that would contribute to long-term environmental deterioration.[48] The immediate and long-term health and welfare of people are linked to their natural, cultural and socio-economic environment. For this reason, and to promote the objective of incorporating the ideas and aspirations of the affected population in the decision process, public participation from the earliest stages and throughout the project development cycle is desirable.

The specific objectives of environmental impact assessment are as follows:

- To promote a comprehensive, interdisciplinary investigation of environmental consequences of the project and its alternatives for the affected natural and cultural human habitat

- To develop an understanding of the scope and magnitude of incremental environmental impacts (with and without the project) of the proposed project for each of the alternative project designs

- To incorporate in the designs any existing regulatory requirements

- To identify measures for mitigation of adverse environmental impacts and for possible enhancement of beneficial impacts

- To identify critical environmental problems requiring further investigation

- To assess environmental impacts qualitatively and quantitatively, as required, for the purpose of determining the overall environmental merit of each alternative

## Phases and structure of environmental impact assessment

The environmental impacts of each phase of the project development cycle will usually differ. During the planning phase, for example, the environmental effects may be strictly social and economic. New political and social alignments may arise among proponents and opponents. The anticipation of a proposed project may have economic consequences for associated resources. The impacts of the construction phase are one-time effects, while those of the operational phase will be recurring. The effects during the phases of planning, implementation, start-up and commissioning, operations and decommissioning, if required, are considered separately and cumulatively.

The performance of an environmental impact assessment also involves the following steps: the definition of the problem; the technology description and forecast; the social description and forecast; and the identification, analysis and evaluation of impacts.[49] Environmental impact assessment of industrial

---

[48]Environment is here understood as the whole, interdependent, natural (ecological) and social (cultural, socio-economic) system, of which an investment project would be an integrated part.

[49]See also chap. VI, sect. B.

131

investment projects is then usually followed by policy analysis and the determination of a suitable investment strategy and corporate environment policy. Finally, and if required, the environment impact statement is prepared.[50]

Sometimes only three phases of environmental impact analysis are distinguished. At first, a preliminary environmental impact assessment is performed using a check-list or standardized set of criteria to ensure consideration of all relevant environmental factors, and to determine which impacts would need to be analysed in detail during the second phase of the assessment, and which administrative actions are to be taken. The check-lists annexed to this chapter may serve as a guideline for the assessment of environmental impacts.

The environmental impact assessment in the second phase consists in the identification and evaluation of environmental impacts resulting from the project. A site visit with all members of the assessment team is essential if the environmental situation is complex and significant for the investment decision. An in-depth study of the incremental impacts (with and without the project) is then prepared, leading to a disciplinary study by each specialist using the full scope of research tools and resources available.

The third phase of environmental impact assessment consists in the preparation of the environmental impact statement. Although closely related to the feasibility study and investment decision, it is not, however, a part of the study itself. This statement, which is now often required as a condition for project implementation, should reflect the interdisciplinary mode in which it was prepared. The final environmental impact statement should specify any mitigation measures that would make the recommended alternative environmentally acceptable.

As a preliminary step, the impacts of production processes and factory operations are examined individually and jointly. Ancillary activities such as the handling of products, raw materials and factory supplies, transport, resource utilization, waste control and disposition measures, and safety and process failure controls are considered. Related operations involving pipelines, transmission lines, docking and road and rail requirements are included. Each project, in one way or another, utilizes natural resources such as land, water, raw materials (minerals etc.) and energy. The aesthetic and social qualities of the site and in the region may be altered or may disappear. The project may emit solid, liquid and gaseous wastes, radiation (including light) or noise.[51] Although it is convenient for the purposes of problem identification and teamwork to classify the totality of the environment in terms of its various components, the analysis must take into account the complex web of component interactions. Apart from the development of analytical models that take into account such interactions to the greatest extent practicable, it is imperative that the team should function in an interdisciplinary mode. Operationally, this requires that frequent coordinated multidisciplinary obser-

---

[50]In the United States, the environmental impact statement is prepared by an environmental authority, and the statement is based on the environmental impact assessment submitted by the promoter of the project (enterprise).

[51]For the operation of each unit a description of the inflow of raw materials and other inputs as well as the products, by-products, wastes and other emissions may be supplemented with a schematic process diagram. Pollution control devices and their effect on waste streams should also be described. Intermittent processes such as start-up, shut-down, testing, cleaning operations, the release of gases, liquids, radiation etc. are described. The temporal distribution of process operations is examined for each phase of the project development cycle indicated above.

vations and analyses of environmental factors should take place. In the first phase of the environmental impact assessment, the definition of the problem arises from the environmental inventory and preliminary environmental impact statement. From these data, the scope of the assessment is determined to arrive at a consensus concerning the impacts to be investigated. Applicable regulations and limitations are determined and preliminary public reaction is sought to identify public concerns and local insights.

The baseline or status quo environment (environmental inventory) represents the foundation for the analysis of project effects. It is described as it exists during the period of analysis and as it is projected to be 10 to 15 years in the future. The incremental effects, or changes induced by the project over time, can then be assessed.

The primary purpose of the environmental impact statement is to serve as a means of including consideration of environmental consequences of the project and its alternatives in the process of project appraisal, to ensure that the policies, goals and aspirations of the proponents, the Government and the affected population are incorporated in the decision process. It should provide full and fair discussion of significant impacts and inform decision makers and the public of reasonable alternatives that would avoid or minimize adverse impacts or enhance the quality of the human environment.[52]

## The assessment process

As shown in figure XXVI, the environmental impact assessment and the techno-economic study should be carried out concurrently and interactively. There are direct parallels between the pre-feasibility study and the preliminary environmental impact statement.

The preliminary environmental impact assessment is reviewed along with the pre-feasibility study, with comprehensive consideration of the technical, socio-economic and environmental features. Screening is intended to determine the level of environmental analysis appropriate to a particular project. If the project warrants no further environmental analysis and is technically and financially feasible, it can be recommended for approval to the environmental authority (for example, an environmental review council), which in the case of industrial projects will normally be at the level of state or province. If approved by this authority, the project can be implemented, provided it complies with all existing environmental regulations. If further assessment is recommended by the authority, the scope of the assessment should be established in consultation between the environmental authority and the promoters of the project. Terms of reference for the level and scope of the assessment should be prepared by the promoters (investors) and the environmental agency. Interim reports should be submitted for review so that all parties concerned may be aware of the project status.[53] The environmental impact assessment and techno-economic feasibility

---

[52]See Council on Environmental Quality, 40 Code of Federal Regulations 1502 (Washington, D.C., Government Printing Office, 1988).

[53]Sometimes the preliminary environmental impact statement may not be sufficiently detailed to satisfy the environmental authorities or the project may not be approved. In such cases, a more detailed environmental impact assessment and environmental impact statement would have to be prepared at the feasibility study level, taking into account the technological, engineering and locational alternatives identified for the project.

**Figure XXVI. Phases of environmental impact assessment**

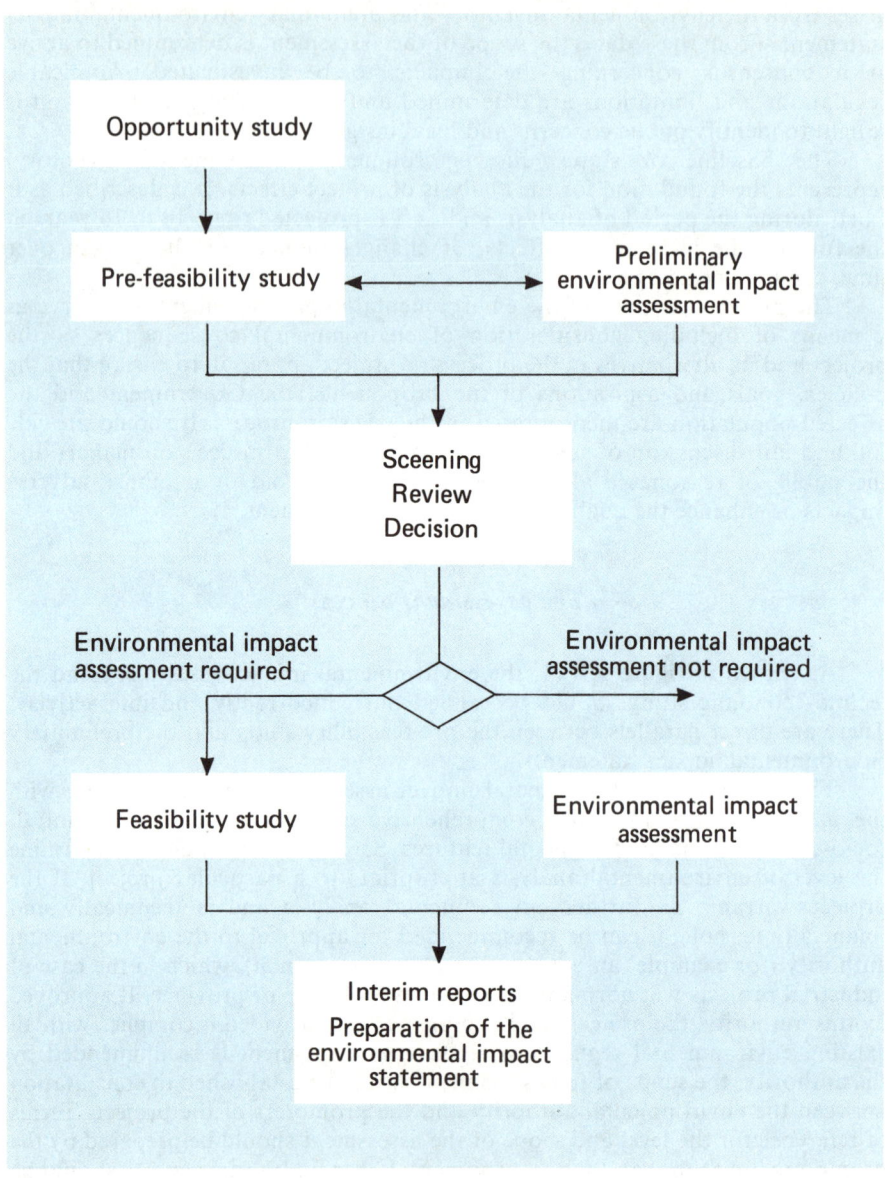

study may be further linked in the sense that certain environmental factors may be appropriately evaluated in economic terms.[54]

A mechanism or organism for monitoring environmental compliance during the construction and operational phases is essential. This body should also monitor any unforeseen environmental consequences and bring them to the attention of the environmental review council for further evaluation.

---

[54]See the notes on environmental cost-benefit analysis later in this chapter.

## Methodologies and tools

Several methodologies and tools that are useful in the performance of environmental impact assessment have been developed. The methodologies should satisfy several important criteria related to the desirability of a comprehensive, interdisciplinary approach to assessment. Ideally the methodology will provide:

- Comprehensive identification of all relevant impacts
- Cause and effect relationships between project and environmental factors and impacts
- Promotion of an interdisciplinary approach to assessment
- The temporal distribution of impacts, for example, differences between impacts in the construction and operational phases
- Criteria for assessment in both qualitative and quantitative terms
- Indication of the dynamic nature of environmental impacts producing primary, secondary, tertiary etc. impacts

In addition, the methodology should be relatively easy to implement and comprehensible to laymen as well as non-technical experts.

The appendix to chapter V contains check-lists suitable for the purpose of feasibility studies.[55] The check-lists include a list of environmental factors that may be affected by the project. The value of using a check-list is the avoidance of the inadvertent omission of a significant factor.

*Interaction matrices.* Matrices are arrays of data with a horizontal list of project activities across the top and a vertical listing of environmental parameters. Matrices can be of varying levels of complexity. A simple interaction matrix indicates linkages between project activities and environmental parameters. Quantified and graded matrices[56] provide a means of analysing impact magnitude and importance. Numerical weightings of the probable impacts using various methods of compilation provide an indication of where the impact is likely to concentrate, spread out, produce compensating

---

[55]Check-lists have been developed in a variety of forms depending on the depth of the study. Simple check-lists indicate only environmental factors. Other information relating to guidelines for measurement and to the scaling and relative weighting of effects may be included. Check-lists are available in several handbooks (such as R. Corwin and others, *Environmental Impact Assessment* (San Francisco, Freeman, Cooper, 1975), and R. N. Burchell and D. Lisokin, *The Environmental Impact Handbook* (New Jersey, Rutgers University, 1975)), in addition to United States government publications (such as Environmental Protection Agency, *Review of Federal Actions Impacting the Environment* (Washington D.C., Government Printing Office, 1975)). A check-list using scaling and weighting, known as the environmental evaluation system, has been adapted for use in Thailand. It was developed by the Battelle Laboratory in the United States. Although designed for assessment of water resource projects, it can be used for other types of industrial projects. It is useful in identifying and quantifying potential environmental impacts for decision makers. Although relatively complex, additional information is required on such matters as the temporal distribution of impacts.

[56]See J. C. Sorenson, "Some procedures and programs of environmental impact", in *Environmental Impact Analysis: Philosophy and Methods,* R. B. Ditton and T. I. Goodale, eds. (Madison, University of Wisconsin, 1972), and B. M. Lohani and N. Halim, "Recommended methods for environmental impact assessment in developing countries: experiences derived from case-studies in Thailand", in *Environmental Impact Assessment for Developing Countries*, A. K. Biswas and Qu Geping, eds. (London, Tycooly International, 1987).

effects etc. Matrices are generally not sufficient for decision-making as they usually do not meet all of the criteria indicated above.

Overlays use a set of transparent sheets on each of which is indicated the degree of impact of the project on a particular environmental parameter. The degree of impact is shown by the intensity of the shading or cross-hatching. These colour-coded transparencies are positioned over the base map and the aggregate impact on various areas is shown by the intensity and colour of the shading. The method is widely used for showing spatial distribution of impacts and is particularly useful in route decisions concerning, for example, transmission lines, rail lines and highways. Computerized overlays have been developed which include not only the shading feature, but also weighting models that indicate the relative importance of each impact. The overlay method is most useful in screening alternative project sites.

Networks are used to analyse the cascaded series of effects resulting from project activities.[57] A set of possible primary, secondary, tertiary etc. impacts is identified from similar experiences, and the likely impacts are identified for the project under study. The network effectively displays factual information, but does not contain information on weightings or social valuations. It is organized in the form of a tree, where primary effects give rise to secondary effects, secondary to tertiary etc.

When the environmental impacts of a system are relatively extensive and complex, more sophisticated techniques may be required to assess impacts properly and choose among alternatives. Systems analysis (usually requiring a computer model) is a method that can deal with multiple criteria for selection among project alternatives. In this approach the criteria must be clearly defined and the project impacts clearly understood. The development of an analytical model requires the interdisciplinary contributions of experts.

Various types of models can be developed. Simulation models provide a replica of the project and its environment. Parameters are varied to gain understanding of the complex interactions between the project and environmental parameters. Stochastic and temporal features can be built into the model. Optimization models seek the best solution in consideration of project and environmental constraints according to an objective function. Techniques such as goal programming permit the simultaneous consideration of multiple objectives that are weighted by "penalties" for deviations from the ideal.

Analytical tools include the instruments of objective measurement of environmental quality. Standards for the use of these instruments must be respected in order to obtain reliable data. Instruments should be selected according to criteria of accuracy and precision. Accuracy refers to the degree to which the instrument indicates the actual value of the parameter. Precision is a measure of tolerance, or the spread of repeated measurements obtained with the instrument. Calibration of the instruments to standards should be checked periodically according to standard practice.

In taking measurements it is important to consider the location and time of measurements to ensure that they are representative and not affected by extraneous factors. Measurements should be taken by qualified individuals. Field analysis permits the constant monitoring of sensitive sites and the opportunity to check unexpected results, but usually is less reliable than analysis in the controlled conditions of the laboratory.

[57]R. Bisset, "Introduction to methods for environmental impact assessment", in *Environmental Assessment* (The Hague, Martinus Nijhoff, 1983).

The following basic steps should be observed when performing environmental impact assessment:

- *Identification of impacts*

    Define development objectives and key constraints on project implementation;

    Identify options for achieving the basic objectives of the project;

    Identify key linkages of proposed development with natural resources, ecological, social and socio-economic systems, and other development activities (see matrix and check-lists in the appendix to chapter V);

    Determine requirements for environmental impact assessment (legal requirements, including procedures for project approval) and environmental impact statements;

    Determine the scope of environmental impact assessment (terms of reference);

    Assemble baseline data for natural and social (socio-economic and cultural) systems, potentially conflicting development policies or projects, and key resource implications;

    Analyse the proposed investment project to identify resource demands and outputs and their environmental impacts;

- *Environmental impact forecast*

    Prepare a projection of the magnitude and severity of the probable future effects of the proposed investment project (see also chapter VI, section B);

- *Evaluation*

    Assess the significance, distribution and permanence of predicted effects from the point of view of the affected population, economic impacts (competition for scarce natural resources, infrastructure, pollution control etc.) and ecological consequences;

    Establish real resource costs and benefits associated with the environmental impacts of the project, and incorporate these costs and benefits into the overall economic evaluation, to the extent that they would be significant for the investment decision;

- *Communications*

    Determine how to present the results of environmental impact assessment, indicating trade-offs, key decision factors, sources of data, levels of confidence, conclusion and recommendations with regard to requirements and possible risks;

    Describe possible measures for reducing and controlling negative environmental impacts, and justify any measures necessary or recommendable, whether during the feasibility study, project implementation or operational phases.


## Cost-benefit analysis of environmental impacts

Environmental impact assessment and cost-benefit analysis are in some respects parallel and overlapping activities. Environmental impact assessment has developed as an instrument for resource allocation and utilization only within the past several decades. Comprehensive environmental protection legislation has been in effect in a number of industrialized countries only since the 1960s.[58] Previously, quantitative economic cost-benefit analysis was the principal means by which policies, plans and projects in the industrial sector were evaluated for their contribution to social objectives, with little regard for the environment. In view of its historical subordination to economic analysis, a deliberate effort may be required to ensure that environmental considerations be included in a comprehensive, interdisciplinary analysis of the socio-economic consequences of a project.

The guidelines of the Council on Environmental Quality, an organ of the executive branch of the United States Government responsible for the elaboration of environmental policy, allude to the primacy of comprehensive analysis relative to quantitative cost-benefit analysis in the environmental review and decision process:

> "If a cost-benefit analysis relevant to the choice among environ-mentally different alternatives is being considered for the proposed action, it shall be incorporated by reference or appended to the statement as an aid in evaluating environmental consequences. The statement shall, when a cost-benefit analysis is prepared, discuss the relationship between that analysis and any analyses of unquantified environmental impacts, values and amenities. The weighting of the merits and drawbacks of the various alternatives need not be displayed in a monetary cost-benefit analysis and should not be when there are important qualitative considerations. In any event, an environmental impact statement should at least indicate those considerations, including factors not related to environmental quality, which are likely to be relevant and important to a decision".[59]

## Cost-benefit analysis models

Several cost-benefit models have been constructed for use in developing countries but are primarily oriented toward the use and management of natural resources. These would include the UNEP Test Model of Extended Cost-Benefit Analysis, the Cost-Benefit Analysis of Natural Systems Assessment and the Extended Cost-Benefit Analysis Graph developed by the Viet Nam Environmental Research Programme.

Cost-benefit analysis is generally applied at the project level to consider all the economic benefits and costs resulting from the employment of national resources of any character and from the production of goods and services. Environmental externalities that are subject to quantification in economic terms may be internalized by including the economic values in the cost-benefit analysis. The environmental impact assessment should include a qualitative assessment of these quantified impacts as well, taking due note of their inclusion in the cost-benefit analysis to avoid, in a sense, double-counting.

---

[58]For example, in the United States the National Environmental Protection Act of 1969 requires that all agencies of the United States Federal Government should "identify and develop methods and procedures, which will ensure that presently unquantified environmental amenities and values may be given appropriate consideration in decision-making along with economic and technical considerations" (Section 102 (B)).

[59]See Council on Environmental Quality, 40 Code of Federal Regulations 1502 (Washington, D.C., Government Printing Office, 1988), chap. V.

As parallel activities, the primacy of cost-benefit analysis versus environmental impact assessment depends upon the context in which the project is being reviewed. For the environmental review and decision process environmental impact assessment is the primary evaluation instrument. In the case of socio-economic evaluation, the reverse is true. Some of the environmental impacts that are economically quantifiable would be included in the cost-benefit analysis, and a comprehensive, interdisciplinary presentation of all environmental impacts would be included in the accompanying environmental impact assessment.[60] At the level of commercial analysis, the environmental consequences of a project are externalities in the sense that they represent neither direct costs for the project nor are they sources of revenue.

Economically quantifiable environmental impacts can be included at the level of economic efficiency. These quantitative values are in this sense internalized, although the beneficial or adverse impacts affect the local, regional or national population rather than the project. In case environmental factors affect specific groups, such as the workforce of the project under study, distributional effects can also be considered. In some cases it may be useful to include subjective quantitative valuations of economically non-quantifiable effects as project merits or demerits, although their inclusion should in no way detract from the value of the comprehensive environmental impact assessment.

The environmental consequences of the project may be in the form of environmental improvement or degradation. If an environmental factor to be affected by the project is regulated, financial costs will accrue to the project for compliance measures. Treatment of environmental impacts within the regulated limit is a matter of judgement. If such impacts are assumed to be environmentally non-deleterious, there would be no corresponding social cost. Any residual effects beyond the regulated limit would be considered a social cost.[61]

Although the project *per se* is evaluated only in financial terms, an environmental externality should be evaluated in economic terms as it has an impact upon a segment of the population external to the project.[62]

In the cost-benefit context the basic principle to apply in assessing the socio-economic impact of the project is to consider the net benefits and costs of the incremental environmental effects of the project, on the basis of the difference in environmental conditions and mitigation measures with and without the implementation of the project.

The alternative circumstances regarding the project impact upon the environment and the assessment of benefits and costs of the environmental

---

[60]The parallel relationship of cost-benefit analysis and environmental impact assessment is described in the United States Environmental Protection Act of 1983 as follows: "In theory (the improvement of economic efficiency) is achieved by selecting ... options that maximize net social benefits. Unfortunately, determining which ... options are best in terms of economic efficiency often is made difficult by uncertainties in data, by inadequacies in analytical techniques, and by the presence of benefits and costs that can be quantified but not monetized or that can only be qualitatively assessed. Thus, even if the criterion of economic efficiency were the sole guide to ... decision-making, the analytical results ... may not always point to a specific ... option as being superior."

[61]On the principle of incremental analysis (with and without the project), it would be useful to supplement the analysis with valuation of the actual incremental effect as if the regulation were not in effect.

[62]In the case of regulation, control or mitigation of the adverse effects of environmental conditions of the workplace, where the affected population is the workforce, the impacts may or may not be wholly internal to the project. However, the same principles apply for financial or economic evaluation as for an environmental externality.

impact require different approaches to valuation based upon the principle of incremental analysis. Various scenarios and the corresponding financial and economic consequences are outlined below.

| Project | Regulation | Cost | Benefit |
|---|---|---|---|
| Exists | Under consideration | Financial and economic cost of compliance | Improvement of environmental quality to regulated limit |
| Under study | Exists | Financial cost of compliance to the project<br><br>Economic cost of compliance may be considered a sunk cost<br><br>Residual environmental degradation | Possible environmental improvement |
| Under study | Concurrently under consideration | Financial and economic cost of compliance | No economic benefit for maintaining environmental status quo |
| Under study | Unregulated | Environmental degradation | Possible environmental improvement |

In the second case outlined above, where the project is under study and environmental regulation exists, although the cost of compliance is considered a sunk cost, it would be a valuable adjunct to the analysis to isolate that part of the investment attributable to compliance as a measure of the social investment in the maintenance of environmental quality.

## Assessment of environmental costs and benefits

The basic principle underlying the quantitative assessment of environmental impacts is the value that may be placed by society or individuals on environmental improvement or degradation. These benefits or costs can be expressed monetarily in terms of willingness to pay for environmental improvement or willingness to accept as compensation for environmental degradation.

## Direct monetary methods

The cost saving (or cost impact) method estimates the changes in household expenditures and in production costs for other industrial activities affected by the environmental change attributable to the project under study. The damage function method develops a dose-response function to assess physical changes in receptor organisms or materials, which is then converted to monetary units by assessing the value of the changes. For example, if a crop yield is altered by a change in environmental quality, the change in the economic value of the crop is a monetary measure of the environmental change. In the case of risks to human life and health, valuation models have been developed using risk-compensation data for occupations with varying levels of risk.[63] An alternative is the human-capital approach, in which the financial costs associated with the health impact, principally medical costs and the present value of lost earnings, are determined.

## Direct survey-based methods

The contingent valuation method uses surveys to determine the value that the affected population places on environmental changes. Subjects have described to them proposed environmental changes and are asked for the maximum amount they are willing to pay for an improvement or the maximum amount they would accept as compensation or to prevent the change in the case of environmental degradation. The data are then statistically analysed and aggregated across households to arrive at a valuation of the environmental change.

The contingent ranking method also uses surveys, but subjects are offered alternatives in terms of environmental change versus payment or compensation combinations which they then rank in order of preference. From this data a model is developed which estimates the change in income that would just offset the utility of the environmental change.

## Indirect market-based methods

The hedonic pricing method attempts to impute values for environmental change by identifying their effect on the market price and price movements of economic resources. The level of environmental quality may be reflected, for example, in local housing prices or labour markets. Prices at different locations of these resources are assumed to reflect the implicit market value of the environmental variation.

The travel cost method identifies the relationship between visits to recreation sites with different levels of environmental quality and the cost of travel to these sites. In the context of industrial development, this method would be applicable in cases where the environmental effect of the project alters transport patterns of the public to recreational or other sites.

## Environmental parameters

For the purposes of environmental impact assessment it is useful to classify the environmental impact factors. Common systems classify environmental impacts according to the affected environment (atmosphere, land, water, flora, fauna, social community etc.) and the nature or types of impact (physical and chemical, economic, aesthetic). These categories are intended to encompass the entire span of attributes of the natural and social human habitat to be assessed and evaluated in terms of changes in the quality of the human habitat.

Physical and chemical impacts, including noise emissions and impacts on energy resources, encompass the effects on physical and chemical characteristics of the whole ecological system consisting of the atmosphere, water, land, fauna

---

[63]See W. K. Viscuse, "Alternative approaches to valuing the health impacts of accidents: liability law and prospective evaluations", *Law and Contemporary Problems*, vol. 47, No. 4 (1983).

and flora. Changes to a physical or chemical attribute of the ecological environment are usually reflected as impacts upon ecological factors, such as population size, growth rates, intra- and inter-species interactions and life cycles, as well as social factors (cultural, economical, aesthetic impacts).

Ecological factors include the flora and fauna separately and conjointly in terms of ecosystems, in which the population, growth rate, intra- and inter-species interactions, life cycle etc. of each species and its habitat is considered.

Aesthetic factors are concerned primarily with sensory impacts, primarily visual, of land use and installations of the proposed project.

Social factors deal with the cultural and economic impacts, such as the quality of human life in terms of health, welfare and social infrastructure. In the case of feasibility studies, such effects include impacts within the corporation or production plant (internal environment), as well as the external environment.

Check-list V-3 in the appendix to this chapter contains a listing of potential environmental factors. However, it is not exhaustive, and should be used only as a guide.

## D. Socio-economic policies

### Role of public policies

Government regulations and restrictions may be critical for the location of a project. Projects with certain characteristics (involving, for example, a particular industry or imported materials) may be allowed only in certain regions. The impact of public policies has increased considerably in recent years, and the extent to which such policies are applicable to a particular investment proposal should be clearly defined. In a number of developed and developing countries there is considerable pressure for the decentralization of industries. In industrialized countries, such dispersal is sought principally on environmental grounds to reduce industrial pollution in areas of heavy industrial concentration. While the emphasis on environmental considerations is increasing also in many developing countries, the main objective of industrial decentralization is to reduce the external diseconomies of urban industrial concentration.

Even when public policies are not very restrictive on industrial growth in particular areas or regions, knowledge of locational policies is necessary to enable the various concessions and incentives that may be a part of such policies to be adequately considered. In some countries, specific geographical zones have been set up and varying patterns of financial incentives have been determined for them. In some developing countries, direct subsidies are given to industries located in particular areas or regions. A similar pattern has emerged in a number of industrially advanced countries in which financial and other incentives are being given to industrial projects located in underdeveloped regions. The impact of such incentives on the economics of a proposed project should be analysed.

Investments in export processing zones and other specified regions are sometimes exempted from taxes or would benefit from other types of subsidy. Such possibilities should be considered in the feasibility study, although such incentives should not serve as the only justification for the choice of a location. On the other hand, locating projects in some regions may necessitate factory-external investments into technical or social infrastructures because of existing laws or regulations.

Apart from the element of persuasion, public policies may directly determine industrial locations when there is a substantial involvement of public or institutional finance. The growth of public-sector enterprises has been significant for industrial growth in a number of developing countries. In these cases, wider policies, such as regional industrial dispersal, tend to play a part in locational decisions. If feasibility studies are sponsored for such projects, however, it is desirable for the project promoters to indicate a specific project location or possible alternatives which should then be evaluated with regard to the basic strategies of the investors, as well as in economic, financial and technical terms, and including social and environmental aspects.

## *Fiscal and legal aspects*

The fiscal and legal regulations and procedures applicable for alternative locations should be defined. The various national or local authorities to be contacted in respect of power and water supplies, building regulations, fiscal aspects, security needs etc. should be listed. The corporate and individual income taxes, excise duties, purchase taxes and other national or local taxes should be ascertained for different locations, together with the incentives and concessions available for new industries. These could vary considerably for different areas and may be a significant locational determinant in some cases. It would also be useful to list any building and other standards and regulations to which the project would need to conform.

## E. Infrastructural conditions

### *Infrastructure dependence*

The availability of a developed and diversified economic and social infrastructure is often of key importance for a project. The feasibility study should identify such key infrastructural requirements because they are vital to the operation of any project. For this purpose it is necessary to have an understanding of the scope and techno-economic characteristics of the project, the capacity to be installed and the technology to be applied.

The size of a project can also constitute a serious constraint regarding possible locations. Quantitative and qualitative requirements for energy, utilities, labour, land etc. during construction and operation might be met in only a few locations if the project is relatively big.

*Technical infrastructure.* The study should analyse whether project requirements regarding technical infrastructure imply a constraint for the choice of location. The analysis should cover not just the quantities required but also other characteristics (such as reliability, quality and physical aspects). The study must distinguish between desirable and critical requirements and demands. There are many elements which are preferable although not essential for the feasibility of a project.

*Transport and communication.* Transport facilities (by rail, road, air or water) may be available for the inflow of various inputs and for the marketing of products. Availability and cost will have to be detailed for the total volume of inputs into the proposed plant and the total outputs leaving the plant, with comparisons for various alternative locations. The amount of detail needed depends on the nature and the extent of the transport involved.

For sea transport, details of port facilities are necessary, including the depth of the relevant harbour basin, crane capacity, the size of ships that could use the port, warehousing facilities and charges, as well as traffic conditions, security aspects etc. For extensive road transport it may be necessary to define the width of roads and bridges, the clearance and bearing capacities of bridges, the category of road and the maintenance obligations that may devolve upon the project, apart from the cost of such transport. If a road has to be constructed to a particular location, estimates will have to be prepared and details of the construction taken into account. For extensive rail transport, it may be necessary to assess the capacity of rolling stock, loading and unloading facilities, warehousing and storage facilities and any seasonal or other bottlenecks that may develop, apart from the cost of rail transport to the principal movement points to and from possible plant locations. Water transport may also be feasible, in which case the width and depth of rivers and canals, the capacity of barges or other vessels that can be used and other related aspects should be considered. In each case, the likely transport costs are to be estimated.

A project that is judged as critically dependent on access to certain means of transport may have a limited number of possible locations. The existing facilities in different regions will often be an obvious restraint, taking into consideration the substantial investments related to the construction of new railways, airfields, ports and roads.

The availability of good communication facilities, including telex and telephone, should also be ascertained for alternative locations. The same reasoning is usually applicable for projects based on a big consumption of power, water and other utilities. An industry can always install its own facilities, but the cost may be discouraging. It is usually much easier and definitely financially more viable to establish such a project at a location with adequate facilities in an existing infrastructure.

### Factory supplies

*Water.* The water supply, apart from such projects as a brewery for which it is also a raw material, should be identified. The water required for a project can be ascertained from the plant capacity and technology. First, the availability of water and the costs entailed should be determined, including: the quantities that could be obtained, if any, from public utilities, together with the conditions of supply and price; and the separate facilities, and their estimated cost, that would have to be provided by the project from surface (for example a river) or sub-surface sources. Secondly, the quality of the water at different locations should be assessed for different purposes, such as drinking, cooling or steam generation.

*Electricity.* The inadequate supply of electricity or its high unit cost in a particular area can constitute a major constraint for a project or for a particular technological process such as electrical smelting. Where the location of a resource-based project cannot be changed, the project has to provide its own power source. Power requirements can be defined in relation to plant capacity, and the supply and cost at various locations should be studied. To determine the impact of energy factors, however, it may be necessary to collect and compare considerably detailed data for alternative locations. In the case of electric energy, such data would need to cover: the amount available; whether high- or low-tension current is required; stability of supply; point of tie-in for a particular area; and the price at different consumption levels.

*Fuel.* For coal, coke, fuel oil or gas, such data should cover, for each item, the quantities normally available, quality, calorific value and chemical composition (to determine pollutants), source, distance to different locations, transport facilities and costs at alternative locations.

## Human resources

The availability of managerial staff and skilled labour may be a critical factor for the success of a project. When considering alternative locations, the availability of human resources, including skilled and semi-skilled workers, and the type of skills, should be taken into account. Labour requirements should be estimated together with allowances for various categories and general living conditions, including housing, social welfare and recreational facilities. Labour history should be identified together with any special labour legislation, conditions and attitudes. Most major projects incorporate training programmes, either during plant construction or as in-plant training.

## Infrastructural services

For certain projects it may be desirable to consider the facilities available at different locations for civil construction, machinery erection or installation and maintenance of plant facilities. This would largely depend on the availability and quality of contractors and building materials. While such facilities would not be a locational determinant, they may affect project costs and should be considered to the extent significant for the feasibility.

## Effluent and waste disposal

Waste disposal may be another critical factor. Most industrial plants produce waste products, in some cases highly toxic substances or emissions that may have significant impacts on the environment. The disposal of such waste products and elimination of emissions can be a critical factor for the socio-economic and financial feasibility of a project. The emissions can be grouped as follows: gaseous (smoke, fumes etc.), which are generally processed till the concentration is reduced to safe levels;[64] physical (noise, heat, vibrations etc.), which are also reduced to tolerable levels often through the use of special equipment; and liquid or solid, which are discharged through pumps and sewers over considerable distances, settled in tanks or mounds, incinerated or specially treated for further use or disposal.

---

[64]There still exists the widespread opinion that such gaseous pollutants may be released to the atmosphere, if diluted below a critical concentration. However, experience shows that such substances or their decomposition products may be accumulated in the biosphere and then become an uncontrollable hazard. The same holds true for liquid and solid pollutants.

Certain effluents that are noxious, unpleasant or even dangerous require special treatment. The location study should determine the extent of effluent discharge and the possible manner of disposal at alternative locations. For this purpose, it may be necessary to take into account any rules on emission treatment that may prescribe the specific steps and levels of treatment and the disposal. In such cases, the cost of the treatment, of pumping and piping facilities, and of establishing and maintaining effluent dumps have to be considered. Climatic and environmental data may need to be collected to determine the impact on a community resulting from waste disposal. This would be particularly applicable in the case of pollutants discharged into the atmosphere or into rivers and the sea.

## F. Final choice of location

The locational requirements and conditions that are significant for the selection of both location and site should be judged against the defined corporate strategies and the financial and economic impacts the final choice might have on the project. In a feasibility study a good starting-point for the final selection of a suitable location is the location of raw materials and factory supplies, or—if the project is market-oriented—the location of the principal consumption centres in relation to the plant.

If transport costs of materials from the sources to alternative locations have a significant impact on the choice of location, the possibilities for substitution of materials and inputs should also be assessed. Infrastructure should then be considered in terms of availability and cost. A combination of these aspects enables a determination of production and marketing costs at alternative locations. Added to these costs should be an allowance for socio-economic and environmental factors. The best choice of location would be one where the costs of products sold (production and marketing costs) are a minimum. However, other environmental (ecological and socio-economic) factors, including the climate and social welfare facilities, such as education, medical services and recreation facilities, will probably also influence the selection of a feasible location and site. Various such locational factors, however, can be assessed in qualitative terms only. In projects where total costs of products sold do not vary much for alternative locations, the qualitative socio-economic environmental considerations could have an overriding effect on locational recommendations.

### Resource or market orientation

Critical to location selection is the impact on a particular project of factors such as the availability of raw materials and inputs, the proximity of centres of consumption and the existence of basic infrastructure facilities. Projects based on specific raw materials are for obvious reasons located at the source. Water, oil, coal, minerals, timber, agricultural products etc. will have to be exploited where the quantities, qualities and other conditions are adequate. Some projects may split their operations to more than one location (as in felling versus processing of timber). The feasibility study should indicate whether the project in question must be located to regions where certain raw materials and conditions exist. Conclusions are to be based on whether, for example, transport of raw materials would be a technically and financially realistic alternative.

The simplest locational model is to calculate the transport, production and distribution costs at alternative locations determined principally by the availability of raw materials and principal markets. A resource-based unit should be located near the source of the basic material, as costs of transport, for example of limestone to a cement factory, may be very high, and copper or nitrate deposits can be most economically processed near the location of the ores. Projects based largely on imported materials may need to be located at ports or near terminals. On the other hand, perishable products or agro-processing industries are market-oriented, and it is advantageous to locate such production near the principal consumption centres. For products that can be determined as resource-oriented or substantially market-oriented, project locations largely follow the location of resources or consumption centres as the case may be.

A great many industrial products, however, are not affected by any one particular factor. Petroleum products and petrochemicals, for example, can be located at source, near consumption centres or even at some intermediate point. A wide range of consumer goods and other industries can be located at various distances from materials and markets without unduly distorting project economics. Even in the case of engineering goods, including machine-building, assembly and subassembly plants, other locational factors exert considerable influence, though the products, in terms of bulk and transport costs, can be said to be primarily market-oriented.

Because of the widening scope of industrial activities, transport costs of materials as compared to products, though still vital for certain projects, have to be viewed in conjunction with such other aspects as production factor substitution, demand elasticity and the possibilities of alternative pricing formulae, all of which could materially affect the weighting of raw material or market factors. The final choice may also depend on the location of the competitors.

For projects that are not unduly resource or market-oriented, an optimum location could well combine reasonable proximity to raw materials and markets, favourable environmental conditions, a good pool of labour, adequate power and fuel at reasonable cost, equitable taxes, good transport, an adequate water supply and facilities for waste disposal. A feasibility study has to take all these factors into consideration.

## Assessment of location

After having assessed the key requirements of a project, usually a limited number of possible locations will have been identified. These alternatives should be subject to a more detailed analysis with various assessment criteria. A continued qualitative analysis, based on the key aspects discussed above, will provide additional information. This should be supplemented by consideration of the financial implications of differences between alternative locations.

As far as the financial feasibility of alternative locations is concerned, the following data—as well as related financial risks—should be assessed:

- Production costs (including environmental protection costs)
- Marketing costs

- Investment costs (including environmental protection)
- Revenues
- Taxes, subsidies, grants and allowances
- Net cash flows

The study should identify significant differences and analyse the underlying causes. A difference in transport costs is fairly easy to estimate but should be related to the financial significance. Transport costs may in other words be, for example, 30 per cent higher in one location than in another, but still be insignificant if the transport costs are marginal in relation to the value added. The assessment is consequently based on a number of aspects and criteria. The difficulties in quantifying the aspects considered in the qualitative analysis should not lead to the mistake of underestimating their importance. The study should analyse and weigh different aspects against each other, both qualitatively and quantitatively and come up with judgements regarding the feasibility and viability of a suitable location.

*Flexibility.* A project concept is based on different conditions, assumptions and judgements. Conditions change, however, and the plant in question can be expected to be subject to modifications and changes in the future. A location that allows greater flexibility may in some cases be preferable. Possible changes may concern restraints regarding emissions from polluting industries, expansion of the plant, new products replacing the original ones, decreasing supply of specific raw materials, need for another market orientation, deteriorating technical infrastructure and difficulties of keeping key personnel.

Potential changes that might affect the choice of location and site should be identified in the feasibility study. A location where the project can be expected to face problems in the future if certain conditions change should be avoided, if better alternatives exist.

*Experiences and preferences.* An important factor for the choice of location and site has in some studies in industrialized countries been identified as the experiences and preferences of the project promoter. Most industrial projects have been located to places where the owners and key decision makers grew up, were educated and trained, were resident at the time of the project establishment, and where they had friends or business connections.

There is no reason to believe that similar aspects would not influence projects in developing countries. Local partners obviously prefer a project to be located in an area where they have personal connections. Foreign partners tend to prefer areas where they have either previous experience of local conditions or resident representatives. Preferences may be based on strictly technical or financial considerations, but can also be due to limited or even inaccurate information and knowledge. Housing, climate and social infrastructure can sometimes play a disproportionate role for the choice of location and site.

## G. Site selection

The feasibility study should analyse and assess alternative sites on the basis of key aspects and site-specific requirements. Qualitative as well as quantitative considerations are to be taken into account. Differences in existing social infrastructure facilities are sometimes as important as transport costs for material inputs and product distribution. The analysis should result in a selection of a specific site and conclusions regarding the feasibility and viability.

Once the location (or alternative locations if this is an objective of the study) is decided upon, a specific project site and, if available, site alternatives should be defined in the feasibility study. This will require an evaluation of the characteristics of each site. The structure of site analysis is basically the same as for location analysis, and the key requirements, identified for the project, may give guidance also for site selection. For sites available within the selected area, the following requirements and conditions are to be assessed:

- Ecological conditions on site (soil, site hazards, climate etc.)
- Environmental impact (restrictions, standards, guidelines)
- Socio-economic conditions (restrictions, incentives, requirements)
- Local infrastructure at site location (existing industrial infrastructure, economic and social infrastructure, availability of critical project inputs such as labour and factory supplies)
- Strategic aspects (corporate strategies regarding possible future extension, supply and marketing policies)
- Cost of land
- Site preparation and development, requirements and costs

The importance of these characteristics varies depending on the nature of the project, the type of civil construction contemplated, the weight of the heavier equipment items, the type of effluent and the number of workers. Different areas within the same region can be subject to various restrictions and incentives, and environmental conditions may discourage the selection of sites close to an existing polluting industry or sites with urban settlements in the immediate neighbourhood. The availability and supply of materials, utilities, means of transport and communication obviously varies within a region. The site selection study should therefore review all the relevant aspects in the context of the proposed project. Full information may not be readily available, and it may be necessary to investigate further.

## Requirements and relevant factors

### Site requirements

A project may depend on particular site conditions, which should be identified and described in the feasibility study. Heavy machinery and foundation works, transports and technical installations may require specific ground conditions. A survey should be made of soil conditions, including bearing qualities and subsoil water level at alternative sites. Special attention should be paid to construction in seismic zones. Some sites may require substantial work on site preparation and development, or it may be exposed to site hazards such as strong winds, fumes and flue gases from neighbouring industries or to risks of floods. The required land area should be specified on the basis of buildings, technical installations and facilities included in the project.

Topography, altitude and climate may be of importance for a project, as well as access to water, electric power, roads and railways or water transport.

149

This analysis is related to materials and inputs as well as technical infrastructure discussed below. The distance to urban centres and the social and economic infrastructure may be important for the availability of labour. The study should also cover existing rights of way (regarding, for example, access roads and water supply) and indicate potential problems.

## Cost of land

The cost of land is an obvious element of site determination and information on this is usually available. Industrial areas are possible site alternatives, and in any event provide indications of land costs in the area. Costs of site preparation and development, as classified in schedule V-1, should be considered for alternative sites and detailed for the selected site.

## Construction requirements

Construction and installation works during the future project implementation may sometimes strongly affect the choice of location and site. Aspects such as the existence of local contractors, availability of building materials, means of transport for heavy machinery and equipment to be brought to the site, a developed social infrastructure and a climate where construction workers and expatriates accept to live for a period of perhaps three to five years are sometimes important. Existing facilities of different kinds may for instance reduce the construction cost and consequently the investment costs as well as financing required. The feasibility study should therefore identify and describe requirements and demands during the construction and installation phase.

## Local conditions—infrastructure

The availability and cost of electricity is common for most sites within a given location. If an independent power facility has to be set up as part of the project, the cost tends to be similar at various sites within an overall location. Similarly, cost of electrical substations and electrical equipment, such as transformers, tend to be the same at different sites. However, the cost of extending power transmission lines to the factory site varies substantially from site to site and has to be estimated.

Transport is very important when comparing the suitability of different sites. Since the volume of inputs and outputs will be known after the plant capacity is determined, transport alternatives and costs could then be calculated and compared for different sites. Preliminary estimates should be made for: terminals for oil, gas or other materials; railway sidings from the nearest railhead; feeder roads connecting with main highways; and water transport.

For a determined plant capacity, it would be easy to define the water required for various purposes, such as cooling, steam generation and drinking. Where water is a requirement for the manufacturing process, as for pulp, such assessment is more important, and the source and cost of the water supply has to be estimated at alternative sites. Such costs can vary considerably and may be a significant element of site selection, particularly if large quantities of water are required.

## Effluent and waste disposal

The disposal of effluent may be a problem for many industries, as discussed earlier in this chapter. The possibilities for effluent disposal at different sites should be carefully studied bearing in mind the type of effluent. The site for a cement plant should not be selected to windward of a dense urban community and refinery effluent discharged upstream of a drinking water supply.

## Human resources

Recruitment of managerial staff and labour may be a critical factor for the viability of a project. Skilled labour and management staff are often in scarce supply, and recruitment of labour with less skill and experience than required might jeopardize the whole project. The study must therefore pay careful attention to the question of labour availability, conditions related to recruitment and facilities for training.

It may be necessary to develop a social infrastructure next to the envisaged site—housing, primary schools, medical and social centres—to attract the required staff and labour force. Such social investment may be imperative for major projects, such as steel plants and heavy engineering industries, involving a large labour complement, but would prove an unduly heavy financial burden in most other cases, at least during the initial stages.

### Final site selection

The selection of plant location and site does not have to be undertaken in two stages. Generally, alternative sites are considered in conjunction with wider locational considerations so that much of the information required is collected simultaneously. It is useful if the location conclusions of the site study are tabulated so that the relevant information can be incorporated into the next stage of project formulation.

It is often necessary to limit the choice of plant site and location in line with the provisions made by the project sponsors, whether public, institutional or private, which reduces the task of the feasibility study. If, however, the study has to indicate the various alternatives without any such guiding principles or constraints, the foregoing factors should be considered.

## H.  Cost estimates

Schedule V-1 is used for the estimates of investment costs at the site. Examples of costs are acquisition of land, taxes, legal expenses, rights of way, site preparation and development. Different cost items are to be identified, quantified (if relevant), estimated and divided into components of foreign and local currency origin. It should be carefully stated whether factory-external facilities, possibly judged as necessary (such as disposal and treatment of effluents, generation of electricity, water supply system, storage, housing and schools) are included in the cost estimates. Schedule V-2 may be used for investment costs related to environmental protection.

Schedules V-3 and V-4 are used for the presentation of annual costs related to the site and environmental protection costs, respectively. This may comprise annual payments for rent, real estate tax, rights of way, annual charges for easements and other cost items. As in the case of investment costs, annual payments are to be specified, quantified (if relevant), estimated and divided into foreign and local currency origin.

## Bibliography

Bisset, R. Introduction to methods for environmental impact assessment. *In* Environmental assessment. The Hague, Martinus Nijhoff, 1983.

Biswas, A. K. *and* Qu Geping. Selected literature on environment impact assessment. Guidelines for environmental impact assessment in developing countries. *In* Environmental impact assessment for developing countries. London, Tycooly International, 1987.

Black, Peter E. Environmental impact analysis. New York, Praeger, 1981.

Burchell, R. N. *and* D. Lisokin. The environmental impact handbook. New Jersey, Rutgers University, Center for Environmental Policy and Research, 1975.

Cheremisihoff, P. N. *and* A. C. Morresi. Environmental impact statement handbook. Ann Arbor, Michigan, Ann Arbor Science, 1977.

Corwin, R., P. H. Heffernan *and* R. A. Johnson. Environmental impact assessment. San Francisco, Freeman, Cooper, 1975.

Council on Environmental Quality. 40 Code of Federal Regulations 1502. Washington, D.C., Government Printing Office, 1988.

————— Environmental quality; the sixth annual report of the CEQ. Washington, D.C., Government Printing Office, 1975.

Greenhut, Melvin L. Plant location in theory and in practice. Chapel Hill, University of North Carolina Press, 1956.

Hamilton, F. E. I. *and* G. J. R. Linge. Spatial analysis; Industry and the industrial environment, v.2: International industrial systems. Wiley, Chichester, 1981.

Hilhorst, J. G. M. Regional planning. Rotterdam, University Press, 1971.

Jacob, H. Zur Standortwahl der Unternehmungen. Wiesbaden, Betriebswirtschaftlicher Verlag Gabler, 1976.

Lohani, B. M. *and* N. Halim. Recommended methods for environmental impact assessment in developing countries: experiences derived from case studies in Thailand. *In* Environmental impact assessment for developing countries. A. K. Biswas *and* Qu Geping *eds.* London, Tycooly International, 1987.

National Environmental Protection Act (NEPA) 1969. Public Law 91-190 USC as amended by Public Law 94-52 3 July 1975 and Public Law 94-83 9 Aug 1975. Washington, D.C., Government Printing Office, 1975.

Schärling, Alain. Où construire l'usine? La localisation optimale d'une activité industrielle dans la pratique. Paris, Dunod, 1973.

Soderman, S. Industrial location planning. New York, Halsted, 1975.

Sorenson, J. C. Some procedure and programs of environmental impact. *In* Environmental impact analysis: philosophy and methods. R. B. Ditton *and* T. I. Goodale *eds.* Madison, Wisconsin, University of Wisconsin Grant Program, 1972.

United Nations. Industrial location and regional development; an annotated bibliography. (ID/43)
  Sales no.: 70.II.B.15.

U.S.A. Environmental Protection Agency (EPA). 40 Code of Federal Regulations.
Ch. 1 6.202. Washington, D.C., Government Printing Office, 1988.

———— Guidelines for performing regulatory impact analysis. Washington, D.C.,
Government Printing Office, 1983.

———— Manual: review of federal actions impacting the environment. Washington,
D.C., Government Printing Office, 1975.

Viscuse, W. K. Alternative approaches to valuing the health impacts of accidents:
liability law and prospective evaluations. *Law and contemporary problems* (Durham,
North Carolina) 47:4, 1983.

## Appendix

## CHECK-LISTS, WORKSHEETS AND SCHEDULES

*V-1.* *Domains of the natural environment subject to and generating environmental impacts*

| | |
|---|---|
| Land<br><br>  Topography<br>  Soil composition<br>  Slope stability<br>  Subsidence<br>  Seismicity (faults, earthquake<br>    potential, volcanic action)<br>  Current and future use<br>  Buffer zones, protected areas<br>    (archaelogical sites, unique<br>    physical features etc.)<br>  Interdependent systems (bodies<br>    of water, mineral and energy<br>    resources, fauna, flora) | Atmosphere<br><br>  Air quality<br>  Flow<br>  Climatic variations<br>  Visibility<br>  Particulates |
| Water (surface water)<br><br>  Shoreline<br>  Bottom interface<br>  Flow variation<br>  Water quality<br>  Drainage pattern<br>  Net flow<br>  Flood plain<br>  Current and future use<br>  Oceanography (where applicable) | Water (groundwater)<br><br>  Water-table<br>  Flow variation<br>  Water quality<br>  Recharge areas and rates<br>  Aquifer characteristics<br>  Current and future use |
| Flora<br><br>  Trees<br>  Shrubs<br>  Grass<br>  Crops<br>  Phytoplankton<br>  Aquatic plants<br>  Rare species<br>  Endangered species | Fauna<br><br>  Terrestrial<br>  Zooplankton<br>  Benthic organisms<br>  Fish and shellfish<br>  Insects<br>  Rare species<br>  Endangered species<br>  Migratory species |
| Energy resources<br><br>  Hydropower<br>  Fuels (fossil, renewable)<br>  Wind<br>  Solar<br>  Geothermal<br>  Tidal<br>  Nuclear | Ecological systems (habitats and<br>complex interdependent<br>ecosystems)<br><br>  Streams<br>  Lakes<br>  Estuaries<br>  Swamps<br>  Deserts and savannas<br>  Marshlands |

*V-2. Domains of the social environment subject to and generating environmental impacts*

| Cultural factors | Social infrastructure |
|---|---|
| Community<br>  Sense of community<br>  Community structure<br>Traditional cultural habits and<br>  customs<br>Historic sites<br>Religious services<br>Social services<br>Recreation | Education<br>Health and well-being<br>  Diseases, physical safety<br>  Health hazards<br>  Population density (urban and<br>  rural) |
| Social development | Economic factors |
| Job opportunities<br>Income distribution<br>Housing<br>Protection of vital natural<br>  resources<br>Internal and external relations<br>  (trade, safety, defence etc.) | Economic development<br>  (agricultural, industrial and<br>  service sectors)<br>Transport and communication<br>Urban and rural area development |

*V-3. Environmental impacts and factors*

| Emissions | Hazards, health risks |
|---|---|
| Liquid waste<br>Solid waste<br>Air pollutants (gases, dust,<br>  fumes, vapours)<br>Noise and vibrations<br>Odours<br>Chemical reactants (producing<br>  colours, odours, poisons)<br>Hazardous substances | Risk of accidents affecting social<br>  and natural environments (during<br>  construction and operation; after<br>  closing down operations; during<br>  transport of hazardous substances)<br>Increase of already existing risks<br>Health risk to workers and staff |
| Degradation and destruction of<br>natural resources and ecosystems | Degradation and destruction of<br>existing social structures |
| Direct and indirect damage to<br>  natural water resources<br>Damage to land resources (soil<br>  erosion, reduced agri-<br>  cultural yields etc.)<br>Uneconomic use of non-<br>  renewable natural resources<br>Damage to plant populations<br>  (forests etc.)<br>Disruption of interlinked<br>  (balanced) ecosystems<br>Displacement, extinction of<br>  species | Migration<br>Displacement of human habitation<br>Displacement of existing economic<br>  activities (informal and small<br>  business sectors, fishing, agri-<br>  culture etc.)<br>Disruption of culture-specific<br>  social relationships and infra-<br>  structures<br>Deterioration of general living<br>  conditions |

## V-4. Matrix for the identification of environmental impacts

| | Construction phase | Operational phase | Post-operational phase | | | | Remarks |
|---|---|---|---|---|---|---|---|
| | | | | | | | |

Key to columns:
- No impact
- Unknown impact
- Design solution
- No design solution
- [2] Type of impact [1]

Activities: Insert project-related activities possibly affecting the environment, such as blasting, building, burning, channelling, trenching, clearing, cutting trees, disposal of hazardous waste and of sewage, draining, drilling, handling and storing hazardous substances and increasing air and automobile traffic.

[4]

Resources subject to impact
[3] Land

Key:

[1] This form may be used first to determine whether there is any impact, and if so, whether design solutions exist. Then the type of impact may be defined on another sheet using a system of notation such as :

[2] (A) = aesthetical; (D) = destructive to ecosystems; (H) = affecting health and wealth; etc.

[3] Insert environmental domains possibly affected (see checklists V-1 and V-2)

[4] Insert environmental parameters possibly affected (see checklists V-1 and V-2)

*Note:* This matrix would have to be adapted to the needs and specific circumstances of each individual project.

## Schedule V-1. Estimate of investment costs: land and site preparation
### (insert in schedule X-1)

Project:
Date:
Source:

[ ]  Construction phase
[ ]  Operational phase

**ESTIMATE OF INVESTMENT COSTS**

| Land/site preparation | | | | | Currency: | | | |
| --- | --- | --- | --- | --- | --- | --- | --- | --- |
| | | | | | Units: | | | |
| | | | | | Cost | | | |
| | | | | Unit | | | | |
| N | Q | U | Item description | cost | Foreign | Local | Total | Year[a] |
| | | | Purchase price of land | | | | | |
| | | | Taxes | | | | | |
| | | | Legal expenses | | | | | |
| | | | . . . | | | | | |
| | | | Lump-sum payments for | | | | | |
| | | | Purchasing options | | | | | |
| | | | Rights of way | | | | | |
| | | | etc. | | | | | |
| | | | Site preparation works | | | | | |
| | | | Equipment | | | | | |
| | | | Site clearing works | | | | | |
| | | | etc. | | | | | |
| | | | | | | | | |
| | | | (for investment costs for environmental protection see schedule V-2) | | | | | |
| **Total investment costs, land and site preparation** (carry over to schedule X-1) | | | | | | | | |

| N = number | U = units | Q = quantity |
| --- | --- | --- |

[a] Of investment.

157

## Schedule V-2. Estimate of investment costs: environmental protection measures
### (insert in schedule X-1)

Project:
Date:
Source:

[ ] Construction phase
[ ] Operational phase
[ ] Post-operational phase

---

**ESTIMATE OF INVESTMENT COSTS**

| Environmental protection measures | | | | | Currency: | | | |
|---|---|---|---|---|---|---|---|---|
| | | | | | Units: | | | |
| N | Q | U | Item description | Unit cost | Cost | | | Year[a] |
| | | | | | Foreign | Local | Total | |
| | | | | | | | | |
| **Total investment costs, environmental protection measures** (carry over to schedule X-1) | | | | | | | | |

N = number      U = units      Q = quantity

[a] Of investment.

## Schedule V-3. Estimate of operating costs related to the site
### (insert in schedule VI-4 or VII)

Project:
Date:
Source:

[ ]   Direct costs
[ ]   Indirect costs

| Product/cost centre:  Code: | First year of production: | Currency:  Units: | | |
|---|---|---|---|---|
| | Cost projections for year: | | | |
| | Local costs | | Foreign costs | |
| Cost item | *Variable per unit* | *Fixed per period* | *Variable per unit* | *Fixed per period* |
| | | | | |
| | | | | |
| | | | | |
| Total unit costs | | | | |
| Total units per period | | | | |
| Total costs per period | | | | |
| Total local and foreign costs related to the site | | | | |

## Schedule V-4. Estimate of operating costs related to environmental protection measures
### (insert in schedules VI-4 or VII)

Project:  
Date:  
Source:

[  ] Operational phase  
[  ] Post-operational phase

[  ] Direct costs  
[  ] Indirect costs

| Product/cost centre:  Code: | First year of production: | | Currency:  Units: | |
|---|---|---|---|---|
| | Cost projections for year: | | | |
| | Local costs | | Foreign costs | |
| Cost item | *Variable per unit* | *Fixed per period* | *Variable per unit* | *Fixed per period* |
| | | | | |
| | | | | |
| Total unit costs | | | | |
| Total units per period | | | | |
| Total costs per period | | | | |
| Total local and foreign environmental costs | | | | |

# VI. Engineering and technology

The scope of an investment project is first of all defined by the project or corporate objectives and strategies determined by the potential investors, taking into account the overall business environment, and secondly by the marketing concept as well as the available project inputs (resources). It is the task of engineering to design the functional and physical layout for the industrial plant necessary to produce the defined products (output), and to determine the corresponding investment expenditures as well as the costs arising during the operational phase. The scope of engineering also includes the plant site and all activities required to deliver both inputs and outputs and to provide the necessary ancillary infrastructure investments. This comprehensive approach should help to determine which technical solution would best serve the intentions of the investors or any third party participating in the project.

An integral part of engineering at the feasibility stage is the selection of an appropriate technology, as well as planning of the acquisition and absorption of this technology and of the corresponding know-how. While the choice of technology defines the production processes to be utilized, the effective management of technology transfer requires that the technology and know-how are acquired on suitable terms and conditions, and that the necessary skills are available or developed. The required machinery and equipment must be determined in relation to the technology and processes to be utilized, the local conditions, the state of the art and human capabilities. Skill development needs to be planned through training programmes at various levels.

The analysis must include all technical, managerial and administrative, as well as external, sociocultural and economic aspects of the required maintenance system. It should also outline the specific requirements of each individual technology, if selected, and specify the need for technical documentation and maintenance procedures. In particular the analysis must include a thorough survey of spare parts and the format of the necessary lists of spare parts.

As discussed in previous chapters, environmental protection devices (such as filters, desulphurization plants, units for the removal of nitrogen oxides, and closed-circuit clarification plants) are an essential part of any company operation, in particular when they form part of the production process. The breakdown of such plant components can, in the worst possible case, lead to a temporary shut-down of the entire plant.

Environmental protection installations often consist of technologically highly complex components. They originate for the most part in countries with a high level of technological development, and are generally not produced in series. For this reason, due care and attention must be given to the problems specific to these installations (spare parts, timely ordering of replacement parts for maintenance work, qualified personnel etc.).

After the determination of an outline of the marketing strategies and the first outline of the production programme and capacity, a preliminary project layout has to be prepared defining the physical features of the plant such as infrastructure, factory and other buildings and civil works and their inter-relationship with utilities, material flows, machinery installation and other aspects of plant construction and operations. It is then necessary to identify the alternative technologies that can be utilized and the implications of such alternatives in terms of costs, foreign participation, use of local raw materials, environmental impact and other factors. These and related aspects need to be highlighted in the feasibility study. Project engineering, therefore, covers a wide range of interrelated activities that have to be carefully planned and assessed and effectively coordinated in terms of their timing and application.

## A.  Production programme and plant capacity

The initial task and scope of engineering is to define the whole range of project activities and requirements, including production levels to be achieved under the technical, ecological, social and economic constraints defined in line with this *Manual*. This necessitates identifying the principal products or product range, including by-products, determining the volume of production, and relating production capacity to the flow of materials and performance of services at the selected site.

### Determination of the production programme

#### Market requirements and marketing concept

The range and volume of products to be produced depends primarily on the market requirements and the proposed marketing strategies. The initial engineering work consists in designing a preliminary production layout suitable for manufacturing the products defined in accordance with the marketing concept, and in the qualities and quantities required. This production programme and volume have to be designed under the constraints determined for the market conditions and the availability of resources, both at various levels of production, the latter determining the minimum sales price for products.

After the required sales programme has been determined, the detailed production programme should be designed in a feasibility study. A production programme should define the levels of output to be achieved during specified periods and, from this viewpoint, should be directly related to the specific sales forecasts. To plan such a programme the various production stages should be considered in detail, both in terms of production activities and timing. Within the overall plant capacity, there can be various levels of production activities during different stages, such levels being determined by various factors in different projects. It would be prudent to recognize that full production may not be practicable for most projects during the initial production operations. Owing to various technological, production and commercial difficulties, most projects experience initial problems that can take the form of only a gradual growth of sales and market penetration, on the one hand, and a wide range of production problems, such as the adjustment of feedstocks, labour and equipment to the technology selected, on the other. Even if full production were to be achieved in the first year, marketing and sales might prove to be a bottleneck.

Depending on the nature of the industry and local factor situations, a production and sales target of 40-50 per cent of overall capacity for the first year should not be considered unreasonably low. It is usually only towards the third or fourth year that full production levels can be achieved and operating ratios effectively determined and adequately planned for. Even in certain process industries where rated plant capacity is capable of being achieved shortly after the commencement of production, during the initial years production may be programmed at well below such capacity in order to adjust to gradual growth of demand for a particular product. Growth of skills in operations can also be a limiting factor in a number of industries, particularly the engineering goods industry, and production has to be tailored to the development of such skills and productivity. Full production capacity may be achieved in such cases only after some years, and it may be unrealistic to plan on any basis other than fairly gradual growth of production and output.

In the case of assembly-type industries, production programming should determine the extent of production integration, which may initially be relatively low and increase only gradually. Production programming can take various forms, and the most suitable production pattern should be determined in relation to projected sales and growth of production, particularly for the initial years of the projection in question.

The determinants of a production programme during the initial production years vary considerably from project to project. This can be illustrated by the different approach that would have to be adopted by the following types of industries: single-product, continuous process manufacture as in cement production; multiple-product, continuous process production as in an oil refinery; batch-job order production such as in an engineering workshop; and assembly and mass manufacture as in the production of motor cars. In the first case, the growth of sales may not be a great problem unless production capacity is in excess of local demand, but production problems may be more critical. In the second case, both production and sales problems may arise. In the third case, though production aspects may present difficulties, obtaining a satisfactory order book would be critical. In the fourth case, the sales aspects in relation to price would be dominant.

*Input requirements*

Once a production programme defines the levels of outputs in terms of end-products, and possibly of intermediate products and the interrelation between various production lines and processes, the specific requirements of materials and labour should be quantified for each stage. For this purpose, a material-flow diagram should be prepared, showing the materials and utilities balances at various stages of production. The nature and general requirements of materials and labour would have been identified prior to the determination of plant capacity, but at this stage the specific quantities needed for each stage of the production programme and the costs that these entail should be determined. The input requirements and costs have to be assessed for: basic materials such as raw materials and semi-processed and bought-out items; major factory supplies (auxiliary materials and utilities); other factory supplies; and direct labour requirements.

Detailed estimates in this regard should be prepared for the stages of initial production and full production, together with one or more intermediate stages if these can be clearly identified. It is also necessary to provide for wastage, damage or rejection elements in preparing the material consumption estimates and for reserve labour needs, as outlined in chapters IV and VIII, which deal with material and human resource requirements. In cases where such a minute procedure cannot be applied to calculate the material and labour costs at different production stages until full capacity is reached, as material and direct labour costs are variable, apportioned material and direct labour costs can easily be calculated for the initial stage on the basis of the cost level at full capacity production. This procedure is applied in schedule X-4/1 (annual production cost estimate) and schedule X-3.

An example of a sales programme is provided in schedule III-1. It should serve as planning base for determining the production programme and scheduling the cash flow table. For this purpose the different envisaged capacity utilization rates should be inserted as the first line of schedule X-3. In this way it will be easily possible to programme the development of variable production costs as production and sales increase.

## Technology

An important factor in determining the production programme and plant capacity is the technology and know-how to be utilized in the project. Specific processes are often related to certain levels of production or become technically and economically feasible only at such levels. This is particularly applicable to the chemical industry, where certain processes can be utilized far more effectively at specific levels of production, but the principle can be extended to other industries. For example, the use of complex machining centres may not be justified in engineering-goods manufacture where relatively low levels of production are envisaged. The nature of technology choice and usage constitutes a key factor in the determination of plant capacity.

Each technically possible alternative must in addition consider social, ecological, economic and financial conditions, because production programmes and plant capacity are functions of various interrelated socio-economic, strategic and technical factors.

## Determination of plant capacity

The term production capacity can be generally defined as the volume or number of units that can be produced during a given period. The following two capacity terms are used in this *Manual*:

(a) *Feasible normal capacity.* This capacity is achievable under normal working conditions, taking into account not only the installed equipment and technical conditions of the plant, such as normal stoppages, down time, holidays, maintenance, tool changes, desired shift patterns and indivisibilities of major machines to be combined, but also the management system applied. Thus, the feasible normal capacity is the number of units produced during one year under the above conditions. This capacity should correspond to the sales derived from the outline of the marketing concept;

*(b)   Nominal maximum capacity.* The nominal capacity is the technically feasible capacity, which frequently corresponds to the installed capacity as guaranteed by the supplier of the plant. A higher capacity—nominal maximum capacity—may be achieved, but this would entail overtime, excessive consumption of factory supplies, utilities, spare parts and wear-and-tear parts, as well as disproportionate production cost increases.

Once the marketing concept and the corresponding sales volume are defined, other components have to be assessed to determine the feasible normal plant capacity. This capacity should in fact represent the optimum level of production as may be determined by the relative interaction of various components of the feasibility study, such as technology, availability of resources, investment and production costs. Though one of these components will be critical for determining the feasible normal plant capacity in respect of a particular project, all the implications of all these aspects should be taken into consideration. The following two factors dominate the capacity determination: the minimum economic size; and the availability of production technology and equipment as related to various production levels.

## Economies of scale

Production capacity must also be related to economies of scale. In most industries, the minimum economic level of production has been generally defined in relation to the technologies applied and the prevailing prices in industrialized countries. This level may, however, differ in different countries depending on the circumstances. While production costs undoubtedly decline with increased levels and volumes of production, the economic, ecological and technical effects may vary considerably from country to country and industry to industry. This is the case, for example, in engineering-goods industries, including durable goods such as automobiles and tractors.

## Minimum economic size and equipment constraints

The concept of minimum economic size is applicable to most industrial branches and projects but is of varying significance for different types of industry. In a number of process-type industries, a minimum production size can generally be defined. A cement plant of less than 300 tonnes per day is not usually considered to be economic, and may therefore necessitate vertical shaft kilns, the production from which would not be able to compete with that of rotary kilns in a competitive market. Ammonia plants need to be of a certain minimum size if the cost of ammonia is not to be unduly high as compared with ammonia supplies obtained by other users. This is true of a large range of chemical industries, including primary and secondary petrochemicals, the economic size of which is increasing rapidly for most products.

Production capacities in a number of industries in industrialized countries have tended to increase rapidly to take greater advantage of economies of scale. Increased capacities involve investment outlays which are proportionately much lower because of the increased output, resulting in lower unit production costs. When determining the minimum economic size of a project, experience gained elsewhere should be used, as there is a relationship between the production costs of the project under study and such costs in the same field of production in other projects. If this is not applicable because of limited resources or size of foreseeable demand, there should be full treatment of the resulting higher production costs and prices, the inability to compete with a cost leadership strategy in external markets, and the degree and type of protection probably required.

Another important factor is that available process technology and equipment are often standardized at specific capacities in different industries. While these can be adapted to lower production scales, costs of such adaptation may be disproportionately high. On this account also, projects in certain industrial branches should conform to a minimum economic size, and if possible it should be so stated. This applies also in assembly-type industries, particularly when series production is involved, as such series must be related to reasonable levels of continuous or semi-continuous production. However, in certain engineering-goods industries involving multi-product manufacture, a much greater degree of flexibility is possible since production capacity can be distributed between a number of products during different periods. Nevertheless, an appropriate economic size can generally be defined in terms of equipment needs and technological application, though various combinations are possible.

### Resource and input constraints

The lack of domestic or external resources, and of basic production inputs, either raw materials or intermediate products, may hinder projects in developing countries. This is because of a shortage of foreign exchange for importing equipment, components or intermediate products, or a shortage of domestic resources, either private or public, for major projects involving large investment outlays. Where effective demand and the possible extent of market penetration are high, plant capacity would then cover only a part of the demand projections, leaving the balance to other projects, imports or subsequent expansions of proposed plant capacity. Even at a minimum economic size, unit production costs are bound to be fairly high compared with production costs in other firms in the same production field, and economies of scale would operate to the least extent consistent with project viability. If the feasible normal plant capacity for the proposed project is below the minimum economic size, the implications in terms of production costs, product prices and such policy aspects as the degree of protection required should be brought out fully in the feasibility study.

### Performance of staff and labour

Industrial experience indicates that a certain time elapses before the staff and labour involved in the manufacturing process have acquired a reasonable level of skill. The learning curve describes this learning process, which is also determined by various factors, such as sociocultural background, physical strength, nutrition, adaptation and adaptability to an industrial environment.

# B.  Technology choice

The selection of appropriate technology and know-how is a critical element in any feasibility study. Such selection should be based on a detailed consideration and evaluation of technological alternatives and the selection of the most suitable alternative in relation to the project or investment strategy chosen and to socio-economic and ecological conditions. Appropriate technology choice is directly related to the conditions of application in particular situations. What may be appropriate in industrialized economies with high labour costs may not necessarily be the optimum for low-wage developing countries, with severe constraints on infrastructure and availability of inputs. On the other hand, a plant in a developing country that produces primarily for export to industrialized countries may need to utilize the latest automated and capital-intensive production processes in order to compete in such markets. Competitive production capability in the intended markets is one of the most crucial factors for technology choice, and the related plant capacity can be a major determinant of such capability.

Technology choice must be directly related to market, resource and environmental conditions and the corporate strategies recommended for a particular project. The industry, the form of foreign participation, national objectives and policies, industrial growth strategy, availability of local resources and skills, and several other factors can impinge directly on technology choice, plant capacity and production costs. It is also necessary to take into account new technological developments and applications and their impact on plant capacity. These may either have general application, as in the case of numerically controlled equipment, or may relate to specific stages of production, with considerable impact on plant capacities in several fields. There may, however, be skill and other constraints on their usage in certain situations, and these are also to be taken into account.

In the light of the world-wide ecological impacts of agricultural and industrial development, technology choice is no longer possible without an assessment of the potential ecological impacts of a project on the natural environment. Consideration of environmental aspects in modern project engineering and technology assessment is not limited to the minimization of pollution, but should also include preservation of natural resources and saving of non-renewable resources. In this respect technology choice is again governed by the principal strategic objectives of the investment project, and at the same time has an interdependent relationship with items covered in previous chapters on marketing, materials and location.

## Ecological and environmental impact

An important aspect in technology selection is represented by the ecological and environmental impacts, and especially any possible hazards that may result from the use of particular technologies. Major disasters in the past have highlighted the need for careful evaluation and assessment of hazardous technologies and the use of toxic materials at different stages of production. It is essential that hazardous production processes and those utilizing toxic substances be clearly identified and appropriate measures taken. The environmental effects of various industrial technologies must also be taken into account. Effluent discharge of toxic substances into rivers and the atmosphere has led to serious pollution and damage in several countries. The measures required to mitigate the use of hazardous technologies and those having an adverse impact on the environment must be identified and assessed as part of the technology choice. Specific measures may need to be prescribed for air pollution control, including limits for discharge of contaminants into the atmosphere, for water pollution control, including determination of quantity of effluents and process wastes, and for control of noise or high frequency sounds. These measures should be incorporated in process designs. In certain projects, involving hazardous processes or toxic substances, buffer zones may need to be provided between the plant site and populated areas.

### Ecological orientation of the preliminary layout

Ideally, an industrial project should not have any negative impacts on the natural and social environment. Since this objective can be achieved economically only in exceptional cases, all efforts should be made to employ production processes with the lowest possible emissions, and to minimize the burden on the environment. Low-emission production can be achieved by considering different techno-economic alternatives during the individual planning stages, such as the use of low-residue raw materials, planning of closed circuits, planning of recycling systems (within the works or outside) and end-of-the-pipe environmental engineering (filters, systems for the removal of sulphur dioxides and nitrogen oxides etc.).

First of all it is important to identify those processes which result in the lowest possible consumption of raw materials. Closed circuits would allow the reutilization of raw and auxiliary materials within the production process by means of a variety of different technologies (such as water recirculation in the paper industry). By applying the appropriate industrial processes, it is possible to recover from waste water or from the exhaust air residual materials that would otherwise place a major burden on the environment. The recovered substances can be reused in the production process. In this case two objectives are achieved, namely the reduction of environment pollution and savings due to the reutilization of raw materials. Recycling of raw materials represents in some cases a considerable advantage in economic and technical terms.

If none of the above-mentioned possibilities can be realized for technological or economic reasons, it is possible to avoid harmful impacts on the environment by incorporating environmental protection technologies at the end of the production process (filter systems, clarification plants, effluent treatment plants etc.).

### Assessment of technology required

The technology required to produce the desired products on the basis of the resources identified for the project may be common (published) knowledge or the property of owners who may be willing to transfer it under certain conditions. The primary goals of technology assessment are to determine and evaluate the impacts of different technologies on the society and national economy (cost-benefit analysis, employment and income effects, satisfaction of human needs etc.), impacts on the environment (environmental impact assessment) and techno-economic feasibility assessed from the point of view of the enterprise.

168

To allow the careful assessment of the suitability of the technological alternatives required and available for the project under study, the following logical sequence of steps should be followed:[65] problem definition, technology description, technology forecast, social description, social forecast, impact identification, impact analysis, impact evaluation, policy analysis and communication of results. In practice these logical steps will usually not be followed in a linear sequence; it may be necessary to apply a process of iteration by repeating earlier steps until satisfactory results are obtained. In order to be able to assess a technological process and its alternatives, a definition of all physical inputs and outputs of the projected plant is needed.

## Problem definition

The technology required is defined not only by the marketing concept (project strategy and product-market relations as described in chapter III) and the available raw materials and factory supplies (as described in chapter IV), but also by various socio-economic, ecological, financial, commercial and technical conditions that may be subsumed under the term business environment. The feasibility study should identify, describe and assess the critical elements of the technology required, and special consideration should be given to existing or possible future constraints on the acquisition and use of available technologies, to further development needs and to the possibility of feasible technological alternatives.

## Technology description and project layout

The preparation of a plant layout and design is essential for every project. This needs to be undertaken in two stages of project planning. The first and initial stage should be the preparation of a preliminary project plan and layout, on the basis of the production activities and the technological alternatives envisaged. The second stage of project layout and design can only be drawn up when the details relating to technology, plant capacity and machinery specifications are finalized.

The preliminary project layout should provide the overall framework of the project, which can serve as a broad basis for plant engineering, order-of-magnitude projections of civil works, machinery requirements and other investment elements. It should define the physical features of the plant such as infrastructure and site development, factory and other buildings, transport facilities (roads, railway sidings etc.) and utility linkages, including electric power substations, water connections, sewage lines and gas and telephone links, both within and outside the plant, together with other construction needs, including possible extensions of production facilities, storage and buildings. A layout chart at this stage should show the interrelationship between buildings and civil works and the equipment to be installed, and provide material-flow diagrams indicating the flow of materials as well as intermediate and final products.

---

[65]See A. L. Porter, *A Guidebook for Technology Assessment and Impact Analysis* (New York, Elsevier, 1980).

The preliminary project layout should include several charts and drawings, which need not be according to scale, but which would define the various physical features of the plant and their relationship with one another. The types and details of charts and drawings to be prepared would vary with the nature and complexity of the project. Nevertheless, for most projects, functional charts and layout drawings at this stage should include the following:

- General functional layout, defining the principal physical, or locational, features and flow relationships of machinery and equipment, civil works and constructions, and various ancillary and service facilities

- Basic characteristics of the technology

- Material-flow diagrams, indicating the flow of materials and utilities

- Transport layout, indicating roads, railways and other transport facilities up to their point of connection with public networks

- Utility lines for electric power, water, gas, telephone, sewage and emissions, both internal and external, up to the point connecting with public networks

- Areas for extension and expansion

Physical layout drawings should be based on survey maps and data on geological and hydrological features and on soil conditions at the selected location. Where layout drawings are prepared according to scale, this can range between 1:1000 to 1:200, but should be large enough to show the essential physical features of the plant, which could then be further elaborated at the stage of preparation of the detailed plant design.

## Technology market and alternatives

At the stage of a feasibility study, the nature of the technology market and the available technological alternatives have to be taken into account. The selection of appropriate technology is undoubtedly one of the key elements of such a study. This needs to be related to the economic plant capacity and the minimum economic production, as well as several other factors that may vary depending on corporate strategy and local conditions. The feasibility study should identify both alternative technologies and alternative sources of technology. The evaluation would then aim at selecting the technology and the source from which it may be secured. The study should also discuss the contractual terms and conditions which may be of special significance in relation to the acquisition of a particular technology. The terms and conditions may vary considerably for process industries, engineering-goods production and the manufacture of durable consumer goods, machinery and equipment. Requirements for the development of skills and of research and design capabilities in the particular field need to be defined.

## Assessment of availability

The market for industrial technology is highly imperfect, with alternative technologies and sources available in most industries. Certain specialized products and processes may be available from only one or a few sources, and alternative production technologies may be difficult to find. There must, however, be adequate knowledge and awareness regarding such alternatives and their potential suppliers, including industrial property rights applicable in each case. Technological information regarding alternative technologies and sources constitutes an important element of the feasibility study. In developing countries information on advanced and other technologies is frequently either not up-to-date or scattered among many sources. The setting-up of data banks for industrial and technological information has therefore become imperative for the promotion of industrial development. In this connection, the UNIDO Industrial and Technological Information Bank (INTIB)[66] became operational in 1980, its main objective being to ensure a quicker, easier and greater flow of information to people who need to select technologies. It is also necessary for the feasibility study to assess technological developments in the particular field and the likely impact of new and emerging technologies on competitive capability.

## Technology forecast

The feasibility study should provide an assessment and forecast of technological trends during the project implementation phase and the project life cycle, on the one hand, or the period limited by the planning horizon for the project, on the other. A technology forecast is especially important for investment projects in highly innovative industries. Developments in new technologies, particularly micro-electronics, biotechnology and new materials and energy technologies are having a significant impact on products and processes in various industries and their implications need to be assessed, together with the corresponding skill applications and development and the absorptive capacity that these may require. The possibility of blending new technologies with more traditional production processes, such as the use of microprocessors at certain stages of production, also needs to be examined. At the same time, the technology to be used should be proven technology that has already been applied and utilized, and which can be related to local conditions.

## Assessment of the local integration

An issue of major significance in technology choice is the level of integration or local value-added that can be achieved with respect to a particular technological usage. The feasibility study should define the extent of integration that should be achieved over a period of time. While this aspect constitutes a key issue in negotiations relating to technology acquisition and transfer, the parameters of the appropriate level of integration should be indicated in the feasibility study, particularly for engineering-goods production, since capital equipment requirements and production planning may largely depend on the integration level sought.

---

[66]INTIB is part of the Industrial and Technological Information Section of the Department for Industrial Promotion, Consultations and Technology. Its overall task is to undertake coordinated activities relating to industrial and technological information, to strengthen information systems in developing countries, and to compile and disseminate information requested by these countries. INTIB operates through its Industrial Inquiry Service and a network system. Detailed information on INTIB may be obtained from the UNIDO Department for Industrial Promotion, Consultations and Technology.

*Description of the socio-economic impact*

Although the socio-economic impact of a project in general and of a selected technology in particular are rather a subject of economic cost-benefit analysis, certain socio-economic aspects cannot be ignored in the feasibility study. Public policies with regard to the acquisition of foreign technologies, technology absorption and development have to be identified, and the socio-economic infrastructure, including the structure of the labour force, may have a significant impact on the feasibility of the technology to be selected for the project.

*Environmental impact assessment*[67]

The environmental impact assessment is a planning and decision process which primarily takes aspects relevant to the environment into account. The environmental impact assessment differs from other approval procedures in two essential respects relating, on the one hand, to the wider scope of the information and greater participation of the public, and, on the other, to the overall approach which also takes into account synergistic effects (interaction of various causes and the potential aggravation of effects on the environment).

During the last two decades, several distinctive procedures for environmental impact assessment have been developed in various industrialized countries in accordance with their respective legal systems. Common to all these procedures is the submission by the prospective plant operator of an environmental impact statement that is assessed under the rules established in the project country. Since the procedures vary greatly from one country to another, it will be necessary to refer to the corresponding literature in the country concerned.

Standards for environmental impact assessment have been determined for application in developed and developing countries by organizations and bodies such as the Economic Commission for Europe, the European Community and UNEP. Such standards may well be applied when planning new industries in developing countries, subject to the legislation of the country concerned.

*Technology evaluation and selection*

Alternative techniques should be evaluated in the feasibility study to determine the most suitable technology for the plant. This evaluation should be related to plant capacity, and should commence with a quantitative assessment of output, production build-up and gestation period and a qualitative assessment of product quality and marketability. The influence of the alternatives on capital investment and production costs should then be assessed for the planning period. Apart, however, from the basic criteria mentioned above, the technology must have been fully proven and be utilized in the manufacturing process, preferably in the company from which it came. While new and unproven or experimental techniques should not be considered appropriate in general, obsolescent technology should be avoided, which means

---

[67]See also chap. V, sect. C.

that technological trends and the possibility of using more developed techniques should be studied. For example, in the production of various types of fertilizer, technological choice should be based on the latest developments rather than on older, though proven, processes that are soon likely to be obsolete.

The selection of technology has to be related to the principal inputs that may be available for a project and to an appropriate combination of factor resources for both the short and the long term. In certain cases, the raw materials could determine the technology to be used. The quality of limestone, for example, is a determinant factor as to whether the wet or dry process is used for a cement plant. The availability of surplus bagasse would determine the type of technology used for the production of paper or newsprint. Furthermore, the non-availability or restricted availability of certain raw materials could be a technological constraint. A technological process based on indigenous raw materials and inputs may be preferable to one for which the principal inputs have to be imported indefinitely, particularly if serious foreign exchange regulations affect the inflow of such materials. Apart from the wider policy implications, supplies of materials and inputs are much better assured if indigenous, and may be less subject to external influences. In fact, progressive integration may be the only practicable means of undertaking production in a developing country for a large number of products.

A specific technology has to be viewed in the context of the total product mix that it generates, and if an alternative technology results in a wider product mix, starting from the same basic production materials and inputs, the value of the total mix, including saleable by-products, should be taken into account. The extent to which a particular technology or production technique can be effectively absorbed by a country could influence the choice of technology. It is often suggested that certain technologies are too sophisticated for particular developing countries because of their inadequate *technological absorptive capacity*. Such an argument may be exaggerated, and has been used to impose obsolete techniques for projects in developing countries. There may, however, be cases where a particular technology, for example involving complex data processing, cannot be effectively absorbed in a country because of the difficulty in training the technical personnel required for the software work within a reasonable period.

The degree of *capital-intensity* considered appropriate could define the technology parameters. In countries with a shortage of labour, or where labour is very expensive as in Western Europe, capital-intensive techniques may be appropriate and economically justified. In countries with excess labour, labour-saving techniques may prove unnecessarily expensive. This situation may apply to the overall technology as well as to the degree of mechanization of projects or particular production operations such as material-handling. The choices from the viewpoint of both labour and capital should be given in the feasibility study so that the most appropriate technique can be selected.

Alternative technologies should also be evaluated with regard to their environmental impacts. Depending on the type of industry and local environment, critical elements such as economic use of raw materials, low-emission technologies (state of the art) and low-waste-production processes must be considered for the selection of suitable technologies. The evaluation should not be based on the optimization of only one variable target, but should aim at an optimal combination of human, techno-economic and strategic requirements.

When new industries or industrial plants are introduced in developing countries, care must be taken to avoid "environmental dumping", which means that polluting industries are transferred to countries where pollution restrictions are either non-existent or less stringent. Another form of environmental dumping is the introduction of obsolete technologies, equipment or production plants with higher pollution factors. Acquisition of previously discarded and disassembled production plants should therefore be checked carefully.

Full account should be taken of investment and operating costs when judging the appropriateness of more capital-intensive techniques. In developing countries the tendency is often to prefer a capital-intensive technique because it is used in industrialized countries. The additional capital cost involved in such technologies should be viewed against the labour costs of less capital-intensive techniques. Both the preference for labour- or capital-intensive technologies and the choice of technology can only be judged on techno-economic grounds, and should be subject to a careful cost-benefit analysis in the feasibility study.

## C.  Technology acquisition and transfer

Together with the selection of technology, alternative sources of supply of such technologies should be located. The sources of unpatented technological know-how can vary with the nature and complexity of the production process and range from individual experts to entire enterprises, domestic or foreign, already engaged in the manufacture of the product in question. Consultancy organizations are usually a valuable source, particularly for specialized products and techniques. An experienced spinning master or a good foundry worker may be quite adequate for the transfer of know-how in a spinning mill or a foundry. However, for much of the engineering-goods industry, where considerable documentation in the form of blueprints and manufacturing drawings may be necessary for a new project, another enterprise in the same industry may be required, although retired experts may also prove adequate where simple products and components are involved. For industries such as petrochemical production, process technology would have to be obtained either from other manufacturing enterprises or specialized consultancy agencies.

### Industrial property rights

Where a desired technology is patented or covered by registered trade marks, it is necessary to secure industrial rights from their holders. The coverage and life of particular patents for a required technology should be investigated. For a large number of products, the use of a particular trade mark or trade name may be of special significance for product marketing, and this should be assessed. In the production, for example, of electric motors or steam turbines, the use of an international brand name could be of considerable significance in product marketing both domestically and for exports. The use of brand names may also affect the marketing of a wide range of consumer products ranging from perishable items to consumer durables, and this should be assessed for each such product.

Technology and know-how are embodied, in varying degrees, in machinery and equipment for a plant, and the choice of particular machinery and equipment can itself be an exercise in technology choice. In several fields, the type, capacity and range of machinery that is acquired and utilized incorporate the various technological aspects of processing and production. Thus, for a sugar factory or a cement plant, the range and capacity of equipment selected would determine production capacity, as also the technological parameters of such projects. In such cases, the management of technology acquisition and transfer largely consists of ensuring efficient operations and maintenance of the equipment. In certain other industries such as chemicals, petrochemicals and fertilizers, on the other hand, the process technology and engineering constitute the primary elements determining equipment size and capacity. In several industries, however, technology is increasingly found to be only partially embodied in equipment and often comprises specialized knowledge that may either be covered by industrial property rights such as patents, trade marks, copyrights and proprietory technology, or be in the form of unpatented know-how that is available from only a limited number of sources. The acquisition of technology in such cases involves negotiations and contractual arrangements for technology licensing and transfer, apart from purchase of equipment for particular technological processes.

## Means of technology acquisition

When technology has to be obtained from some other enterprise, the means of acquisition have to be determined. These can take the form of technology licensing, outright purchase of technology or a joint venture involving participation in ownership by the technology supplier. The implications of these methods of acquisiton should be analysed.

### Licensing

Technology licensing has developed into a popular and effective mechanism for trade in technology. A licence gives the right to use patented technology and provides for the transfer of related know-how on mutually agreed terms. Most licences for industrial projects in developing countries have to be obtained from foreign enterprises holding industrial property rights or possessing unpatented know-how, though in some developing countries they can also be obtained from domestic enterprises, particularly where no patents are involved. In cases where technology licensing is considered necessary, it is desirable to have the technology package disaggregated and to identify critical contractual elements. Though both these aspects relate to the post-feasibility implementation stage, if they are considered in the study it would greatly assist in the subsequent negotiations of the technology licence contract.

### Purchase of technology

For certain industrial branches it is desirable to acquire the technology by outright purchase, and if this is so it should be emphasized in the feasibility study. Outright purchase is appropriate when "one-time" technological rights or know-how are to be secured, and when there is little likelihood of subsequent technological improvements or need for continued technological support to the prospective licensee.

An important issue in technology negotiations may relate to the development of exports and export capability on the part of the licensee. Such capability would depend on various factors, including plant capacity, local production costs and geographical proximity to major export markets. The implications for the development of exports and the measures necessary in this regard should, however, be examined in the feasibility study.

## *Participation of the licence-holder in the joint venture*

Equity participation by a technology supplier is a policy matter for the project sponsors and is beyond the scope of the feasibility study. However, the study should consider such participation in the following terms: continuing technological support on a long-term basis; possible access by the technology supplier to both domestic and external markets that may be served by the proposed projet; participation in the risk associated with new products not tested in a particular market; and effects of participation from the viewpoint of covering resource gaps in projects involving a large outlay. Such an evaluation should, at the same time, highlight the financial benefits that would accrue to the technology supplier both as a supplier and as an equity participant.

The detailed technological services that would be required in conjunction with the use of a particular technology should be stated in the study, and the type of agencies listed that perform such services. These services include: detailed engineering, plant design and equipment layout; providing for auxiliary facilities at the pre-implementation stage; supervision during implementation; and testing, commissioning and start-up in the post-implementation period. The nature and scope of such technical services should be defined. In certain instances, the technology and the engineering services are combined as in a consultancy organization, but even then, the costs should be separately considered and judged.

Since most industrial technology in developing countries is acquired from external sources, an important issue is the form of participation of the technology supplier. Apart from equipment imports, technology can be acquired through *non-affiliate licensing* or through foreign subsidiaries or joint ventures in which the technology supplier participates in the ownership of the project. Such participation is often largely limited to the capitalized value of the technology, equipment and technical services provided by the technology supplier. In recent decades, non-affiliate licensing has emerged as an important channel for technology acquisition and transfer, and there has been a substantial increase in licensing agreements between enterprises in industrialized economies, as also in several developing countries. Non-affiliate licensing, however, requires a certain level of technological absorptive capacity, and where this is not adequately available and continuing technological support is necessary from the licensor, a joint venture with varying levels of foreign equity participation may be more appropriate. The extent of equity participation, if any, by the technology licensor is generally an issue for negotiations between the parties concerned.

Nevertheless, the feasibility study should indicate whether equity participation by the selected licensor would be desirable in view of the nature and complexity of the technology that may be involved. Such participation may be particularly useful if continuing technical assistance and supply of inputs and services is necessary over a period of time, or where technology is undergoing rapid change, or in situations where the technology supplier can provide access to external markets that may otherwise be difficult to penetrate. At the same time, where foreign participation in a joint venture is primarily limited to the capitalization of technology, caution must be exercised, and capitalization of such costs should be assessed in terms of the overall returns that would accrue to the technology supplier over the lifetime of the enterprise as against technology payments in the form of fees and royalties.

## Disaggregation

The technology package should be disaggregated into various component parts, such as the technology proper, related engineering services, phasing of domestic integration, supply of intermediate products and even the supply of equipment by the licensors, because prospective licensees from developing countries are often in a weak bargaining position, and technology suppliers tend to load the technology package with features that are not essential to the technology. A distinction should be made between essential technological features and others that should be evaluated separately. The feasibility study should indicate the level of such disaggregation or "unpackaging" of technology for the project in question.

## Technological absorption and adaptation

The feasibility study should indicate the measures and action to be taken for technological absorption and adaptation of the acquired technology to local conditions. The absorption of technology within the duration of a technology agreement requires the planned development of skills and capabilities in various stages of plant operations. An essential element is staff planning, and an efficient recruitment policy has to be combined with a comprehensive training programme for various categories of plant personnel. The feasibility study should identify the various categories of personnel to be recruited and the training programmes they need to undergo. The training activities of the technology licensor can only complement and supplement the training provided in the plant of the licensee. It is also necessary that the inflow of technology, when provided in stages and at different levels of local manufacturing integration, is closely linked with the development of the skills and capabilities of the workforce in the licensee enterprise. Technological adaptation requires not only the adjustment of special know-how to local factor conditions, but the capability to modify products and processes to suit local preferences and requirements and to initiate a process of innovative development in a particular field. This would require both design skills and facilities for research and development, and the measures and requirements in this regard should be identified in the feasibility study.

## Contract terms and conditions

The contractual terms and conditions for technology acquisition and transfer, which are likely to be of particular significance to the project, need to be highlighted in the feasibility study. These may differ in emphasis from project to project, but certain contractual issues would be of significance in most cases.

*Definition.* The details of the technology, including processes and products, together with the technical services required from the technology supplier, should be clearly defined. This should include all necessary documentation, such as blueprints, specifications, production drawings etc. It is important, in this context, to disaggregate the various elements of technology and services and to assess their cost and other implications separately.

*Duration.* Since the duration of a technology agreement must be adequate for effective technological absorption, the period required for such absorption should be defined. A reasonable period for the agreement should also be indicated in the feasibility study, together with the scope for progressive technological upgrading and renewal.

*Warranty.* The appropriate warranty or guarantee relating to the technology and know-how supplied should be indicated in the feasibility study.

*Access to improvements.* Provision should be made for the licensee to have access to improvements made by the licensor during the period of agreement.

*Industrial property rights.* Patents and other industrial property rights pertaining to a particular technology should be identified and suitable provisions suggested for listing patents and acquiring usage rights for the period of validity of the patents, and also for possible violation of third-party rights. The implications of use of a foreign trade mark or brand name should be reviewed in terms of their marketing advantages, on the one hand, and continuing payment for use of foreign brand names, on the other.

*Payments.* Technology payments can be in the form of a lump-sum payment or continuing royalties or a combination of the two. The suggested form and appropriate level of payment should be indicated in the feasibility study, taking into account the fees and royalties paid for similar projects in other countries and allowing for variations and differences.

*Territorial sales rights.* The implications of exclusive and non-exclusive sales rights for the country where the project is located and neighbouring countries or other geographical regions should be examined, in the feasibility study.

*Supply of imported inputs.* The implications of securing imported inputs, such as intermediate products and components, from the technology licensor should be examined and suggestions made as to appropriate provisions in this regard, including provisions on pricing of such intermediate products.

*Training.* For the absorption of technology, training is essential. The study should indicate where and when training would be required, either in the plant of the licensor or through supply of expert personnel in the plant of the licensee. The specific fields of training, the number of persons to be trained and the period of training for each category should be defined.

Several other provisions that are fairly standard in technology agreements need not be specifically discussed in the feasibility study unless they are particularly relevant for the project in question. These include provisions on assignability, confidentiality, reporting, maintenance of records, quality control, governing law, *force majeure* and settlement of disputes.

In discussing the contractual provisions described above, the feasibility study should, in effect, provide fairly specific guidelines for negotiating suitable terms and conditions for technology acquisition and transfer. In several developing countries, regulatory authorities have prescribed guidelines on technology agreements, but these necessarily deal only with broad policy parameters. In order to assist developing countries in their negotiations on technology acquisition and transfer, UNIDO has established a Technology Exchange System that provides information abstracted from technology transfer agreements of participating countries. The information is accessible only to those who provide it on a confidential, reciprocal and mutually beneficial basis.

The negotiating strategy should also be indicated, and a draft of the principal terms and conditions from the viewpoint of the prospective licensee should be prepared.

### Cost of technology

The costs of the selection and acquisition of technology and the related technical services should be estimated in the feasibility study. This may present difficulties, as negotiations on technology acquisition and technical services between the prospective licensee and licensor come after the preparation of the study, and, in a number of developing countries, may depend on the degree of regulatory control of licensing arrangements by governmental bodies. An assessment of this question in the feasibility study could, however, provide guidelines on technology negotiations for the project sponsors, and set the framework within which such negotiations could be conducted.

An assessment has to be made of the proper remuneration for technology and services. For this purpose, technology payments made in other cases for the same industry may be referred to if the information can be obtained. An assessment could also be made of various payment alternatives such as a lump sum, a running royalty rate or a combination of the two. A royalty payment may be more appropriate when the technology necessitates a relationship with the technology licensor over a period of time. This rate tends to range from fractional percentages up to 3 to 5 per cent of actual sales, depending on the nature of the industry and plant capacity. For most technical services, assessment of appropriate costs would be easier, as the cost of comparable services can generally be obtained, except when they are highly complex or proprietory in nature. Schedule VI-1 may be utilized for this purpose. Lump-sum payments for patents and trade marks, for special rights and concessions and for unpatented know-how can be capitalized (under incorporated fixed assets in schedule VI-3/2) and amortized according to the regulations in force in a country. Royalty payments, however, are generally not capitalized and are included in production costs.

## D.   Detailed plant layout and basic engineering

### Detailed plant layout

While the preliminary layout would define the principal physical features of the plant and their relationship with one another, a detailed final plant layout needs to be prepared prior to project implementation. This can only be done when the technology and production processes are determined and the list of capital equipment and material inputs is finalized. A close relationship exists between technological processes, equipment requirements and the plant layout and design, and the latter must necessarily be based on and closely linked with the former. In some projects, this may not result in significant differences from the initial preliminary layout, and the detailed plant layout would only be more detailed in coverage. In other projects, however, there may be considerable variations from the preliminary layout. These may relate not only to the type and configuration of equipment to be used in particular processes, but also to the implications of the use of particular technologies in terms of safety requirements, emission control, waste disposal etc. This would be particularly applicable to chemical and other process industries, where the nature of the technology utilized would constitute a major determinant of the detailed plant layout. In any event, a detailed plant layout needs to be prepared for all projects prior to the stage of implementation.

## Basic engineering

It will be necessary, at this stage, to prepare the plant design together with the engineering work that it may entail. The detailed plant layout and basic engineering design are required in a feasibility study to allow the preparation of cost estimates, while detailed engineering work would usually not start before a project enters the implementation phase. In case the scope of detailed engineering work is significant, the volume of work, the time required and costs must be projected. Basic engineering essentially comprises the detailed configuration of construction facilities, equipment and production processes, and of material flows and linkages between different stages of production. The nature of plant design and engineering would vary from project to project. In major projects such as petrochemical and fertilizer production or smelting of ore, considerable basic and detailed engineering work is necessary. This is often incorporated as part of the process technology and know-how to be acquired. In other projects, however, plant design and engineering would need to be undertaken by the project authorities as a key element of project planning. The plant design in all projects would define the functional relationships between various processes and stages of production, including flows of material at different production stages.

## Detailed charts and drawings

The plant layout and basic engineering should comprise charts and drawings, including several features added to those prepared for the preliminary layout. These should be as detailed as required to comply with the financial evaluation of the project or project alternative, and should include:

- Functional layout related to site conditions and indicating the position of principal structures and buildings, major equipment, roads, railways and other transport facilities, various utility and service facilities, and areas for future expansion. The layout should be done on a scale of between 1:1000 and 1:2000, and be based on a survey of geological, soil and other data;
- Location of main production units, including loading areas, electrical outlets and instrumentation, and of auxiliary production units, repair, storage and research and development facilities etc.;

- Material-flow diagrams, showing the flow of materials, utilities and emissions, as well as intermediate and final products, through various sections of the plant, and quantity-flow diagrams, indicating quantities entering or leaving the production process;

- Production line diagrams, defining various stages of production and indicating location, space requirements, dimensions of principal capital equipment, of foundations and of mounting devices, electric power and utilities etc.;

- Final physical layout for transport, utility lines, consumption, linkages and communications facilities.

## E. Selection of machinery and equipment

The selection of equipment and technology are interdependent. In certain projects, such as a cement plant, production and operational technology is part and parcel of the supply of equipment and no separate arrangements for technology acquisition are necessary. However, in cases when technology has to be independently acquired, the selection of equipment should follow the determination of technology as the two are closely linked. The requirements of machinery and equipment should be identified in the feasibility study on the basis of plant capacity and the selected production technology.

Equipment selection at the feasibility study stage should broadly define the optimum group of machinery and equipment necessary for a specific production capacity by using a specific production technique. This selection differs in emphasis with the type of project. For most process-oriented industries, machinery, or groups of machines, have to be defined for various processing stages so that the various stages merge into one another. In all projects the capacity rating of equipment has to be defined for each processing stage and related to the capacity and machinery requirements at the next production stage. The requirements of machinery and equipment must therefore be directly related to capacity needs at different stages of processing. The equipment choice for manufacturing industries is much wider, since different machines can perform similar functions with varying degrees of accuracy. The complex of machine tools required for the manufacture of diesel engines or certain kinds of compressors could thus take alternative forms. From an investment viewpoint, equipment costs would be kept to a minimum, consistent with the needs of various machinery functions and processes. To determine the equipment required for a machine-building enterprise, for example, it is necessary to define various machining and other operations required for projected production volumes over a certain period, the breakdown of the machine-hours required for each operation, the selection of specific machine tools to perform each function and the number of machines required for different production levels to be achieved over that period.

### Relationship with other study components

The determination of equipment requirements should be related to other study components. While most of the components should be covered in the determination of plant capacity and technological processes, others may prove pertinent since the choice of equipment even within the framework of a defined plant capacity and technology may still be fairly wide. In certain cases there may be infrastructure constraints relating, for example, to the availability of power for a large electric furnace or the transport of heavy equipment to a remote interior site. In some instances, the use of highly sophisticated equipment, such as machine tools with numerical controls, may not be appropriate in initial production stages because of the length of time required for training. The use of more sophisticated equipment may also be ruled out or postponed when such equipment has to be imported, on account of overall investment constraints or limitations on the availability of foreign exchange. Maintenance requirements and the availability of maintenance facilities could also be an important factor. Government policies, such as import controls, may restrict the import of certain types of equipment, and equipment selection has then to be tailored to available domestic products.

## Level of automation

An important issue in equipment choice is the degree of automation that may be required. Automation may take the form either of process automation or of functional automation, the latter relating primarily to the automation of certain functions. In certain high-precision industries, such as production of instruments and controls, where computerized production operations are being rapidly extended, the use of computerized equipment may need to be considered.

At the same time, capital costs of automation tend to be very high, and, while the replacement of high-cost labour by automated capital equipment may be economically viable in highly industrialized economies, the same considerations may not be equally applicable in developing countries. Where the competitive nature of production or the corporate strategy require the use of automated equipment, however, the necessary skills must be developed to meet such needs, as production operations would otherwise become obsolete. Thus, the use of computer-aided designs for production of ready-made garments for export, or the use of numerically controlled machine tools or machining centres for capital goods production, could represent significant cost advantages and production flexibility in developing countries. On the other hand, the extensive use of robotics in automobile manufacture may have fewer advantages in developing countries because of lower labour costs, the high costs of automation and the degree of skills and capability that the use of robotics and automated production may require. Equipment choice, therefore, has to assess the balance of factors and advantages in relation to the degree of sophistication and automation that may be required in specific fields of production and even in certain stages of production in particular projects.

## Categories of equipment

Equipment can be variously categorized. One classification can take the form of the machinery requirements for each stage of the production process. In other cases, the machinery can be listed under plant machinery, mechanical equipment, electrical equipment, instrumentation and controls, transport and conveying equipment, testing and research equipment and other machinery items. Whatever classification is used, the machinery requirements should be listed in their totality. The rated performance required from various items of equipment should also be defined, so as to ensure that the production capacity of equipment in various stages of processing and manufacture are uniform and consistent.

*Production equipment*

The list of plant machinery and equipment should include all movable and immovable machines and equipment for production, processing and control and related facilities that form an integral unit with the machines and that serve no other purpose. Such equipment can be variously classified for different types of projects, one classification being to divide the items into the following subgroups: plant (process) machinery; mechanical equipment; electrical equipment; instrumentation and controls; process conveying and transport equipment; and other plant machinery and equipment. The erection and installation of machinery may necessitate special foundations, supporting structures, walls, beams and ceilings. The equipment groups and machines for various functional processes or production centres should be subdivided to the level of individual machines and facilities, and the machinery list should be complete so as to cover the requirements for each stage of production from the receiving of raw materials to the dispatch of the final products. The rated performance required for various pieces of process equipment should be defined, and for each project component a list of equipment should be tabulated in accordance with schedule VI-2 given in the appendix to chapter VI.

However complete the list and evaluation of machinery and equipment may be at the stage of a feasibility study, it may have to undergo substantial modification if the parameters of a project are modified in the course of investment decisions, including changes in the technological process adopted. Such modifications would, however, have to be elaborated during the post-feasibility study stages.

*Spare parts and tools*

A list should be prepared of required spare parts and tools with their estimated prices, including the parts to be obtained with original equipment and parts and tools required for operational wear and tear. Spare part needs would depend on the nature of the industry, availability of spare parts, the capacity to manufacture such items in the country concerned and import facilities. Generally, it is sufficient to stock a three- to six-month supply, under certain conditions, although the stock could be higher. In any case, the stock requirements have to be carefully evaluated, as they may have an impact on plant inventories and the working capital required.

*Testing and research equipment*

Provision should be made for testing equipment, including quality control and research equipment for technological development and adaptation.

*Imported and domestic equipment*

Machinery and equipment requirements, including spare parts, should be broken down in terms of imported equipment and domestically available machinery. Cost estimates for imported equipment should be on the basis of c.i.f. and landed costs, as well as internal transport, insurance and other costs up to the plant site. Transport and other costs of domestic equipment should be incorporated up to the plant site. The cost of erection of equipment should be estimated, particularly when this is undertaken as an independent operation. In other cases, installation costs should be provided for, though separately, in the cost estimates. The installation costs may vary from a relatively low figure of approximately 1 to 2 per cent, to a range of from 5 to 15 per cent or more, depending on the equipment and the type of erection and installation involved. Provision for price escalation should be made where appropriate, particularly when delivery is extended over a period of 18 months or more. The cost of domestically produced equipment usually tends to be higher in developing than in developed countries, particularly where there are rigorous import controls, and this has to be allowed for in investment cost estimates. Delivery periods for domestic equipment tend to vary considerably from those for equivalent imported machinery, and this must be taken into account in time-scheduling.

*Limitations and constraints*

Equipment requirements have to be related to the local industrial and technological infrastructure and to other aspects of the feasibility study. There may be infrastructure constraints such as limited electric power availability for large electric furnaces or for electrolytic processes having large power requirements at low rates. The use of computerized equipment, including machine tools and machining centres may be limited especially at initial stages because of inadequate skill availability and the period required for training skilled personnel. Foreign exchange requirements may constitute a major constraint, both for sophisticated, capital-intensive equipment and for imported inputs required for operations, including spare parts, components and intermediate products. Equipment choice has also to be related to maintenance facilities that may be available or can be developed, and to the availability of other maintenance inputs for particular machinery. It is necessary that the feasibility study should take into account such constraints in defining the parameters for selection of machinery and equipment. At the same time, the techno-economic implications of such constraints, particularly with respect to the development of exports of manufactured products, should be clearly spelt out.

*Procurement lead time*

The matching of imported and locally produced equipment also involves assessment of the procurement lead time for different groups and items of equipment. Procurement lead time has to be estimated in all cases, including the administrative lead time for the issue of tenders and bids, evaluation of offers and finalization of contracts, and the lead time of the supplier for equipment manufacture and transport. This subject is dealt with in chapter IX.

*Erection and installation*

Provision has to be made for the erection and installation of machinery and equipment. This may include special foundations and support structure for heavy equipment that have to be provided as part of the civil works. The erection function itself may be fairly specialized for certain types of equipment, particularly in process industries, and may require a separate contract for plant erection and installation.

*Tenders and bids*

The detailed list of machinery and equipment will later form the basis for the preparation of tender or bid documents for equipment supply. These should specify the details of the equipment required, together with conditions of supply.

## F.  Civil engineering works

The feasibility study should provide plans and estimates for the civil works related to the project. This should cover site preparation and development, factory and other buildings, civil engineering works relating to utilities, transport, emissions and effluent discharge, internal roads, fencing and security, and other facilities and requirements of the plant.

Civil engineering works are fairly project-specific and have to be related to a particular plant site and the facilities that may be required. While plans and estimates for the principal buildings required for a specific type of plant follow a fairly uniform pattern, there may be major variations in estimates because of site conditions and for other civil engineering works because of local conditions.

*Buildings*

Plans and estimates for buildings and structures should include: the main factory or plant building; buildings for ancillary production facilities such as foundries and forges, or for preparation or initial processing of raw materials; ancillary buildings for maintenance and repair, testing and research and development; storage and warehouses for stocks of raw material or finished products; non-factory buildings, including administrative buildings; staff welfare facilities such as cafeterias, medical facilities and recreation areas; residential buildings, if any, for supervisory and shift personnel; and other buildings required for plant personnel. These requirements can vary considerably from project to project, depending on site conditions, proximity of urban facilities and the nature of production activities. A project at a fairly remote site may require considerable expenditure on buildings for personnel, since such buildings may not be available. In large resource-based projects, entire townships may have to be developed, since no alternative facilities may be available, and project estimates must take such costs into account from the earliest stage.

*Ancillary construction needs*

Construction requirements should also be assessed and estimated for constructions, structures, pipelines etc. for utilities and other basic plant facilities. Water storage facilities may be necessary, apart from water connections; an electricity substation may be required; and approach roads and internal roads must be planned, in addition to railway sidings or other transport facilities such as ropeways. Ventilation, heating and air-conditioning, where necessary, will need to be provided, and sewage lines and plumbing should be planned, together with other such construction facilities.

*Plans and estimates*

The plans and estimates for civil engineering works should be detailed for cost estimates and implementation scheduling. The nature of each construction should be defined, including modular construction where appropriate, the quality of construction materials and the quantities and cost of materials required. Detailed civil engineering drawings are usually not required before the start of project implementation.

The estimates for buildings and other constructions should be based on unit costs such as building costs per square metre in the plant surroundings. While the final costs will depend on the bids and quotations that are received, the plans and estimates at the project engineering stage should be complete for all the necessary constructions and accurate to the extent required for projecting the overall project investment costs.

## G. Maintenance and replacement requirements

An important aspect of project engineering is the determination of critical maintenance and replacement requirements for the project. Satisfactory maintenance of plant, buildings and various facilities is essential for efficient plant operations. Similarly, replacement requirements for various parts, components and materials at different stages of construction and production need to be identified and planned for. Both these aspects should be covered in the feasibility study.

Maintenance requirements should be assessed in terms of both the maintenance equipment that may be necessary for efficient maintenance of the plant and facilities, and the maintenance skills and capability[68] that need to be developed. Maintenance equipment can range from relatively simple equipment and materials necessary for cleaning and maintaining plant equipment, buildings and facilities in good condition, to fairly complex maintenance equipment required in certain process industries. The development of maintenance skills and capability is of particular importance, especially in developing countries where efficient maintenance may be both more difficult and more important because of difficulties in obtaining replacements. Such skills should be developed, through training programmes at the project implementation stage,

---

[68]The organization of plant maintenance is discussed in chap. VII, sect. B.

for general-purpose maintenance and with respect to maintenance of specific, complex equipment and facilities.

Replacement requirements need to be determined for wear-and-tear parts, tools, jigs and fixtures in engineering-goods industries, and for spare parts, components and materials for plant, buildings and other facilities in all projects. An efficient balance has to be maintained between replacement requirements and stocks of parts, components and materials. Such a balance constitutes a critical feature of financial planning of inventories during the project implementation stage.

Inventory requirements for maintenance and replacement items will vary with each project and depend on the nature of the project, the extent of utilization of particular parts or materials, and the speed with which such items can be replaced. In several fields, fairly standard stock levels are prescribed for various maintenance and replacement items. These may, however, need to be adjusted in situations where such items have to be imported and there are foreign exchange constraints. Estimates should be prepared in this regard and incorporated in the factory cost estimates in schedule VI-4.

## H.  Estimates of overall investment costs

### *Capital cost estimates*

Once the production programme and plant capacity are defined, a preliminary order-of-magnitude estimate can be drawn up regarding the broad investment requirements of the project, particularly if a plant capacity is set at a fairly standardized level, and prices are available for plant and equipment at such capacities. In the case of preliminary cost estimates for opportunity or pre-feasibility studies, this can also be done through the use of certain broad ratios. For example, it is often estimated that the machinery and equipment for a project would constitute about 50 per cent of total investment costs, with the main plant costing about 30 per cent. Buildings and civil works are generally assumed to cost from 10 per cent to 15 per cent of total investment. Similar, though much smaller, percentages can be set for utilities, instrumentation, piping and other ancillary facilities and requirements. Such percentages, however, vary considerably from industry to industry and country to country and should be utilized with a great deal of caution. At the same time, these figures may be useful at the project appraisal stage when analysing the structure of investment costs. If, for example, the civil engineering cost estimates are relatively low in relation to plant machinery and equipment as compared with similar projects,[69] then the plant machinery costs could be overestimated, or the cost projections for civil engineering may not cover all civil engineering works probably required for project implementation. To check the reliability of cost estimates, a detailed breakdown to the various cost items would be necessary (see also check-list VI-2 in the appendix to chapter VI).

---

[69]The technology, type of project (turnkey greenfield site, industrial site with existing infrastructure etc.), battery limits, plant capacity and plant location must be comparable, to permit the use of such indicators for complete plants. Published ratios are, however, fairly reliable for the estimating costs of equipment and services forming part of the main plant items (pipings, electrical equipment, civil engineering design etc.).

On the basis of the estimates for technology, machinery and equipment and civil engineering works, the feasibility study should provide an overall estimate of the capital costs of the project. Such an estimate will undergo modification in accordance with the bids and offers received from suppliers and contractors, but will nevertheless provide a fairly realistic estimate of capital costs. These costs should be reflected in schedules VI-1 (technology costs), VI-2 (equipment) and VI-3 (civil engineering works). Schedule VI-4 summarizes the overhead costs.

The accuracy of cost estimates in relation to project development has already been described in part one of this *Manual*. The preliminary estimate is based on the process flow sheet after the scope of the project has been determined by those concerned with the preparation of an opportunity or pre-feasibility study. A physical contingency allowance is commonly added, but it would be preferable to have the probable cost range quoted.

The budget estimate required at the feasibility study level must be founded on a properly developed flow sheet and a full assessment of the site. It will be based on a fairly detailed equipment list, and costs of special or main plant items may be obtained through preliminary tendering. A typical degree of accuracy would be $\pm 10$ per cent. Careful consideration must be given to this estimate, and in particular to the contingencies allowed.

*Reliability of cost estimates*

The precision of cost estimates will be aided by a clear definition of the scope of the project. Incomplete or wrong technical information, over-optimistic construction programmes and inexperienced estimating engineers are usually the main causes of incorrect and misleading capital cost estimates.

*Estimating methods*

*Exponential cost estimating*

When historical data are available on similar types of plants or plant items, then it is possible to arrive at reasonably accurate cost estimates of plants or plant items differing in size and capacity. However, it is very important to understand that exponential factors are only valid if the technical scope of the project and process technologies are similar. If this is not the case, the margin of error of cost estimates may be greater than the required reliability of estimates. Exponential cost estimating is based on the following function: if the relative size of two plants or plant items is $S_1/S_2$, then the relative costs would be $(C_1/C_2)^n$, where $n$ is the exponential factor that for many plants and equipment lies between 0.6 and 0.7.

$$\left(\frac{C_1}{C_2}\right)^n = \frac{S_1}{S_2}$$

Exponential cost factors are published,[70] but should be checked regularly against prices obtained through tendering. It is also necessary to update

---

[70]For example, by the Institution of Chemical Engineers, London.

historical data because of inflation. Some typical exponential factors are as follows:

| Plant item | Exponential factor |
|---|---|
| Tanks (spherical) | 0.7 |
| Electric motors | 0.8 |
| Columns, towers | 0.7 (constant diameter) |
| | 1.0 (constant height) |
| Heat exchangers | 0.65 = 0.95 |
| Piping | 0.7 = 0.9 |
| Instruments and control | 0.0 |

For rough order-of-magnitude estimates, an overall plant exponential factor based on experience may be used. Caution must be exercised in applying the method of exponential estimating for complete plants. For example, in the case of chemical plants with batch reactors, the exponent will be greater than for similar plants designed for a continuous process. Furthermore, exponential factors may vary considerably for different locations, as when a greenfield project in a developing country is compared with a similar larger plant in another location with a different locational infrastructure. A satisfactory estimate may be obtained if such plants are broken down into discrete plant units or sections and a suitable exponent is used for estimating the costs of each unit.

## Factorial estimating

This technique consists in determining the costs of main plant items and then adding up factors for subsidiary items in order to build up an estimate of total costs. For example, if the cost of a large tank is estimated at $20,000, the costs of erection on site, piping, instrumentation and electrical equipment may be calculated at 32 per cent, or $6,400 dollars. The corresponding factors vary depending on the type of subsidiary items. Erection costs may be between 1 and 24 per cent, depending on construction work required on site; piping costs may be between 2 and 20 per cent, depending on the type of equipment and technological process.

Estimating starts with the design of a process flow sheet. From this a list of equipment, civil works etc. is derived with basic technical data. Quotations for main items would be required for feasibility studies, while in the case of pre-feasibility studies the method of factorial estimating may be applied, provided that suitable and updated historical data are available.

## Estimating based on full design

The most accurate estimate of investment costs must be based on a detailed and complete design of each project component. Since competitive quotations should be obtained for plant equipment, machinery, erection, civil works etc., estimating based on full design would usually not be appropriate for a feasibility study, but would occur during the project implementation phase, once the project has been approved.

## Typical investment cost structures

Experience shows that investment costs are typically distributed among such items as civil, mechanical and electrical engineering, instrumentation, installation and project overheads and design. Although cost distribution varies considerably with production capacity, project scope (overseas greenfield site, existing local industrial site etc.), battery limits, location and technology selected, it is possible to develop typical cost structures for well-defined industries, locations and battery limits. The ratios indicating the percentage distribution of costs may be used as a valuable guide when analysing project cost estimates or for the preparation of first order-of-magnitude cost projections of opportunity studies.

## Bibliography

Aggteleky, B. Fabrikplanung. Munich, Hanser, 1970.

Asian Development Bank. Environmental guidelines for selected industrial and power development projects. Manila, 1988.

Baranson, Jack. Industrial technologies for developing countries. New York, Praeger, 1969.

Bhalla, A. A., *ed.* Technology and employment in industry: a case study approach. 3. ed. Geneva, International Labour Office, 1985.

Contractor, F. J. The role of licensing in international strategy. *Columbia journal of world business* (New York) 4, Winter, 1981.

Dreger, Wolfgang. Projekt-Management, Planung und Abwicklung von Projekten. Wiesbaden Bauverlag, 1975.

Economic Development Foundation. Manual on plant layout and material handling. Tokyo, Asian Productivity Organization, 1971.

Frey, Siegmar. Plant layout. Munich, Hanser, 1975.

Beanlands, Gordon E. *and* Peter N. Duinker. An ecological framework for environmental impact assessment in Canada. Hull, Canada, FEARO, 1983.

Grant, E. L., W. G. Ireson *and* R. S. Leavenworth. Principles of engineering economy. 8. ed. New York, John Wiley, 1976.

Griffiths, R. F. Dealing with risk; the planning, management and acceptability of technological risk. Manchester, University Press, 1982.

Marsh, P.D.V. Contracting for engineering and construction projects. 3. ed. Aldershot, Gower, 1988.

Marton, K. Multinationals, technology and industrialization. New York, Lexington, 1986.

Moore, J. H. Plant layout and design. New York, Macmillan, 1962.

Netherlands. Ministerie van Volkhuisvesting, Ruimtelyke Ordening en Milieubeheer and Ministerie van Landbouw en Visserij. Netherlands handling uncertainty in environmental impact assessment. 's-Gravenhage, 1985.

Porter, A. L. A guidebook for technology assessment and impact analysis. New York, Elsevier North-Holland, 1980.

Pratten, C. F. Economies of scale in manufacturing industry. London, Cambridge University Press, 1971.

Schörner Georg, Umweltverträglichkeitsprüfung in der Verwaltungspraxis. Berichte und Dokumente der Akademie für Umwelt und Energie. Laxenburg, Austria, Akademie für Umwelt und Energie, 1988. Workshop Report, Heft 23.

Singh, Rana K. D. N. Long-term needs of developing countries in technology licensing. Cleveland, Ohio, Les Nouvelles Licensing Executives Society, December 1982.

Singh, Rana K. D. N. *and* W. Bogner, *eds.* Technology management and acquisition. Washington, D.C., International Law Institute, 1984. 3 v.

Stumpf, H. Der Know-how Vertrag. 3. ed. Heidelberg, Verlag für Recht und Wirtschaft, 1977.

Symposium: Ost-West-Symposium Umwelttechnologie, eine grenzüberschreitende Herausforderung. Vienna, Europaverlag, 1987.

United Nations. Guidelines for the acquisition of foreign technology in developing countries with special reference to technology licence agreements. 1973. (ID/98) Sales no.: 73.II.B.1.

_____ Economic Commission for Europe. Airborne sulphur pollution, effects and control. 1984.

_____ Report. Seminar on environmental impact assessment, Warsaw. Geneva, 1987.

United Nations Centre for Science and Technology for Development. Impact of new and emerging areas of science and technology on the development of developing countries. Substantive theme paper for Intergovernmental Committee on Science and Technology. 1987. (A/CN.11/80)

United Nations Conference on Trade and Development. Legislation and regulations on technology transfer. Geneva, August 1980.

United Nations Industrial Development Organization. National approaches to the acquisition of technology. 1987. Development and transfer of technology series, No. 1. (ID/187)

Walsh, L., R. Wurster *and* R. J. Kimber. Quality management handbook. New York, Marcel Dekker, 1986.

World Bank. Environment and development: implementing the World Bank's new policies. Washington, D.C., 1988.

_____ Manual of industrial hazard assessment techniques. Washington, D.C., 1985.

_____ The environmental guidelines. Washington, D.C., 1984.

# Appendix

# CHECK-LISTS AND SCHEDULES

It would be useful to check whether the various aspects discussed in chapter VI have been adequately weighed and the necessary measures taken at various stages of project engineering and technology selection, acquisition and management. The following check-list is provided for this purpose.

## VI-1.   Engineering and technology

*Production programme and plant capacity*

- Describe and justify the production programme and plant capacity in relation to:

    Market requirements and marketing strategy
    Input requirements and supply programme
    Technology and economies of scale in the industry
    Minimum economic size and equipment constraints
    Resource and input constraints
    Project alternatives

*Technology choice*

- Describe the technology to the extent significant for the project, and state the reasons for selection in relation to:

    The basic project objectives and strategy
    Socio-economic impacts
    Ecological impacts (environment impact assessment)
    Technology development (technology forecast)
    Input requirements and constraints
    Availability and possible alternatives

- Describe and justify the preliminary project plan and layout selected and prepare diagrams and data as required for technology assessment and evaluation

- Assess the technology and identify and consider alternatives and critical elements relating, for example, to:

    Market and input requirements
    Production programme and plant capacity
    Economies of scale and minimum economic capacity
    Infrastructure required and available
    Technology absorption capacity
    Hazards and ecological (environmental) impacts
    Availability, industrial property rights etc.

- Evaluate the technologies assessed and justify the choice

*Technology acquisition and transfer*

- Describe in the feasibility study critical elements of technology acquisition and transfer, including any significant conclusions and recommendations with regard to:

    Licensing
    Disaggregation of the technology package
    Suppliers and available alternatives
    Contractual terms and conditions
    Negotiation strategies and purchase of technology

Participation of the licence-holder, foreign equity participation
Costs of technology
Technology transfer

- Describe technology, know-how and related services to be performed by the licensor, in particular:

    Duration and renewal of agreement

    Non-restricted use of unpatented know-how after expiry of agreement

    Full and complete transfer of know-how available with licensor

    Warranty on technology

    Access to improvements during period of agreement

    Industrial property rights—usage rights on all patents and proprietary know-how and choice as to use of brand names

    Supply of imported components and intermediate products by licensor—exercise of option by licensee and determination of suitable pricing formula

    Training, both in-plant and in the plant of the licensor

    Territorial sales rights—avoidance of undue restrictions

- Other licensing terms:

    Payments: lump-sum or royalty or combination

    Other provisions relating to governing law; settlement of disputes; confidentiality; quality control; sublicensing; reporting; assignability, *force majeure* etc.

- Define adequate measures to be undertaken for technology absorption

- Identify and recommend a programme for continuing technology assessment, monitoring and forecasting in the relevant field of production

*Plant layout and basic engineering*

- After selection of technology, prepare the plant layout, drawings, basic design and engineering. These charts and drawings should adequately reflect the interrelationship between environmental conditions and constraints, socio-economic infrastructure, technology, equipment, constructions and material flows and inputs.

- Make sure that the plant layout and basic engineering:

    Are in accordance with the technology and know-how selected

    Are determined in relation to various equipment categories such as basic plant and production, auxiliary, testing and research, and replacement equipment, including spare parts and tools

    Provide for the levels of local integration or value-added sought to be achieved in the various processes of production

    Provide for the required levels of automation considered necessary for competitive production, and where a substantial level of automation is required, provide for skill development for operations and maintenance

    Consider any possible constraints and limitations in ordering capital equipment, including foreign exchange and government policies on machinery and maintenance equipment imports

    Take into account the availability of locally manufactured machinery and equipment, including costs and delivery period

    Provide for specialized erection and installation of machinery that may be necessary

*Site*

Land purchase, including all costs of purchase
Soil survey
Survey of special hazards, such as earthquakes, flooding and abnormal meteorological
   conditions

*Site preparation and development*

Location and relocation of structures, pipes, cables, power lines, roads
Demolition and removal of existing structures and foundations
Wrecking, grubbing

Site grading, cutting and filling to establish general job levels but not detailed grading
Diversion of streams etc.
Road improvements and diversions
Railway sidings and improvements
Pipe corridors
Dock and wharfage requirements
Water supply contribution
Electric power supply contributions (high and low tension)
Sewerage and waste disposal works
Communications (telephone, telex, fax etc.)

Temporary work for plant construction, if not covered under unit prices of civil works
   (site overheads)
Landscaping, including plants, grass, sods, water basins etc.

*Civil works—outdoor works, structures*

Foundations, pile foundations, slurry trench walls, walls, soil consolidation
Drainage, lowering of groundwater table
Steel sheet piling, ramps
Foundations for all kinds of heavy equipment

*Civil works—buildings*

Main plant buildings
Plant structural steelwork
Chimneys and stacks
Buildings for service plants
Stores, storage buildings, warehousing
Laboratories, workshops, offices
Medical and first aid centres, fire station
Canteen, change rooms, lavatories
Site security, fencing, gate houses
Traffic lights, outdoor lights
Garages, car parks, cycle sheds
Customs and excise offices, weighbridge
Drainage, sewage system
Pipe and cable ducts
Land reinstatement, landscaping etc.
Railway tracks
Residential buildings

*Process plant*

Process plant machinery and equipment

Special erection costs for plant items
Special materials, such as catalysts, if they entail investment costs
Inspections and tests
Safety and fire protection equipment
Ventilation, air conditioning (to remove toxic gases, vapours etc.)
Effluent treatment plant
Instrumentation and control
Pipework and valves
Insulation and painting
Costs of process development and prototype testing
Stand-by plant

*Service plant and equipment*

Steam-generating plant and auxiliaries
Power generation plant and auxiliaries
Electricity connection charges
Transformer and switch gear
Cabling
Starters
Stand-by power supplies
Plant and pipework for water storage, treatment and distribution
Process, cooling and drinking water supplies

Emission-handling and treatment
Oil and grease separators
Pumping stations and screw conveyors
Waste storage boxes
Refuse burning plants etc.

Internal transport, conveying and storage of materials
Supplies, fuel, intermediate and finished products
Elevators, cranes etc.
Heating and lighting services
Cooling, refrigeration equipment
Compressed air, inert gas supplies

Maintenance and repair equipment
Spare parts, if investment costs are involved
Operating and maintenance manuals, instructions, drawings
Test equipment

Lightning protection
Communication equipment and installations (telephone, telex etc.)

*Overhead costs, incorporated fixed assets*

*Engineering costs*
Process and plant design, basic engineering
Detailed engineering if not covered under civil works or machinery and equipment
Inspections costs, consultants and specialists, including travel
Cost of models, prototype design

*Temporary facilities required for construction*
Site engineer: office etc.
Temporary supply of power, water etc.
Temporary access, storage facilities, site security (fencing etc.)
Construction workshops
Camp, canteen

*Other direct costs of project implementation*

Preparation and issue of bid documents for construction of civil works and other
 facilities in accordance with a phased programme
Evaluation of bids, negotiations and purchasing
Inspection, commissioning (including travel)
Supervision of construction and start-up
Direct labour, contract labour, including overtime work
Transport costs, unloading and handling charges

*Pre-production expenditures*

Process or patent fees, agent fees
Legal and insurance fees
Consultant fees

Research and development expenditures
Central administration expenditures
Pre-production marketing costs
Training expenditures
Miscellaneous taxes and duties

Commissioning and start-up expenditures

*Working capital*

Inventories built up during the construction phase
Raw materials
Factory supplies
Spare parts
Products

## Schedule VI-1. Estimate of technology costs
*(insert in schedules VI-4, X-3 and X-1 or X-2)*

(a) Technology selected (description, specifications, suppliers ...)

(b) Costs:

### Lump-sum payments (incorporated fixed assets) [a]

| Technology, know-how | Lump-sum payments | | | Year |
| | Foreign | Local | Total | |
|---|---|---|---|---|
| | | | | |
| Total | | | | |

### Fixed royalty payments (operating or marketing costs) [b]

| Year | Technology, know-how | Royalty payments | | |
| | | Foreign | Local | Total |
|---|---|---|---|---|
| 1 | | | | |
| 2 | | | | |
| 3 | | | | |
| . | | | | |
| . | | | | |
| n | | | | |

### Royalty payments ( __% of annual sales revenues) [b]

| Year | Technology, know-how | Royalty payments | | |
| | | Foreign | Local | Total |
|---|---|---|---|---|
| 1 | | | | |
| 2 | | | | |
| 3 | | | | |
| . | | | | |
| . | | | | |
| n | | | | |

[a] Insert in schedule X-1 (or VI-2/2) or X-2.
[b] Insert in schedules VI-4 and X-3.

## Schedule VI-2/1. Estimate of investment costs:
## plant machinery and equipment
### (insert in schedule VI-2/2)

Project:
Date:
Source:

[ ] Construction phase
[ ] Operational phase

## ESTIMATE OF INVESTMENT COSTS

| Plant machinery and equipment | | | | | Currency: | | | |
|---|---|---|---|---|---|---|---|---|
| Main plant item or plant unit[a] | | | | | Units: | | | |

| N | Q | U | Item description[b] | Unit cost | Cost | | | Year[d] |
|---|---|---|---|---|---|---|---|---|
| | | | | | Foreign | Local | Total | |
| | | | Plant machinery[c]<br>Pre-mixing unit<br>Heat exchanger<br>Distilling column<br>Rectification unit<br>etc.<br><br>Plant equipment<br>...<br>...<br>... | | | | | |
| **Total investment costs,**<br>**plant unit (item)**<br>(carry over to schedule VI-2/2) | | | | | | | | |

N = number     U = units     Q = quantity

[a] Insert name or description of plant or main plant item.
[b] Plant machinery, plant equipment, auxiliary and service equipment, primary stock of spare parts, wear and tear parts, tools etc.
[c] Insert detailed list of individual items.
[d] Of investment.

198

## Schedule VI-2/2. Summary sheet of investment costs: machinery and equipment
### *(insert in schedule X-1)*

Project:
Date:
Source:

[ ] Construction phase
[ ] Operational phase

---

### SUMMARY SHEET OF INVESTMENT COSTS

| | |
|---|---|
| Plant machinery and equipment [ ]<sup>a</sup> | Currency: |
| Auxiliary and service plant [ ] | |
| Environmental protection, | Units: |
|   plant machinery and equipment [ ] | |
| Incorporated fixed assets [ ] | |
| Stock of primary spare parts etc. [ ] | |

| N | Main plant item or plant unit (cost centre) | Cost | | | Year[b] |
|---|---|---|---|---|---|
| | | Foreign | Local | Total | |
| | Insert from schedule VI-2/1 | | | | |
| **Total investment costs** (carry over to schedule X-1) | | | | | |

N = number

*Note:* For the purpose of economic cost-benefit analysis, local (foreign) cost elements contained in imported (national) equipment should be identified.

<sup>a</sup> Use different sheets for each item.
<sup>b</sup> Of investment (if necessary show subtotals for each year and plant item).

## Schedule VI-3/1. Estimate of investment costs:
## civil engineering works
### (insert in schedule VI-3/2)

Project:
Date:
Source:

[  ]  Construction phase
[  ]  Operational phase

| ESTIMATE OF INVESTMENT COSTS | | | | | | | | |
|---|---|---|---|---|---|---|---|---|
| Civil engineering work[a] | | | | | Currency: | | | |
| Main plant item or plant unit[b] | | | | | Units: | | | |
| N | Q | U | Item description[c] | Unit cost | Cost | | | Year[e] |
| | | | | | Foreign | Local | Total | |
| | | | Structures[d]<br>...<br>...<br>... | | | | | |
| **Total investment costs,**<br>**plant unit (item)**<br>(carry over to schedule VI-3/2) | | | | | | | | |

| N = number | U = units | Q = quantity |
|---|---|---|

[a] Covering construction works, structures, buildings etc., but <u>not</u> site preparation (see schedule V-1).
[b] Insert name or description of plant or main plant item.
[c] Structures, stores, factory buildings, office buildings, office equipment etc.
[d] Insert detailed list of individual items.
[e] Of investment.

## Schedule VI-3/2. Summary sheet of investment costs: civil engineering works
### (insert in schedule X-1)

Project:
Date:
Source:

[ ] Construction phase
[ ] Operational phase

| SUMMARY SHEET OF INVESTMENT COSTS | | | | |
|---|---|---|---|---|
| Civil works, structures, outdoor works etc. [ ]$^a$<br>Buildings [ ]<br>Incorporated fixed assets [ ]<br>Civil works for environmental protection [ ] | Currency:<br><br>Units: | | | |

| N | Main plant item or plant unit (cost centre) | Cost | | | Year$^b$ |
|---|---|---|---|---|---|
| | | Foreign | Local | Total | |
| | Insert from schedule VI-3/1 | | | | |
| **Total investment costs**<br>(carry over to schedule X-1) | | | | | |

N = number

*Note:* For the purpose of economic cost-benefit analysis, local (foreign) cost elements contained in imported (national) equipment should be identified.

$^a$ Use different sheets for each item.
$^b$ Of investment (if necessary show subtotals for each year and plant item).

## Schedule VI-4/1. Estimate of factory costs
### (insert in schedule VI-4/2)

Project:
Date:
Source:                                           [  ]  Direct costs
                                                  [  ]  Indirect costs

| Product/cost centre:<br><br>Code: | First year of production: | Currency:<br><br>Units: | | |
|---|---|---|---|---|
| | Cost projections for year: | | | |
| | *Local costs* | | *Foreign costs* | |
| *Cost item* | *Variable per unit* | *Fixed per period* | *Variable per unit* | *Fixed per period* |
| Raw materials (from IV-1)<br>Factory supplies (from IV-1)<br>Overhead costs of raw materials and factory supplies (from IV-1)<br>Spare parts consumed<br>Repair, maintenance material<br>Royalties (payable on production) (from VI-1)<br>Labour (from VIII-2)<br>  Skilled labour<br>  Unskilled labour<br>Labour overheads (taxes, labour benefits etc.)<br>Factory overhead costs<br>  Salaries, wages<br>  Materials, services<br>  etc. | | | | |
| Total unit costs | | | | |
| Total units per period | | | | |
| Total costs per period | | | | |
| Total local and foreign factory costs | | | | |

## Schedule VI-4/2. Projection of factory costs
### (insert in schedule X-3)

Project:
Date:
Source:

| Product/cost centre: | | | First year of sales: | | Currency: | | |
|---|---|---|---|---|---|---|---|
| Code: | | | | | Units: | | |
| | Total local costs | | | Total foreign costs | | | Grand total |
| Year | Variable | Fixed | Total | Variable | Fixed | Total | |
| | | | | | | | |

*Note*: Units of products sold are defined in schedule III-1 for each product. The grand total for each profit centre may be computed using the same forms. However, data may also be introduced directly into the data input file of the UNIDO COMFAR system.

# VII.    Organization and overhead costs

This present chapter deals with the development and design of the organization needed to manage and control the entire operation of the factory, and with the related overhead costs. The preceding chapters have explored and described the problems of product marketing, providing the necessary material inputs, locating the plant at the optimal site and preparing the engineering design. Project engineering and organizational planning are closely related, and should therefore be undertaken jointly in a series of feedback operations.

The aim of this chapter is to describe the process of organizational planning and the structure of overhead costs, which can be decisive for the financial feasibility of the project. A division of the company into organizational units in line with the marketing, supply, production and administrative functions is necessary not only from the operational point of view, but also during the planning phase, to allow the assessment and projection of overhead costs. Furthermore, it is essential for the feasibility of a project that a proper organizational structure should be determined in accordance with the corporate strategies and policies.

The recommended organization will depend on the social environment as well as on techno-economic necessities. The organizational set-up depends to a large extent on the size and type of the industrial enterprise and the strategies, policies and values of those in a position of power in the organization. It should also be borne in mind that organizations are not static but develop with the project (pre-investment and investment phases, start-up and operation).

While other chapters specifically deal with direct costs, this chapter will deal with indirect or overhead costs. Past experience shows that many feasibility studies neglect or underestimate these costs, which in some projects may have a significant impact on their profitability. Considerations regarding the project organization will help the analyst to identify and quantify these costs. The design and establishment of cost centres in line with the organizational structure will facilitate this task.

## A.    Plant organization and management

Organization is the means by which the operational functions and activities of the enterprise are structured and assigned to organizational units, represented by managerial staff, supervisors and workforce, with the objective of coordinating and controlling the performance of the enterprise and the achievement of its business targets.

The organizational structure of an enterprise indicates the delegation of responsibilities to the various functional units of the company, and is normally shown in a diagram, often referred to as an organigram. Usually, the organization is designed primarily in line with the different functions in the enterprise, such as finance, marketing, purchasing and manufacturing. However, there is no unique organization pattern. It is also possible to base organizational structures on products or production lines (for instance, profit or cost centres), or on geographical areas or markets; the latter are typical for marketing organizations.

The problem of structuring and organizing the work and the delegation of executive responsibilities must not be seen only from the functional point of view, because various sociocultural factors may militate against the mere copying of such organizations in other countries. This aspect is also very important in developing countries, when special organizational structures are required for the optimal use of imported technologies.

### Organizational functions

The organizational functions are the building blocks of the company. As reflected in figure XXVII, they may be grouped into the following organizational units in line with the specific requirements of the individual company:

- General management of the enterprise
- Finance, financial control and accounting
- Personnel administration
- Marketing, sales and distribution
- Supplies, transport, storage
- Production:
    Main plant
    Service plants
    Quality assurance
    Maintenance and repair

**Figure XXVII.   Example of an organization chart for an industrial enterprise**

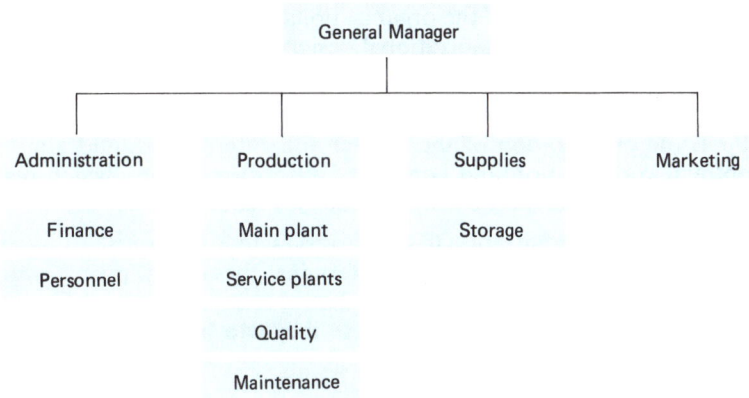

The organizational structure of the company can take a number of shapes, the most common being the pyramid shape, which has the following three organizational levels:

- Top management, normally entrusted with long-term strategic planning, budgeting, coordination and control
- Middle management, normally entrusted with the planning and control of the organizational functions, such as sales, production, purchasing and finance
- Supervisory management that plans and controls the day-to-day operations and activities within the organizational units under its supervision

Regardless of the type of manufacture engaged in by a plant, the analysts will have to consider the establishment of a number of cost centres that are common to most manufacturing companies. These cost centres are explained below in the section on accounting and financial control. Cost centres will be described in terms of:

- Placement within the organization
- Operational purpose, responsibilities and authorities
- Main tasks
- Labour and skill requirements
- Inputs and outputs

## B. Organizational design

A rough outline of organizational structures and of related costs may be included in a pre-feasibility study (rarely in an opportunity study), especially when organizational aspects could have a significant impact on the feasibility of a project. Usually the design of the organizational set-up of a project is covered in the feasibility study. The organizational design for both the construction and the operating phase depends on internal and external project requirements and conditions, and is prepared for the following two reasons:

- First, the organization of the project and enterprise should aim at the optimal coordination and control of all project inputs, which make it possible to implement the project strategies economically;
- Secondly, the organizational set-up serves to structure the investment and production costs and to determine the costs linked with the corresponding organizational units. For accounting purposes these costs are treated as overhead costs, unless they can be directly related to a specific product or cost centre.

The design of the organization usually includes the following steps:

- The goals and objectives for the business are stated;

- The functions that are necessary to achieve the goals are identified;
- The necessary functions are grouped or related;
- The organizational framework or structure is designed;
- All key jobs are analysed, designed and described;
- A recruiting and training programme is prepared.

The organizational planner will then have to consider some of the fundamental aspects of optimal organization. These may include:

- The span of control, that is, the numbers of employees reporting to a supervisor
- The number of organizational levels
- A subdivision of activities by function, process, equipment, location, product or classes of customers
- The distribution of responsibilities and authority

Later, once the project is approved, all information applicable to the organization will be collected in an organization manual, which may include:

- An overall description and identification of the strategic objectives and policies of the company
- A description of the various functional units, sections or divisions of the company, specifying the main tasks to be performed by the individual units
- Job descriptions for at least all key personnel
- Administrative procedures according to which transactions are to be carried out, both internally and externally, and covering all functions and all levels of the company

Other descriptive material may be included according to the local conditions and the way in which the company operates.

## General management

Depending on the type and size of an enterprise, the general manager with his office is responsible for the entrepreneurial functions. These are management functions that are fundamental for the existence of an enterprise and may not be delegated. Often, especially in the case of medium-sized industrial plants, the general manager is also in charge of general administrative functions, such as personnel and finance. In cases where technical and technological aspects are essential for the enterprise, the production manager could be in charge of the enterprise.

The feasibility study should determine the staffing requirements for the office of the general manager in order to allow estimates of personnel and other overhead costs related to this office. Cultural and social aspects should be considered, and the study team should not try to blindly copy organizational patterns that have proven successful in other countries.

An administrative unit or department has to be planned to provide the management with the financial and accounting information required for the efficient and economic operation of the enterprise. National business laws and fiscal regulations also require that the financial situation of the enterprise should be reported regularly and in line with standards determined by the authorities.

The accounting department is usually ranked as a staff function because it has no supervisory functions within the enterprise. In some cases all administrative operations are centralized in one department, combining for example the functions of accounting, purchasing and personnel. Specialized staff is required for cost accounting, bookkeeping, calculation of salaries and wages, budgeting etc. Again the number and qualifications of the required staff have to be determined to allow the projection of personnel costs. Estimated office overhead costs for materials, services and communications must be included in the projection of administrative overhead costs.

To facilitate cost planning and control already during the pre-investment phase the project should be divided into cost centres. It is not possible within the framework of this *Manual* to enter into the intricacies of cost-centre accounting. In the appendix to this chapter a brief check-list is provided of cost centres that may occur in any plant.

Production cost centres are those areas of activity where all major industrial operations are performed within the context of a manufacturing establishment, for example a vegetable-oil-processing factory. These centres are delinting, decorticating, pressing, solvent extraction, bagging, neutralizing, bleaching, deodorizing, winterizing, filling and packing.

Service cost centres are those areas of activity that render the supplementary services necessary to the smooth running of the plant, such as:

- Social services, including housing, health services, cafeterias, transport and company food stores

- Plant management, production workshops

- Off-site transport: all transport activities that are not related to connected production processes

- Purchasing of raw materials, spare parts and other supplies

- Stores for purchased raw materials, spare parts, packing materials, supplies and equipment

- Repair and maintenance of machinery and equipment, buildings, vehicles etc.

- Power supply and distribution for production and general use

- Steam generation and distribution

- Water supply (when the company has its own supply)

- Laboratories, process control

- Effluent disposal

Changes may be made according to the organizational structure of the factory under study.

Administrative and financial cost centres comprise all activities related to managerial planning, control and performance evaluation. Practice varies with respect to the number of centres in which these activities are grouped. Larger factories maintain specialized centres for planning, budgeting, costing, statistics, personnel training, accounting and finance. Smaller factories have fewer such centres. Hence, all expenses related to administration and finance should be accumulated in one centre under the designation of administration and finance.

## Marketing organization

The marketing department is the organizational unit carrying out the marketing functions described in chapter III. Usually it has an independent line function, but the individual structure of the unit varies according to type of customer, the nature of the product, its geographical distribution and the sales and distribution pattern. Establishing a marketing organization for a new project (or product) requires the prior careful determination of both the marketing objectives and the means required and available.

Sales and distribution of a product in a country where the infrastructure and the means of communication are limited may also require a more costly marketing organization, and seriously restrict the competitiveness of the company in some cases. There are many examples of production plants based on economies of scale that could not compete with the local traditional suppliers, owing to a large and costly sales and distribution system.

## Organization of supplies

The supply system includes the provision of inputs of materials and services, shipping of the goods, storage and inventory control. A number of placements within the organization are possible. Some companies may have a central purchasing department and stores attached to the production units. The purchasing department may be an independent line function or it may be placed under the supervision of the production unit. If a company is divided into production plants that are geographically separated, it may be practical to attach a small decentralized purchasing unit to each of these production plants.

In some large companies the entire supply system is entrusted to a purchasing or supplies department. Its purpose is to purchase goods and services from selected suppliers according to approved specifications and bills of quantity, and to place them at the disposal of the production plant according to a supply schedule derived from the production programme. In some cases it may be necessary to include in the duties of the purchasing department the transport of goods from suppliers.

It is the responsibility of the purchasing department to contribute to the overall profit generation of the company by obtaining the best possible prices, while avoiding the storage of larger quantities of input materials than are required for reasonably safeguarding the production requirements. In developing countries procurement can be critical because of various infrastructural and other socio-economic constraints. Supply stocks must therefore often be considerably higher than in industrialized economies.

Purchasing will normally cover the provision of both goods and services from domestic and overseas suppliers. Typical tasks will therefore include:

- Selection and evaluation of suppliers

- Requesting bids or arranging international competitive bidding
- Ordering and dispatch
- Shipping and clearing, quality control of incoming goods
- Warehousing
- Invoice control and payments of suppliers

## Organization of storage

The flow of materials, from the moment of purchasing through the entire manufacturing process until the point of selling or delivery of the products, needs to be organized in order to secure the undisturbed operation of the factory. Stock control must aim at keeping stocks of materials and products low to avoid unnecessarily high net working capital requirements, while maintaining the minimum stock required for safe and uninterrupted operation.

Often the control of the entire material and product flow, including storage, remains within the production department. In this case the production programme as well as products in stock would be planned jointly with the marketing department, and supplies would be ordered through the purchasing department. The stock of spare parts is usually controlled by the maintenance unit.

## Organization of production

The organization of the production plant is designed in accordance with the production process, as discussed in chapter VI, and in line with the availability of human recources determined in chapter VIII. Like the other organizational units, the production department causes indirect costs, such as costs of plant management, general supplies and services, which have to be assessd in the feasibility study. These costs are subsumed under factory overheads.

## Organization of quality assurance

The quality assurance department is responsible for the total quality of a product from its conception to its delivery to the end-user (including, for example, the quality of an automobile service system). The type and scope of quality assurance depends, however, on the industry and the size of the project. Its placement in the organization often reflects the wish that the quality assurance department must be independent of other departments, whose activities it monitors and evaluates (engineering and research, production, after sales service etc.). Quality assurance may, however, be placed elsewhere in the organization. It may be part of the production department or be subordinated to the purchasing department. In the latter cases, the responsibilities of the quality assurance department are usually more restricted and the tasks limited to the control of production, incoming goods and outgoing products.

If the company depends on imported raw materials, intermediate products or factory supplies, quality control and inspections on the premises of the suppliers may be necessary. In this case quality control may have to be subcontracted to specialized enterprises.

Labour and skills requirements vary in accordance with the level of quality assurance, and with the extent to which the department will be responsible for quality monitoring of research, engineering, production and perhaps also service. Inputs required for the activities of a quality assurance department also vary in accordance with the responsibilities of the department. A fully integrated department will need almost all technical documentation from functional specifications to the final production and works specifications, and in addition engineering schedules, production plans and copies of orders to suppliers. Output material from the same department will include design reviews, quality control reports and recommendations and quality statistics.

## Organization of maintenance

The maintenance function is often placed within the production department. However, the placement of the maintenance unit within the individual company organization depends on where it can best fulfil its main objective of ensuring that plant equipment is ready and functioning as required in accordance with the production programme. The structure of the maintenance unit also depends on the maintenance policy that is adopted by the individual company. In a highly industrialized environment where equipment suppliers or their agents are at hand, and where maintenance contractors can be easily found, the unit may only have to deal with preventive maintenance and emergency repairs. As the environment becomes less industrialized, more maintenance operations will have to be undertaken by the maintenance unit.

If a maintenance unit is wholly dependent on its own resources it will be responsible for both preventive and corrective maintenance of all plant equipment, auxiliary equipment and buildings. Consequently, a complicated manufacturing plant will require a highly developed, well-staffed maintenance organization. It will probably also need a vast amount of imported spare parts and materials that will increase the foreign exchange and working capital requirements of a project. For such a plant it will be necessary to prepare a comprehensive maintenance analysis, before the technology choice can be made, because maintenance requirements and costs for sustaining plant operation may be prohibitive under the conditions assessed for the project.

Understanding of the role of maintenance has proven to be extremely important in industrialized countries, where it has taken many years to develop the necessary motivation. In some developing countries this problem may be the most serious hindrance to the establishment of an efficient maintenance organization. The unit should be mainly staffed with the technicians who would be directly involved in the daily maintenance operations.

## Organization of personnel

The personnel unit deals with all subjects related to human resources, such as recruitment and training of personnel and updating and developing skills and knowledge. If management of the company staff and workforce is relatively simple, there may be no need for a separate personnel unit. In that case personnel matters may be placed as a staff function or could be incorporated in the administrative department. However, if human resource

211

management is of significant importance for the feasibility of a project, a special personnel department would be required.

The sociocultural environment of the project usually has a great impact on the organization and overhead costs of the personnel department. For example, labour laws directly applicable to the hiring and laying-off of personnel, local cultural habits or customs may have a decisive impact on recruitment, employment and development of the human resources required in the project. In some countries religious rules or customs may restrict women from working with men, or require special prayer facilities at the factory. In other projects potential conflict between different ethnic or social groups may require special measures and entail significant costs.

*Human resource development* may be an important task of a personnel department. Training may have to be organized to increase skills of staff and workers, to secure or increase the quality of products etc. Other important subjects could be training related to health protection, the introduction and maintenance of safety measures, and the operation of machinery and plants in accordance with environmental protection measures.

The feasibility study should determine the costs relating to this organizational unit, and special attention should be given to costs arising during the start-up phase of the project.


## C.  Overhead costs

In most feasibility studies little attention is paid to the planning of overhead costs. Overhead costs are frequently computed as a percentage surcharge on total material and labour inputs or other reference items, a procedure that, in most cases, is not sufficiently accurate. Admittedly, the amount of time and effort required to calculate overhead costs should be positively related to the results to be obtained. Overhead costs should be grouped as outlined below.


### Factory overheads

Factory overheads are costs that accrue in conjunction with the transformation, fabrication or extraction of raw materials. Typical cost items, with chapter references, are listed below.

- Wages and salaries (including benefits      Chapter VIII
  and social security contributions) of
  manpower and employees not directly
  involved in production

- Factory supplies, e.g.      Chapter IV

  Utilities (water, power, gas, steam)

  Effluent disposal

  Office supplies

- Maintenance      Chapter VII

These cost items should be estimated by the service cost centres where they accrue.

## Administrative overheads

Administrative overheads should only be calculated separately in cases where they are of considerable importance, otherwise they could be included under factory overheads. Typical cost items, with chapter references, are listed below.

- Wages and salaries (including benefits and       Chapter VIII
  social security contributions

- Office supplies                                  Chapter IV
  Utilities
  Communications

- Engineering                                      Chapter VII
  Rents
  Insurances (property)

- Taxes (property)                                 Chapter VII

These cost elements should be estimated for administrative cost centres such as management, bookkeeping and accounting, legal services and patents, traffic management and public relations.

## Marketing overheads

Direct selling and distribution costs, such as special packaging and forwarding costs, commissions and discounts, should be calculated separately for each product, as described in chapter X. Indirect marketing costs that cannot be easily linked directly with a product are usually treated as marketing overhead costs. These costs are often included under administrative overheads. However, marketing costs should be shown in the feasibility study as a separate cost group, if the total represents a significant share of the total costs of products sold. Typical cost items, with chapter references, are listed below.

- Wages and salaries (including benefits and       Chapter VII
  social security contributions)

- Office supplies, utilities, communication        Chapter III
  Indirect marketing costs, advertising,
      training etc.

## Depreciation costs

Depreciation is an accounting method used to distribute the initial investment costs of fixed assets over the lifetime—usually the fiscal standard lifetime—of the corresponding investment. Annual depreciation charges are frequently included under overhead costs. Since, however, these costs are treated differently for the discounted cash flow method, depreciation costs should be shown separately from overhead costs. In this way it is still possible to include them for the calculation of factory and unit costs, as well as for financial evaluation.

Depreciation costs should be calculated on the basis of the original value of fixed investments, according to the methods applicable (straight line, declining balance or accelerated depreciation method etc.) and rates adopted by management and approved by the tax authorities. The same applies for non-tangible assets, such as capitalized pre-production expenditures.

## Financial costs

Financial costs such as interest on term loans, should be shown as a separate item, because they have to be excluded when computing the discounted cash flows of the project, but are to be included for financial planning, as described in chapter X. When forecasting overhead costs, attention should be given to the problem of inflation. In view of the numerous cost items in overhead costs, it will not be possible to estimate their growth individually, but only as a whole. A sound judgement has therefore to be made as to the magnitude of the overall inflation rate of overhead costs.

**Bibliography**

Aggteleky, Béla. Fabrikplanung. Munich, Hanser, 1970.

Anthony, R. N. Essentials of accounting. 3. ed. Reading, Massachusetts, Addison-Wesley, 1983.

Barnes, M. C. Company organization—theory and practice. London, Allen and Unwin, 1970.

Beams, F. A. Advanced accounting. 2. ed. Englewood Cliffs, New Jersey, Prentice-Hall, 1982.

Blunt, P. Organizational theory and behaviour; an African perspective. London, Longman, 1983.

Fess, P. E. *and* C. S. Warren. Accounting principles. 14. ed. Cincinnati, Ohio, 1984.

Grant, E. L. *and* L. F. Bell. Basic accounting and cost acounting. 2. ed. New York, McGraw-Hill, 1964.

Grant, E. L., W. G. Ireson *and* R. S. Leavenworth. Principles of engineering economy. 6. ed. New York, John Wiley, 1976.

McBeath, G. Organization and manpower planning, 3. ed. London, Business Books, 1974.

Nystrom, P. C. *and* W. H. Starbuck. Handbook of organizational design. Oxford, Oxford University Press, 1981. 2 v.

Schmalensee, R. *and* R. D. Willig. Handbook of industrial organization. Amsterdam, North-Holland, 1989.

Seicht, G. Moderne Kosten- und Leistungsrechnung. Vienna, Linde, 1977.

Seidler, L. J. *and* D. R. Carmichael. Accountants' handbook. 6. ed. New York, Wiley, 1981.

Tirole, J. The theory of industrial organization. Cambridge, Massachusetts, Massachusetts Institute of Technology, 1989.

# Appendix

## CHECK-LISTS AND SCHEDULES

### VII-1.   Cost centres

*Production cost centres*

Production cost centres usually comprise the main production (or plant) units or production lines, for which costs must be determined.

*Service cost centres*

Social service
Plant management
Off-site transport
Purchasing
Stores
Repair and maintenance
Power, heat, light, air-conditioning
Steam
Water supply
Laboratories, quality control
Effluent disposal

*Administration and finance cost centres*

General administration
Personnel
Training
Accounting and bookkeeping

### VII-2.   Overhead costs[71]

Plant maintenance
Storage costs (personnel, materials and services etc.)
Internal transport services
External transport costs
Insurance

Administrative and service personnel
   Salaries, wages

Social overhead costs (health etc.)

Communications and travel
Office supplies
Rents
Leasing fees (unless covered under financial costs)
Recurring land charges
Property taxes

---

[71]Use schedules for indirect costs: marketing costs (schedule III-2); factory costs (schedule VI-4); and estimate of overhead costs (schedule VII-1).

215

Royalties, licence fees
Environmental protection costs
    Costs for preventive measures
    Costs for curative measures
    Duties, taxes etc. payable as emission charges

Depreciation charges (costs)

Costs of financing

## Schedule VII-1. Estimate of overhead (indirect) costs
### (insert in schedule VII-2)

Project:
Date:
Source:

| Product/cost centre:<br><br>Code: | First year of production: | | Currency:<br><br>Units: | |
|---|---|---|---|---|
| | Cost projections for year: | | | |
| | Local costs | | Foreign costs | |
| Cost item | Variable per period | Fixed per period | Variable per period | Fixed per period |
| | | | | |
| Overhead (indirect) costs | | | | |
| Total units per period | | | | |
| Total costs per unit | | | | |
| Total overhead costs | | | | |

## Schedule VII-2. Projection of overhead (indirect) costs
### (insert in schedule X-3)

Project:
Date:
Source:

| Product/cost centre: | First year of sales: | Currency: |
| Code: | | Units: |

| Year | Total local costs | | | Total foreign costs | | | Grand total |
|------|----------|-------|-------|----------|-------|-------|-------|
| | Variable | Fixed | Total | Variable | Fixed | Total | |
| | | | | | | | |

# VIII.  Human resources

This chapter deals with human resource planning. Once the production programme, plant capacity, technological processes to be employed and plant organization have been determined, the human resource requirements at various levels and during different stages of the project must be defined, as well as their availability and costs. The successful implementation and operation of an industrial project needs different categories of human resources—management, staff and workers—with sufficient skills and experience. The feasibility study should identify and describe such requirements and assess the availability of human resources as well as training needs. The study should pay particular attention to the definition and assessment of those skills and experiences which may be critical for the success of the project.

On the basis of the qualitative and quantitative human resource requirements of the project, the availability of personnel and training needs, the cost estimates for wages, salaries, other personnel-related expenses and training are prepared for the financial analysis of the project. In case an economic evaluation is intended, the costs of unskilled labour should be shown separately.

## A.   Categories and functions

The determination of human resources required, as well as the assessment of the resources available for the project, are often an important part of a feasibility study, because managerial or supervisory staff and skilled labour can be a critical factor for the success of a project. The successful operation of even the most professionally designed and well-equipped industrial project will ultimately depend on the skill, experience and productivity of workers, staff and management. A promising and carefully planned project can easily be jeopardized by bad management or the inadequate skills and experience of personnel in key positions. A project with great risks and uncertainties may on the other hand prove to be successful thanks to good management and qualified labour.

Human resources as required for the implementation and operation of industrial projects need to be defined by categories, such as management and supervision personnel and skilled and unskilled workers, and by functions, such as general management, production management and supervision, administration (accounting, purchasing etc.), production control, machine operation and transport. The numbers, skills and experience required depend on the type of industry, the technology used, plant size, the cultural and socio-economic environment of the project location, as well as the proposed organization of the enterprise.

The definition of personnel requirements by categories and functions is necessary for the preparation of a detailed manning table, including the calculation of the total costs of management, staff and labour, and for a comparison of the needed personnel with the resources available in the project region. This comparison will facilitate the assessment of training needs. For the determination of training requirements and overhead costs it is necessary to describe also the required functions and professions or skills, such as those of electricians, drivers, machine operators and accountants.

### Managerial and supervisory staff

The provision of qualified and experienced managers is a basic prerequisite for successful project implementation and operation. It is therefore essential that the requirements of such personnel should be defined in the feasibility study so that they can be recruited in time by the project authorities. In many projects, key senior personnel need to be associated with the project during the pre-production stage and even during the prior stage of project formulation and the feasibility study. The timely provision of qualified staff to manage all the functions of the plant is most important.

Another serious bottleneck to project implementation in many developing countries is the lack of suitably experienced supervisory personnel, and planning for this category should be undertaken well in advance. The feasibility study should define the requirements only on a shift-by-shift basis or at the department level, and state the qualifications and experience necessary. Given the typical lack of such experienced personnel, the timing of recruitment, possible sources of availability and the nature of necessary training programmes should be indicated.

Experience has shown that in most cases it is not too difficult to finance a project proposal, and that even its implementation is not too difficult provided the project has a good management structure. Many poorly performing investment projects suffer mainly from bad management. Thus, before approving a new project, a major rehabilitation or extension of an existing project, the source and cost of managerial and supervisory staff should be determined. It is costly to count on remedial action taken as late as the operating phase of the project.

Local entrepreneurial and managerial capabilities,[72] social factors (for example, the cultural environment and social policies), and sectoral and project-specific requirements, including training and intercultural transfer of such capabilities, should be covered in the feasibility study.

### Skilled and unskilled workers

The timely provision of skilled and unskilled workers is of equal importance to the availability of managerial and supervisory staff. Experience

---

[72]The term entrepreneurial is used here basically to embrace functions and capabilities that are central to the operation and survival of a firm, such as the setting up of corporate objectives and strategies and the motivation and supervision of staff and workers. In large and medium-sized firms such functions are usually divided between the members of the team forming "the management" of a firm, whereas in the small business sector usually one or two persons have to cover all these functions. The role of the "owner-entrepreneur"—bearing the investment risk—is of less importance in this chapter.

shows that the level of skilled labour available in developing countries will in many cases not be in line with the exigencies of the production process and of the machinery and equipment to be installed in the plant under study. The specification of requirements for professionals and skilled and unskilled workers, as well as estimates of the necessary number of workers, are therefore a precondition for the preparation of the manning table, recruitment planning and the design of a training plan.

A definition of the kinds of professional staff, skilled labour and unskilled workers needed should be provided in order to specify the minimum training and professional experience required in order to qualify for the different posts identified. This is even more necessary because of the substantial differences in the available public training programmes for skilled workers in developing countries.

## B.  Socio-economic and cultural environment

Human resource requirements not only depend on techno-economic and financial or commercial factors, but also are determined to a certain extent by social and socio-economic conditons in the country and location of the project.

### Labour conditions, standards and health care

### Legislation and labour terms

Labour terms can be regulated by legislation or trade union contracts or be based on common practice. Employment of women may be subject to specific conditions, traditions and policies. The prevailing rules regarding national holidays, shift work, working hours, and annual, sick and training leave will have an impact on the effective number of working hours and days per year, and therefore affect the human resource requirements, given the production targets and other conditions.

### Labour norms

A common error in the definition of human resource requirements is the adoption of labour norms prevailing in industrialized countries. This might result in over-optimistic estimates of effective machine-hours and productivity, and hence of the resulting production and the financial outcome. Realistic estimates should instead be made, on the basis of experience of and comparisons with similar industrial projects in the project country and region. Differences in skills, experience, productivity and other respects, as compared with industrialized countries, should be accounted for. This is particularly important in the initial stages of production operations.

### Occupational safety

In many developing countries minimum standards of occupational safety have not been established or are not enforced strictly enough. This situation has lead to a shifting of hazardous industries from developed to developing countries, a redeployment of industries that has in some cases dramatically affected the occupational safety of the workers, not to mention the often severe environmental impacts. A feasibility study must therefore also assess the relevant existing regulations on occupational safety, including future trends, and analyse their impact on investment and production costs.

### Health care and social security

The project analyst should also identify and consider necessary plant components regarding arrangements for health care and social security for the human resources to be employed. The cost of such components will have to be estimated and included in the cost tables of the study. ILO has published a number of documents on the subjects of occupational safety, health and working conditions in developing countries and in different employment situations.

## C. Project-related requirements

### Identification of requirements

Staff and labour requirements have to be planned for the implementation or pre-production phase as well as for the start-up and operating phases. Particular attention should be paid to those enterprise functions which are essential for the feasibility of the investment, and for which special professional skills and experience of employees and workers are required, as in the areas of enterprise management (entrepreneurial and management functions), marketing, raw materials and factory supplies, production processes and product characteristics, organization and personnel and construction management. Environmental and other locational aspects, including infrastructural services, may also require special personal skills. An export-oriented project may for instance call for particular attention to staffing in critical functions, such as quality control, marketing and transport of finished goods. A remote plant location with no existing infrastructure but with a sophisticated technology and equipment might put the personnel department (recruitment, training, social infrastructure etc.) in focus. A complicated production process and a high value added might require special skills and experience in maintenance and quality control.

The identification of these significant requirements already at the stage of the feasibility study is both difficult and important. Some common examples of mistakes and their consequences are:

- Failure to provide the project implementation team with experienced and committed personnel often leads to delays and additional costs;
- Bad timing of recruitment may lead to delays and poor utilization of production capacity during the first operating years. Over-optimistic estimates regarding duration and quality of training as well as bad timing often have similar consequences;
- Inadequate maintenance and supply of raw materials and utilities may lead to unplanned and costly production stops that could have been avoided with more experienced and skilled personnel;

- Bad timing of marketing and sales, inexperienced salespersons and sales managers, lack of legal advice before signing of contracts etc. may result in sales volumes and revenues not keeping pace with production;

- Unskilled drivers may cause transport delays, damage, losses and a deterioration in quality of the products being transported.

### Timing of requirements

#### Pre-production phase

When estimating labour requirements, a distinction should be made between the pre-production and the operational phases. During the pre-production phase, it may be assumed that labour requirements occur mainly in conjunction with preparatory measures needed to start the operational phase. Thus, the managerial staff, supervisors, and some foremen and specialized machine operators have to be recruited in advance, not only to be trained, but also to attend to the construction of buildings and the installation of equipment that they will later be operating. Estimates should be made by category of staff and workers, as well as by function, applying standard pro-forma man-month costs to arrive at the labour costs that need to be capitalized. The persons required at this phase should be kept to a minimum to maintain pre-production costs as low as possible.

Foreign expertise may also be required for such functions as detailed engineering or supervision of construction or equipment erection. The number of persons required, together with costs and periods of service, could in each case be indicated. It should be specified when foreign expertise is provided at this stage on a lump-sum basis. When such expertise is provided at the plant site or within the country of the project, the man-months and periods of service should be specified in each case. This is to ensure that suitable training programmes can be set up for domestic personnel easily enough to keep both the number of foreign personnel and the time they are required to a minimum.

#### Operational phase

Requirements during the operating phase may vary over time. Capacity utilization is usually improved gradually and additional shifts may be introduced, bringing about increased production and possibly additional requirements in certain personnel categories.

When estimating labour requirements for the operational phase, the functions and skill levels needed should be determined by departments (schedule VIII-1) and aggregated for the project (schedule VIII-2). A distinction should be made between variable and fixed wage and salary costs, as well as between the local and foreign labour components. The number of shifts should be considered. When calculating the total wage and salary costs, it should be noted that the hourly wage rate and monthly salaries do not constitute the only personnel costs, but that provision should also be made for the following:

- Annual, sick and training leave, which reduce the number of effective working days

- Social security, fringe benefits and welfare costs, annual deposits to pension funds etc., which increase the human resource costs

- Installation grants, subsistence payments and similar cash costs, which occur with recruitment and employment of manpower
- Costs of training
- Payroll taxes

In the case of both wage and salary estimates, it is suggested that these extra labour costs should be covered by surcharges; these should be computed separately for wage- and salary-earners. An example is provided in the appendix to this chapter.

When estimating labour requirements, the qualifications and skills required should be described by categories of labour and staff in order to provide a framework for recruitment and for arranging suitable training programmes. When estimating these requirements, the technology selected, labour availability and changing levels of productivity should be considered.

## Manning tables

Human resource requirements should be defined for the different departments and functions of the project, in accordance with the organizational set-up.

*Organizational set-up.* Human resource requirements will obviously also depend on the management structure, organizational layout, operating plan and other factors related to the financial and commercial features of the project. A close study of chapter VII, which deals with plant organization, is therefore recommended. The number of shifts and production lines, the policy regarding in-house versus external facilities and services, and characteristics of the market and the products are just a few examples of such an influence.

*Manning tables.* Labour planning should start at the departmental level, defining the labour and staff requirements by functions and categories (workers—skilled, semi-skilled and unskilled; staff—managerial, supervisory, administrative and sales). The departmental manning table can be set up according to schedule VIII-1. The manning table of the entire project can be obtained by simply aggregating the departmental manning tables in schedule VIII-2 for labour and staff.

The number of working days in a year is frequently overestimated—planners should be aware of losses of working days because of Sundays, national holidays etc. Often only 200 to 250 working days are actually available each year. In order to provide more information, the manning tables could be related to a certain production level and show how requirements are expected to develop over a period of time. The feasibility study should at least state clearly the underlying conditions and assumptions (for example, whether the requirements refer to the first year of operation or some future year, the production level or the number of shifts).

The manning tables will also be used to analyse availability and recruitment of human resources as well as to estimate operating costs related to these resources. It is therefore advisable to structure the manning tables in such a way as to simplify future work. A specification of requirements related to changes in production (that is, leading to variable costs) and of more fixed requirements is recommended.

# D.  Availability and recruitment

The feasibility study should analyse and assess the general availability of human resources required and describe briefly the background situation, focusing on employment, progress of economic development and of industrialization, urbanization etc. Particular attention should be paid to the availability (supply and demand) of management staff, supervisors and relevant categories of skilled labour. The existence of educational and training institutions and plans for the establishment of new institutions may increase the availability of staff and labour for the project, whereas competing investment plans would increase the demand for human resources.

## Assessment of supply and demand

The feasibility study should not only provide a national outlook, but also briefly describe and assess the employment situation in the region, given its relevance for the project. The assessment of human resources available should cover sectoral employment conditions in the region, unemployment, technical and social infrastructure and migration trends. General economic development, infrastructure development and plans regarding industrial projects should be analysed with regard to possible future changes of the employment situation and availability of personnel.

The following factors should be given due consideration when the availability and employment of human resources are analysed:

- The general availability of relevant human resource categories in the country and the project region
- The supply and demand situation in the project region
- Recruitment policy and methods
- Training policy and programme

Assessments and estimates should as far as possible be explained and justified. For example, a certain technology, safety hazards, sophisticated machinery and equipment, international market orientation and other factors may justify special skills and experience.

It is not sufficient to show only general statistical figures regarding human resource availability. The study should indicate the current supply and demand situation in the region as well as possible shortages in relevant categories. Strong demand from existing industries and expected demand from projects under construction might make it more difficult for the project in question to recruit human resources with the professional background and skills required. The study should also indicate common employment conditions prevailing in the region, and describe significant differences between different parts of the region (such as free schools and housing and special allowances granted in remote areas).

## Recruitment planning

The study should analyse the ability of the project to attract the human resources required. The competitiveness will depend both on the wages and salaries offered and on social security and fringe benefits. A developed and diversified infrastructure in the project region is usually of importance in a situation where certain categories are scarce and difficult to recruit.

Recruitment policy and methods should therefore be assessed in the feasibility study. The methods and means of retaining key personnel for long periods, probable terms of employment and possible fringe benefits to employees and their families should be identified. The policy regarding key personnel is obviously of particular interest.

Difficulties in the recruitment of key personnel (such as managers, supervisors and skilled labour) can be dealt with in different ways:

- Recruitment is combined with intensive training of key personnel in order to meet quality requirements;
- Foreign expertise is recruited.

The use of foreign experts is often subject to debate. It is sometimes regarded as an expensive solution and not in conformity with the general objective of giving priority to domestic human resources. It may on the other hand be the only way in the short term to provide the project with skilled key personnel.

*Foreign experts*

The lack or inadequacy of managerial skills at the technical, administrative and commercial levels can only be offset by sound recruitment policies together with extensive training programmes.

A feasibility study should indicate the qualifications and experience required by key managerial personnel. Persons with basic educational qualifications can generally be found. Insufficient experience can be made up only through intensive training during the pre-production stage. In many cases, such training will have to be arranged in foreign countries and negotiated as part of the technology supply arrangement.

An attempt is often made to compensate for the lack of experience of local managerial talent through the employment of foreign personnel, either by hiring individual expatriates or by signing management contracts with foreign companies. Although this is an expensive course and does not immediately serve the important aim of developing indigenous managerial skills (especially if it extends over long periods, as is often the case), the employment of expatriates may be necessary for the successful implementation of a project.

The study of labour needs should assess the availability of suitable domestic managerial skills and, when foreign assistance is necessary, the duration and conditions of obtaining such assistance should be prescribed. The duration should be for the minimum period possible, and an important condition should be the selection and training of suitable domestic counterpart personnel to take over gradually such responsibilities. The timely arrangement for transferring industrial management skills to developing countries is of great importance, and may be seen as being parallel to the transfer of technologies. The feasibility study should indicate whether such plans for the transfer of know-how are included in the project concept. Very often the domestic and foreign training requirements are underestimated in order not to burden the viability of the project with too high training costs.

## E.    Training plan

Since the lack of experienced and skilled personnel can constitute a significant bottleneck for project implementation and operation in developing countries, extensive training programmes should be designed and carried out as part of the implementation process of investment projects. Such training may be organized already during the pre-production stage at the plant site, at the plant of joint-venture partners or suppliers of technologies and equipment, in similar factories in the country or abroad, or at specialized training institutes. Training can be provided at the factory by managerial and technical personnel and others, by specially recruited experts or by expatriate personnel. This can constitute an important element of technical assistance in cases of technology licensing and joint ventures. Training programmes may need considerable funds. In terms of growth of efficiency and productivity, this may well prove to be the most necessary and appropriate investment. The requirements of training for various levels of plant personnel, the duration of such training for each category, and the location of and arrangements for training should be defined.

The timing of training programmes is of crucial importance, since persons should be sufficiently trained to be able to take up their positions as and when required. Thus, personnel at various levels should already have undergone any training necessary before production starts, during the pre-production and construction stages. In the case of managerial and key non-technical personnel, such training would cover aspects of management and procedure. The training of supervisory and production personnel would cover production processes in sufficient detail to enable them to train others in the same fields. Provision for training is required not only before production starts but also thereafter, since the upgrading of skills, management development and compensation for retirements and resignations is a continuous process.

Training requirements should be defined separately for the pre-production and for the operational phases, in order to provide adequately for pre-production and operational training costs. This is of great importance, since training costs accruing during the pre-production phase will have to be capitalized as pre-production expenditures, whereas training costs originating during the operational phase become part of the production costs. Although it is well known that the labour force in developing countries is in many cases not sufficiently trained to operate modern plants and equipment, provisions for training are still far from sufficient. In some cases pre-production training expenses were between 10 and 15 per cent of total investment costs. However, since training requirements vary from project to project, no generally applicable percentage rates can be given in this *Manual*. If sufficient financial provisions are not made in advance, such unexpected project costs can easily put the project in a critical financial situation.

A training programme can be prepared through the following steps:

- Analysis of personnel characteristics and conditions. Verifiable capabilities, numbers, experience and other characteristics are to be analysed. Restrictions relating to unions and labour laws may be relevant. Socio-cultural characteristics (such as religion, tribal traditions, attitudes regarding women and men working together, traditions regarding job stability and working hours) should be considered;

- Analysis of training requirements. A job (task) analysis will provide information about the different tasks to be carried out. This is related to judgements regarding performance characteristics of different personnel categories. This knowledge will, together with estimates regarding learning curves, form a basis for defining the scope of the training required;

- Formal training is usually related to management and supervisory personnel. It can be carried out in the country or abroad, depending on training facilities, industrial traditions, trainers available and other factors;

- On-the-job training can be carried out in the form of individual or group training. It is usually carried out at the plant in question, but can take place partly in other industries. This kind of training should not be exclusively technical, but should also cover administrative and other duties;

- Updating during future plant operations may be required for management and administrative staff as well as labour. The introduction of new plant equipment and methods of work will require motivated staff to maintain high standards of proficiency and productivity.

## F.   Cost estimates

The manning tables prepared for each department can be used for estimating labour costs. A distinction should be made between variable and fixed costs. There is a tendency to consider non-production labour costs as fixed and production labour costs as variable. This is generally too great a simplification, as most labour costs are semi-fixed or fixed in the short term.[73]

The feasibility study should present the estimated labour costs for each department and function. Underlying assumptions (such as average wages and salaries for different categories) are to be presented. The costs are to be divided into foreign and local currency components. When estimating the total wage and salary costs, provision should be made for the following personnel overhead costs:

- Social security, fringe benefits and welfare costs
- Installation grants, subsistence payments and similar cash costs that occur in connection with recruitment and employment
- Annual deposits to pension funds
- Direct and indirect costs of training
- Payroll taxes

The total labour costs are to be aggregated and transferred to schedule X-3.

---

[73]The feasibility study should provide information not only about the extent of these costs at a certain production level, but also how they vary with production and over time. An identification of fixed and variable cost components as well as foreign and local currency components should be made.

# Bibliography

Arthur, D. Managing human resources in small and mid-sized companies. American Management Association. New York, 1987.

Craig, R. L. *and* L. R. Bittel. Training and development handbook. 2. ed. London, McGraw-Hill, 1976.

Franke, G. Stellen- und Personalbedarfsplanung. Wiesbaden, Gabler, 1977.

Harper, S. Personnel management handbook. Aldershot, Gower, 1987.

Henemann, H. G., D. P. Schwab *and* J. A. Fossum. Managing personnel and human resources; strategies and programmes. Homewood, Illinois, Dow Jones-Irwin, 1981.

Miller, E. L., E. H. Burack *and* M. H. Albrecht. Management of human resources. Englewood Cliffs, New Jersey, Prentice-Hall, 1980.

Odiorne, G. S. Strategic management of human resources. San Francisco, Jossey-Bass, 1984.

Taylor, B. Management development and training handbook. London, McGraw-Hill, 1975.

Tracey, W. R. Human resources management and development handbook. New York, Amacom, 1985.

**Appendix**

# CHECK-LISTS, WORKSHEETS AND SCHEDULES

Human resource planning will have to take into account the needs of the project, that is, the previously determined production (chapter VI) and marketing (chapter III) requirements that form the basis of an organizational concept (chapter VII), as well as the availability of human resources and training needs (chapter VIII) assessed in connection with the choice of location (chapter V). The main steps involved in the assessment of data and preparation of manning tables, including personnel costs, are reflected in the following check-list.

## VIII-1.  Human resource planning

*Labour*

Data and alternatives

Describe data required for the determination of labour inputs

Prepare alternative manning tables, taking into account the following

- Organizational layout
- Strategies and objectives of management for operating the factory
- Skill requirements and level of training of labour
- Availability of labour, local and foreign

Selection of labour

Select and describe in detail the manning table for labour

State reasons for selection

Describe in detail the selected alternative

- Show the structure (organization)
- Prepare detailed manning table considering the subdivision into production labour and non-production labour (administration etc.)

Cost estimate

Estimate annual labour cost at nominal feasible capacity, subdivided into

- Cost of production labour (variable)
- Cost of non-production labour (fixed)

Use schedules VIII-1 and VIII-2 and insert totals in schedule X-10

*Staff*

Data and alternatives

Describe data required for the determination of staff inputs

Prepare alternative manning tables, taking into account the following

- Organizational layout
- Strategies and objectives of management for administering and operating the factory, marketing the products etc.
- Skill requirements and level of staff training
- Availability of staff, local and foreign

Selection of staff

Select and describe in detail the manning table for staff

State reasons for selection

Describe in detail the selected alternative
- Show structure (organization)
- Prepare detailed manning table

Cost estimate

Estimate annual cost of local and foreign staff

Use schedules VIII-1 and VIII-2 and insert totals in schedule X-10

The following worksheet provides a typical example of the computation of surcharges on wages and salaries. All figures given in this example depend on the working programme (working days per week, number of shifts etc.) and on the labour laws and benefits granted to staff and labour. The figures should be checked carefully before being introduced into the projections of production and marketing costs.

*VIII-2. Computation of surcharges on wages and salaries*

| *Effective working days per year* | | *Days* |
|---|---|---|
| Number of days per year (including leap year) $(3 \times 365 + 1 \times 366)/4 =$ | | 365.25 |
| Deduct days not paid | | |
| Sundays $(365.25/7) =$ | | 52.18 |
| Saturdays (if applicable) 52.18 | | 52.18 |
| | | 260.89 |
| Number of paid days per year | or | 261 |
| Deduct paid unproductive working days (typical figures) | | |
| Official and religious holidays, not falling on Saturdays or Sundays | 11 | |
| Leave (according to labour laws) | 20 | |
| Sickness (according to statistics) | 15 | |
| Training etc. | 10 | |
| Others | 5 | |
| Total paid unproductive working days | | −61 |
| Number of effective working days per year | | 200 |

| *Computation of surcharges* | *Days* | *Percentage* |
|---|---|---|
| Unproductive working days $(61/200) \times 100$ | | 30.0 |
| Social security (insurance of all kinds, according to local labour jurisdiction) | | 15.0 |
| Social security for unproductive working days (15 per cent of 30 per cent) | | 4.5 |
| Allowances | | |
| Leave, equivalent to | 20 | |
| Christmas, equivalent to | 20 | |
| Subsistence, equivalent to 1 day per month | 12 | |
| Total allowances in "days", corresponding to $(52/200) \times 100$ per cent | 52 | 26.0 |
| Payroll tax, according to laws in force | | 2.5 |
| Total surcharge | | 78.0 |

*Note:* If shift work or regular overtime work is necessary for plant operation (as in a steelworks), the allowances should be added to the surcharges.

## Schedule VIII-1. Manning table

| MANNING TABLE: | Staff [ ] | | | | | | | | | Labour [ ] | | |
|---|---|---|---|---|---|---|---|---|---|---|---|---|
| Department (cost centre): | Number of persons by salary (P1, P2 ...) or by wage (W1, W2 ...) category[a] and shift | | | | | | | | | | | |
| Function | | _[b] 1 | | _ 2 | | _ 3 | | _ 4 | | | | |
| | S[c] | F | L | F | L | F | L | F | L | F | L | T |
| | 1 | | | | | | | | | | | |
| | 2 | | | | | | | | | | | |
| | 3 | | | | | | | | | | | |
| | 4 | | | | | | | | | | | |
| | 1 | | | | | | | | | | | |
| | 2 | | | | | | | | | | | |
| | .. | | | | | | | | | | | |
| | .. | | | | | | | | | | | |
| Total labour | | | | | | | | | | | | |

> S = shift
> F = foreign personnel (recruited from abroad)
> L = local personnel (recruited nationally)

[a] Use separate schedules for staff (P) and labour (W).
[b] Insert code for salary (P) or wage (W) category.
[c] Note that four shifts will have to be manned in case a plant is operating in three shifts for seven (six) days a week.

## Schedule VIII-2. Estimate of personnel costs
### (insert in schedules VI-4 and VII-1, depending on type of personnel)

Project:
Date:
Source:

| Product/cost centre: Code: | First year of production: | | | Currency: Units: | |
|---|---|---|---|---|---|
| | Cost projections for year: | | | | |
| Direct costs by category | | | | Annual costs per person | | | Total costs per year | |

| Code | F/L | V/F$^a$ | U$^b$ | Costs$^c$ per U | U per year | Costs per person | No. of persons | Total | Variable share of total$^d$ |
|---|---|---|---|---|---|---|---|---|---|
| | | | F | | | | | | |
| | | | L | | | | | | |
| | | | T | | | | | | |
| Total foreign costs | | | | | | | | | |
| Surcharge (%) | | | | | | | | | |
| Surcharge (costs) | | | | | | | | | |
| Grand total, foreign costs | | | | | | | | | |
| Total local costs | | | | | | | | | |
| Surcharge (%) | | | | | | | | | |
| Surcharge (costs) | | | | | | | | | |
| Grand total, local costs | | | | | | | | | |
| Total (foreign + local) | | | | | | | | | |
| Total surcharge | | | | | | | | | |
| Grand total, personnel costs | | | | | | | | | |

| F = foreign | L = local | T = total (foreign + local) | U = unit of time |
|---|---|---|---|

$^a$ Indicate whether number of persons varies with capacity utilization (V) or remain fixed (F).
$^b$ Indicate whether costs are given by hour (H), day (D), week (W), month (M) or year (Y).
$^c$ Indicate foreign (local) cost components, if applicable.
$^d$ Indicate personnel costs, varying proportionally with capacity utilization (production volume).

# IX. Implementation planning and budgeting

The project implementation phase embraces the period from the decision to invest to the start of commercial production. It is very important carefully to plan and analyse this critical phase of the project cycle, because deviations from the original plans and budgets could easily jeopardize the entire project. A primary objective is therefore to determine the technical and financial implications of the various stages of project implementation, with a view to securing sufficient finance to float the project until and beyond the start of production. The choice of financing as well as the financial implications of investment and production delays should receive particular attention.

A series of simultaneous and interrelated activities taking place during the implementation phase have to be identified, including the financial implications they might have for the project. When preparing the implementation plan for the feasibility study it should also be borne in mind that, at a later stage, this plan will be the basis for monitoring and controlling the actual project implementation. The implementation schedule must present the costs of project implementation as well as the schedule for the complete cash outflows (for all initial investments), in order to allow the determination of the corresponding inflows of funds, as required for financing the investments.

This chapter deals with the objectives of implementation planning and budgeting and describes the characteristics of the main implementation work tasks as well as the major constraints that normally have a particular impact on project implementation. Planning techniques commonly applied in implementation planning are briefly introduced, including the use of computers for planning large investment projects. A check-list and a schedule for the preparation of the implementation budget are provided in the appendix to this chapter.

## A. Objectives of implementation planning

To implement a project means to execute all the on- and off-site work tasks necessary to bring a project from the feasibility study stage to its operational stage. While the preparation of the preliminary implementation plan is a part of the feasibility study, the execution of the implementation plan is usually entrusted to a project implementation team.

A realistic schedule should be drawn up for the various stages of the project implementation phase. This is an essential part of the feasibility study, as the implementation of every project must be related to a time schedule. Such a schedule must initially define the various implementation stages in terms of the resources and duration of activities required for each stage. The implementation plan should then establish a time schedule that combines the various stages into a consistent pattern of activities that dovetail into each other. This comprehensive schedule should cover the entire investment phase, including the period between the investment decision and the initial production stage, of which the actual construction period is only one, although the most important, part. Project implementation planning is considered here mainly in order to draw the attention of the project planner to the financial implications of project scheduling and to the possibilities of the early detection of implementation delays and their financial consequences.

Varying periods of time are required for various stages of implementation in different projects. These depend on the circumstances prevailing in a country and the specific nature and requirements of a particular project. A considerable amount of time may elapse between the moment when the investment decision is taken and the actual start of construction. This period comprises the following main activities: appointment of the implementation team, company formation, financial planning, organizational build-up, technology acquisition and transfer, basic engineering, pre-qualification of contractors, consultants and suppliers, preparation of tender documents, tendering, opening of bids, evaluation of bids, negotiations and award of contracts, detailed engineering, acquisition of land, construction works, installation of equipment, purchase of materials and supplies, pre-production marketing, training and plant commissioning, start-up and initial production. Both local and foreign parties may be involved, and many problems will have to be referred to the local authorities.

In some cases the implementation period may be so long that the cost data given in the feasibility study become outdated and need to be reviewed. If a construction period of two, three or more years follows, the cost data used for the investment decision may be several years old by the time of the start-up. Thus it is imperative that all cost data are dated and documented to allow for a continuous cost monitoring by way of both projections and gathering actual data. By comparing the actual data accruing during the construction stage with the data provided in the feasibility study, it will be possible to detect the implications any cost overruns may have on the liquidity, financing requirements and overall profitability of the project.

Implementation planning and budgeting includes the following major tasks:

- Determination of the type of work tasks, on- and off-site, that are necessary to implement the project

- Determination of the logical sequence of events in the work tasks

- Preparation of a time-phased implementation schedule, positioning all the work tasks correctly in time and allowing for adequate time to complete each individual task

- Determination of the resources needed to complete the individual tasks and the extraction of the corresponding costs

- Preparation of an implementation budget and cash flow that will ensure the availability of adequate funds throughout the implementation phase

- Documentation of all implementation data allowing the implementation plan and budget, as well as the forecasts made in the feasibility study, to be updated

# B. Stages of project implementation

The main stages of project implementation planning, which are dealt with in further detail for the case of a new industrial investment project, do not always lend themselves to a stage-by-stage analysis with one stage invariably leading to the other. A great deal of overlapping and simultaneous planning of various activities is inevitable. Training activities, for example, may start very early when key personnel from the company participate in out-of-the country training for a long period, while the training of maintenance technicians and operators is undertaken later during construction and start-up. It is particularly important to link socio-economic conditions of a country, or indeed a region of a country, to many activities of the implementation period in order to evaluate their consequences for the scheduling of the individual activities. An effective port organization may be important to a specific project, but if the highway that connects the port with the company premises is badly maintained because the staff of the responsible authority is inexperienced and underpaid, the project could be critically affected.

## Appointment of the implementation team

The realization of a project is usually entrusted to a project implementation team. If the company in process of formation has qualified personnel, it may decide to establish a project implementation team under its own management. Alternatively, a professional consultant may be selected to act on behalf of the investor.

The team may undertake the entire work or only a part of it. Particularly in the case of large projects some of the tasks, for example detailed engineering or supervision of construction and installation works, are often subcontracted. The main objective in the appointment of a project team is to ensure that the execution of all works comply with the implementation plan and budget, and that proper countermeasures can be enforced in case the actual implementation work and costs deviate from the plan.

## Company formation and legal requirements

The formation of a new company would be necessary, for example, if the investors are starting a new business and the project will not or cannot be embedded within an existing enterprise. In case the investment is to take place within an existing enterprise, some of the legal requirements described below may not be valid.

## Legal process, registration and authorization

If the formation of a company is necessary, the feasibility study should identify for this next stage in project implementation any local, national, bilateral or international rules and regulations to be adhered to, and which procedures prescribed by the local authorities are to be followed. To avoid unnecessary delays, the use of legal assistance may be mandatory. A number of national and international documents and guides exist that describe the contents of contracts between companies and of documents that have to be submitted to the authorities. Rules and customs vary from country to country, and the procedures can be rather time-consuming.

Company formation can generally be divided into the following four steps:

- Signing of a letter of intent between business partners to establish a company. In case of an international joint venture,[74] such a letter of intent is signed by the local and foreign partners. One of the subjects covered by the letter of intent may be the joint preparation of a feasibility study for the venture. Should this study lead to positive conclusions during the pre-investment phase, the subsequent three steps will follow as part of the investment phase;

- Agreement between the business partners on the financial arrangements and the drafting of the documents required by the authorities;

- Formal application to the authorities;

- Official approval or registration of the new company.

The legal procedure of forming a joint venture can be rather complicated and time-consuming. Before a project can be executed as a joint venture, a legal framework must be established. The main element in this framework is the legal formation of a limited liability company in the host country with the joint venture partners as shareholders. In many developing countries this may take 4 to 6 months, and expert assistance may be required.

In case of a joint venture, a memorandum and articles of association will be drafted. Sometimes this will have to correspond to the joint venture agreement signed earlier by the partners. Depending on the local regulations for the establishment of enterprises, as well as the type and size of the new company, various costs may arise during this stage of project implementation (covering, for example, obligatory publication of company by-laws, appointment of a board of directors, meetings, travel, appointment and authorization of general managers, establishment of bank accounts, duties and taxes and legal assistance). These costs may form a significant part of the pre-production capital expenditures, and have to be included in the feasibility study to the extent significant for financial budgeting.

### Governmental approvals

Government approval procedures may take considerable time in certain developing countries, even at the initial stage, particularly if foreign investment is involved. Government approval is required, in many cases, to import machinery and equipment and in respect of technology supply arrangements.

---

[74]As a rule, the legal document between partners in the formation of a joint venture includes information on the following subjects: identification of the parties; power of attorney; name, objective and starting date of the company; obligations of the partners; finance; management; accounting and auditing; termination clauses; and other legal requirements. After the conclusion of the internal agreement between the partners, the new company should be registered and its establishment authorized by the local authorities. This may require drawing up a number of documents in the countries of both the foreign joint venture partner and the local partner. To avoid delays, the official procedure should be studied in detail well ahead of registration and authorization.

The import of intermediate goods, including processed materials, parts and components, may also require the sanction of governmental agencies at the production stage. In all these cases, adequate time should be provided to obtain the necessary approvals and to avoid creating bottlenecks. It is difficult to specify a fixed time-frame, as conditions differ from country to country, but in those countries in which approvals have to be obtained, from 1 to 6 months is necessary in most cases.

## Financial planning

After the decision to invest has been taken and once the total investment costs and their scheduling are known, detailed arrangements for project financing need to be initiated in line with the financial requirements of project implementation. A sound debt-equity ratio should be aimed at, taking into account supplier credits, institutional loan financing and investor funds. There must be a good understanding at the feasibility stage of all the implementation costs. Only with such a comprehensive assessment will it be possible to determine the financial requirements and the accruing financial costs that also constitute a part of the initial investment costs.

## Project management and organization

The implementation plan and schedule prepared for the feasibility study will normally form the basis for the future work of a project management team. When implementing a project, the investor should first set up a project management team. It is usually advisable to appoint a key person who would build up a company-internal management team, or select outside project management consultants. The team should have the necessary authority *vis-à-vis* contractors and consultants to ensure the efficient and timely implementation of the project. It would also be an asset if the team members have an intimate knowledge of local conditions. The team should not only remain active during the implementation period, but should ideally form the nucleus of the managerial, technical and operational staff that is to be put in charge of operating the plant.

## Organizational build-up

During the stage of organizational build-up the recruitment of human resources is initiated. The recruitment schedule outlining when personnel in the various categories is needed depends on the type of manufacture, and the availability of labour and staff. Training of new employees may begin at a very early stage, and might require that some of the key people be trained abroad. Moreover, to begin other training activities, expatriate instructors may have to be mobilized, training materials provided and training facilities made ready. Consequently, the training plan that has been prepared earlier in the feasibility study is an important planning tool for the implementation team. Recruitment is too often left to a very late stage, and training programmes are initiated only when the plant is ready to commence production, leading to unnecessarily poor capacity utilization in the early production stages.

## Technology aquisition and transfer

The acquisition of technology is a key element of the implementation phase. The selected technology has many legal, economic, financial and technical aspects, and negotiations with technology suppliers may take considerable time in certain cases, particularly if minority or significant participation is sought from the licensors. Legal problems such as patent rights, exploitation limitations, or restrictions on the transfer of technology and trade names may sometimes have to be solved. If the contractual obligations of the technology suppliers include training, this should be included in the training plan (see chapter VIII). The feasibility study should contain a projection of the time schedule and the costs related to the acquisition and transfer of the technology chosen for the project. Moreover, the time allocated for the detailed engineering design will depend on the kind and complexity of the technology (see also chapter VI).

## Detailed engineering and contracting

### Detailed engineering

The final plant layout and design as prepared in the feasibility study (see chapter VI) will be the point of departure for detailed engineering. During the implementation phase the entire documentation for site preparation, ordering of machinery and equipment, civil works and plant erection will be elaborated. The generation of drawings, descriptions, bills of quantity and equipment specifications engages many engineers, architects and planners, and will require efficient coordination. The time required and the cost of this work have to be estimated in the feasibility study.

A complete set of technical documentation must be supplied to the implementation team well ahead of the start of the construction and installation stage. If detailed technical information is available already in the feasibility study stage, it may be useful to annex it to the study.

An important aspect usually not receiving proper attention is the provision of operating and maintenance manuals. In case of different suppliers the manuals should be uniform in layout and arranged in such a way that the text, drawings and diagrams can be easily utilized by the future operators and maintenance personnel.

### Tendering, negotiations and award of contracts

The phase of tendering, negotiations and contract awards includes prequalification of contractors, consultants and suppliers, preparation of tender documents, tendering, evaluation of tenders, contract negotiations and award of contracts. It is beyond the scope of this *Manual* to outline in detail the contents of this stage of project implementation. However, reasonable time must be allowed for these activities in order to obtain the best proposals.

There is usually a considerable lapse of time between the invitation for quotations and the final award of contracts. This period can, however, be projected without too much difficulty. The time elapsing until equipment is delivered may also be very long. It ranges normally from a few months for relatively simple plant and equipment to two years or more for more complex installations.

When ordering the equipment, the delivery time should be planned according to the progress of the erection work on site and the requirements for the various construction stages, to ensure that the equipment arrives in a sequence that is optimal from both the delivery and construction points of view. All problems related to the transfer of construction and plant equipment must be solved before delivery to avoid undue delays. The feasibility study should identify any such problem areas that could be critical for the feasibility of the project. It may, for example, be necessary to simulate all transport stages for critical supply items, such as very bulky or heavy machinery and equipment. Quality control must have been performed at the factories of the suppliers, shipping and transport routes determined, and commercial and customs documents prepared according to the local laws and regulations. Even the greatest care taken to ensure an optimal delivery sequence will not, however, rule out the need for interim warehouses where some of the equipment can be safely stored until it is installed in the plant.

In cases where both imported and domestic equipment is installed, problems relating to the sequence of delivery become all the more significant. In many instances, equipment manufactured domestically in developing countries takes considerably longer to deliver than imported equipment, and orders need to be planned in advance to a greater extent, owing to the limited capacities available locally.

The performance testing of the plant is sometimes a serious problem. These tests, in particular their duration and the conditions of testing, will have to be specified in the contract documents with such detail and clarity that future disputes and claims can be avoided. Although performance tests may be a matter that is handled directly between suppliers and the purchaser, an independent consultant will often be appointed to conduct the tests. The feasibility study should indicate which performance tests are recommended or required, and also contain a projection of a time schedule as well as of the related costs.

The outcome of the performance test is critical to both suppliers and purchasers because it has contractual implications. The approval of the test by the purchaser is normally the condition for the release of a retained payment instalment to the supplier. But the test is equally critical for the investors, inasmuch as an unsuccessful performance test inevitably means a delayed start-up of plant operation and production. Although suppliers or contractors will normally have to issue a performance bond, its value may only be marginal compared with the production loss suffered by the investors. It is a common experience that a badly specified performance test, without a clear statement of objectives, plant operation and testing procedures, as well as of the obligations of all parties concerned, often leads to delays and legal problems.

In many contracts performance tests are followed by a guarantee period. The acceptance of a performance test would then be provisional only, and the final acceptance certificate is issued after expiry of the entire period, subject to satisfactory performance by the supplier or contractor.

### Model forms of contract

In recognition of the growing sophistication of purchasing contracts for industrial plants and the shortcomings of many commercial contracts concluded in the past, especially by various developing countries, UNIDO took the initiative in the early 1980s to draft model forms of contract[75] for the erection of fertilizer plants in developing countries under the following terms: turnkey lump sum; semi-turnkey; cost-reimbursable; and supply of know-how and engineering services. These model forms of contract are guidelines that clearly spell out the obligations of the parties in a balanced way, and although conceived for fertilizer plants, they may also provide a useful basis for the design of similar contracts for other industrial plants.

In drafting these model forms of contract emphasis was put on the following: timely completion of an integrated fertilizer plant guaranteed to be capable of sustaining a high operating efficiency and producing specification-grade products; establishment of the total investment costs instead of the contract price only; payment terms linked to the fulfilment of the obligations of the contractor instead of to agreed time periods; continuing validity of mechanical warranties; involvement of the purchaser at all stages of procurement; and effective use of performance bonds to secure the performance of the contractor.

In order to guide and assist users of model forms of contract in contract negotiations, UNIDO prepared guidelines that would cover pre-contracting practices, the preparation of technical specifications and the scope of work, as well as an explanatory commentary on the principal clauses of the model form of contract, together with a description of recommended additional arrangements, both within and outside the contract, to cover training of local personnel required by inexperienced plant operators.

### Acquisition of land

A critical step in a project is the acquisition of land, which sometimes may lead to long-drawn-out negotiations. Options for the acquisition of land may be considered at an early stage, but it should be borne in mind that for each alternative site a comprehensive utilization plan must be prepared. Adequate access to the plant site must be granted, and roads must be designed to withstand the load of heavy traffic during construction and the transport of goods manufactured at the plant. Severe climatic conditions may hamper and delay the construction work on site. Extension of existing railways will have to be considered. Installation of interim and permanent power and water lines must be undertaken in time to allow construction work and production. The installation of telecommunication facilities must be ready by the time site activities begin.

As described in chapter V, the acquisition of land may require approval by the authorities of an environmental impact statement for the project. Obtaining such approvals may be very time-consuming, and if local regulations to avoid

---

[75]"UNIDO model form of turnkey lump-sum contract for the construction of a fertilizer plant including guidelines and technical annexures" (UNIDO/PC.25/Rev.2); "UNIDO model form of semi-turnkey contract for the construction of a fertilizer plant including guidelines and technical annexures" (UNIDO/PC.74/Rev.1); "UNIDO model form of cost-reimbursable contract for the construction of a fertilizer plant including guidelines and technical annexures" (UNIDO/PC.26/Rev.2); "Guidelines containing illustrative articles of a licensing and engineering services agreement for the construction of a fertilizer plant including technical annexures" (UNIDO/PC.141/Rev.1). The four model forms of contract drafted follow a uniform list of 46 main articles and 29 technical annexures. The essential differences between these model forms of contract relate to the scope of work of the contractor, the method of payment and the type of site.

safety hazards are not properly dealt with in the feasibility study, additional work on or off the site may be necessary, probably resulting in extension of the construction work and additional costs.

## Construction and installation

The time and cost projections for construction and installation work on site are basically part of the engineering work described in chapter VI. At the stage of the feasibility study the realistic planning of construction works and installation of equipment is of crucial importance. Any delays during the actual construction phase will have an immediate impact on the costs and income projections made in the feasibility study. For scheduling of the construction and installation work it is important to understand that such work can begin only when the final plant layout has been prepared, land has been acquired at the selected site, and all necessary approvals have been obtained from local authorities.

Site preparation can generally be planned without major problems, but care must be taken to perform the necessary tests and technical investigations to ensure that the projected civil works are adequate. Site preparation must also cover requirements during construction, with an assessment of locally available offices, living quarters, means of transport, the size and layout of camp facilities etc.

The sequence of civil works and construction activities needs to be carefully defined in relation to infrastructure requirements and availability and the arrival and erection schedule of different types of plant equipment. The material flow on site must be considered carefully to ensure that the location of open-air stores and warehouses do not hamper other activities on the site.

Arrangements for erection and installation of equipment need to be undertaken in good time, both when erection work is subcontracted and when it is carried out by the project authorities. Aggressive follow-up and expediting of equipment deliveries is important, and the provision of technical assistance to local suppliers and contractors may be considered in order to interpret or explain complicated technical specifications or work procedures.

## Supply of materials and services

It is necessary to finalize arrangements for the delivery of basic production materials during the implementation phase. If domestic suppliers are used, it is sometimes advisable to undertake a survey of their facilities to ensure that they are capable of delivering the specified quality and quantity of materials in accordance with the supply schedule. For imported goods the supplier-buyer transfer constraints must be studied, and all problems that may arise during transit must be resolved before shipping commences.

Although an initial delivery of spare parts normally is provided by the equipment suppliers, it may not be sufficient to support the work of still inexperienced maintenance technicians. Funds (foreign currency) must therefore be provided for additional procurement of spare parts and expendable materials.

The application of an efficient quality control system is mandatory for critical production items. Quality control may be executed by agencies operating in the countries of foreign suppliers. In agro-industries some input materials (for example, sugar cane for a sugar factory) must be grown before they are delivered, which makes the scheduling of the availability of such materials especially important.

## Pre-production marketing

The preparation of the sales market must start early enough to ensure that the output can be sold as scheduled. Otherwise, a stock of unsold products may accumulate, and the major assumptions concerning the commercial profitability of the product may no longer be valid. Market preparation ranges from advertising and training of salesmen and dealers to the organization of the distribution network and the provision of special sales facilities (such as deep-freezing equipment, showrooms, workshops).

## Plant commissioning

One of the most critical stages during the implementation period is the commissioning of the plant. This stage normally comprises the following activities:

- Pre-operational checks
- Trial runs
- Performance test
- Acceptance and take-over

The commissioning stage—which is often rather long—can be most effectively used as a valuable training period, particularly for the maintenance technicians. That requires, however, appropriate training of the technicians before commissioning starts.

Commissioning activities require the supply of inputs, materials and labour to the site. A supply programme must therefore be included in the implementation plan.

## C. Implementation scheduling

Effective and balanced timing of the delivery of various input requirements must be established. This can only be done by accurate project scheduling. The periods required for various implementation activities can be defined for such activities on the basis of a project schedule that has to be well-knit, coordinated and developed through a systematic analysis and simulation of the entire process.

Various methods of analysis and scheduling are available. The most simple and popular method involves the bar or Gantt chart, which divides project implementation into various time-phased activities and shows the duration of each activity. The implementation schedules are normally prepared in three steps as described below.

In step one the planner determines the logical sequence of events in implementation without paying too much attention to the exact duration of each task. The positioning of some of the tasks is self-explanatory. Detailed engineering must necessarily precede construction and installation; company formation must have been completed before the assignment of staff is considered. Other tasks may need more analysis before they can be positioned correctly.

In the second step the planner will analyse how specific tasks are to be undertaken. This analysis will normally reveal that some tasks can be further subdivided into subtasks. Detailed engineering, for example, is the result of the coordinated effort of several groups of architects and engineers. Again the subtasks must be properly timed to show the interdependence between various tasks. The analyst will then proceed to an analysis of the work content of each subtask, which will make it possible to determine how much time it takes to complete the individual subtasks.

The analyst can then establish the implementation schedule showing the proposed start and duration of project implementation and the correct positioning and duration of all activities and tasks. The description of each task should include:

- The work to be done
- The resources needed
- The time it takes to complete the task
- The responsibility for the task
- Information inputs required for the task
- Results to be produced
- Interrelationship with other activities

Suppliers of plant equipment will be able to provide information concerning installation and commissioning. Shipping or forwarding companies can provide valuable information on transport times, the handling of documents and customs clearance procedures.

### Network planning and use of computers

In some projects there is a need to define the interdependent relationship between the tasks and subtasks involved. In such cases it may be useful to apply a network planning method such as the critical path network (CPN) procedure. Any project that has a large number of tasks will greatly benefit from the application of computers. A number of planning programmes are commercially available. The costs of preparing and constantly updating a CPN plan for a project may be substantial. If such costs are significant for the project, the feasibility study should include them as part of the project monitoring and control costs.

### Alternative planning techniques

The bar-chart planning method can be applied to every project, usually without difficulty. This method sometimes gives the best overview of the main sequence of events, even if a more sophisticated scheduling method must be applied at a later stage. The bar chart is usually a sufficient planning tool for implementation planning in the pre-investment phase, particularly in a feasibility study.

## D.   Projecting the implementation budget

The objective of implementation budgeting is to determine the cost of resources required to implement an investment project, once the project has been approved and the investment decision is made. The feasibility study should determine the cost of resources in accordance with the timing of the various stages of project implementation described above. The estimated implementation costs are capitalized pre-production costs forming part of the total initial investment costs.

The cost estimates are based on the implementation activities and tasks determined for the project. For various cost items standard costs can be found in publicly available reference material. For example, associations of architects and engineers in many countries have established unit costs per man-day and rules for calculating fees for architectural and engineering services (calculated on the basis of the type and scope of the project and the work). Other cost items such as housing, transport, legal fees and duties may require local surveys. Price and cost estimates should include contingencies for probable price increases, projected for the most likely starting date of project implementation. In case the actual starting date is delayed, it will be necessary to update all cost and income projections and recompute the schedules required for project financial analysis (see chapter X).

### Bibliography

Choudhury, S. Project scheduling and monitoring in practice. New Delhi, South Asian Publishing, 1983.

Cleland, D. I. *and* W. R. King. Project management handbook, 2. ed. New York, Reinhold, 1988.

Coombs, W. E. *and* W. J. Palmer. The handbook of construction accounting and financial management. 3. ed. New York, McGraw-Hill, 1984.

Harrison, F. L. Advanced project management. 2. ed. London, Gower, 1985.

Hed, Sven R. Project control manual. Windsor, Hed, 1984.

Marsh, P. V. D. Contracting for engineering and construction projects. London, Gower, 1971.

Stuckenbruck, L. C. The implementation of project management: the professional's handbook. Reading, Massachusetts, Addison-Wesley, 1981.

United Nations. Contract planning and organization. (ID/117)
    Sales no.: 74.II.B.4.

_____ The initiation and implementation of industrial projects in developing countries: a systematic approach. (ID/146)
    Sales no.: 75.II.B.2.

## Appendix

## CHECK-LISTS AND SCHEDULES

*IX-1.   Sample breakdown of project implementation costs*

*Costs of project implementation management*

Salaries and wages of managerial staff
Rent and operation of offices, motor cars, living quarters etc.
Travel and communication expenses
Fees for specially assigned consultants
Fees and cost of quality control inspections abroad
Printing and photocopying
Duties and taxes during the implementation period
Costs of legal assistance

*Costs of company formation and organizational build-up*

Costs and expenses directly related to company formation, such as financial costs,
   duties, taxes, fees and costs of legal assistance
Salaries and wages of managerial and administrative staff
Recruitment costs (advertising costs, fees paid for recruitment services etc.)
Salaries and wages of recruited staff and labour from date of recruitment until
   commercial production
Rent and operation of offices, training facilities, motor cars, living quarters etc.
Travel and communication expenses
Fees for specially assigned consultants
Fees for consultants and experts as well as possible additional allowances for
   foreign staff
Fees for external training (locally and abroad) including travel and subsistence
   payments
Training documentation and training material (if not part of supplier contracts)

*Technology acquisition and transfer*

Travel and communication expenses
Consulting fees
Testing, technology assessment costs
Detailed process engineering for lump-sum know-how payments and royalties (see
   also chapter VI)
Costs of know-how transfer (training costs)

*Detailed engineering of equipment and civil works, tendering, evaluation of bids,
negotiations and contract awards*

Salaries and wages of planning staff
Rent and operation of offices, motor cars etc.
Travel, transport, communication, subsistence
Fees for various types of consultants on detailed engineering costs (see also
   chapter VI)
Site and laboratory tests
Printing of tender documents, drawings and specifications
Stamps and duties
Legal assistance

*Supervision and coordination of construction work, installation, testing, trial runs, start-up and commissioning*

Salaries and wages of site staff
Costs of local and foreign experts and consultants
Rents (living quarters, offices etc.)
Erection, operation and camp maintenance
Raw and auxiliary materials, factory supplies for test runs, performance testing and initial production
Cost of interim warehousing off site
Cost of spare parts and maintenance
Insurance paid during project implementation

*Arrangements for supplies*

Salaries and wages for purchasing staff
Travel and other related expenses
Communications

*Arrangements for pre-production marketing*

Salaries and wages for sales and marketing staff
Advertising
Training of salesmen and dealers
Travel expenses
Communications
Cost of establishing distribution network including special equipment
Printing expenses for public relations materials etc.

*Preliminary expenses and costs involved in capital issues (unless included already in cost groups listed above)*

Registration and incorporation fees
Printing and incidentals expenses
Public relations expenses
Underwriting commissions
Brokerage
Legal fees
Insurance
Interest during construction (on term loans, current bank accounts etc.)
Other pre-production expenses

## Schedule IX-1. Project implementation charts

### Project implementation chart: Level 1

| No. Main tasks | Year | 1 | 2 | 3 | 4 | 5 | 6 | 7 |
|---|---|---|---|---|---|---|---|---|
| | Quarter | 1 2 3 4 | 1 2 3 4 | 1 2 3 4 | 1 2 3 4 | 1 2 3 4 | 1 2 3 4 | 1 2 3 4 |
| 1 Company formation[a] | | ▨□▨ | | | | | | |
| 2 Governmental approval[a] | | ▨ | | | | | | |
| 3 Organizational build-up | | ▨▨▨ | | | | | | |
| 4 Technology acquisition & transfer | | ▨▨ | | | | | | |
| 5 Detailed engineering | | ▨▨ | | | | | | |
| 6 Tenders, negotiations, contracting | | □▨▨ | | | | | | |
| 7 Acquisition of land | | ▨ | | | | | | |
| 8 Construction and installation | | ▨▨▨▨ | | | | | | |
| 9 Supply of materials and services | | ▨ | | | | | | |
| 10 Pre-production marketing | | ▨▨ | | | | | | |
| 11 Plant commissioning | | ▨ | | | | | | |
| 12 Build-up of full plant operation | | ▨▨▨▨ | | | | | | |

[a] If applicable.

### Project implementation chart: Level 2

| Main task No. 5 | Year | 1 | 2 | 3 | 4 | 5 | 6 | 7 |
|---|---|---|---|---|---|---|---|---|
| No. Tasks | Quarter | 1 2 3 4 | 1 2 3 4 | 1 2 3 4 | 1 2 3 4 | 1 2 3 4 | 1 2 3 4 | 1 2 3 4 |
| .1 Site preparation, infrastructure | | ▨ | | | | | | |
| .2 Architectural and structural | | ▨ | | | | | | |
| .3 Electrical and mechanical | | ▨ | | | | | | |
| .4 Production programme | | ▨ | | | | | | |
| .5 Equipment specifications | | ▨ | | | | | | |
| .6 Documentation (operat., maint.) | | ▨ | | | | | | |
| .7 Tests & acceptance standards | | ▨ | | | | | | |
| .8 Technical bid documents | | ▨ | | | | | | |

### Project implementation chart: Level 3

| Equipment specifications | Year | 1 | | | | 2 | | |
|---|---|---|---|---|---|---|---|---|
| | Quarter | 1 | 2 | 3 | 4 | 1 | 2 | 3 |
| .51 Main plant units: line1 | | | | ▨▨ | | | | |
| .52 Main plant units: line 2 | | | | ▨▨ | | | | |
| .53 Main plant units: line 3 | | | | ▨ | | | | |
| .54 Interphase wiring | | | | | ▨ | | | |
| .55 Instrumentation | | | | | ▨ | | | |
| .56 Emergency generator | | | | □▨ | | | | |
| .57 Cranes and trucks | | | | ▨ | | | | |

## Schedule IX-2. Estimate of investment costs:
## project implementation
### (insert in schedule X-1)

Project:
Date:
Source:

| ESTIMATE OF INVESTMENT COSTS | | | | | | | | |
|---|---|---|---|---|---|---|---|---|
| Project implementation (insert main task from IX-1) | | | | | Currency: | | | |
| Main plant item or plant unit[a] | | | | | Units: | | | |
| N | Q | U | Item description | Unit cost | Cost | | | Year[b] |
| | | | | | Foreign | Local | Total | |
| | | | | | | | | |
| Total investment costs, project implementation (carry over to schedule X-1) | | | | | | | | |

> N = number     U = units     Q = quantity

*Note:* For the purpose of economic cost-benefit analysis, local (foreign) cost elements contained in imported (national) equipment should be identified.

[a] Insert name or description of plant or main plant item.
[b] Of investment (if necessary show subtotals for each year and plant item).

# X.  Financial analysis and investment appraisal

Given the conditions for investment appraisal, project preparation should be geared towards the requirements of financial and economic analysis. In this chapter, after an introduction to the scope and objectives of financial analysis, the principal aspects of the analysis and the concept of investment appraisal are explained. Basically, financial analysis should accompany the design of the project from the very beginning, which is only possible when the financial analyst is integrated into the feasibility studies team at an early stage. From a financial and economic point of view, investment can be defined as a long-term commitment of economic resources made with the objective of producing and obtaining net gains (exceeding the total initial investment) in the future. The main aspect of this commitment is the transformation of financial resources (that is, the investor's own and borrowed funds) into productive assets, represented by fixed investment and net working capital. While the interest in future net gains is common for each party investing in a project, the expected gains or benefits may differ considerably between them, and may also be valued differently.

Important aspects of financial analysis, such as basic criteria for investment decisions, pricing of project inputs and outputs, the planning horizon and project life, as well as risks and uncertainty, will be discussed, and then detailed consideration will be given to cost analysis, basic accounting principles, methods of investment appraisal (discounting and conventional methods), financing, financial efficiency and ratios, and financial analysis and project evaluation in conditions of uncertainty.

The chapter concludes with a brief characterization of the objectives and commonly accepted methods of economic evaluation. Examples of the various schedules required for financial analysis are given in the appendix to the chapter. The example presented in annex I to this *Manual* contains the background information and data needed for the computation of all schedules shown in chapter X.

## A.  Scope and objectives of financial analysis

A feasibility study, as mentioned earlier, is a tool for providing potential investors, promoters and financiers with the information required to decide whether to undertake an investment, and whether and how to finance such a project. The scope and objectives of financial analysis are determined to a great extent by the definition of what investment is.

Investment may be defined as a long-term commitment of economic resources made with the objective of producing and obtaining net gains[76] in the

---

[76]The term net gains is used to indicate that the objectives of investment projects are not limited to the net income as computed in a net income statement.

future.[77] The main aspect of this commitment is the transformation of liquidity—the investor's own and borrowed funds[78]—into productive assets, represented by fixed investment and net working capital, as well as the generation of liquidity again during the use of these assets.

The above definition comprises all types of investment, including industrial investments. With this characterization in mind, it becomes evident that financial analysis and final project appraisal involves the assessment, analysis and evaluation of the required project inputs, the outputs to be produced and the future net benefits, expressed in financial terms. The methods applied for this purpose are as follows: analysis of the reliability of projected data; analysis of the structure and significance of costs and income projections in order to identify the critical variables that could have a significant impact on the feasibility of an investment; determination and evaluation of the annual and accumulated financial net benefits, expressed as profitability, efficiency or yield of the investment; and consideration of the time factor with regard to prices, cost of capital, and decisions taken in conditions of uncertainty (norm 1 business risks and specific project risks).

The above-mentioned transformation of liquid financial resources (funds) into productive assets (fixed assets and net working capital) corresponds to the financing of an investment. Project financing includes the design of a proper financial structure, considering the conditions under which funds would be available, and the optimization of project financing from the point of view of the enterprise and the investors.

As noted earlier, the conditions for the appraisal of an investment are that a technically feasible solution is also financially feasible, can be implemented within the socio-economic and ecological environment identified for the investment project (socio-economic and ecological feasibility), and is likely to continue to be feasible for the minimum time determined by decision makers as the planning horizon for their decisions. The scope and objectives of financial analysis are therefore to determine, analyse and interpret all the financial consequences of an investment that may be relevant to and significant for the investment and financing decisions.

Furthermore, financial analysis and evaluation[79] should ensure that for the objectives determined by the decision makers, and within the given confidence levels of a feasibility study, the following conditions are fulfilled:

---

[77]See P. M. Hawranek, "Investitionsentscheidungen—Entscheidungen ueber die Umstrukturierung von Leistungen in der Wirtschaft", in *Entwicklungsmanagement, Beiträge zu einer neuen Dimension im internationalen Management,* M. Hofmann and K. Schedl, eds. (Berlin, Duncker and Humblot, 1982).

[78]In order to achieve or maintain a particular capital structure, a project could obtain funds from preferred and common stocks, bonds, use of retained earnings, leases and loans from banks (see chap. X, sect. F). The cost of capital is the weighted average cost of each money source. This weighted average takes into account the joint cost and the desired long-run relative proportions of each type of capital, including the impact of inflation.

[79]The term analysis (financial and economic) as used in this *Manual* comprises the pure analytical work required to identify the critical variables likely to determine the success or failure of an investment. The analysis must not be limited to mathematical computations, but would have to include the critical interpretation of all relevant data.

The term evaluation refers to the determination of the values of project inputs and outputs. In the case of feasibility studies the evaluation of a project is made by the investors and financiers who may approve or reject the proposed project. Formalized ex-ante evaluation corresponds to the concept of project appraisal used by the World Bank. Evaluation in the terminology of the World Bank is an ex-post evaluation of projects financed by that institution.

- The most attractive of the possible project alternatives is determined under the prevailing conditions of uncertainty;
- The critical variables and possible strategies for managing or controlling risks are identified;
- The flow of financial resources required during the investment, start-up and operational phases is determined, and the financial resources available at the lowest cost are identified for the time required and used in the most effective way.

These objectives are interrelated. Their conversion into project reality requires sound judgement, useful concepts, techniques for analysing situations and principles for the guidance of action. Financial analysis uses a family of highly developed concepts and techniques for decision-making, planning and monitoring, which have to be mastered by drawing on related subjects and techniques such as financial and management accounting, economics, quantitative methods, law and taxation. As the financial analyst must work with all specialists engaged in the preparation of the feasibility study, he or she must have a broad appreciation of their functions and working methods. These matters are dealt with in the following sections, which present an accepted conceptual framework from a practical point of view.

## B. Principal aspects of financial analysis and concept of investment appraisal

Financial analysis of industrial investment projects is not an isolated activity performed only towards the end of the project design in order to complete a primarily technical study or project proposal and to show the financial implications of a project for promoters and potential investors. It should rather accompany the various alternatives and the design of the *project strategies* that basically determine the marketing strategies, project scope, resources, location, production capacities and technology, as already described in this *Manual*, thus providing a yardstick for the evaluation of the financial and economic success or failure of a project. This will make it possible to avoid being burdened, after detailed technical design work and data assessment, with a project proposal that is found to be financially unfeasible because investment, production and marketing costs are not sufficiently covered by projected incomes from operations in the business environment assessed during the feasibility study. If found unfeasible at this terminal stage of the study, it is usually too late, and definitely too costly, to start the whole work again for another project alternative.[80]

Another important aspect to be considered when undertaking financial analysis is that the decision makers usually give different weights to the various criteria used for investment appraisal. This would force the analysts to identify such criteria[81] and select proper methods to produce the information required

---

[80]A typical reaction in such situations is to propose an increase in production capacity, making use of economies of scale, but ignoring the possible consequences for the marketing concept (the demand and market volume may not be large enough, or a supply increase may result in a considerable drop in market prices) or other consequences with regard to location, availability and supply of resources, total finance available for a single project etc.

[81]For example, rapid amortization at a lower profitability might be given priority over high long-term profitability, or investors may wish to expand their market position *vis-à-vis* a major competitor even at marginal returns because they hope that such a strategy will help to maintain high profitability in an already existing firm.

by investors. However, financial analysis should not limit itself to answering questions raised by investors, but should also indicate and highlight any other critical impacts that would have to be considered when appraising a project. The orientation of financial analysis towards the needs of decision makers and their investment and financing criteria, as well as the principal conceptual aspects, are discussed below.

### Interest of parties involved

While the interest in future net benefits is common for each party participating in a project, the expected benefits may differ considerably between them and may also be valued differently. To cope with this situation the financial analysis should begin with the determination of the required project inputs and generated outputs, valued at market prices, and determine the annual as well as accumulated net surpluses. Using the methods described in the following sections, the net benefits (yield or profitability) generated by the investment are determined in financial terms. Basically, two groups of financial resources can be distinguished: equity provided by the investors; and loans of financing institutions or other similar sources of funds (including owners).[82] The conditions under which the project may obtain funds reflect the interest of the financiers, in particular their *opportunity cost of capital* and the margin added for the various risks expected and evaluated by each party individually.

The expected net benefits may not always be the only gains resulting from participation in an investment project. An investor may expect to obtain additional financial gains elsewhere as a result of the investment. For example, a joint venture partner could have additional cash flows in the parent company as a result of participation in the venture. Such additional flows may include the supply of components and services (technical assistance, marketing research, management contracts etc.), transfer of technology and know-how (lump-sum and royalty payments), marketing of products (including exports) etc. These activities of joint venture partners, as well as any other advantages resulting from their participation (obtaining supplies possibly at lower prices, securing or opening new markets etc.), would have to be taken into account when determining the feasibility of participation for each individual party.[83] When assessing the criteria applied by individual investors and financiers, it is also important to determine their individual profits net of income tax. For example, an annual dividend of 10 per cent payable to shareholders would correspond to an effective profitability of 5 per cent in the case of a 50 per cent

---

[82]The debt-equity mix affects the flow of funds from and to the different sources of finance. As a result of the leverage effect, the IRR on equity would increase with an increasing debt-to-equity ratio if the IRR of the project is higher than the cost of loan capital. On the other hand, the profitability of equity capital would become lower with a decreasing debt-equity ratio. This effect would be the reverse if the cost of loan capital exceeded the overall profitability of the total capital invested. The debt-equity ratio also has an impact on overall profitability, in so far as the cash outflow for the payment of corporate (income) taxes usually is a cost item for the firm. Therefore, any increase of the annual interest payable on the debt balance—owing in the present example to an increase of the debt-equity ratio—would reduce the gross or taxable profit, and consequently also the cash outflow of the project. This tax effect on the net cash flow and the leverage effect are important criteria for the determination of an optimal combination of the sources and types of finance. See also sect. F on project financing.

[83]Similarly, such indirect gains may determine the financing decisions of commercial banks. If development finance institutions are likely to participate, various development objectives requiring the incorporation of economic cost-benefit analysis in the feasibility study may have to be taken into account.

income tax. It may therefore be interesting for the shareholder to leave the profit in the firm and reinvest at a profitability rate above 5 per cent.[84] The computation of discounted net cash returns on equity and of the profitability of invested equity capital is described later in the section on investment appraisal methods.

## Public interest

Investment has been identified as oriented towards the generation of future net gains. This objective can be achieved only when an investment is properly integrated within the business environment, as described in chapter III. Therefore, any industrial investment is not only a part of a system of supply and demand of goods and services, but also an integrated part of a socio-economic and ecological system within which it performs. To be successful, investments also have to serve the needs and development objectives of this socio-economic system. Since it is in the public interest that investments make efficient use of scarce resources and contribute as much as possible to national development, various fiscal and administrative measures are applied to control investment. These measures, in the form of incentives as well as restrictions, must be identified and included in the financial analysis and appraisal of a project in so far as they affect or could affect the financial feasibility of an investment.[85]

## Basic criteria for investment decisions

Although the return on capital invested is the main criterion for investment decisions, it is not the only one in the case of industrial investments, because if financial returns alone counted, financial resources could as well be invested in bonds, securities etc. However, for the purpose of industrial feasibility studies, investment is defined not only as a benefit-oriented long-term commitment of resources, but also as the transformation of liquidity into productive assets. Considering that the net benefits would be solely the result of the productive use of such assets, any decision on industrial investments should be based on the following criteria relating to the overall feasibility of investment projects:

- Is there any possible conflict, at present and in the long run, between the basic project (corporate) objective and the development objectives valid for the socio-economic environment?

- How suitable is the proposed strategy[86] for the achievement of the project objective; have alternative strategies been taken into consideration; and why has the proposed strategy been selected?

- How does the project design, that is, the scope of the project, the marketing concept, the production capacity and the technology and location selected, match with the project strategy and the availability of the required resources?

---

[84]This example is a simplification, since risk elements and the market value of the share have not been taken into account.

[85]The role of public policies and possible conflicts is also dealt with in chap. V.

[86]See the sections on marketing and project strategy in chap. III.

- Will the project make efficient use of economic resources, and are there better alternative uses of the main inputs required for the project?
- Are projections of total investment costs and production and marketing costs within the acceptable confidence level?
- Are the total investment costs within the financial limits determined by the availability of capital?
- Does the structure of cash outflows and inflows and of the corresponding net cash returns meet with the minimum requirements and expectations of the investors and financiers?
- Will the supply of local money and foreign exchange be sufficient to meet outstanding financial obligations at any time during the life of the project?
- How sensitive are the accumulated discounted returns and the annual returns to the planning horizon, to errors in data assessment and project design, to inflation and relative price changes and to changes in the business environment (mainly those involving competitors, consumers, markets, supplies and public policies)?
- Have critical variables been identified? What risks are associated with these variables, and what strategies exist to manage or control those risks?
- What are the financial consequences of the risks; in other words, do they entail additions to investment costs, to the funds required, to production and marketing costs, and to finance costs, or lower than expected production, sales volumes and sales prices?
- How likely is the projected scenario or business environment required as a minimum condition for the investment to be appraised by investors, by financing institutions etc.

The methods applied for financial analysis and investment appraisal are described in detail in the following sections, starting with cost analysis, then dealing with discounting and conventional methods, project financing, ratio analysis and financial evaluation in conditions of uncertainty.

### Accounting systems

Financial analysis relies on a systematic presentation and processing of relevant business data on assets and liabilities, costs and income, and the related flows of goods, services and financial resources. Accounting systems serving the various purposes of management have been developed, and basic accounting methods are as old as business itself. The quality of financial analysis and investment appraisal depends basically on the reliability of the information processed and on the methodology applied. Although accounting systems are not always identical in different countries, basic accounting principles are the same everywhere.[87]

Accounting systems always cover the financial status of the firm in terms of the wealth (assets) and obligations (liabilities) recorded in its balance sheet,

---

[87]While there are many ways of determining net income, there is only one way of determining cash flow.

the costs accounted for over the reporting period, and the corresponding income shown in the net income statement. In addition, a cost accounting system is needed in order to determine production and marketing costs, which is necessary not only for the preparation of the net income statement, but also for efficient financial planning, product pricing and cost control.

For liquidity planning the cash flow statement is used. It should be pointed out that depreciation allowances are not classified among the cash outflows. The inclusion of depreciation charges (costs) would result in the double-counting of fixed project costs, since they are already accounted for as fixed capital investments. This is why depreciation charges are regarded as a cost item, but not as a cash item. The financial costs (interest paid) are included among the cash outflows. However, for the computation of the discounted cash flow (IRR and NPV), the financial costs must be excluded, because they constitute—like the dividends paid on equity—a yield generated by the investment and are reflected in the discount rate.

Cost accounting is intended to provide a measurement of budgeted material costs, wages and salaries, and other expenses involved in producing and marketing the goods and services generated by the project. These contemplated costs are examined in an effort to establish the relationship between them and the level of business activity of the project, for which an indication of the variable and fixed costs is required. With this information a profit plan that defines the cost-volume-profit relationships may be constructed. Measuring profits involves separating costs applicable to units sold from the cost applicable to the units remaining in inventories. Finally, to establish rational sales prices requires a knowledge of both the costs and their relationship to the sales volume (see also chapter III). The contemplated costs budgeted for normal capacity permit the analyst to price goods and services for the recovery of costs and a normal profit.

Standard costs representing a predetermined cost may be calculated in advance of operations for later comparison with actual costs. During plant operation costs may be recorded on a chronological or other predetermined basis under any applied system, such as job-order costing or process costing. After completion of the operations, the actual costs incurred are recorded chronologically. Both, chronological and pre-determined costs may be utilized in a cost accounting system.

The classification of costs is necessary in order to facilitate cost planning (budgeting) and to permit the determination of cost items that could be critical for the feasibility of a project. The classification described below in the section on the analysis of cost estimates has already been used in the schedules given in the appendices to chapters III to IX.

### Pricing of project inputs and outputs

The inputs and outputs of a project appear in physical form, and prices are used to express them in value terms in order to obtain a common denominator. Ideally, for the purpose of the feasibility study prices should reflect the real economic values of project inputs and outputs for the entire planning horizon of the decision makers. Prices may be defined in various ways, depending on whether they are:

- Market (explicit) or shadow (imputed) prices

- Absolute or relative prices
- Current or constant prices

Market or explicit prices are those present in the market, no matter whether they are determined by supply and demand or by the Government; in other words, they are the prices at which the firm will buy the inputs and sell the outputs. In financial analysis market prices are applied. Later, at the stage of economic cost-benefit analysis, the question will have to be raised as to whether market prices reflect the real economic value of project inputs and outputs. If this is not the case, that is, if market prices are distorted, then shadow or imputed prices will have to be introduced for economic analysis.

Absolute prices reflect the value of a single product in an absolute amount of money, while relative prices express the value of one product in terms of another. For instance, the absolute price of 1 tonne of coal may be 100 monetary units and an equivalent quantity of oil may be 300 monetary units. In this case the relative price of coal in terms of oil would be 0.33, meaning that the relative price of oil is three times the price of coal.[88]

The level of absolute prices may vary over the lifetime of the project because of inflation or productivity changes. This variation does not necessarily lead to a change in relative prices, in other words, relative prices may sometimes remain unchanged despite variations in absolute prices. Both absolute and relative prices are relevant for the financial analysis.

Current and constant prices differ over time as a result of inflation, which is understood as a general rise of price levels in an economy. If inflation can have a significant impact on project input costs and output prices, such an impact must be dealt with in the financial analysis presented in the feasibility study. Whenever relative input and output prices remain stable, it is sufficiently accurate to compute the profitability or yield of an investment at constant prices. Only when relative prices change and project input prices grow faster (or slower) than output prices, or vice versa, then the corresponding impacts on net cash flows and profits must be included in the financial analysis. If inflation impacts are negligible, the problem of choosing between current and constant prices does not exist, since they are equal and the planner may use either.

Inflation may have to be considered in financial planning, even when the relative prices remain basically unchanged, because additional equity and loan financing may be needed to deal with significant annual inflation rates, especially during the project implementation phase (construction and start-up).[89] Working capital requirements should be checked in view not only of the gradual attainment of full capacity, but also of the increased inflationary pressure on the cost items to be financed from working capital. Consequently, different inflation rates should be applied to local and imported materials, utilities, labour etc. when projecting working capital. As far as sales forecasts are concerned, it will not be sufficient to project the quantities of sales; price changes must also be anticipated.

If relative prices change significantly over time, the analyst is confronted with the delicate task of estimating the future inflation rate and its impact on

---

[88]Depending on whether tonnes or calorific values are used as a reference, relative prices may be different.

[89]In the case of hyperinflation, it is also necessary to re-evaluate the fixed and current assets on a yearly basis, or even for shorter periods, and to convert unemployed liquidity into short-term investments (such as bonds).

relative prices, and of deciding whether to use current or constant prices. The use of constant prices may still require some adjustments to account for the expected change in relative prices. If the analysis is made using current prices, the analyst will have to anticipate the future inflation rate. In this case, possible inflation rates should be projected by item—for the main cost and revenue items—in order to consider any significant changes in relative prices of locally produced and of imported goods and services.

## Planning horizon and project life

Planning is understood as a consciously programmed activity having as its focus the objective consideration of the future. The anticipations and assumptions about the future need to be made explicit and should be analysed in order to find the optimal development path. This is why the planning process integrates futuristic thinking with careful analysis. The project planning horizon of a decision maker may be defined as the period of time over which he decides to control and manage his project-related business activities, or for which he formulates his investment or business development plan. The planning horizon determined by decision makers must also consider the lifetime of a project.

The economic life, that is, the period over which the project would generate net gains, depends basically on the technical or technological life cycle of the main plant items, on the life cycle of the product and of the industry involved, and on the flexibility of a firm in adapting its business activities to changes in the business environment. When determining the economic life span of the project various factors have to be assessed, some of which are as follows:

- Duration of demand (position in the product life cycle)
- Duration of the raw material deposits and supply
- Rate of technical progress
- Life cycle of the industry
- Duration of building and equipment
- Opportunities for alternative investment
- Administrative constraints (urban planning horizon)

It is evident that the economic life of a project can never be longer than its technical life or its legal life; in other words, it must be less than or equal to the shorter of the latter. For project planning purposes only the economic life is relevant.

Considering that the accumulated net cash flows of an investment project are a function of the time period covered in the feasibility study, the planning horizon may have a considerable impact on the results of the financial analysis. Since the values obtained for the discounted cash flows and the various profitability and efficiency ratios vary sometimes considerably with the length of the planning period, the determination of the planning horizon of a feasibility study is often a very critical task. The relationship between the planning horizon and project life should therefore be considered when appraising an investment project.

258

## Risk and uncertainty

Investment projects are by definition related to the future, which a project analyst cannot forecast with certainty. Thus financial analysis and evaluation have to be carried out under conditions of risk and uncertainty. The difference between risk and uncertainty is related to the decision maker's knowledge of the probable occurrence of certain events. Risk is present when the probabilities associated with various outcomes may be estimated on the basis of historical data. Uncertainty exists when the probabilities of outcomes have to be assigned subjectively, since there are no historical data. The aspects and methods of financial analysis under uncertainty are discussed later in this chapter in the section on break-even analysis, sensitivity analysis and probability analysis.

## C. Analysis of cost estimates

Since reliable cost estimates are fundamental to the appraisal of an investment project, it is necessary to check carefully all cost items that could have a significant impact on financial feasibility. The sensitivity analysis described later permits the identification of critical cost items, and the cost structure analysis helps to identify possible inconsistencies and unbalanced cost structures, especially when data for similar projects are available from a feasibility-studies data bank. In case of questionable estimates, it may be necessary to verify such cost projections by using other data sources. The preparation of cost estimates has been described in chapters III to IX and comprises the pre-investment, project implementation (investment) and operational phases. It covers the corresponding costs of initial investment, production, marketing and distribution, plant and equipment replacement, working capital requirements and decommissioning at the end of the project life.

The estimates should be grouped into local and foreign components and may be expressed either in constant or current prices (real or nominal terms). Depending on the price basis used in the feasibility study and for the financial analysis, allowances for price increases (contingencies) should be provided for. Since inconsistency in the use of accounting and financial terminology often causes problems for the analysis, it is recommended that the terms defined and explained below be strictly adhered to.[90]

### Total investment costs

### Initial investment costs

Initial investment costs are defined as the sum of fixed assets (fixed investment costs plus pre-production expenditures) and net working capital, with fixed assets constituting the resources required for constructing and equipping an investment project, and net working capital corresponding to the

---

[90]The terminology introduced with the first edition in 1978 is based on the most important publications in the fields of project appraisal, analysis of capital projects, accounting and financing, and has been widely accepted.

resources needed to operate the project totally or partially. At the pre-investment stage, two mistakes are frequently made. Most commonly, working capital is included either not at all or in insufficient amounts, thus causing serious liquidity problems for the nascent project. Furthermore, total investment costs are sometimes confused with total assets, which correspond to fixed assets plus pre-production expenditures plus current assets. The amount of total investment costs is, in fact, smaller than total assets, since it is composed of fixed assets and net working capital, the latter being the difference between current assets and current liabilities (see below).

## Investment required during plant operation

The economic lifetime is different for the various investments (buildings, plant, machinery and equipment, transport equipment etc.). In order to keep a plant in operation, each item must therefore be replaced at the appropriate time, and the replacement costs must be included in the feasibility study. Other types of investment occurring during the operational phase are investments for rationalization, modernization and plant expansion. In general these investments should be analysed in separate studies, and only in exceptional cases should the costs be incorporated in the feasibility study of the initial investment project.

## Pre-production expenditures

In every industrial project certain expenditures due, for example, to the acquisition or generation of assets are incurred prior to commercial production. These expenditures, which have to be capitalized, include a number of items originating during the various stages of project preparation and implementation. They are briefly outlined below.

*Preliminary capital-issue expenditures.* These are expenditures incurred during the registration and formation of the company, including legal fees for preparation of the memorandum and articles of association and similar documents, and for capital issues. The capital-issue expenditures include basically the preparation and issue of a prospectus, advertising, public announcements, underwriting commissions, brokerage, expenses for processing of share applications and allotment of shares. Preliminary expenditures also include legal fees for loan applications and land purchase agreements.

*Expenditures for preparatory studies.* There are three types of expenditures for preparatory studies:

- Expenditures for pre-investment studies: opportunity, pre-feasibility, feasibility and support or functional studies (for example, project design reports) undertaken for the implementation of the project;
- Consultant fees for preparing studies, engineering, and supervision of erection and construction, although consulting services may be debited to the relevant fixed investment costs, and are not included under pre-production expenditures in cases where they can be directly related to the creation of an asset;
- Other expenses for planning the project.

*Other pre-production expenditures.*[91] Included among other pre-production expenditures are the following:

- Salaries, fringe benefit and social security contributions of personnel engaged during the pre-production period;
- Travel expenses;
- Preparatory installations, such as workers' camps, temporary offices and stores;
- Pre-production marketing costs, promotional activities, creation of the sales network etc.;
- Training costs, including fees, travel, living expenses, salaries and stipends of the trainees and fees payable to external institutions;
- Know-how and patent fees;
- Interest on loans accrued or payable during construction;
- Insurance costs during construction.

*Trial runs, start-up and commissioning expenditures.* This item includes fees payable for supervision of start-up operations, wages, salaries, fringe benefits and social security contributions of personnel employed, consumption of production materials and auxiliary supplies, utilities and other incidental start-up costs. Operating losses incurred during the running-in period up to the stage when satisfactory levels are achieved also have to be capitalized. Pre-production expenditures can be tabulated according to schedule X-2.

In allocating pre-production expenditures, one of two practices is generally followed:

- All pre-production expenditures may be capitalized and amortized over a period of time that is usually shorter than the period over which equipment is depreciated;
- A part of the pre-production expenditures may be initially allocated, where attributable, to the respective fixed assets and the sum of both amortized. Pre-production expenditures that are not attributable are capitalized as a total and also amortized over a certain number of years. For the phasing of pre-production expenditures on an annual basis see schedule X-2.

*Plant and equipment replacement costs.* Such costs include all pre-production expenditures as described above and related to investments needed for the replacement of fixed assets. Again, the estimates include the supply, transport, installation and commissioning of equipment, together with any costs associated with down time, production losses as well as allowances for physical contingencies.

*End-of-life costs.* The costs associated with the decommissioning of fixed assets at the end of the project life, minus any revenues from the sale of the assets, are end-of-life costs. Major items are the costs of dismantling, disposal

---

[91]Investment in current assets, such as stocks of spare parts, raw materials and factory supplies, as required for the start-up of plant operation, is dealt with below in the section on net working capital.

and land reclamation. It is often reasonable for a feasibility study to assume that these costs can be offset against the salvage value of the corresponding asset.

## Fixed assets

As indicated above, fixed assets comprise fixed investment costs and pre-production expenditures.

### Fixed investment costs

Fixed investments should include the following main cost items, which may be broken down further, if required:

- Land purchase, site preparation and improvements
- Building and civil works
- Plant machinery and equipment, including auxiliary equipment
- Certain incorporated fixed assets such as industrial property rights and lump-sum payments for know-how and patents

The estimates include supply, packing and transport, duties and installation charges. Depending on the type and accuracy of the pre-investment study, provisions should also be made for physical contingency allowances, providing a safety factor to cover miscellaneous (unforeseen or forgotten) minor cost items. To arrive at the total fixed investment costs, the final amounts derived from schedules V-1 and V-2, and schedules VI-1, VI-2 and VI-3, should be inserted in schedules X-1 and X-2,[92] respectively, and added up. Total annual fixed investment costs are projected for each year of the construction period until the planned production level is reached. Any investment required during the operational phase to maintain the operation of the plant should be inserted in schedule X-1.

### Net working capital

Net working capital[93] is defined to embrace current assets (the sum of inventories, marketable securities, prepaid items, accounts receivable and cash) minus current liabilities (accounts payable). It forms an essential part of the initial capital outlays required for an investment project, because it is required to finance the operation of the plant. Any changes in current assets or liabilities, such as an increase or decrease of production volumes or inventories (raw materials, work-in-progress, finished products etc.), has an impact on the financial requirements. Any net increase of working capital corresponds to a cash outflow to be financed, and any decrease would set free financial resources

---

[92] These schedules are given in the appendix to this chapter.

[93] In the literature quite often the term working capital is used as a synonym for net working capital. This term should not, however, be mixed up with the net increase or net changes of working capital, which result from changes in current assets and liabilities.

(cash inflow for the project). Since the working capital is computed net of creditors, that is, net of short-term finance, it is quite logical that working capital should be financed from equity or long-term debt (short-term seasonal peaks occurring within a production year may, however, be financed by short-term or medium-term capital).

In the analysis of investment costs it should be carefully checked whether the initial working capital requirements as well as the changes during plant operation are properly considered in the cost estimates. Only thus can it be ensured that there is no unexpected shortage of finance during start-up of operations, and that working capital outlays are included for the appraisal of the investment project.

The above classification makes no mention of time, and since time is vital in the formulation of procurement policies, working capital should furthermore be classified as either permanent or temporary. Permanent working capital is that amount of funds required to produce the goods and services necessary to satisfy demand at its lowest point. The funds representing permanent working capital never leave the business process. Temporary or variable working capital is not always gainfully employed. For example, project businesses that are seasonal or cyclical in nature require relatively more temporary working capital. Therefore, capital that is temporarily invested in current assets should be obtained from sources that will allow its return when not in use.

The net concept is used in determining the amount and nature of assets that may be used to pay current liabilities. The amount that is left after these debts are paid may be used to meet future operational needs. If the analyst abstained from classifying permanent and temporary working capital, then net working capital is used as the average long-term level of working capital and has to be covered by medium or long-term financing or equity (schedules X-4 and X-7).

The amount of working capital invested should be optimal, that is, neither too large nor too small, to avoid penalties for the project. Working capital should be carefully estimated and adequately controlled and monitored.


*Accounts receivable (debtors)*

Accounts receivable are trade credits extended to product buyers as a condition of sale; the size of this item is therefore determined by the credit sales policy of the company. Since the ratio of credit sales to gross sales differs from company to company depending on the competitive situation prevailing in the industry, it is difficult to come up with a valid generalization. Each case should therefore be assessed individually according to the following formula:

$$\text{Debtors} = \frac{\text{Credit terms (in months)}}{12} \times (\text{Value of annual gross sales})$$

In the case of accounts receivable the value of annual gross sales should be calculated as costs of the product sold (that is, production costs plus marketing and distribution costs) minus depreciation and interest, with the understanding that the latter are to be covered by the sales revenues and not by the working capital.

*Inventories*

Working capital requirements are considerably affected by the amount of capital immobilized in the form of inventories. Every attempt should be made to reduce inventories to as low a level as justifiable.

*Production materials.* In computing inventories of production materials, consideration should be given to the sources and modes of supplies of raw materials and factory supplies. If the materials are locally available and in plentiful supply and can be rapidly transported, then only limited stocks should be maintained unless there are special reasons for keeping a higher stock (such as price fluctuations). If the materials are imported and import procedures are dilatory, then inventories equivalent to as much as six months' consumption may have to be maintained. Other factors influencing the size of inventories are the reliability and seasonality of supplies, the number of suppliers, possibilities of substitution and expected price changes.

*Spare parts.* Levels of spare-parts inventories depend on the local availability of supplies, import procedures and maintenance facilities in the area, and on the nature of the plant itself. The plant is usually provided with an initial set of spare parts.

*Work-in-progress.* To assess capital requirements for covering work-in-progress, a comprehensive analysis should be performed of the production process and of the degree of processing already reached by the different material inputs during each stage. The requirements are expressed in months (or days) of production, depending on the nature of the product. In machinery production, this can extend to several months. The valuation is based on the factory costs of work-in-progress.

*Finished products.* The inventory of finished products depends on a number of factors, such as the nature of the product and trade usage. The valuation is based on factory costs plus administrative overheads (schedule X-3).

*Cash-in-hand and cash-in-bank*

Interest is sometimes added to the working capital. If the interest is charged on a half-yearly basis, which is often the case, no provision is normally necessary. However, if at the end of such a six-month period the surplus of receipts over payments does not fully cover the interest payments, additional short-term finance would be required. It may also be prudent to provide for a certain amount of cash-in-hand. This could be done by including a contingency reserve on working capital, which, depending on the case, could be around 5 per cent.[94] Schedule X-5/2 provides an example of how to calculate the cash requirements in the case of seasonal fluctuations of such requirements.

---

[94]For the purpose of feasibility studies and in the case of a similar distribution of receipts and payments during each year, the approximate minimum cash/overdraft to be included in the computation of the net working capital may be computed on the basis of annual costs of labour, factory and administrative overheads, as well as direct marketing costs (or operating costs less the costs of raw materials, factory supplies and indirect marketing).

## Accounts payable (creditors)

Accounts payable will depend on credit terms provided by suppliers. Hence raw materials, factory supplies and services are usually purchased on credit with a certain period elapsing before payment is effected. Accrued taxes are also paid after a certain period has elapsed (unless tax advances have to be paid), and may be another source of finance similar to accounts payable. The same holds true for wages payable. Such credited payments reduce the amount of net working capital required.

It is very important to understand that creditors related to investment are to be excluded from the computation of working capital requirements, because by definition investments are long-term commitments and must therefore be financed by long-term resources (equity or debt).

## Calculation of net working capital requirements

When calculating the working capital requirements, the minimum coverage of days for current assets and liabilities has to be determined first. Annual factory costs, operating costs, and costs of products sold should then be computed, since the values of some components of the current assets are expressed in these terms. Since working capital requirements increase as a project gradually becomes fully operational, it is necessary to obtain the above cost data for the complete start-up period until and including production at full capacity (schedule X-3). If however the project generates sufficient cash surplusses (self-financing capacity), it may not be necessary to finance any net increase in working capital from outside resources.

The next step is to determine the coefficient of turnover for the components of current assets and liabilities by dividing 360 days by the number of days of minimum coverage (schedule X-4). Subsequently, the cost data provided in schedule X-3 for each item of the current assets and liabilities are divided by the respective coefficients of turnover and put in schedule X-4. Finally, the net working capital requirements for the different production stages are obtained by deducting the current liabilities from the sum of current assets. The required cash-in-hand is calculated separately (schedule X-5/2) and inserted at the bottom of schedule X-4.

Working capital for seasonal factories (such as a sugar factory) needs to be calculated on a slightly different basis. A year is divided into operational and non-operational periods. The working capital requirements during the operational phase are calculated on a normal basis. For the off-season, the working capital needed has to be scaled down, since only fixed costs are maintained. However, during the operational season, inventory must be increased, and therefore working capital requirements will grow. A seasonal factory has to build up the working capital in the operational period and decrease it during the non-operational period. The calculation of the working capital for seasonal firms is based on an annual forecast of payments and receipts.

All payments are listed and compared with monthly receipts coming from sales. In schedule X-5/1 the net working capital requirements are projected for the case of seasonal fluctuations. Schedule X-5/2 provides an example of the calculation of short-term liquidity. The last column of the schedule shows the deficits aggregated over the year, NCU 90,000 being the lowest and NCU 2,710,000 the highest deficits. In case of a permanent net working capital of approximately NCU 2 million, the credit would peak at about NCU 600,000 and the debt at about NCU 700,000.

The calculation of working capital requirements at the stage of the feasibility study is of particular importance since it forces the project promoter, investors and financing institutions to think about the funds needed to finance the operation of the project as compared with invested funds, such as pre-production expenditures and fixed investment costs.

Conceptually, the term net working capital should not be confused with the term current assets, which normally ought to be larger. Figure XXVIII shows how working capital should be financed out of permanent capital, which is composed of equity capital, reserves and long- and medium-term liabilities.

Current liabilities (mainly accounts payable) represent financial means usually considered to be put at the disposal of the project at no interest cost. However, in case a discount is offered for payment on delivery or receipt of the invoice, such a discount, if not used, is equivalent to an interest payable to creditors. It is a generally accepted practice to deduct current liabilities from current assets and to compute the return on capital employed as well as the discounted cash flows only for the permanently employed capital, that is, the finance corresponding to fixed investment plus working capital (see schedules X-6/1 and X-6/2).

### Schedules for total investment costs and total assets

From the figures of fixed investments, pre-production expenditures, and net working capital estimates, the total initial investment costs of the project under consideration can be calculated. The phasing of such costs, including plant and equipment replacement costs and end-of-life costs (if any), is shown in schedules X-6 and X-9. It should be noted that, when phasing the total investment outlay, the initial investments should be inserted in the schedule first, and then all subsequent increments, until operation at full capacity is reached.

In order to establish the projected balance sheets (schedule X-11) and to obtain sufficient data for ratio analysis,[95] a schedule covering total assets should be provided at the stage of project preparation. This can easily be done by substituting current assets for net working capital in schedule X-6. When phasing current assets, the initial amounts should be inserted in the schedule first, and then all subsequent changes, until operation at full capacity is reached.

### Production costs

It is essential to make realistic forecasts of production or manufacturing costs for a project proposal in order to determine the future viability of the project. One of the major deficiencies encountered in pre-investment studies is the inaccuracy of production cost estimates. This frequently leads to unexpected losses which, if reinforced by low capacity utilization caused by wrong sales forecasts, may quickly push a nascent establishment out of operation. The analysis of cost structures and identification of critical cost items, as well as

---

[95]See sect. G below.

## Figure XXVIII. Structure of the balance sheet

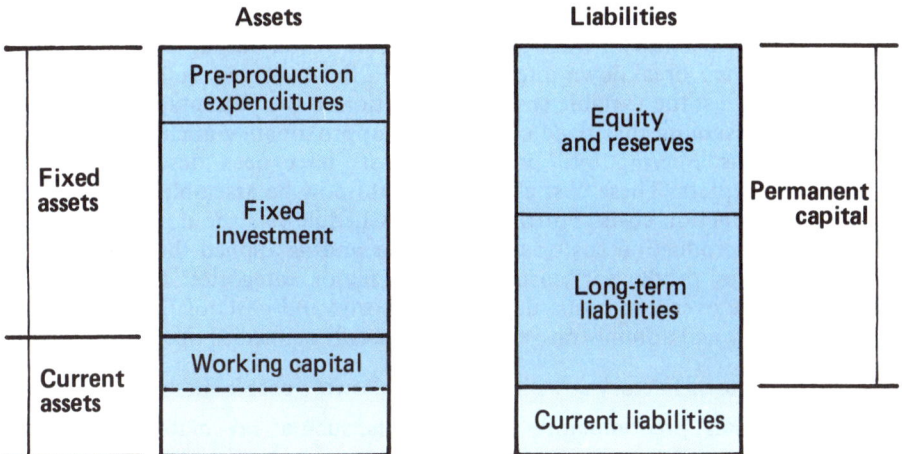

critical comparisons with similar projects, are proper means of improving the reliability and accuracy of cost projections and predictions of the financial feasibility of an investment.

Production costs should be calculated as total annual costs and preferably also as cost per unit produced (unit costs). Often pre-investment studies deal only with overall production costs, which should then be broken down at least into the main cost items (raw materials, factory supplies, personnel, overheads etc.). The computation of unit costs, which is relatively simple for single-product factories, may become rather complicated for certain technologies and the manufacture of a variety of products. For the analysis and justification of an envisaged production programme and for the break-even analysis, it is necessary to determine the main cost items directly related to each individual product. Production costs must be determined for the different levels of capacity utilization, and for an operational period corresponding to the planning horizon of the investors and financing institutions interested in the project.

Frequently overlooked in feasibility studies is the fact that fixed costs may be constant within only a limited range of production increases or decreases.

### Definition of production cost items[96]

As has been indicated, this *Manual* is geared towards the use of discounting methods for financial analysis and investment appraisal. All cost

---

[96]In the first edition of this *Manual* sales and distribution costs were treated as a part of total production costs. With the revision and extension of chapter III, the term marketing costs has been introduced, covering direct and indirect costs of all marketing activities (including sales and distribution costs). Since marketing costs are, strictly speaking, costs relating to the marketing of products and not to the manufacturing process, it has been decided to differentiate between these two types of costs.

elements required for the calculation of total production costs therefore have to be projected and scheduled in line with the production programme and for the full planning period. It is, however, not necessary to prepare a schedule for each cost item separately. Once production costs at full output level have been defined and their breakdown into variable and fixed costs is established,[97] it is possible to adjust the variable costs in proportion to the percentage of capacity utilization, assuming that fixed costs remain approximately unchanged. All of the cost items entering into production costs have been described in the preceding chapters. These cost elements should now be assembled in order to arrive at production costs. For this purpose schedule X-3 should be used. The definition of production costs as given earlier and as applied throughout this *Manual* divides production costs into four major categories: factory costs; administrative overhead costs; depreciation costs; and costs of financing. The sum of factory and administrative overhead costs is defined as operating costs.

*Factory costs.* Factory costs include the following cost items:

- Materials, predominantly variable costs, such as raw materials, factory supplies and spare parts
- Labour (production personnel) (fixed or variable costs, depending on type of labour and cost elements)
- Factory overheads (in general, fixed costs)

To arrive at factory costs (schedule VI-4), the final amounts derived from schedules IV-1, V-3, V-4, VI-1 (if applicable), VII-1 and VIII-2 should be inserted in schedule VI-4 and schedule X-3.

*Administrative overheads.* The composition of administrative overhead costs as well as procedures for their computation were described in chapter VII. All that is needed at this stage is to transfer the final amounts from schedules VII-1 and VIII-2 to schedule X-3.

*Depreciation costs.* Depreciation costs are charges made in the annual net income statement (profit-loss account) for the productive use of fixed assets. While depreciation costs have to be considered in accounting for the computation of the balance sheet and net income projections, they present investment expenditure (cash outflow during the investment phase) instead of production expenditure (cash outflow during production). Depreciation charges must therefore be added back if net cash flows are calculated from the net profit after corporate tax, as obtained from the net income statements. Depreciation costs do have an impact on net cash flows, because the higher the

---

[97]Variable costs change roughly in proportion to the variations in the level of production. Typical variable costs include materials, production labour and utilities. Variable costs can be divided further into: proportional costs, which change proportionally with the volume of production (for example, raw materials); degressive costs, which change at a lower rate than the volume of production (for example, maintenance and repair); progressive costs, which change at a higher rate than the volume of production (for example, overtime); and regressive costs, which decrease with an increase in the volume of production (for example, maintenance costs of unutilized machines).

Fixed costs remain unchanged regardless of changes in the level of activity, and include mainly overhead and depreciation charges, the latter only if the calculation is time-based. Fixed costs include long-term contractual services, rents, and administrative salaries.

This differentiation is a considerable simplification, and is only valid for a specific range of capacity utilization. It should be kept in mind when break-even analysis is discussed later in this chapter—the assumed cost curve may actually have a different shape.

depreciation charges, the lower the taxable income, and the lower the cash outflow corresponding to the tax payable on income.

*Financial costs.* Financial costs (interests) are sometimes considered as part of the administrative overheads, particularly if they relate to an existing establishment or one that is being expanded and for which the financing scheme is already known. For the purposes of financial analysis and investment appraisal, however, it is necessary to determine financial costs separately. Most feasibility studies show a declining amount of external finance and, correspondingly, decreasing financial costs. The computation of financial costs is described later in this chapter.[98] Financial costs are computed in schedule X-7 and inserted into schedule X-3.

Figure XXIX shows the interaction of the various cost elements in a feasibility study and indicates the chapters of the *Manual* in which they are covered. This should help the reader to obtain a better understanding of the cost structure and its impact on the profitability (return on investment and equity, respectively) of a project.

## Unit costs of production

For the purpose of cash flow analysis it is sufficient to calculate the annual costs. At the feasibility stage, however, an attempt should also be made to calculate unit costs to facilitate the comparison with sales prices per unit. For single-product projects, unit costs are calculated simply by dividing production costs by the number of units produced (therefore unit costs usually vary with capacity utilization). In the case of a multi-product project it is recommended to apply direct costing and compute both the direct costs and the margin generated per unit produced and sold. The overall margins serve to cover the indirect costs or overheads, that is, those costs which have not been directly related to a certain product. A common accounting method for computing unit overhead costs is to allocate overhead costs to direct material and direct labour unit costs by means of different percentage surcharges. For new investment projects the determination of these surcharges may be difficult, and for projects in developing countries in particular, comparative data may be difficult to obtain or may not be available at all. Cost accounting surcharges vary from factory to factory and country to country, and are computed with the help of a specially designed cost-centre accounting scheme. For an ongoing project, surcharges are based on historical data. In the absence of such data it might perhaps be thought that for new, large-scale projects an ex-ante cost-centre accounting scheme should be built up to compute ex-ante surcharges. There are, however, too many imponderables for this procedure to be generally practicable.

### Direct and indirect costs

From the viewpoint of product costing (calculation of unit cost prices), production costs and marketing costs should be divided into direct and indirect costs. Direct costs are easily attributable to a product unit or service in terms of

---

[98]See sect. F below.

270

**Figure XXIX. Origin of cost items for profitability calculation (return on equity)**

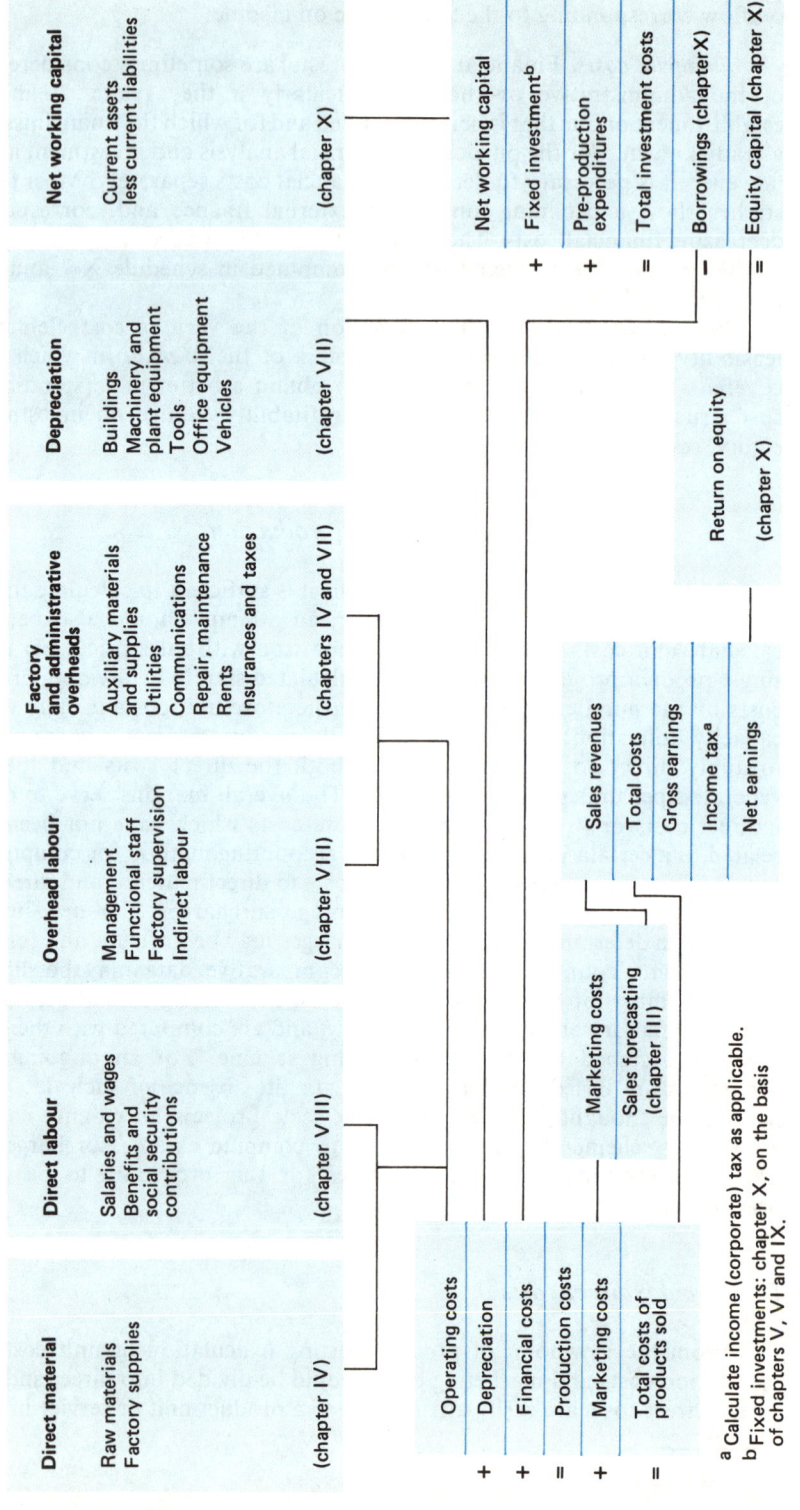

a Calculate income (corporate) tax as applicable.
b Fixed investments: chapter X, on the basis of chapters V, VI and IX.

cost of production materials and production labour. Since indirect costs (factory administrative overheads such as management and supervision, communications, depreciation and financial charges) cannot be easily allocated directly to a particular unit of output, they must first be apportioned to cost centres, and thereafter to the unit cost price by way of surcharges obtained from the cost accounting department. *Direct costing* is an accounting method that avoids the problem of determining surcharge rates. The direct variable and direct fixed costs are deducted from the revenues generated by a certain product (or product group), and the remaining surplus or margin together with the margins generated by other products is then available to cover the indirect costs. The surplus then remaining is called the *operational margin* (excluding or including costs of finance). This method may be extended for the computation of margins on different production or enterprise levels, such as a production line (first level), then a plant unit composed of more than one production line (second level), then the complete factory (third level), and finally the entire enterprise, which may operate more than one factory. Direct costs are often mixed up with variable costs and indirect costs with fixed costs, probably because most of the indirect costs are invariable or fixed. However, as described above, both direct and indirect costs may be variable or fixed. The distinction between direct and indirect costs is made to indicate the relationship between a cost item and a cost centre or profit centre, while the variability (or non-variability) describes the relationship between a cost item and the volume of production.

The solution adopted in this *Manual* is to deduct from the anticipated unit sales price the variable unit costs and then multiply the remaining margin by the units produced.[99] The annual margin must then be sufficient to cover all fixed costs arising in the period, and should also generate a sufficient surplus, as required by the investors.

### Marketing costs

Marketing costs comprise the costs for all marketing activities as described in chapter III (see also schedule III-2), and may be divided into direct marketing costs for each product or product group, such as packaging and storage (if not included in the production costs), sales costs (salespersons, commissions, discounts, returned products, royalties, product advertisements etc.), transport, interim storage (if required) and distribution costs, indirect marketing costs, such as overhead costs of the marketing department (personnel, materials and communications, market research, public relations and promotional activities not directly related to a product or product group etc.). The analysis of these costs involves their assignment to various costing groups such as territories, certain classes of customers (wholesalers, retailers, governmental institutions etc.), and products or product groups.

Marketing and distribution costs fall into the category of period costs, even if variable, and as such are charged against the operations of the accounting period in which they are incurred (while production costs are frozen in inventory until the units are sold). For depreciable investments as required

---

[99]It is also possible to deduct the total annual variable costs from the total sales income to compute the annual margin, in this case the variable margin. The computation of the variable margin is necessary when a break-even analysis is required.

for marketing and distribution (for example, delivery trucks), depreciation charges are to be included in the computation of total marketing costs. The analysis of marketing costs together with direct costing can be a very useful instrument for evaluating a marketing mix and for determining an optimal production programme and product mix.

# D. Basic accounting statements

Although the cash flow analysis has been adopted as the principal instrument of investment appraisal, it is necessary for the analyst and for those finally deciding whether to invest and finance a project to have an understanding of basic accounting principles and statements. The accounting statements are also important for the analysis of the structure of project financing and for the computation of the capital costs of a company. In the case of rehabilitation, modernization and expansion projects, the accounting records of the existing company are usually the best source of information and the basis for starting the financial analysis.

There are basically two categories of accounting statements: the net income statement or profit and loss account which is linked to the balance sheet; and the cash flow table for financial planning. In many countries the balance sheet and net income statement must be published in the case of certain types of corporations.

## Net income statement

The net income statement (schedule X-10) is used to compute the net income (net earnings) or deficit of the project arising each year. The projections are required for the entire duration of the planning period chosen for the project. The net income statement differs from the cash flow statement inasmuch as it shows costs and incomes (and not expenditures and revenues)[100] by period, following the accrual concept, according to which income from operations is associated with the costs that were needed to achieve this income during the period under consideration. To keep computations simple, in feasibility studies it is usually assumed that inventories of raw materials, work-in-progress and final products are the same at the beginning and end of each accounting period (usually the calendar year).

The net income statement is linked with the projected balance sheet in so far as the annual profit (or loss) shown in the net income statement (schedule X-10) increases (or reduces) the wealth of a company as represented on the balance sheet. Annual profits, if retained, increase the reserves (schedule X-11), while losses are accumulated under the assets.[101] As dividends are usually not paid in the same year, the annual balance contains also a line for dividends payable (schedule X-11).

---

[100]The cash flow concept is described in the section on accounting terminology in part one of this *Manual*.

[101]In United States accounting, accumulated losses are not shown on the asset side, but are deducted from accumulated profits, making the account negative if the losses exceed the profits.

272

For the purpose of a feasibility study the net income statement should show at least how the net earnings are divided between different classes of equity shareholders, the different suppliers of loan capital and the tax authorities. For the break-even analysis the variable costs, the variable margin, fixed costs (including depreciation and financial charges) and the operational margin should be shown (schedule X-10). No explanatory notes on the concept of net income statements are provided here, since this has been sufficiently covered in the literature.

### Balance sheet

A balance sheet is a statement showing the accumulated assets—the wealth—of a company and how this wealth is financed. The sources of finance are treated as the aggregate liabilities of the company *vis-à-vis* those providing it with funds, namely the investors (equity shareholders) and the group of creditors, banks and debenture holders. By definition both sides of a balance sheet, representing assets and liabilities,[102] are equal. For the purpose of a feasibility study the balance sheet should be broken down at least as shown in schedule X-11.

The projected balance sheet in the feasibility study should consist of estimates of key items, such as cash and other current assets (in particular, raw materials, accounts receivable, work-in-progress, and finished products), fixed assets, as well as equity and loan capital and current liabilities that are required for the smooth performance of the enterprise. The series of projected balance sheets shows then the projected development of the accumulated assets and how these are financed.[103]

All components of the balance sheet are contained in the schedules already designed, although a number of adjustments still have to be made. Current assets are shown in schedule X-4,[104] and fixed assets may be computed from the data contained in schedule X-6 (it should be noted that annual depreciation allowances are required in order to arrive at the book value). Short- and medium-term loans and equity capital are derived from schedule X-7/3, whereas current liabilities are inserted from schedule X-4. The balance between total assets and long-term liabilities, however, may show the need for additional, usually short-term, finance. On the other hand, a cash surplus (unemployed liquidity) may be shown on the asset side, resulting from retained profits (build-up of reserves, as shown in schedule X-10).

It is a matter of company policy whether to maintain high accumulated reserves and retained profits as compared with equity capital, or to convert such reserves into equity capital. Often business laws demand that a minimum amount of reserves (related, for example, to dividend payments) is maintained. Retained profits are available for financing new investments, and under some taxation laws these funds may be cheaper for the firm than new equity paid in by shareholders.

---

[102]In the United States, the term "liabilities" does not include equity and reserves.

[103]The discussion of the rate of turnover presented at this point in the first edition has been transferred to the later section on financial and efficiency ratios.

[104]Changes in inventories of raw materials, work-in-progress and finished products have been taken into account when calculating the working capital (see schedule X-4 for the growth of current assets).

*Source and application of funds (cash flow table for financial planning)*

It is not sufficient to determine the total amount of financial means required and to identify sources of available finance. The timing of the inflow of funds (paid-in equity, loan disbursements, sales revenues, short-term loans, bank overdrafts or creditors) must be synchronized with the various expenditures (cash outflow) for investments as well as the plant operation. If this timing of financial flows is not properly done, the project may experience periods with accumulated financial surpluses not employed but costing interest, or face sudden shortages of funds and liquidity problems. The latter case may have a serious financial impact, for example, forcing the project to borrow short-term finance at usually higher costs, or there may be delays in project implementation if a financial bottleneck cannot be covered during the construction phase. During the operational phase liquidity problems would lead to reduced supplies and under-utilization of the installed production capacities.

The net income statement and the balance sheet, designed to show the wealth of a firm, are not directly suitable for financial planning, that is, the assurance of the liquidity of the firm. It is therefore necessary to prepare a cash flow schedule showing the sources and application of funds, in particular, the overall cash inflows and outflows. During the project implementation and operational phases detailed financial planning is required at least on a monthly basis. For the purpose of the feasibility study, however, an annual cash flow schedule is generally sufficient.

Just as financial planning for the investment phase should ensure that capital is available to finance investment expenditures, and that financial inflows and expenditures (cash outflows) are synchronized, financial planning for the operational phase must ensure that cash inflows, or sales revenues, from operations will be adequate to cover all production expenses and all financial commitments, such as debt service (both interest and principal), taxes and payment of projected dividends. This aspect is particularly significant in the early years of operation, when output is usually considerably below the installed capacity, while the burden of debt service is often the highest. This is the case, for example, with supplier credits, which usually have to be repaid over a period from 5 to 8 years in equal instalments.

In schedule X-8, an example of integrated cash flow (comprising operational (real) and financial cash flows) is given, covering the periods of construction, start-up and operation at full capacity. The preparation of a separate cash flow schedule showing also the foreign exchange requirements and foreign cash inflows is recommended. Data for the financial planning schedule are obtained from schedules X-1, X-2 and X-4 (fixed investment, current assets and current liabilities), X-7 (sources of finance and corresponding debt service) and X-10 (sales revenues). The cash flow tables are closely linked to the projected balance sheet, since the cumulative cash balance obtained in the cash flow schedule for financial planning—which should never be negative—corresponds to the figure in the balance sheet. The cash outflow for tax payments is obtained from the net income statements, assuming that the tax is paid at the end of the same year, in other words, that no tax credits are granted.

Since capital is frequently scarce, it is the general tendency of inexperienced promoters to keep the projected financial requirements as low as possible. A project analyst should resist the temptation to please the sponsors of the study by such unreasonably low figures. Bad financial planning in the pre-investment study will hamper the progress of the project either while obtaining clearance by financial institutions or at an even more crucial stage of project implementation.

In order to shed more light on the financial structure of investment proposals and to facilitate the final choice of financing, alternative modes of financing must be considered and provided for in every pre-investment study. For each financing alternative the cash flow tables, net income and balance sheet projections have to be computed, as well as those ratios and indicators of the efficiency of investment projects which vary with the structure and costs of finance.

The following two approaches are generally taken in projecting cash needs:

- A cash flow forecast based on the income statement, in which the statement is adjusted for non-cash items. The resulting figure refers to funds provided by operations. Considering cash flows not recognized in the income statement leads to the final funds position of the project;

- A cash receipts and disbursement statement, or the cash budget, reflecting the initial cash balance, the receipts for the period, the expected disbursements and the ending cash balance. This statement is typically divided into subperiods, possibly in terms of weekly or monthly time intervals.

## E.  Methods of investment appraisal

As far as the investor is concerned, the investment criterion overruling all other project-related business objectives is the financial feasibility of an investment project. This means that the financial return on both the total capital invested and on the paid-in equity capital is sufficiently high. However, the interest of the parties involves a wider field of decision criteria than that represented by net returns on capital invested.[105] Although sufficient returns are essential for a project to be approved, investments must be justified usually within a wider context, which for investors and financiers includes any gains, whether net profits or non-cash benefits, resulting directly or indirectly from an investment. For investment appraisal such external or indirect benefits should be expressed in monetary terms whenever possible, if the decision makers want to include such criteria for the approval of a project.

As mentioned in discussing financial statements, different sources of finance are usually involved in financing a project. Each of the parties interested in co-financing would logically have their own appraisal criteria, including the acceptable minimum return on the corresponding capital share. The feasibility study should therefore consider the various decision criteria. The financial evaluation should be carried out and presented in such a way that all parties concerned with the investment and financing decision obtain the information needed to ascertain their share of the projected return in relation to other parties as well as in relation to their inputs and the expected financial risks of the project.

An entrepreneur, as a rule, finances a project partly through equity capital and partly through borrowed funds. The prime interest of the entrepreneur is

---

[105]See sect. B above.

usually to know the profitability of the equity capital, that is, the net profit after tax over the paid-in equity (or share) capital. When preparing a feasibility study, however, it is generally not known how the project will be finally financed. Apart from the impact of loan financing on income tax computations (cost of finance is deductible from the operational margin),[106] the profitability rate for equity capital depends entirely on the overall profitability of total capital invested and the interest paid on the debt balance (leverage effect). It is therefore necessary first to determine the financial feasibility of the investment project as a whole, and only then assess the individual feasibility for each participating source of finance (equity holders including joint venture partners, commercial banks and development finance institutions).[107]

Cash-flow concept

Investment has been defined[108] as a long-term commitment of economic resources made with the objective of producing and obtaining net gains in the future. The conventional methods of investment appraisal, which will be discussed later, basically evaluate the expected net profit (sales income less costs and income taxes) against the capital invested. For the purpose of investment appraisal it is, however, necessary to assess and evaluate over a certain period (in this *Manual* defined as the planning horizon of the decision makers) all inputs required and all outputs produced by the project. The information contained in the net income statements and projected balance sheets is, however, not sufficient for this purpose, and therefore the discounted cash-flow concept has become the generally accepted method for investment appraisal.

Similarly, the cash-flow concept is needed for planning of the flow of financial means, in other words, of the sources and application of funds.

### Definition and computation of cash flows

Cash flows are basically either receipts of cash (cash inflows) or payments (cash outflows). For the purpose of financial planning and the determination of the net cash returns of an investment, it is necessary to distinguish between financial flows, which are related to the financing of an investment, and cash flows (expenditures and revenues) representing the performance or operation of the project (operational cash flows).

Financial cash flows are shown in schedules X-7/2 (financial resources, inflow), X-7/4 (debt service, outflow) and X-8, and include, for example:

| *Financial inflows* | *Financial outflows* |
|---|---|
| Paid-in equity capital | Dividends paid |
| | Buying back of shares |

---

[106]See schedule X-10.

[107]Profitability ratios for capital invested are computed from the figures contained in the balance sheet and net income statement of the project. Since the net profit is usually not identical with the profit distributed (dividends paid), two different values can be computed for the profitability of equity capital. As compared with the cash-flow concept, there is also a difference between the net cash return on equity capital and the profitability computed for the same source of funds. The differences are explained in detail below in the analysis of cash-flow discounting methods.

[108]See sect. B. above.

| Financial inflows | Financial outflows |
|---|---|
| Subsidies, grants | Repayments (if required) |
| Long- and medium-term loans | Interests paid on loans and other costs of finance |
| | Amortization (repayment) of loans |
| Short-term loans, bank overdraft | Interest paid on short-term loans and overdraft, repayments on short-term loans and overdraft |
| Increase in accounts payable | Decrease in accounts payable |

Operational cash flows are shown in schedules X-9 (discounted cash flow):

| Operational cash outflows | Operational cash inflows |
|---|---|
| Increase in fixed assets investment) | Revenues from selling of fixed assets |
| | Recovery of salvage values (end of project) |
| Increase in net working capital | Revenues from decrease of net working capital |
| Operating costs[109] | Sales revenues |
| Marketing expenses | |
| Production and distribution losses | Other income due to plant operations |
| Corporate (income) taxes | |

## Basic assumptions underlying cash-flow discounting

This *Manual* does not undertake to justify and explain the methods and basic assumptions of cash-flow discounting and compounding, because the subject is extensively dealt with in the literature. The basic assumption underlying the discounted cash-flow concept is that money has a time value in so far as a given sum of money available now is worth more than an equal sum available in the future. This difference can be expressed as a percentage rate indicating the relative change for a given period which, for practical reasons, is usually a year. Considering that a project may obtain a certain amount of funds $F$, if this sum is repaid after one year including an agreed interest $I$, the total sum to be paid after one year would be $(F + I)$, where

$$F + I = F(1 + r)$$

and $r$ is defined as the interest rate (in percentage per year) divided by 100 (if the interest rate is, for example, 12.0 per cent, then $r$ equals 0.12).

---

[109]It should be noted that depreciation charges (costs) and interest payments are not classified among the operational cash outflows, because inclusion of depreciation of assets would provoke a double-counting of the costs to the project, since they are already accounted for as investment costs when capitalized in the balance. However, for accounting purposes (including taxation) assets are to be depreciated over the project lifetime. This is why the depreciation of assets is a cost item in the net income statement only, and must be deducted from the annual total costs of products sold (production and marketing costs) when determining the annual cash outflows. Interest and any other cost of finance are also included for the computation of the yield or return on the total capital investment, because they are part of this total yield. However, interest on loans (but not net profits distributed) is a cost item in the net income statement.

Supposing that $CF_n$ is the nominal value of a future cash flow in the year $n$, and $CF_p$ the value at the present time (present value) of this expected inflow or outflow, then (assuming that $r$ is constant):

$$CF_p = CF_n/(1 + r)^n$$

$$\text{or } CF_p = CF_n(1 + r)^{-n}$$

## Main discounting methods

There are two main discounting methods used in practice for the appraisal of investment projects, as far as the evaluation of financial feasibility is concerned: the net-present-value method (often referred to as NPV method), and the internal-rate-of-return (IRR) method, sometimes also referred to as the discounted-cash-flow method.

### Net present value

The net present value of a project is defined as the value obtained by discounting, at a constant interest rate and separately for each year, the differences of all annual cash outflows and inflows accruing throughout the life of a project. This difference is discounted to the point at which the implementation of the project is supposed to start. The NPVs obtained for the years of the project life are added to obtain the project NPV as follows:

$$NPV = NCF_0 + (NCF_1 \times a_1) + (NCF_2 \times a_2) + ... + (NCF_n \times a_n)$$

$$\text{or } NPV = \sum_{n=0}^{n=j} \frac{NCF_n}{(1 + r)^n}$$

where $NCF_n$ is the annual net cash flow of a project in the years $n = 1, 2, ..,$ $j$, and $a_n$ is the discount factor in the corresponding years, relating to the discount rate applied through the equation

$$a_n = (1 + r)^{-n}$$

Discount factors ($a_n$) may be obtained from present value tables.

The *discount rate or cut-off rate* should be equal either to the actual rate of interest on long-term loans in the capital market or to the interest rate (cost of capital) paid by the borrower.[110] The discount rate should basically reflect the *opportunity cost of capital,* which corresponds to the possible returns an investor (financier) would obtain on the same amount of capital if invested elsewhere, assuming that the financial risks are similar for both investment alternatives. In other words, the discount rate should be the *minimum rate of return,* below which an entrepreneur would consider that it does not pay for him to invest.

---

[110]The market rate for long-term loans is usually valid for borrowers with the best credit rating. In case additional risks, exceeding the normal investment risks, are expected, financing institutions as well as private investors would increase the costs of finance for the project by adding a safety margin to the base rate to cover the various country risks etc.

If the computed NPV is positive, the profitability of the investment is above the cut-off discount rate. If it is zero, the profitability is equal to the cut-off rate. A project with a positive NPV can thus be considered acceptable, provided a sufficient margin of error above zero NPV to account for uncertainty has been included. If the NPV is negative, the profitability is below the cut-off rate (usually the opportunity cost of capital for this type of project), and the project should be dropped.

An important decision criterion of the investor is often not only the profitability of his investment, but also the answer to the question: how long does it take to get the money back including a certain minimum interest rate? He may decide, for instance, to invest only if the investment is repaid in five years at an interest rate of 15 per cent per year, which would mean that the NPV must not be negative for a discounting rate of 15 per cent and a planning horizon of five years. The net cash return on equity would have to be used for discounting.

Using the data of the example, the NPV of the total investment outlay (schedule X-9/1) and the NPV of the equity capital (schedule X-9/2) can be determined. The relevant schedules are given at the end of this chapter.

Schedules X-9/1 and X-9/2 show that the working capital and the salvage value of fixed assets will be recovered by the end of the project life. For the computation of the discounted return on equity capital invested, any outstanding debt balances would have to be deducted from these salvage values in order to obtain the real end-of-life net worth for the shareholders.

The NPV and the IRR for the total investment (schedule X-9/1) shows the yield of the project as a whole. In case there is no loan (outside) financing, the NPV and IRR are the same as in schedule X-9/2.[111] However, if part of the investment is financed from loan capital (outside financing), the NPV and IRR are different because of the tax effect of the debt service (interest is a cost item, and therefore the taxable profit is lower in the case of interest payments). The cash flow corresponding to payment of the income (corporate) tax is taken from the net income statement (schedule X-10).

## Net-present-value ratio

If one of several project alternatives has to be chosen, the project with the largest NPV should be selected. This needs some refinement, since the NPV is only an indicator of the positive net cash flows or of the net benefits of a project. In cases where there are two or more alternatives, it is advisable to know how much investment will be required to generate these positive NPVs. The ratio of the NPV and the present value of the investment (PVI) required is called the net-present-value ratio (NPVR),[112] and yields a discounted rate of return. This should be used for comparing alternative projects. The formula is as follows:

$$NPVR = \frac{NPV}{PVI}$$

[111]It should be borne in mind that if a project is financed without loan capital, the production costs will not contain any financial costs.

[112]In some textbooks this is called the profitability index.

If the construction period does not exceed one year, the value of investment will not have to be discounted. A comparison of the two alternative ways of financing the project in the example yields the NPVRs shown in table 1.

Table 1.  Computation of net-present-value ratios

| Schedule | $NPV^a$ at 12 per cent | PVI | NPVR |
|---|---|---|---|
| X-9/1 | 3 798 | 3 291 + 4 578 + 761 = 8 630 | 0.44 |
| X-9/2 | 4 106 | 2 600 + 804 + 8 = 3 412 | 1.20 |

$a$ Accumulated for 18 years (schedules X-9/1 and X-9/2).

In summary, the NPV has great advantages as a discriminatory method compared with the payback period or the annual rate of return, discussed later, since it takes account of the entire project life[113] and of the timing of the cash flows. The NPVR can also be considered as a calculated investment rate which the profit rate of the project should at least reach. The shortcomings of the NPV are the difficulty in selecting the appropriate discount rate and the fact that the NPV does not show the exact profitability of the project. For this reason the NPV is not always understood by business people used to thinking in terms of a rate of return on capital. It is therefore advisable to use the internal rate of return.

*Internal rate of return*

The internal rate of return is the discount rate at which the present value of cash inflows is equal to the present value of cash outflows. In other words, it is the discount rate for which the present value of the net receipts from the project is equal to the present value of the investment, and the NPV is zero. Mathematically, it means that in the NPV equation discussed earlier, the value for $r$ has to be found for which—at defined values for $CF_n$— the NPV equals zero. The solution is found by an iterative process, using either discounting tables or a suitable computer programme.

The procedure used to calculate the IRR is the same as the one used to calculate the NPV. The same kind of table can be used, and, instead of discounting cash flows at a predetermined cut-off rate, several discount rates may have to be tried until the rate is found at which the NPV is zero. This rate is the IRR, and it represents the exact profitability of the project.[114]

The calculation procedure begins with the preparation of a cash flow table. An estimated discount rate is then used to discount the net cash flow to the

---

[113] An investor may be willing to invest if the NPV on his paid-in equity is above zero for a shorter period—his planning horizon adopted for the investment decision—than the project lifetime. In this case the net cash return on equity is estimated for this shorter period and discounted using the cut-off rate of the investor. If the value of the plant at the end of the planning horizon (assuming, for example, that the investor could sell his equity share at that time) is taken into account in the decision, then the net value, that is, the total value net of all obligations towards others, is taken as a net cash inflow occurring at the end of the discounting period.

[114] The IRR is known also as marginal efficiency of capital, interest rate of return, discounted cash flow, or financial rate of return (as opposed to the economic rate of return used in economic analysis).

present value. If the NPV is positive, a higher discount rate is applied. If the NPV is negative at this higher rate, the IRR must be between these two rates. However, if the higher discount rate still gives a positive NPV, the discount rate must be increased until the NPV becomes negative.

If the positive and negative NPVs are close to zero, a good approximation of the IRR value can be obtained, using the following linear interpolation formula:

$$i_r = i_1 + \frac{PV\,(i_2 - i_1)}{PV + NV}$$

where $i_r$ is the IRR, PV is the positive NPV (at the lower discount rate $i_1$), and NV is the negative NPV (at the higher discount rate $i_2$).

The absolute values of both PV and NV are used in the above formula. It should be noted that $i_1$ and $i_2$ should not differ by more than one or two percentage points (absolute). The above formula will not yield realistic results if the difference is too large, since the discount rate and the NPV are not related linearly.

For the total capital invested the NPV equals $3,801,000 at a 12 per cent discount rate (for the example shown in schedule X-9/1). In order to find the IRR, several discount rates greater than 12 per cent are tried until the NPV is approximately zero. The NPVs at discount rates of 18 per cent and 20 per cent are shown in table 2.[115]

Table 2.   Example of cash flow discounting

| Year | Annual net cash flow (thousand dollars) | Discount factor at 18 per cent | NPV (thousand dollars) | Discount factor at 20 per cent | NPV (thousand dollars) |
|---|---|---|---|---|---|
| 1 | (3 291) | 1.000 | (3 291) | 1.000 | (3 291) |
| 2 | (5 127) | 0.847 | (4 343) | 0.833 | (4 271) |
| 3 | (88) | 0.718 | (63) | 0.694 | (61) |
| 4 | 1 722 | 0.609 | 1 049 | 0.579 | 997 |
| 5 | 2 700 | 0.516 | 1 393 | 0.482 | 1 301 |
| 6 | 3 343 | 0.437 | 1 461 | 0.402 | 1 344 |
| 7 | 2 259 | 0.370 | 836 | 0.335 | 757 |
| 8 | 1 208 | 0.314 | 339 | 0.279 | 337 |
| 9 | 2 192 | 0.266 | 583 | 0.233 | 511 |
| 10 | 2 170 | 0.225 | 488 | 0.194 | 421 |
| 11 | 2 170 | 0.191 | 414 | 0.162 | 352 |
| 12 | 1 995 | 0.162 | 323 | 0.135 | 269 |
| 13 | 1 805 | 0.137 | 247 | 0.112 | 202 |
| 14 | 1 805 | 0.116 | 209 | 0.093 | 168 |
| 15 | 1 805 | 0.099 | 177 | 0.078 | 141 |
| 16 | 1 805 | 0.084 | 152 | 0.065 | 117 |
| 17 | 1 805 | 0.071 | 128 | 0.054 | 97 |
| 18 | 2 723 | 0.060 | 163 | 0.045 | 123 |
| Accumulated total | — | — | 265 | — | (486) |

Note: Figures in parantheses are negative.

---

[115]The IRR is sensitive to the length of the cash flow array (planning horizon). For example, if the cash flow is discounted for 16 years only, the IRR would be approximately 18 per cent, and less if a shorter planning horizon is chosen.

Table 2 shows that, discounted at 18 per cent, the net cash flow is still positive, but it becomes negative at 20 per cent. Consequently, the IRR must lie between 18 and 20 per cent. For practical purposes this would be sufficiently close to be able to calculate the exact IRR using the formula or a graphical interpolation.

## Interpretation of the internal rate of return

The IRR may be interpreted as the annual net cash return (gain or yield in financial terms) produced on capital outstanding per period, or understood, in other words, as the highest net-of-tax annuity rate (annual debt service rate) at which the project could raise funds, provided the annual net cash flows are rather constant.[116]

When analysing the equations for the computation of the NPV of a series of annual cash flows $CF_n$, it can easily be shown that the same NPV may be obtained for different cash flow arrays, and similarly, for investment projects with completely different cash flow structures, the same IRR may be computed (see table 3). In addition, the value computed for the NPV depends also on the lengths of the cash flow array (that is, the planning horizon adopted as a criterion for the investment decision). The IRR or NPV should therefore never be used as the only decision criterion, and the financial evaluation of investment projects should always include a critical analysis of the structure and timing of discounted cash flows.

### Table 3. Comparison of project alternatives

(Thousands of dollars)

| Invested capital | Discounted annual net cash flow | | | | | | | | NPV | Rate of discount or IRR (per cent) |
|---|---|---|---|---|---|---|---|---|---|---|
| | 1 | 2 | 3 | 4 | 5 | 6 | 7 | 8 | | |
| *Project A* | | | | | | | | | | |
| (950) | 150 | 170 | 190 | 210 | 230 | 250 | 270 | 375 | 895 | — |
| (950) | 130 | 129 | 125 | 120 | 114 | 108 | 102 | 122 | — | 15 |
| (950) | 134 | 136 | 135 | 134 | 130 | 127 | 152 | 152 | 120 | 12 |
| (190)[a] | 34 | 34 | 34 | 33 | 32 | — | — | — | (17) | 12[b] |
| *Project B* | | | | | | | | | | |
| (780) | 166 | 180 | 190 | 200 | 200 | 200 | 200 | — | 556 | — |
| (780) | 144 | 136 | 125 | 115 | 99 | 86 | 75 | — | — | 15 |
| (780) | 148 | 144 | 135 | 127 | 113 | 101 | 91 | — | 79 | 12 |
| (156)[a] | 37 | 36 | 34 | 32 | 28 | — | — | — | 9 | 12[b] |

*Note:* Figures in parentheses are negative.

[a]Assuming 20 per cent equity participation and a 25 per cent share in net cash flows.

[b]Assuming investor's opportunity costs of capital at same rate as for total project.

---

[116]When the assets of a project sufficiently cover all liabilities at the end of the discounting period, the IRR would only then correspond to the highest net-of-tax interest rate, provided that the firm has the option to repay its obligations at will.

The investment proposal may be accepted if the IRR is greater than the cut-off rate (the cost of capital plus any margin for risk), which is the lowest acceptable interest rate for the invested capital.[117]

If several projects or alternatives are being compared, it is not necessarily the project with the highest IRR which should be selected, provided the IRR is greater than the cut-off rate for at least two of the projects or alternatives. In this case, known as the ranking problem and the problem of mutually exclusive investment projects, the two discussed discounting methods may lead to contradictory results.[117]

*The ranking problem*

It has been shown above that different cash flow arrays can produce an identical IRR, and it is also possible that a project with a lower IRR (still above the cut-off rate, however) should be given preference to a project with a higher IRR but showing an undesirable cash flow structure. Furthermore, projects **may be ranked differently if the NPV method is applied. Figure XXX below illustrates the problem.**

The IRR of project B ($IRR_B$) is higher than for project A ($IRR_A$), and for any rate of discount between $i_2$ and the IRR, the NPV is higher for project B than for project A. If the cut-off rate is below $i_2$, then both projects would be still acceptable from the profitability point of view. In this case, however, project A would be given priority if the NPV dominates project selection. The rate of discount for which the NPVs of both projects are identical is called the crossover rate ($i_2$). Under the rather theoretical conditions of completely identical project risks, identical project life and a comparable amount of investment, the project earning the higher yield would normally be ranked first. Since these assumptions would rarely apply in real life, the investors' evaluation of the different project risks and of possible risk minimization strategies would finally determine the investment decision.

*Mutually exclusive projects*

For the reasons explained above the IRR method should also be applied with care in the case of two or more mutually exclusive projects. Projects are mutually exclusive if the acceptance of one project means the rejection of the other. This situation is typical, for example, if only one site is available to the

---

[117]The IRR should be applied with care in cases where major negative net cash flows occur repeatedly during the later life of the project. Although this occurs very seldom (occasionally in the oil and mining industry, for example), the NPV may go positive and negative more than once when applying different rates of discount. In this case, there would be more than one solution for the IRR (a polynomial equation has as many solutions as there are changes in the sign of the cash flows series, although most likely not all solutions would be real), and the IRR method may produce meaningless results. To overcome this deficiency, the adjustment of the cash flows in accordance with the yield method and the following procedure has been recommended. The point is determined from which the future cash flows—discounted at the yield rate—are negative. These cash flows are then discounted at the normal cost of capital to bring them back in time to the point at which they are largely absorbed by the preceding positive cash flows. A revised yield calculation is then performed on the cash flows modified in this way. This method is explained and justified in detail in A. J. Merrett and A. Sykes, *The Finance and Analysis of Capital Projects* (London, Longman, 1974).

**Figure XXX.  NPV method and ranking problem**

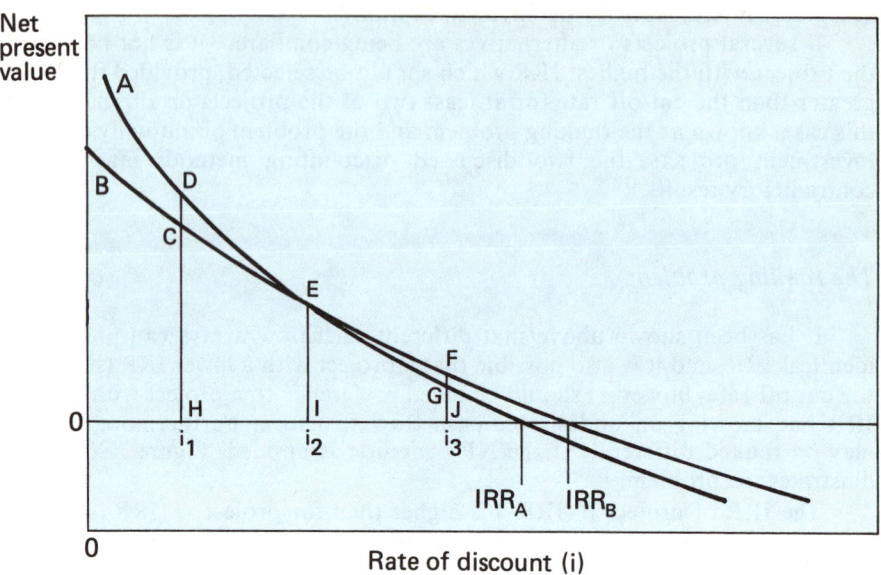

investors, or if they have a choice between extending an existing plant or establishing additional but smaller production facilities at a distant location (total capacity being limited by total demand). This problem is not a question of accepting or rejecting a project, but of determining which of two feasible alternatives should be chosen. Figure XXX can again be used to illustrate the problem.

When applying the IRR criterion project B would be chosen because the value of the IRR is greater for project B than for project A. Using the NPV as a selection criterion, the solution depends on the rate of discount applied. In figure XXX, for example, if the opportunity cost of capital corresponds to an interest rate $i_2$, both projects would show an identical NPV ($\overline{IE}$) for this rate of discount. In case the opportunity cost of capital is lower, project A may be chosen because of the higher NPV ($\overline{HD}$). If the discounting rate is higher than $i_2$ (as is the case with $i_3$) the choice would probably be in favour of project B, owing to its higher NPV ($\overline{JF}$). The application of the IRR method would also lead to the selection of project B.

Of the three appraisal methods discussed above, the NPV allows the evaluation of the expected accumulated net gains of an investment discounted to the present time. The NPVR shows the accumulated net gain as generated by one unit of capital invested, while the IRR indicates the net return (gain) expressed as a profitabilty rate per year, but does not allow any direct conclusion to be drawn with regard to the accumulated gains. Furthermore, all three methods have in common that there is no direct assessment of the distribution of cash inflows and outflows over the planning horizon (increasing, decreasing, constant or fluctuating net cash flows). Therefore, when applying these methods, the financial objectives and decision criteria of the investors (and financing institutions) with regard to amortization periods, risk acceptance etc. must be observed. This may be especially important in cases where one method would not produce a clear indication of which project alternative to choose. For example (see table 3), suppose there are two projects A and B with the same IRR, as follows:

| Project | IRR (per cent) | NPV at 12 per cent |
|---------|----------------|--------------------|
| A       | 15             | 120                |
| B       | 15             | 79                 |

Since both projects have the same IRR of 15 per cent, an investor would be indifferent to the choice of either if the IRR method alone is applied. However, project A would produce a higher NPV at 12 per cent, and is also better if the NPVR is taken as an efficiency measure (0.126 for A and 0.101 for B). Project A should therefore be recommended for implementation, provided the projects are similar with regard to other investment criteria (risk, markets, total funds available etc.). On the other hand, an investor sharing, for example, 20 per cent of the initial investment and—as a simplification—25 per cent of the annual net cash flows would prefer project B, if the aim is to recover the investment at 12 per cent within five years.

The discounted net cash return on equity (NPV and IRR on equity) is computed by deducting from the net cash flows of the entire project the financial cash flows related to loans (outside financing), that is, the debt service (interest and amortization of the loan) as well as the repayment of any debt balance outstanding at the end of the planning period (see schedule X-9/2).

### Discounted return on equity capital

The concept of cash flow discounting can also be applied to determine the NPV of an investment from the point of view of the shareholders. Two positions may be distinguished:

- The cash returns on equity as represented by annual payments of dividends are discounted at the opportunity cost of capital of the shareholders. The NPV for shareholders is obtained by deducting the total of discounted paid-in equity from the accumulated discounted dividend payments. If this NPV is positive for the planning period of shareholders, the investment would be able to pay the required returns. The IRR for this cash flow shows the profitability of equity capital, as represented by dividends paid.

- The cash surpluses generated annually, that is, after debt service and corporate tax, but before payment of dividends, is discounted. The discounted net cash flow from the point of view of the shareholders is obtained by deducting the total discounted equity payments from the accumulated discounted cash surpluses (that is, the accumulated discounted return on equity capital). The computation of this discounted return on equity[118] is demonstrated in schedule X-9/2.

---

[118]The discounted return on equity corresponds to the "present value for a project with outside financing", as described in schedule X-14 in the first edition of this *Manual*.

## Conventional methods

### Payback period

The payback, also called pay-off period, is defined as the period required to recover the original investment outlay through the accumulated net cash flows earned by the project. It is important to note that the cash flows of a project are used to calculate the payback. It would be entirely wrong to compute the payback on the basis of the accumulated net profit after tax. Even when accumulated interest and depreciation are added back, there is the danger that investments for replacement, as usually necessary for continuing the operation of the plant, will not be included in the calculations.

The payback method[119] is mainly criticized for its concentration on the initial phase of the production period, without taking into account, for the investment decision, the performance of the plant after the payback period. This critical argument would be justified if an investment decision is entirely based on the payback method. However, if applied for assessing risk and liquidity, and if used in combination with profitability measures as discussed in this *Manual*, the payback can be a very practical and useful instrument.

### Interpretation of the payback

*Risk.* The payback is useful if a new project would have to expect rapid technological change in the industrial sector, in particular when the technological life cycle is much shorter than the technical life cycle of the project or its main components. Another typical situation would be that the entry barriers (see chapter III) are relatively low in a highly competitive market. In such business environments the investors may choose a project strategy to recover the investment outlay, including a certain minimum interest within a period related to the phase of the life cycle of the industrial sector as well as to the expected technology and product life. The decision makers would then be able to determine the payback points first for the recovery of all investment outlays (conventional payback), and secondly for the recovery of all investment outlays including a minimum profitability (the NPV at the required discounting rate would be equal to zero for a payback period of $n$ years, thus breaking even at this point, and then earning additional interest in the following years).

The experienced financial analyst can use this information to determine the sensitivity to cost and sales price variations in each of these periods. After allowing for debt service, the net cash generation capacity (self-financing capacity) may be computed for the payback period—indicating the capacity of the project to finance the new investments probably needed to cope with the development of the industrial sector (innovation and modernization investments, rationalization etc.).

*Approximate measure of profitability.* A short payback period corresponds on average to a high annual net cash flow. The reciprocal of the payback

---

[119] While the payback is usually interpreted as a break-even point at which accumulated net cash flows become positive, the method is sometimes adapted, in so far as those assets which could be converted into cash easily, such as working capital, are added to the accumulated net cash flows, thus shortening the payback period. This method is not recommended, because it would mean assuming that the plant would cease operations at the moment the initial investment outlay is paid back, no longer being able to earn the necessary return (interest) on capital.

period can therefore be used as an appropriate measure of the profitability of an investment.[120] A long payback period would also imply that the ratio between the annual net cash flows and the initial investment is relatively poor. If at the same time the output-capital ratio (expressing the value of the annual output produced by investing one unit of capital) is also low, the project is likely to be unattractive to investors and financiers.

## Simple or annual rate of return

The simple rate of return method relies on the operational accounts.[121] It is defined as the ratio of the annual net profit on capital. This ratio is often computed only for one year, generally a year of full production. However, it may also be calculated for various degrees of capacity utilization (sensitivity analysis) or for different years during the start-up phase. For investment appraisal two rates of return—on total capital employed (total investment) and on equity capital—are usually of interest.

The (annual) rate of return on total capital invested $R_j$ is

$$R_j \text{ (per cent)} = \frac{NP + I}{K} \times 100$$

and the (annual) rate of return on equity capital paid $RE$ is

$$RE_j \text{ (per cent)} = \frac{NP}{Q} \times 100$$

where $NP$ is the net profit (after depreciation, interest charges and taxes), $I$ the interest, $K$ the total investment costs (fixed assets and working capital, [122] and $Q$ the equity capital.

The retained profits (reserves accumulated in a firm) should, however, be included when calculating the efficiency of the investor's financial share. The sum of equity capital and retained profits ($PR$) is also known as the net worth of a company. For the computation of the return on net worth, $Q$ in the above formula would have to be replaced by $Q + PR$. A shareholder, if mainly interested in the dividends paid, would evaluate the profitability of involvement by comparing the annual (average) dividend received net of tax with capital investment.

In conclusion, the value of the simple rate of return depends on how the terms profit and capital are defined. The ratios used should therefore be

---

[120]The approximation is relatively good if the investment phase is short, the annual net cash flows are fairly constant and the project life exceeds 10 to 15 years. In case of a perpetual net cash flow, the reciprocal of the payback exactly equals the IRR.

[121]Without going into too much detail, it should be mentioned that the simple rate of return method is based on accounting conventions that frequently change from country to country depending on existing legislation, and that do not allow the method to reflect the real profitability of the project. However, existing legislation has to be considered in terms of profitability, so as to be able to assess the project under prevailing conditions. The net income statement (schedule X-10) shows the various types of profits (gross, taxable and net) derived by applying accounting conventions. If depreciation allowances are to be shown separately, they should be deducted from the gross profit to obtain the taxable income.

[122]Sometimes the value of total long-term liabilities as shown in the balance sheet is used for the computation. For example, in the case of the rehabilitation of existing firms, the balance sheet (after revaluation) may be the only source of information available.

explained before a final judgement is made. Using the figures of the example presented in annex A, the rates of return shown in table 4 could also be considered for year 6, the first year of full capacity, and for year 8, after the expiry of tax holidays:

**Table 4. Example of different rates of return**

|  | Year 6 | Year 8 |
|---|---|---|
|  | *(thousand national currency units)* | |
| Net profit plus interest | 2 720 | 1 428 |
| Total investment outlay | 8 720 | 8 720 |
| Rate of return (per cent) | 31.2 | 16.4 |
| Net profit plus interest and depreciation | 3 500 | 2 208 |
| Total investment outlay | 8 720 | 8 720 |
| Rate of return (per cent) | 40.1 | 25.3 |
| Net profit | 2 381 | 1 292 |
| Total equity paid | 3 500 | 3 500 |
| Return on equity (per cent) | 68.0 | 36.9 |
| Net profit | 2 381 | 1 292 |
| Total net worth | 4 830 | 7 192 |
| Return on total net worth (per cent) | 49.3 | 18.0 |

The simple rate of return method has a few serious disadvantages. For example, which year is the normal (representative) year to be taken as a basis for computing the rate of return? Since the simple rate of return uses annual data, it is difficult and often impossible to choose the most representative year of the project. In addition to the varying levels of production, especially during the initial years, and the payment of interest, which can also differ annually, there are certain other factors that cause changes in the level of net profit in particular years (tax holidays, for instance).

In years in which a tax concession is to be applied, the net profit will obviously be quite different from that in years when the profit is subject to normal taxation. This shortcoming of the simple rate of return—which is a consequence of its static character—can to some extent be alleviated by calculating the profitability of the project for each year as shown in schedule X-10. The difficulty of choosing the "normal" year is revealed by the varying annual rates of return shown in table 5.[123]

Even after this calculation, however, the main shortcoming of the simple rate of return remains: it does not take into account the time value of the equity payments and of the annual returns on equity. Furthermore, the annual return on equity is lower than the net cash flow remaining after debt service. Thus, unless the annual depreciation is reinvested without delay, the rate-of-return method always underestimates the financial gains (yield) of an investment as expressed by means of the IRR. Income obtained in an early period is

[123]The computation of an average rate of return (accumulated net profits divided by the number of years) would solve the problem of selecting a representative year. However, the problem of the time value of money would still remain unsolved. The rate of return method is often used when alternative technologies are compared by determining the total annual production costs assuming full capacity utilization. The margin between sales prices and costs of products sold (production costs plus marketing costs) is then related to the respective investment costs and the alternative with the higher rate of return is given priority, ignoring all other factors relevant for investment appraisal, as discussed in this *Manual*.

**Table 5. Annual rate of return on equity capital**

| Item | Year of project | | | | | | | | |
|---|---|---|---|---|---|---|---|---|---|
| | Construction | | | Start-up and full capacity | | | | | |
| | *1* | *2* | *3* | *4* | *5* | *6* | *7* | *8* | *9* |
| | *(thousand national currency units)* | | | | | | | | |
| Net profit after tax | — | — | (434) | 712 | 1 682 | 2 381 | 1 241 | 1 292 | 1 308 |
| Equity capital | — | — | 3 500 | 3 500 | 3 500 | 3 500 | 3 500 | 3 500 | 3 500 |
| Rate of return (per cent) | — | — | — | 20.3 | 48.1 | 68.0 | 35.5 | 36.9 | 37.4 |
| Net worth | — | — | 3 500 | 3 066 | 3 778 | 4 830 | 6 581 | 7 192 | 7 869 |
| Return on net worth (per cent) | — | — | — | 23.2 | 44.5 | 49.3 | 18.9 | 18.0 | 16.6 |

*Note:* Figure in parentheses is negative.

obviously preferable to income obtained later. It is very difficult, however, to choose between two project alternatives that have different profitabilities over a number of years. For instance, how can one of the two alternatives shown in table 6 be selected, assuming both had the same total investment costs?

**Table 6. Net profit of project alternatives**

| Item | Net profit per year after taxes | | | | | Total |
|---|---|---|---|---|---|---|
| | *1* | *2* | *3* | *4* | *5* | |
| | *(thousand national currency units)* | | | | | |
| Net profit, project A | 50 | 60 | 120 | 160 | 200 | 590 |
| Net profit, project B | 170 | 120 | 90 | 80 | 70 | 530 |

In such a case it is not sufficient to rely on an annual calculation of the profitability. It is necessary instead to determine the overall profitability of the projects, and this is only possible by using discounting methods.

In conclusion, the simple-rate-of-return method can be used for computing the profitability of total investment costs when more or less equal gross profits are expected throughout the lifetime of the project. In such a case, it can be useful for a preliminary evaluation of competing projects and an elimination of the poor ones, keeping in mind that each country applies different legislative rules to depreciation and taxation, and that such rules make it difficult to evaluate the real benefits of the projects.

## F. Project financing

The allocation of financial resources to a project constitutes an obvious and basic prerequisite for investment decisions, for project formulation and pre-investment analysis, and for determining the cost of capital (without which the decision to accept or reject a project on the basis of the NPV and IRR cannot be made). A feasibility study would serve little purpose if it was not backed by a reasonable assurance that resources were available for a project if the conclusions of the study proved positive and satisfactory. A preliminary assessment of project financing possibilities should already have been made in most cases before a feasibility study is undertaken. This is especially true if a project opportunity or pre-feasibility study has previously been performed, as such studies would indicate the order of magnitude of the required capital outlay. A feasibility study should only be made if financing prospects to the extent indicated by such studies can be defined fairly clearly.

As discussed earlier, resource constraints may define the parameters of a project well before an investment decision is made, and at various stages of project formulation. A large steel plant may not be practicable in a small country with extensive iron ore deposits but with very limited financial resources. Such resource constraints may limit the consideration of certain projects or restrict project capacity to the minimum economic levels. Financial constraints could exist at all levels of project sponsorship and occur whether a particular project is under consideration by an individual entrepreneur, a major industrial group (domestic or foreign), or a governmental or semi-governmental agency.

Apart from some instances where resource constraints constitute a major limiting factor in the consideration of project possibilities and project size, it is only when the basic techno-economic parameters of a project are defined that the detailed requirements of financing can be adequately assessed. Thus, in a feasibility study, the capital outlay of a project can be appropriately determined only after plant capacity and location have been decided, together with estimates of the costs of a developed site, buildings and civil works, technology and equipment.

Defining the financial requirements of a project at the operational stage in terms of working capital is equally necessary, although too often neglected. This can only be determined once estimates are made of production costs, on the one hand, and sales and income, on the other. These estimates should cover a period of time and be reflected in a cash flow analysis. Unless both estimates are available and unless the available resources are sufficient to meet the fund requirements, both in terms of initial capital investment and working capital needs over a period of time, it would not be prudent to proceed to the financing decision and project implementation. There are innumerable instances of projects that ran into serious financing problems because of inadequate estimates of fund requirements at the initial investment or operational stages, because investment, production costs and marketing costs were underestimated, or sales and income were overestimated.

## Sources of finance

### Equity

A generally applied financing pattern for an industrial project is to cover the initial capital investment by equity and long-term loans to varying extents, and to meet working capital requirements by additional short- and medium-term loans from national banking sources. However, as explained before, the minimum net working capital requirements should be financed from long-term capital. Within this framework various permutations are possible and need to be assessed.

In certain projects, equity capital covers not only the initial capital investment but also net working capital requirements, for the most part. This generally occurs in situations where institutional capital is scarce and available only at high cost. Since earnings from capital through term deposits are also high in such situations, a project would need to be very attractive financially before it could mobilize adequate investible resources. In other cases, where relatively inexpensive long- or medium-term credit is available, there is a growing tendency to finance projects through such loans.

In all cases, a balance needs to be struck between long-term debt and equity. The higher the proportion of equity the less the debt service obligations and the higher the gross profit before taxation. The higher the proportion of loan finance, the higher the interest payable on liabilities. In every project, therefore, the implications of alternative patterns and forms of financing must be carefully assessed; a financing pattern should be determined that is consistent with both availability of resources and overall economic returns.

Equity can be raised by issuing two types of shares: ordinary shares (common shares in United States terminology); and preference shares. Preference shares usually carry a dividend at least partly independent from profit, without, or with only limited, voting rights. Preference shares can be convertible to common shares, they can be cumulative or non-cumulative in terms of dividends, or they can be redeemable or non-redeemable, with the redemption period varying between 5 and 15 years. Dividends on ordinary shares with full voting rights, however, depend on the profitable operation of the company. There is currently a trend towards more than one class of common shares, involving greater voting rights combined with lower dividends and receipts and fewer privileges, or vice versa.

## Loan financing

Since it is relatively easy for a sound project to obtain loans, the process of project financing may well start by identifying the extent to which loan capital can be secured, together with the interest rate applicable. Such loan capital would need to be separately defined in the following forms: short- and medium-term borrowings from commercial banks for working capital purposes, or supplier credits of various forms; and long-term borrowings preferably from national or international development finance institutions.

*Short-term loans.* Short-term loans from commercial banks and local financial institutions are available against hypothecation, or pledging, of inventories. The limits to which inventories are financed by commercial banks are fixed by the banks, and depend on banking practices in the country, the nature of the project and inventories, and the credit rating of the enterprise and its management. The limits usually vary between 50 and 80 per cent, leaving a margin of from 20 to 50 per cent of inventories to be financed from other sources, preferably venture capital.

Bank borrowing for working capital can be arranged on a temporary basis. If at any time the cash flow statement suggests that sufficient liquid funds are available, such commercial bank borrowings should be substantially reduced or entirely eliminated, without however jeopardizing the overall liquidity of the project. In some cases, such a cash-flow surplus may be needed for further capacity expansion, so that the enterprise may need to rely on long-term bank credits for some time. Working capital needs should even be partly met out of long-term funds (equity capital and long-term loans), since the largest portion of working capital is permanently tied in inventories (raw materials, work-in-progress, finished goods and spare parts).

In the example case presented in annex A to this *Manual*, 20 per cent of the total liabilities are financed from equity funds. As shown in schedule X-7/2, the loan capital is repaid during five years starting in the second year of operation. The change in the ratio of net worth to debt is possible because the project generates a sufficient cash surplus (over interest payments) to repay the debt. Other short-term funds are trade credits (creditors or accounts payable), bills of exchange, deferred tax payments and wages payable.

*Long-term loans.* Loan financing is usually subject to certain regulations, such as restrictions on the convertibility of shares and declaration of dividends. Apart from these regulations, certain ratios in the capital structure of the company need to be maintained. Investment may also be financed partly by issues of bonds and debentures. The market for bonds and debentures tends to be fairly limited as far as new projects are concerned, but such securities are often issued to finance the expansion of existing enterprises.

An important source of finance is also available at government-to-government level for many developing countries. This can take the form of general bilateral credit or tied credit, which may be related to the purchase of machinery and equipment from a particular country or even from a particular source.

In addition to share capital and loan finance, an important financial category at the operational stage is the internal cash generated by the project itself. This can take the form of accumulated reserves (retained profits and depreciation).

*Supplier credits.* Imported machinery and spares can often be financed on deferred credit terms. Machinery suppliers in industrialized countries are generally willing to sell machinery on deferred-payment terms with payments spread over 6 to 10 years, and sometimes even longer. Deferred payment terms are available against bank guarantees; this enables such machinery suppliers to obtain refinancing facilities from financial institutions in their own countries.

## Example

*Cost of the project and means of finance.* In table 7, part A, the total initial investment outlay (schedule X-6/1) amounts to NCU 8.72 million (including interest accrued during construction). Financing of the total initial investment outlay is shown in part B.

## Leasing

Instead of borrowing financial means it is sometimes possible to lease plant equipment or even complete production units, in other words, productive assets are borrowed. Leasing, as the borrowing of productive assets is called, requires usually a down payment and the payment of an annual rent, the leasing fee. These assets are, however, contained in the balance sheet of the lessor and not in the balance sheet of the borrowing firm, the lessee.[124] Therefore, leasing essentially represents a form of off-balance sheet financing. This aspect may be important in situations in which a firm prefers to maintain

---

[124]In United States accounting, financial leases are included directly in the balance sheet.

Table 7. Example of investment outlay and structure of finance

| Item | Funds (thousand national currency units) |
|---|---|
| *A. Investment outlay* | |
| Fixed-investment costs | |
| Land | 80 |
| Buildings | 2 900 |
| Equipment | 4 000 |
| Other | 730 |
| Total initial fixed investment | 7 710 |
| Working capital (including bank borrowing) | 400 |
| Pre-production capital expenditures[a] | 610 |
| Total initial investment costs | 8 720 |
| *B. Structure of investment* | |
| Source | |
| Equity capital | 3 500 |
| Supplier credit | 2 600 |
| Commercial credit (including NCU 200 for start-up year) | 3 000 |
| Total long-term capital | 9 100 |
| Surplus (long-term capital) during construction phase | 380 |
| Start-up year | |
| Short-term finance (bank overdraft) | 400 |
| Cash deficit (start-up year) | (10) |
| Financing of net increase in assets (start-up year) | (600) |
| Finance available | 170 |

*Note:* Figures in parentheses are negative.

[a]Including interest of NCU 302,000 accrued during construction.

a certain debt-equity ratio or is not in a position to further increase its debentures.

Provided that both the lessor and lessee fall under the same tax regulations, purchase equipment under the same conditions and enjoy identical financing conditions, the accumulated leasing costs should not differ significantly from the costs of purchasing and financing of the purchase of the same assets. Only when lessors enjoy certain advantages, owing, for example, to their position in the capital-goods or financial markets (credit rating), may the leasing costs be lower for the lessee than total costs in case the items are purchased.

In the case of investment projects the problem is basically to decide which alternative should be preferred, leasing or purchasing of capital assets. For the evaluation of the two financing alternatives the discounted cash flow method should be applied. The initial down payment, the current leasing fees and any additional payments[125] under the leasing agreement are then part of the cash outflows, replacing all initial investment costs computed for the purchasing alternative. Since the duration of leasing contracts is in general much shorter

---

[125]If the lessor is responsible for maintenance and insurance, as is usually the case with an operating leasing contract, the leasing payments include these costs. In the case of financial leasing, maintenance and insurance are usually the responsibility of the lessee, and the corresponding costs must be included in the production cost estimates.

than the technical and economic life of an asset, it is necessary to include the residual value (cash inflow) of the leased asset when comparing leasing with loan financing. The inflow for the lessee would usually not be the book value but either the book value or the market value (minus the lessor's cost of selling the used items), whichever is lower.[126]

If the investor has a choice between loan and leasing financing,[127] he would compare the discounted cash flow for both cash flow arrays to determine which alternative would bring the higher yield (IRR, NPV), bearing in mind, however, the liquidity aspect and risks involved. If tax regulations have different effects on leasing financing, these tax impacts need to be included in the cash flow discounting.

Funds to finance leases may be obtained from independent leasing companies (service or financing leasing companies, lease brokers), banks, insurance companies, pension funds and industrial development agencies. Leasing financing of investment projects in developing countries has been introduced by international financing institutions such as the International Finance Corporation, and may become an interesting financing alternative, especially in cases where leasing has certain advantages over loan financing.

## Cost of capital

Capital for financing of investments may be obtained from private and institutional resources (banks, insurance companies, funds etc.). However, behind these institutions stand again private investors. In all cases private savings are therefore the ultimate source of capital.[128] Basically, all savings are made to provide for future needs, but this alone would not be an incentive to invest or lend money to an investor, because lending would mean a long-, medium- or short-term commitment reducing the liquidity of the lender, and would also imply uncertainty concerning the full return of the funds lent. To obtain finance, an investor must therefore pay a charge—the cost of capital or of finance—for the funds lent. This charge comprises an interest rate, usually expressed as a percentage per annum, as well as certain fixed charges (commitment fee, charge on capital not drawn, commissions etc.). Interest is usually computed for the outstanding balance of the corresponding liabilities of a firm, for example, interest payable on a bank loan, dividends payable on equity capital (such as preference shares) and interest payable on a current account.

For the investor the cost of capital is determined by the conditions that can be obtained for the project on the capital market. For the amount stemming from own funds (savings) investors should charge their opportunity cost of capital, that is, the interest they would obtain if they invested in another feasible venture (provided such alternatives exist).

---

[126]If the market value is greater than the book value, usually the margin is split between the lessor and the lessee, at a rate determined in the contract. The lessee may also have the option to purchase the equipment from the lessor at the market price or book value.

[127]Apart from the above described situations, when the financing policy of a firm requires leasing financing, or when the investor cannot raise the necessary funds on the capital market, or when the firm has exceptionally high marginal capital costs, there is little justification for a company to undertake lease commitments on plant and machinery or any assets.

[128]Similarly, most public sources of finance stem from individual savings (individual income which is not or cannot be consumed).

## Impact of financing cost on financing policies

The cost of equity capital for the project or firm is basically determined by the minimum accumulated return,[129] expressed as the NPV of the future income of the shareholders, and the minimum annual rate of return, expressed as the rate of return on equity capital. The acceptable minimum rates depend on the opportunity cost of capital, the expected business risks, and the valuation of any gains or benefits obtained in addition to the payment of dividends. The purpose of the concept of equity is to give the management of the firm more flexibility with regard to the best use of the annual net profits in the interest of the shareholders or owners and the firm.

The debt service (interest and amortization) is fixed and legally binding for the firm, and has to be paid even when the generation of cash is insufficient in certain years, whereas payment of dividends is in general linked to a sufficiently high profit and cash generation. The determination of the right (optimal) capital mix is therefore essential when a financing strategy is designed for an investment project.[130]

Different financing institutions impose different financing conditions. A government guarantee is even sometimes required for multilateral financing. It is important that the enterprise is not obliged to start with loan amortization before the start-up of operations. Very often financial costs are capitalized during the implementation period, and debt service starts when sufficient cash is generated through the operation of the new production facilities.

It may be possible to combine relatively short-term supplier credits (for instance, a three-year grace period and a four-year amortization period) with longer-term financing from multilateral banks. In this case, supplier credits could be disbursed last and amortized first, while leaving multilateral financing for early disbursement and late amortization. Thus, generally suitable loan terms can be obtained.

In new as well as expansion projects, the kind of debt service will also have to be decided on. The following two systems are possible: periodical debt service with equal amortization instalments (constant principal) plus gradually decreasing interest; and periodical debt service with constant payments (annuities), in which case the sum of the declining amortization and increasing interest payments is constant over the amortization period of the loan. The first system requires less total financing cost but a fairly substantial initial debt service during the start-up of the project. The second system, although it has a higher total financing cost, is preferable for the new enterprise because the initial debt-service burden is smaller than under the first system.

The various forms and sources of financing have different implications in terms of impact on different projects and may even affect project formulation. Supplier credits and other forms of medium-term credit, though initially advantageous in terms of coverage of resource gaps at the initial stage, constitute a heavy debt burden during early years of production; their incidence on production costs should be determined and accounted for in the cash flow analysis. National and international institutions that provide loan finance require that projects should be formulated in considerable detail, so that their

---

[129]For an investor, the return net of all taxes will of course be taken into account when deciding whether to finance or co-finance an investment project.

[130]A rule applied by consultants suggests that the total equity capital should be able to cover possible losses over a five-year period (assuming the worst case).

full implications are adequately highlighted. In some cases, they insist that the feasibility study should be prepared by recognized independent consultants or that management responsibilities for certain major projects be assumed by experienced and acceptable parties.

## Public policy and regulations on financing

The hard core of the entrepreneurial decision in respect of financing is to choose between equity raised through the sale of shares and that raised through payments by the project sponsor. In most cases, the initial equity base is provided only by the project sponsors. The extent of such initial equity depends on the anticipated profitability and on availability of funds for this purpose and of alternative sources of capital participation, all under the prevailing regulations on financing and taxation of income from capital investment.

Where a project is expected to yield a high rate of profitability, maximum participation would be sought by the sponsors within an appropriate equity-debt pattern and subject to fund constraints. In the case of any resource gap, or where the sponsors wish to limit their risks to a particular proportion of equity, outside participation can be invited to provide additional equity or loans. Funds can be mobilized either from national sources (individual or institutional), or through foreign participation. When a developing country has a reasonably well developed capital market, equity funds can be raised through public issues of shares. Such share issues are usually underwritten by banks and other financial institutions. In some cases, financial institutions, including specialized institutions dealing in industrial financing, participate in share capital to varying extents. Usually such participation is in the form of minority share-holding. In some developing countries, it may be necessary for institutional agencies to acquire majority holdings initially and release them gradually to domestic entrepreneurs as and when domestic entrepreneurship is willing to take over all, or a part of, such holdings.

In considering foreign equity participation, a basic policy question may arise regarding the extent (if any) of foreign influence after such participation. In a number of developing countries, foreign equity participation requires governmental approval. In some countries, such approval is often not granted, particularly to non-priority sectors of investment. In other cases, only minority foreign participation is generally permitted. In certain countries, however, even majority foreign participation is welcomed, particularly in sectors involving large investments or in projects with a great employment potential.

Thus, in cases where foreign equity participation is considered, the first need is to assess the policy implications and the reaction of government authorities. Thereafter, the implications of foreign equity participation on the project should be evaluated. In some cases, where foreign technological assistance and support may be required for a number of years, or where access to improved and new technologies may be required, it may be desirable to have the technology supplier or licensor also participate in capital ownership.

Technical management may sometimes have to be entrusted to a foreign company, usually a licensor, in which case foreign capital participation may be desirable. The extent of foreign participation would, however, have to be considered on a case-by-case basis and be determined within the framework of national policies by such factors as the nature and magnitude of investment outlay, and the technological and management support required, the extent of the resource gap that could otherwise develop, and the relations between a technology licensor and licensee. It may not be possible to discuss all these aspects at the stage of a feasibility study; often the policy and general implications of foreign capital participation can be elaborated.

## Financing institutions

Most developing countries have established development financing institutions, usually called industrial finance corporations or industrial development banks. In most developing countries, there is more than one institution available to finance projects. Most countries have established financial institutions at the state and national levels. Some of the national institutions provide foreign currency loans which are financed by international institutions, such as the World Bank and its affiliates.

Various international institutions and funding facilities exist for the financing of industries in developing countries. Some of these, such as the World Bank, including the International Development Association as well as the International Finance Corporation, the Special Fund of the Organization of Petroleum Exporting Countries, the Kuwait Fund for Arab Economic and Social Development, and the International Investment Bank of the Council for Mutual Economic Assistance, operate on a world-wide scale. Even though many of these funds will be used primarily for infrastructure and agricultural development rather than for industry, the provision of funds on soft terms for infrastructure is one of the fundamental prerequisites of successful industrialization.

There are also institutions operating on a regional basis, such as the African Development Bank, the Asian Development Bank, the European Investment Bank and the Inter-American Development Bank. Funds have been set up by the oil-exporting countries, such as the Arab Fund for Economic and Social Development and the Islamic Development Bank. Bilateral institutions have been established in most of the countries of the Organisation for Economic Cooperation and Development and, in some oil-exporting countries, including Kuwait, the United Arab Emirates and Venezuela.

In this context, the role of the export financing and guaranteeing agencies must be mentioned.[131] The primary task of such agencies is to provide financial support of exports from industrialized countries; only as a secondary task are they designed to help developing countries. Commercial banks, including those in the Eurocurrency market and the currency markets of the Association of South-East Asian Nations, are becoming increasingly active in industrial development financing. However, they lend to only a few developing countries. A major step towards easier terms and availability of loans would be achieved with the establishment of a multilateral guarantee system for commercial loans.

In many developing countries, the availability of industrial finance in the form of institutional finance and from other sources has grown to such an extent that new entrepreneurs can start industrial ventures while providing a

---

[131]Supplier credit guarantees are given, for example, by *Compagnie française d'assurance pour le commerce extérieur* (France), *Compañia española de Seguros de Crédito a la Exportación* (Spain), Export Credits Guarantee Department (United Kingdom), Export Development Corporation (Canada), *Exportkreditnamnden* (Sweden), Export-Import Bank (Japan), Export-Import Bank (United States), Ministry of International Trade and Industry (Japan), Nederland se Crediet Maatschappij (Netherlands), *Office national du ducroire* (Belgium) and *Sezione Speciale per l'Assicurazione Crediti Esportazioni* (Italy).

relatively small share of the total equity required. The situation varies widely, but in some countries, the initial portion of equity to be raised by sponsors of industrial projects can be as low as 10-25 per cent of the total finance needed.

The various aspects discussed above need to be fully assessed before evolving a financing package suitable for a project under consideration. Invariably, the package is determined by identifying the most economic pattern in terms of cost of finance, assessing the feasibility of obtaining capital on such a basis, and ensuring that the pattern is consistent with both public policies and regulations, and the projected cash flows of the proposed enterprise. The various sources of finance can then be tabulated in schedule X-7/1. Schedule X-7/2 shows the flow of financial resources and schedule X-8/2 the utilization of these funds during construction, start-up and full capacity operation.

## G.  Financial and efficiency ratios

The figures appearing in the balance sheet, the net income statement and the cash flow tables convey a considerable amount of information in terms of their absolute values. In financial analysis it is usual to refer to several well-known ratios that facilitate the analysis and specially the comparison of projects and alternatives.[132]

The ratios discussed below are those most frequently used. Other ratios may be applied as well. Whichever choice is made by the project evaluator, the ratios should not be applied automatically. The computation of such ratios alone would little serve the purpose of project appraisal, if not accompanied by an interpretation of their meaning. Analysts and decision makers should also bear in mind that ratios may not automatically be regarded as good or bad, but have to be evaluated in the light of the characteristics of the corresponding industry, the type and scope of the project and the country of investment.

### Financial ratios

### Long-term debt-equity ratio and long-term debt-net-worth ratio

The long-term debt-equity ratio is an indicator of the financial project risk for both the equity and the loan capital. Considering that the debt service represents a legally binding commitment of a firm, the financial risk is higher for the firm as well as the bank or financing institution, the higher the debt in relation to equity capital. The ratio also indicates the extent to which the outstanding debt balance is covered by the total assets of a firm in the event of liquidation of the project before it goes into operation. In case of an existing firm the earned surplus and reserves (retained profits) must be added to the equity capital to reflect the true ratio between the shareholders' interest in the firm and the long-term debt. This sum of equity and reserves is known as the net worth of the firm or the shareholders' interest. Financial prudence sets certain norms for this ratio.

Usually, the ratio is expressed as a fraction, for example, debt to net worth is 4:1 or 80:20, meaning that for this example the total long-term debt is four

---

[132]The financial and efficiency ratios, if properly interpreted, are valuable analytical tools, especially for the comparison of projects and in rehabilitation studies.

times the net worth or one fifth or 20 per cent of the total liabilities. In a number of projects of large or medium size, an ideal debt-equity ratio of 50:50 tends to be adopted, but this is by no means a standard pattern. A feasibility study should define the appropriate financing arrangement, taking the availability of resources and the nature and requirements of funds fully into account. Equity-debt ratios of 33:67 or 25:75 or even higher are practised in many countries. A generalization, however, cannot be made, since each project should be assessed on its own merits.

The debt-equity is also a measure of *investor leverage.* The smaller the equity capital, the higher the income per unit share. From the profitability point of view, equity owners therefore favour high debt-equity ratios, since such ratios give leverage to equity capital and allow equity owners to control projects even with a small amount of capital. However, since the financial risk is growing with an increasing debt balance, it is also in the interest of the shareholders to establish a sound balance between risk and loan capital.

Investment banks ask for a sound debt-equity ratio, since the largest portion of equity capital is always tied in land, buildings and equipment, which can be liquidated only with difficulty or only at a loss in case of bankruptcy of the project. Banks therefore frequently refuse to finance a project with loans greater than the amount the promoter is prepared to invest, thus limiting the loan to 50 per cent of the required investment outlay.

### Current ratio or current-assets-to-current-liabilities ratio

The current ratio is a liquidity measure computed by dividing current assets by current liabilities. This ratio measures the short-term solvency and is a very rough indicator of the ability of a company to meet current liabilities. It is so rough that, for example, even a "satisfactory" ratio would be misleading as far as the liquidity situation is concerned, if the inventory could not, for example, be sold for cash. To guard against this possibility, the quick ratio is frequently used in addition to the current ratio. The quick ratio is computed by dividing cash plus marketable securities and discounted receivables by current liabilities. The ratio thus eliminates inventory and prepaid expenses from current assets. In view of the danger of possible misinterpretations, the following ranges of satisfactory values can only be offered with great caution.

| | |
|---|---|
| Current ratio | 2.0-1.2 |
| Quick ratio | 1.2-1.0 |

### Long-term debt-service coverage

The long-term debt-service coverage should be looked at in order to make sure that all long-term loans and the related financial expenses can be repaid in the agreed yearly instalments without depriving the firm of needed funds. Debt-service coverage is defined as the ratio of cash generation[133] to debt service

---

[133]The annual cash generation may be obtained from the cash flow schedule for financial planning (schedule X-8), or may be derived from the figures contained in the balance sheet and net income statement (net profit after tax plus interest and depreciation plus net increase of liabilities (equity or debt), minus new investments.

(interest plus repayment of principal). Ratios of 1.5-3.0 range between acceptable and satisfactory. This ratio often increases considerably if the long-term debt service gradually decreases and no new borrowing is projected.

## Debtors—creditors ratio

The ratio between debtors (accounts receivable) and creditors (accounts payable), if determined for a number of consecutive periods, helps to identify overtrading, as in the case of rehabilitation projects. Overtrading, which is often found in developing countries, is a situation where too high a level of production is maintained with insufficient cash resources. The effects of overtrading can be disastrous for a company, and usually lead to a complete failure of a business. Overtrading is in most cases the result of rising prices (inflation), increasing stocks, heavy taxation, depletion of working capital or overexpansion of production in relation to the market. The cure for overtrading is the provision of additional (long-term) funds, increasing marketing efforts to reduce stocks, and the reduction of operations.

The following indicators help to detect overtrading in the balance sheet:
- A progressive fall of the debtors—creditors ratio;
- There is an increase in the creditor accounts, or in the stocks and work-in-progress, or in the total debt (loan), without a corresponding increase of sales (turnover);
- New bills or promissory notes are issued;
- Receivables decrease;
- Above all, there is a reduction of liquid resources and a failure to raise fresh cash by borrowing, as one pledgeable asset after the other is mortgaged.

## Efficiency ratios

The operational performance and profitability of an investment is measured by relating the financial net benefits—expressed as net cash flows, profits before and after corporate tax or profits plus interest payable on debt—to the corresponding capital investments. For the comparison of projects the *profitability of sales* is sometimes computed, where gross or net profits are expressed as a percentage of annual sales. The profitability figures of both investment and sales are mathematically related to each other through the output-capital ratio (annual sales divided by total capital investment).

## Output-capital ratio

The efficiency of an investment may also be expressed in terms of the annual output produced by investing one unit of capital. Although this ratio is used more in economic analysis, it can be a very useful yardstick when assessing investment ideas at an early stage (opportunity study and pre-feasibility study phase of a project).

*Net present value ratio*

When the present value of the accumulated net benefits of a project (that is the annual output of the project net of annual operating expenditures and income taxes, discounted and accumulated over the planning horizon) is related to the present value of the total capital invested, the NPVR, which has already been described in this chapter, is obtained.

*Relation between personnel employed and investment*

The relation between total initial investment and the number of workers and staff employed is used when comparing alternative technologies. However, when the problem is to choose between alternatives with different labour intensities, it may be advisable to compute the ratio between investment and total costs of personnel. Similarly, the efficiency of personnel employed may be computed by determining the value of output produced by one unit of personnel costs. These ratios, including the capital-output ratio, complement the cash flow and financial analysis in so far as additional information may be obtained with regard to possible risks, suitable investment strategies and positioning of a project in a competitive environment.[134]

*Turnover of inventories*

The rate of turnover of products in stock is a measure of the marketing capabilities of management. It is specific to particular industries, but differs from country to country, as it depends also on the overall business environment. However, provided that comparable project data are available from a data bank, these ratios may serve for financial planning as well as for the final project appraisal. In general, the faster the turnover, the better for the finance of the company.

## H.    Financial evaluation under conditions of uncertainty

Forecasts of the future business environment and of demand, production and sales can be only an approximation, because it is not possible, on the basis of past data, to determine more than a past trend, which may be extrapolated into an uncertain future. Of primary importance in the appraisal of an investment project is the reliability of the data assessed and of the project design[135] (marketing concept and sales programme, selection of project inputs and location, choice of technology, engineering design, management, personnel

---

[134]The estimate of the IRR and NPV obtained by competitors is usually not possible on the basis of published data (balance and net income statement). The various ratios may however be estimated with sufficient approximation. Ratios may also be obtained from research institutions and industrial associations for various industries.

[135]Risks may be categorized as follows: risk from undertaking insufficient numbers of similar projects; risk from misinterpretation of data; risk from bias in the data and in its assessment; risk from a changing external economic environment invalidating much of the usefulness of past experience; and risk from errors of analysis (see A. J. Merrett and A. Sykes, op. cit., p. 143).

and organization, as well as the implementation of the project). To minimize uncertainty with regard to the reliability of project data and design, the financial analyst should check whether the feasibility study covers all aspects relevant to the investment and financing decisions. Then the study must indicate all sources of data, and any assumptions made should be explained and justified.[136] Only when the feasibility study fulfils these basic requirements should the analysis of the business risks begin. The most common reasons for uncertainty, however, are inflation, changes in technology, false estimates of the rated capacity, and the length of the construction and running-in periods. The problem of uncertainty is aggravated by the phasing of a project over time. Investments also underlie many developments and changes in the political, social, commercial and business environment, as well as changes in technology, productivity and prices.

To cope with the risks involved in any significant investment, management has basically the following two options with regard to a policy on risks: to seek insurance against various risks identified for an investment project; to identify the possibilities for active risk control or *risk management.* The main instrument of the insurance strategy is to invest (finance) only when the expected returns are higher than the cost of capital plus the risk margin. This concept, however, can be successful only when the investor has an *investment portfolio,* in other words, when his risks are spread over a number of carefully selected investments. Practically, only large business groups and financing institutions have this possibility, while most of the owners of firms do not dispose of enough funds to invest in different projects.

The insurance strategy, which is based on an assessment of the probability of risks,[137] is a basic strategy for financing institutions. However, in a very dynamic business environment this concept cannot be satisfactory, and the debt burden accumulated by many developing countries may, to a large extent, be the result of focusing on the projected investment yields (expressed as the internal rate of return). The feasibility study should therefore identify possible strategies for risk control and design the project following the strategic orientation, as described in part one and elaborated further in chapter III of this *Manual.*

When deciding about the desirability of a project, all the elements of uncertainty have to be taken into account by evaluating, on the one hand, any foreseeable risks that could have significant impacts on its feasibility, and, on the other, the possible means of risk control. The allowance to be provided for such risks may have a decisive impact on the profitability of the project, and may, in the case of a marginal proposal, tip the balance against project implementation.

When the aspects of uncertainty are to be included in the financial evaluation, three variables in particular should be examined, namely sale revenues, costs of products sold and investment costs. A host of individual items enter into these variables, all of which are composed of a price and a quantity. The project planning team should identify the variables that could

---

[136]For example, assumptions concerning estimates of production and investment costs, prices or the lifetime of the project may not always be correct, or the decision makers may evaluate a scenario differently.

[137]For example, the country risk is evaluated on the basis of the economic and political situation in the country, the total outstanding foreign debt in relation to the domestic product etc. A country risk may be insured through a government guaranty, possibly from an exporting country.

have a decisive influence on the profitability of a project, and that should be subjected to risk analysis. Sensitivity analysis is a proper instrument for identifying these critical variables and the extent to which they could affect the financial feasibility of a project.

### Sensitivity analysis

With the help of sensitivity analysis it is possible to show how the net cash returns or the profitability of an investment alter with different values assigned to the variables needed for the computation (unit sales price, unit costs, sales volume etc.). Sensitivity analysis should be applied already during the project planning stage, when decisions concerning major inputs are being taken. The element of uncertainty could be reduced at this stage by finding the optimistic and pessimistic alternatives, and thus determining the commercially most realistic combination of project inputs for the business environment (or scenario) favoured by the decision makers.

To determine the critical variables the structure of cash flows should be analysed first. The variables having the greatest share of cash inflows and outflows are then subject to variations of quantities or prices or both parameters at the same time. For example, usually a few products out of a product range generate most of the sales revenues, but this does not necessarily mean that these products also make the greatest contribution to the return or gross profits. The direct costing method should therefore be applied to identifying the variable margin generated by one unit of each product having a significant share of sales revenues. Similarly, those cost items need to be identified which, in case of prices or quantities deviating from the forecasts, would have a significant impact on the variable margin and the operating profit as well.[138]

This exercise can be performed by assigning values to the critical variables corresponding to reasonably pessimistic, normal and optimistic scenarios, and by the computation of the discounted cash flows (IRR or NPV) and any ratios etc. chosen as a yardstick for investment appraisal. With the help of sensitivity analysis it is possible to identify the most important project inputs, such as raw materials, labour and energy, and to determine any possibilities of input substitution, as well as the critical elements of the marketing concept.[139]

To illustrate the application of sensitivity analysis in project formulation, the impact of changes in the unit sales price, variable production and fixed production costs (including depreciation) on the break-even point is dealt with below.

### Break-even analysis

The purpose of break-even analysis is to determine the equilibrium point at which sales revenues equal the costs of products sold. When sales (and the

---

[138]Cost structure analysis, direct costing, and the computation of variable and operational margins is described above in sect. C of this chapter.

[139]When analysing the critical variables, it is important not only to estimate confidence levels, but also to determine the possible reasons for deviations from the projections. This analysis should include the determination of critical factors possibly affecting the defined critical variables, such as possible transport and supply problems for critical materials, possible price fluctuations for critical products and supplies caused by highly speculative, competitive or volatile markets etc.

corresponding production) are below this point, the firm is making a loss, and at the point where revenues equal costs, the firm is breaking even. Break-even analysis serves to compare the planned capacity utilization with the production volume below which a firm would make losses. The break-even point can also be defined in terms of physical units produced, or of the level of capacity utilization at which sales revenues and production costs are equal. The sales revenues at the break-even point represent the break-even sales value, and the unit price of a product in this situation is the break-even sales price. If the production programme includes a variety of products, for any given break-even sales volume there would exist a variety of combinations of product prices, but no single break-even price.

Before calculating the break-even values, the following conditions and assumptions should be satisfied:

- Production and marketing costs are a function of the production or sales volume (for example, in the utilization of equipment);
- The volume of production equals the volume of sales;
- Fixed operating costs are the same for every volume of production;
- Variable costs vary in proportion to the volume of production, and consequently total production costs also change in proportion to the volume of production;
- The sales prices for a product or product mix are the same for all levels of output (sales) over time. The sales value is therefore a linear function of the sales prices and the quantity sold;
- The level of unit sales prices and variable and fixed operating costs remain constant, that is, the price elasticity of demand for inputs and outputs is zero;
- The break-even values are computed for one product; in case of a variety of products, the product mix, that is, the ratio between the quantities produced, should remain constant.

Since the above assumptions will not always hold in practice, the break-even point (capacity utilization) should also be subject to sensitivity analysis, assigning different fixed and variable costs as well as sales prices. For the interpretation of the results of break-even analysis, a graphical presentation (see figure XXXI) is very useful, because from the angle of the cost and sales curves, and the position of the equilibrium point in relation to total capacity, analysts can often identify potential weaknesses.

*Algebraic determination of the break-even point*

Break-even production is the number of units $U$ necessary to produce and sell in order fully to cover the annual fixed costs $C_f$ for a given unit sales price $p_s$ and the variable unit costs $c_v$, or

$$(p_s - c_v)\, U = C_f$$

$$\text{or } U = \frac{C_f}{(p_s - c_v)}$$

**Figure XXXI. Determination of the break-even conditions**

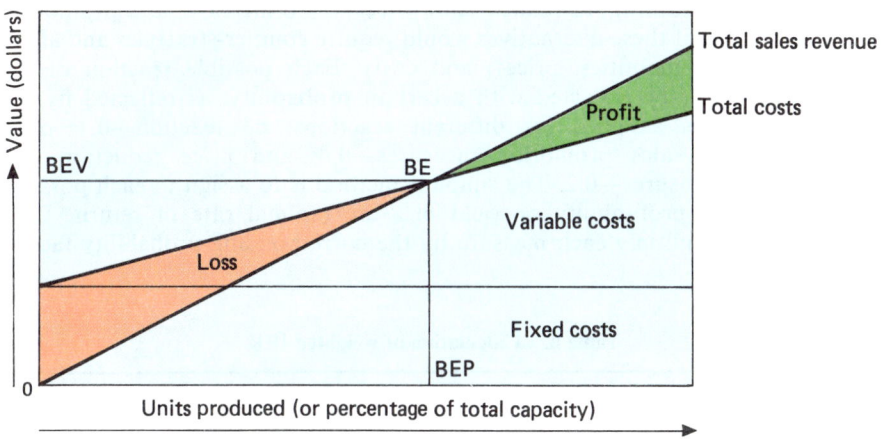

*Notes:* All costs an sales are annual values.
BEV = Break-even value
BEP = Break-even production

In the above equation, the number of units $U$ (or the rate of capacity utilization) is computed for given values of $p_s$, $c_v$ and $C_f$. It is also possible to compute $p_s$, **the break-even sales price for a given production volume and** defined costs. In case of more than one product, for example, products $A$ and $B$, the break-even sales value would be computed as follows:

$$(p_{sA} - c_{vA})U_A + (p_{sB} - c_{vB})U_B = C_{f(A+B)}$$

The break-even analysis may be carried out excluding and including costs of finance. In the latter case, the annual costs of finance need to be included in the fixed costs. Since the interest payable depends on the outstanding debt balance, the total annual fixed costs are usually not constant over the start-up and initial operating period. The break-even analysis should therefore be carried out for each year during this phase of the project.[140]

### Probability analysis

The sensitivity analysis already described allows the identification of the most critical variables, in particular those which, if they deviate from the forecast, could affect the feasibility of the investment significantly. In real life not all variables are likely to deviate to the same extent and in the same direction, and deviations may occur at any time during the construction and operating phase of the investment. The methods offered by the probability analysis allow the inclusion of possible deviations in the financial evaluation and appraisal of an investment project.

---

[140]The same is true for the production and marketing costs, because various cost items may change as a result of extra costs arising during initial operation.

First of all, the investor would have to estimate the probability of a certain scenario materializing. For example, the possible reaction of competitors[141] could be to do nothing, to reduce sales prices, or to increase sales promotion activities. Each of these alternatives would require counter-strategies and affect sales revenues (quantities, prices) and costs. Each possible reaction of the competitors may be expected with a certain probability, as reflected by the following values assigned for different reactions: no reaction—0.1; price reduction—0.4; sales promotion measures—0.3; and price reduction and promotional measures—0.2. The simplest method is to assign to each possible alternative one profitability or yield measure (annual rate of return, IRR, NPV), and to multiply each measure by the corresponding probability factor, as in table 8.

**Table 8.   Calculation of weighted IRR**

| Alternative | Probability | IRR | Weighted IRR |
|-------------|-------------|-----|--------------|
| No reaction | 0.1 | 20.0 | 2.0 |
| Price reduced | 0.4 | 18.5 | 7.4 |
| Promotion | 0.3 | 19.0 | 5.7 |
| Price reduction and promotional measures | 0.2 | 17.5 | 3.5 |
| *Total* | 1.0 | — | 18.6 |

The weighted IRR, 18.6, given in table 8 in the example has a limited value for investment appraisal, because it does not imply that the investment would yield 18.6 on an average. However, it may be useful for ranking projects. What analysts can deduce from the above table is that there is a 4 out of 10 chance that the investment would yield 19 per cent or more, and a 60 per cent chance of earning between 17.5 and 18.5 per cent as a result of the reactions of competitors. Supposing an 18 per cent cut-off rate applied by the investors, the project could be rejected on the assumption of a ±0.5 per cent confidence level of the IRR (that is the IRR is expected to be between 17.5 and 18.5, with the probability of 0.6).

For the appraisal of a project, however, it is important to determine not only the critical variables and their probable values and impacts, but also when deviations from the forecast may happen. For example, it makes a great difference whether a drop in sales prices occurs during start-up or during or after the payback period. In case there are a number of critical variables, stochastic models may be applied, where for each critical variable a confidence level is determined, and within these limits each variable is assigned a random value. For such a random combination of cash flows, the financial ratios etc. are computed, sometimes repeatedly in order to obtain a data series for project appraisal. While the introduction of stochastic models may be an interesting complementary method, it can also give analysts and decision makers an impression of accuracy that does not really exist.[142]

---

[141]See the analysis of competition in chap. III, sect. B.

[142]One of the problems is that various variables are not independent; e.g. nitrogen fertilizer production costs depend to a considerable extent on energy costs, while their market prices depend on supply and demand, and production costs as well. To identify such interrelations is a precondition for the application of stochastic models and for the development of investment, production and marketing strategies.

The value of probability analysis, however, lies in the identification and analysis of what could affect and seriously endanger a project, if implemented, and the determination of possible strategies to manage such situations.

With the introduction of sensitivity and probability analysis the number of computations increases considerably, since for each variable several values need to be computed in addition to the probability forecasts of occurrence. Access to suitable and reliable (well-tested) computer models is therefore a condition for the application of such methods.

### Evaluation of inflation risks

The question as to whether and when to use constant or current (inflated) prices in financial analysis has already been discussed in section B of this chapter. It has been shown that for the evaluation of net cash flows and the profitability of the project, inflation effects may be ignored, provided the relative prices of the major project inputs and outputs are likely to remain constant for the project lifetime. However, if relative prices are likely to change (for example, in the costs of labour, imported goods and services, replacement of fixed assets, and of local or international market prices of the goods produced), the sensitivity of the projected cash flows to such inflation effects should be analysed in the feasibility study. The analysis should not be limited to the determination of the sensitivity to changes in relative prices of project inputs and outputs, but should also identify possible strategies to cope with inflation risks (for example, any contractual obligations should include proper price escalation clauses).

In the case of hyperinflation, the yield or profitability of an investment project may best be computed assuming constant prices. If significant relative price changes are to be anticipated, the relative increase or decrease should be introduced. For example, assuming that the annual inflation rate is $x$ per cent and the average increase in labour costs is ($x + 1.5$ per cent), the cash flows should be computed at constant prices, with the exception of labour costs, which would be inflated by 1.5 per cent per annum. In case the annual average price increase is lower than the general inflation, a negative inflation rate should be introduced for the corresponding item.

Financial planning in the case of significant inflation rates, especially hyperinflation, requires the application of special accounting methods, which must comply with the rules and regulations valid in the country where the project is located.[143] These methods include the frequent revaluation of the **book values of fixed and current assets (including the adaptation of the corresponding annual depreciation charges), as well as of the liabilities of the firm.**

*Leasing.* The inflation risk may have an impact on the decision whether to lease or buy a plant. If future payments on leases are fixed in money terms, as is usually the case, inflation tends to increase the attractiveness of leasing, because the inflation risk would then be partly transferred to the lessor.

## I. Economic evaluation

As pointed out earlier, the financial evaluation aims at assessing the financial and commercial feasibility of a project from the point of view of the

---

[143]See the bibliography at the end of this chapter.

investors and financiers. The enterprise performance within a business environment is analysed, taking all expenses for project inputs as cash outflows, and the income from operations (sales revenues) as cash inflows. Financial resources required to implement and utilize the investment are inflows from the point of view of the firm (outflows for the banks, shareholders etc.), and the costs of finance as well as repayment of liabilities are financial outflows for the firm. All inputs and outputs are valued at market conditions. This means that the analyst and decision makers measure the net gains or benefits generated by the investment in financial terms, including the net benefits from the overall investment as well as the surplus left to investors (equity or share capital), taking into consideration the individual time preferences of the investors and financing institutions.

An investment project should also be justified within the wider context of the national economic and social environment. This is important because the corporate objectives and investment policies as determined by the investors may not always be in harmony with the national socio-economic policies of the country or area of investment. For that reason, and in order to allow the determination of public investment policies,[144] the net benefits generated from the national and socio-economic point of view should be determined. Although the investors generally have little interest in such an evaluation, there are two reasons why it may be useful to include the assessment and analysis of matters of public interest in the feasibility study. First, the economic environment and its future development could have significant impacts on the financial feasibility of the project, involving policies on income distribution, environmental protection, international trade etc. Secondly, the economic benefits generated by an investment may be used as an argument in favour of required public policy measures (such as protection from imports at dumping prices, granting permission or licences for the acquisition of foreign technology, approval of foreign equity participation and governmental guaranties).

There are various reasons for definite public interest in the economic evaluation of investment projects. For example, in the absence of "perfect" markets, the market mechanism cannot ensure the optimal allocation of resources from the national point of view under any circumstances. The maximization of financial surplus at the level of the firm does not fully reflect all other national development objectives. Sometimes there is inadequate competition, which enables some firms to develop a monopolistic position in the market. On the other hand, government intervention (through taxes, subsidies, customs duties, interest rates, price controls, import quotas etc.) often distorts the market prices of traded goods and services, resulting in the failure of those prices to reflect the true economic value of such goods and services.

The economic evaluation of investment projects may be characterized as follows.

- The national development impact of a project is assessed and evaluated;

---

[144]For example, incentives in case the investment is beneficial for the economy but not sufficiently attractive from the point of view of the investors, or prohibitive measures such as higher taxes and duties in certain areas or for certain technologies in case the investment has negative impacts in the form of social costs to the economy etc.

- Project inputs and outputs are valued at shadow prices[145] that reflect their true value to the national economy;

- Direct effects on the economy (involving imports, exports, employment, foreign exchange, supply and demand, ecological conditions etc.), as well as indirect effects (affecting performances in other sectors, through reduced under-utilization of installed capacities, new investment initiatives etc.), are included in the analysis where significant (these effects may be economic benefits or costs, both tangible and intangible);

- Social time preferences[146] are accounted for.

The economic evaluation of investment projects is beyond the scope of this *Manual*. When an evaluation of the contribution of industrial projects to the national economy is required, one of the methods developed for this purpose should be used. The principal methods are described in detail in various publications recommended in the bibliography to this chapter.

---

[145]Shadow prices indicate the value of goods and services assuming no market distortions. While market prices are to be used for the financial evaluation, shadow prices reflect the value of project inputs and outputs better than market prices, and may be considered as their necessary correction for the economic evaluation. Shadow prices are usually determined only for major production factors and project inputs and outputs, as well as when market distortions are significant.

[146]Social time preferences reflect the weight that society attaches to future as opposed to present consumption. For the economic evaluation, time preferences are expressed by the social discount rate, which differs from the individual discount rate applied in the financial evaluation.

## Schedule X–1/1.  Total fixed investment costs

### TOTAL FIXED INVESTMENT COSTS (thousand NCU)

| Investment category | From schedule | Total[a] construction | Total[b] production | Construction 1991 | Construction 1992 | Production 1993 | 1994 | 1995 | 1996 | 1997 | 1998 |
|---|---|---|---|---|---|---|---|---|---|---|---|
| 1. Land purchase | V-1 | 20 | – | 20 | – | – | – | – | – | – | – |
| 2. Site preparation and development | V-1 | 60 | – | 50 | 10 | – | – | – | – | – | – |
| 3. Civil works, structures and buildings | VI-3 | 2900 | – | 1000 | 1900 | – | – | – | – | – | – |
| 4. Plant machinery and equipment | VI-2 | 3500 | 500 | 1500 | 2000 | – | – | – | – | – | 500 |
| 5. Auxiliary and service plant equipment | VI-2 | 500 | 500 | – | 500 | – | – | – | – | – | 500 |
| 6. Environmental protection | | – | – | – | – | – | – | – | – | – | – |
|     Site preparation | V-2 | – | – | – | – | – | – | – | – | – | – |
|     Civil works | VI-3 | – | – | – | – | – | – | – | – | – | – |
|     Plant machinery and equipment | VI-2 | – | – | – | – | – | – | – | – | – | – |
| 7. Incorporated fixed assets (project overheads) | | 730 | – | 430 | 300 | – | – | – | – | – | – |
|     Technology | VI-1 | – | – | – | – | – | – | – | – | – | – |
|     Project implementation | IX-2 | – | – | – | – | – | – | – | – | – | – |
|     Miscellaneous project overhead costs | IX-2 | – | – | – | – | – | – | – | – | – | – |
| 8. Contingencies | | – | – | – | – | – | – | – | – | – | – |
| TOTAL FIXED INVESTMENT COSTS | | 7710 | 1000 | 3000 | 4710 | – | – | – | – | – | 1000 |
| Foreign share (%) | | 36.2 | 40.0 | 33.3 | 38.0 | – | – | – | – | – | 40.0 |

[a] Initial fixed investment.
[b] Fixed investment during plant operation.

Project/alternative: sample case, annex I.
Date: 19xx/xx/xx

---

[147]The figures shown in the schedules are based on the data given in the case-study presented in annex A to this *Manual*.

*Schedule X–1/2. Total fixed investment costs: foreign or local components*

| TOTAL FIXED INVESTMENT COSTS (thousand NCU) | | | | Construction | | Foreign [X]    Local [ ] Production | | | | | |
|---|---|---|---|---|---|---|---|---|---|---|---|
| Investment category | From schedule | Total^a construction | Total^b production | 1991 | 1992 | 1993 | 1994 | 1995 | 1996 | 1997 | 1998 |
| 1. Land purchase | V-1 | – | – | – | – | – | – | – | – | – | – |
| 2. Site preparation and development | V-1 | 10 | – | – | 10 | – | – | – | – | – | – |
| 3. Civil works, structures and buildings | VI-3 | 100 | – | – | 100 | – | – | – | – | – | – |
| 4. Plant machinery and equipment | VI-2 | 2500 | 200 | 1000 | 1500 | – | – | – | – | 200 | – |
| 5. Auxiliary and service plant equipment | VI-2 | – | 200 | – | – | – | – | – | – | – | 200 |
| 6. Environmental protection | | | | | | | | | | | |
| Site preparation | V-1 | – | – | – | – | – | – | – | – | – | – |
| Civil works | VI-3 | – | – | – | – | – | – | – | – | – | – |
| Plant machinery and equipment | VI-2 | – | – | – | – | – | – | – | – | – | – |
| 7. Incorporated fixed assets (project overheads) | | 180 | – | – | 180 | – | – | – | – | – | – |
| Technology | VI-1 | – | – | – | – | – | – | – | – | – | – |
| Project implementation | IX-2 | – | – | – | – | – | – | – | – | – | – |
| Miscellaneous project overhead costs | IX-2 | – | – | – | – | – | – | – | – | – | – |
| 8. Contingencies | | – | – | – | – | – | – | – | – | – | – |
| TOTAL FIXED INVESTMENT COSTS | | 2790 | 400 | 1000 | 1790 | – | – | – | – | – | 400 |
| Share of total (%) | | 36.2 | 40.0 | 33.3 | 38.0 | – | – | – | – | – | 40.0 |

^a Initial fixed investment.
^b Fixed investment during plant operation.

Project/alternative: sample case, annex I.
Date: 19xx/xx/xx

311

*Schedule X–2/1. Total pre-production expenditures*

## TOTAL PRE-PRODUCTION EXPENDITURES (thousand NCU)

| Investment category | From schedule | Total[a] construction | Total[b] production | Construction 1991 | Construction 1992 | Production 1993 | Production 1994 | Production 1995 | Production 1996 | Production 1997 | Production 1998 |
|---|---|---|---|---|---|---|---|---|---|---|---|
| 1. Pre-investment studies | II-1 | – | – | – | – | – | – | – | – | – | – |
| 2. Preparatory investigations | II-1 | – | – | – | – | – | – | – | – | – | – |
| 3. Company formation costs, fees etc. | IX-2 | – | – | – | – | – | – | – | – | – | – |
| 4. Project management, organization | IX-2 | – | – | – | – | – | – | – | – | – | – |
| 5. Technology acquisition | IX-2 | – | – | – | – | – | – | – | – | – | – |
| 6. Detailed engineering, contracting | IX-2 | – | – | – | – | – | – | – | – | – | – |
| 7. Pre-production supplies/marketing | IX-2 | – | – | – | – | – | – | – | – | – | – |
| 8. Plant commissioning, trial run etc. | IX-2 | – | – | – | – | – | – | – | – | – | – |
| 9. Other capital (issue) expenditures | IX-2 | 308 | – | 291 | 17 | – | – | – | – | – | – |
| 10. Contingencies | IX-2 | – | – | – | – | – | – | – | – | – | – |
| PRE-PRODUCTION EXPENDITURES (net of interest) | | 308 | – | 291 | 17 | – | – | – | – | – | – |
| 11. Interest paid/accrued | X-7/4 | 302 | – | 29 | 273 | – | – | – | – | – | – |
| TOTAL PRE-PRODUCTION EXPENDITURES | | 610 | – | 320 | 290 | – | – | – | – | – | – |
| Foreign share (%) | | 34.4 | – | 21.9 | 48.3 | – | – | – | – | – | – |

Project/alternative: sample case, annex I.
Date: 19xx/xx/xx

[a] Initial expenditures.
[b] Expenditures during plant operation.

*Schedule X–2/2. Total pre-production expenditures: foreign or local components*

## TOTAL PRE-PRODUCTION EXPENDITURES (thousand NCU)

Foreign [X]  Local [ ]

| Investment category | From schedule | Total[a] construction | Total[b] production | Construction 1991 | 1992 | Production 1993 | 1994 | 1995 | 1996 | 1997 | 1998 |
|---|---|---|---|---|---|---|---|---|---|---|---|
| 1. Pre-investment studies | II-1 | – | – | – | – | – | – | – | – | – | – |
| 2. Preparatory investigations | II-1 | – | – | – | – | – | – | – | – | – | – |
| 3. Company formation costs, fees etc. | IX-2 | – | – | – | – | – | – | – | – | – | – |
| 4. Project management, organization | IX-2 | – | – | – | – | – | – | – | – | – | – |
| 5. Technology acquisition | IX-2 | – | – | – | – | – | – | – | – | – | – |
| 6. Detailed engineering, contracting | IX-2 | – | – | – | – | – | – | – | – | – | – |
| 7. Pre-production supplies/marketing | IX-2 | – | – | – | – | – | – | – | – | – | – |
| 8. Plant commissioning, trial run etc. | IX-2 | – | – | – | – | – | – | – | – | – | – |
| 9. Other capital (issue) expenditures | IX-2 | 48 | – | 41 | 7 | – | – | – | – | – | – |
| 10. Contingencies | IX-2 | – | – | – | – | – | – | – | – | – | – |
| PRE-PRODUCTION EXPENDITURES (net of interest) | | 48 | – | 41 | 7 | – | – | – | – | – | – |
| 11. Interest paid/accrued | X-7/5 | 162 | – | 29 | 133 | – | – | – | – | – | – |
| TOTAL PRE-PRODUCTION EXPENDITURES | | 210 | – | 70 | 140 | – | – | – | – | – | – |
| Share of total (%) | | 34.4 | – | 21.9 | 48.3 | – | – | – | – | – | – |

[a] Initial expenditures.
[b] Expenditures during plant operation.

Project/alternative: sample case, annex I.
Date: 19xx/xx/xx

Schedule X-3/1. Total annual costs of products sold

## TOTAL ANNUAL COSTS OF PRODUCTS SOLD (thousand NCU)

| Cost item | From schedule | Production | | | | | | | | | | |
|---|---|---|---|---|---|---|---|---|---|---|---|---|
| | | 1993 | 1994 | 1995 | 1996 | 1997 | 1998 | 1999 | 2000 | 2001 | 2002 | 2003 - 2007 |
| Capacity utilization (%) | | 55 | 75 | 90 | 100 | 100 | 100 | 100 | 100 | 100 | 100 | 100 |
| 1. Raw materials | | | | | | | | | | | | |
| Raw material A | VI-4/2 | 1265 | 1725 | 2070 | 2300 | 2300 | 2300 | 2300 | 2300 | 2300 | 2300 | 2300 |
| Raw material B | VI-4/2 | 1182 | 1612 | 1935 | 2150 | 2150 | 2150 | 2150 | 2150 | 2150 | 2150 | 2150 |
| 2. Factory supplies | VI-4/2 | 248 | 338 | 405 | 450 | 450 | 450 | 450 | 450 | 450 | 450 | 450 |
| 3. Spare parts consumed | VI-4/2 | 250 | 250 | 250 | 250 | 250 | 250 | 250 | 250 | 250 | 250 | 250 |
| 4. Repair, maintenance, material | VI-4/2 | 193 | 263 | 315 | 350 | 350 | 350 | 350 | 350 | 350 | 350 | 350 |
| 5. Royalties | VI-4/2 | 30 | 30 | 30 | 30 | 30 | 30 | 30 | 30 | 30 | 30 | 30 |
| 6. Labour | VIII-2 | 687 | 937 | 1125 | 1250 | 1250 | 1250 | 1250 | 1250 | 1250 | 1250 | 1250 |
| Skilled labour | | – | – | – | – | – | – | – | – | – | – | – |
| Unskilled labour | | – | – | – | – | – | – | – | – | – | – | – |
| 7. Labour overheads (taxes etc.) | VIII-2 | – | – | – | – | – | – | – | – | – | – | – |
| 8. Factory overhead costs | VI-4/2 | 1320 | 1320 | 1320 | 1320 | 1320 | 1320 | 1320 | 1320 | 1320 | 1320 | 1320 |
| Salaries, wages | | – | – | – | – | – | – | – | – | – | – | – |
| Social costs etc. (on salaries) | | – | – | – | – | – | – | – | – | – | – | – |
| Materials and services | | – | – | – | – | – | – | – | – | – | – | – |
| Rents, leasing costs (factory) | | – | – | – | – | – | – | – | – | – | – | – |
| Insurance | | – | – | – | – | – | – | – | – | – | – | – |
| FACTORY COSTS | | 5175 | 6475 | 7450 | 8100 | 8100 | 8100 | 8100 | 8100 | 8100 | 8100 | 8100 |

| Item | Ref. | | | | | | | | | | | |
|---|---|---|---|---|---|---|---|---|---|---|---|---|
| 9. Administrative overhead costs | VII-2 | 500 | 500 | 500 | 500 | 500 | 500 | 500 | 500 | 500 | 500 | 500 |
|   Salaries, wages | | – | – | – | – | – | – | – | – | – | – | – |
|   Social costs etc. (on salaries) | | – | – | – | – | – | – | – | – | – | – | – |
|   Materials and services | | – | – | – | – | – | – | – | – | – | – | – |
|   Rents, leasing costs | | – | – | – | – | – | – | – | – | – | – | – |
|   Insurance | | – | – | – | – | – | – | – | – | – | – | – |
| OPERATING COSTS | | 5675 | 6975 | 7950 | 8600 | 8600 | 8600 | 8600 | 8600 | 8600 | 8600 | 8600 |
| 10. Depreciation | X-7/4 | 780 | 780 | 780 | 780 | 780 | 780 | 840 | 840 | 840 | 490 | 110 |
| 11. Financial costs | | | | | | | | | | | | |
|   Interests | | 522 | 546 | 453 | 339 | 238 | 136 | 45 | – | – | – | – |
|   Leasing costs | | – | – | – | – | – | – | – | – | – | – | – |
| TOTAL PRODUCTION COSTS | | 6997 | 8301 | 9183 | 9719 | 9618 | 9516 | 9485 | 9440 | 9440 | 9090 | 8710 |
| 12. Direct marketing costs | III-3 | 70 | 70 | 70 | 70 | 70 | 70 | 70 | 70 | 70 | 70 | 70 |
|   Salaries etc. | | – | – | – | – | – | – | – | – | – | – | – |
|   Rents, leasing costs | | – | – | – | – | – | – | – | – | – | – | – |
|   Other direct costs | | – | – | – | – | – | – | – | – | – | – | – |
| 13. Marketing overhead costs | III-3 | 263 | 292 | 315 | 330 | 330 | 330 | 330 | 330 | 330 | 330 | 330 |
|   Salaries etc. | | – | – | – | – | – | – | – | – | – | – | – |
|   Rents, leasing costs | | – | – | – | – | – | – | – | – | – | – | – |
|   Other indirect costs | | – | – | – | – | – | – | – | – | – | – | – |
| COSTS OF PRODUCT SOLD | | 7310 | 8663 | 9568 | 10119 | 10018 | 9916 | 9885 | 9840 | 9840 | 9490 | 9110 |
| Foreign share (%) | | 26.0 | 27.2 | 27.8 | 28.1 | 28.0 | 27.8 | 27.6 | 27.7 | 27.7 | 26.1 | 26.7 |
| Variable share (%) | | 50.0 | 57.6 | 62.6 | 65.7 | 66.4 | 67.1 | 67.3 | 67.6 | 67.6 | 70.1 | 73.0 |

Project/alternative: sample case, annex I.
Date: 19xx/xx/xx

## Schedule X–3/2. Total annual costs of products sold: foreign or local components

**TOTAL ANNUAL COSTS OF PRODUCTS SOLD** (thousand NCU)  Foreign [X]  Local [ ]

| Cost item | From schedule | 1993 | 1994 | 1995 | 1996 | 1997 | 1998 | 1999 | 2000 | 2001 | 2002 | 2003 - 2007 |
|---|---|---|---|---|---|---|---|---|---|---|---|---|
| | | | | | | Production | | | | | | |
| Capacity utilization (%) | | 55 | 75 | 90 | 100 | 100 | 100 | 100 | 100 | 100 | 100 | 100 |
| 1. Raw materials | | | | | | | | | | | | |
| Raw material A | VI-4/2 | 1265 | 1725 | 2070 | 2300 | 2300 | 2300 | 2300 | 2300 | 2300 | 2300 | 2300 |
| Raw material B | VI-4/2 | – | – | – | – | – | – | – | – | – | – | – |
| 2. Factory supplies | VI-4/2 | – | – | – | – | – | – | – | – | – | – | – |
| 3. Spare parts consumed | VI-4/2 | – | – | – | – | – | – | – | – | – | – | – |
| 4. Repair, maintenance, material | VI-4/2 | – | – | – | – | – | – | – | – | – | – | – |
| 5. Royalties | VI-4/2 | 30 | 30 | 30 | 30 | 30 | 30 | 30 | 30 | 30 | 30 | 30 |
| 6. Labour | VIII-2 | | | | | | | | | | | |
| Skilled labour | | – | – | – | – | – | – | – | – | – | – | – |
| Unskilled labour | | – | – | – | – | – | – | – | – | – | – | – |
| 7. Labour overheads (taxes etc.) | VIII-2 | – | – | – | – | – | – | – | – | – | – | – |
| 8. Factory overhead costs | VI-4/2 | – | – | – | – | – | – | – | – | – | – | – |
| Salaries, wages | | – | – | – | – | – | – | – | – | – | – | – |
| Social costs etc. (on salaries) | | – | – | – | – | – | – | – | – | – | – | – |
| Materials and services | | – | – | – | – | – | – | – | – | – | – | – |
| Rents, leasing costs (factory) | | – | – | – | – | – | – | – | – | – | – | – |
| Insurance | | – | – | – | – | – | – | – | – | – | – | – |
| FACTORY COSTS | | 1295 | 1755 | 2100 | 2330 | 2330 | 2330 | 2330 | 2330 | 2330 | 2330 | 2330 |

| Item | Ref | | | | | | | | | | | | |
|---|---|---|---|---|---|---|---|---|---|---|---|---|---|
| 9. Administrative overhead costs | VII-2 | — | — | — | — | — | — | — | — | — | — | — | — |
| Salaries, wages | | — | — | — | — | — | — | — | — | — | — | — | — |
| Social costs etc. (on salaries) | | — | — | — | — | — | — | — | — | — | — | — | — |
| Materials and services | | — | — | — | — | — | — | — | — | — | — | — | — |
| Rents, leasing costs | | — | — | — | — | — | — | — | — | — | — | — | — |
| Insurance | | — | — | — | — | — | — | — | — | — | — | — | — |
| OPERATING COSTS | | 1295 | 1755 | 2100 | 2330 | 2330 | 2330 | 2330 | 2330 | 2330 | 2330 | 2330 | 2330 |
| 10. Depreciation | X-7/5 | 300 | 300 | 300 | 300 | 300 | 300 | 300 | 300 | 300 | 300 | 50 | — |
| 11. Financial costs | | | | | | | | | | | | | |
| Interests | | 208 | 198 | 156 | 114 | 73 | 31 | — | — | — | — | — | — |
| Leasing costs | | — | — | — | — | — | — | — | — | — | — | — | — |
| TOTAL PRODUCTION COSTS | | 1803 | 2253 | 2556 | 2744 | 2703 | 2661 | 2630 | 2630 | 2630 | 2630 | 2380 | 2330 |
| 12. Direct marketing costs | III-3 | 70 | 70 | 70 | 70 | 70 | 70 | 70 | 70 | 70 | 70 | 70 | 70 |
| Salaries etc. | | — | — | — | — | — | — | — | — | — | — | — | — |
| Rents, leasing costs | | — | — | — | — | — | — | — | — | — | — | — | — |
| Other direct costs | | — | — | — | — | — | — | — | — | — | — | — | — |
| 13. Marketing overhead costs | III-3 | 30 | 30 | 30 | 30 | 30 | 30 | 30 | 30 | 30 | 30 | 30 | 30 |
| Salaries etc. | | — | — | — | — | — | — | — | — | — | — | — | — |
| Rents, leasing costs | | — | — | — | — | — | — | — | — | — | — | — | — |
| Other indirect costs | | — | — | — | — | — | — | — | — | — | — | — | — |
| COSTS OF PRODUCT SOLD | | 1903 | 2353 | 2656 | 2844 | 2803 | 2761 | 2730 | 2730 | 2730 | 2730 | 2480 | 2430 |
| Share of total (%) | | 26.0 | 27.2 | 27.8 | 28.1 | 28.0 | 27.8 | 27.6 | 27.7 | 27.7 | 27.7 | 26.1 | 26.7 |
| Variable share (%) | | 34.6 | 34.6 | 34.6 | 34.6 | 34.6 | 34.6 | 34.6 | 34.6 | 34.6 | 34.6 | 34.6 | 34.6 |

Project/alternative: sample case, annex I.

Date: 19xx/xx/xx

*Schedule X–3/3. Total annual costs of products sold: variable or fixed components*

## TOTAL ANNUAL COSTS OF PRODUCTS SOLD (thousand NCU)    Variable [X]    Fixed [ ]

| Cost item | From schedule | Production 1993 | 1994 | 1995 | 1996 | 1997 | 1998 | 1999 | 2000 | 2001 | 2002 | 2003 - 2007 |
|---|---|---|---|---|---|---|---|---|---|---|---|---|
| Capacity utilization (%) | | 55 | 75 | 90 | 100 | 100 | 100 | 100 | 100 | 100 | 100 | 100 |
| 1. Raw materials | | | | | | | | | | | | |
|     Raw material A | VI-4/2 | 1265 | 1725 | 2070 | 2300 | 2300 | 2300 | 2300 | 2300 | 2300 | 2300 | 2300 |
|     Raw material B | VI-4/2 | 1182 | 1612 | 1935 | 2150 | 2150 | 2150 | 2150 | 2150 | 2150 | 2150 | 2150 |
| 2. Factory supplies | VI-4/2 | 248 | 338 | 405 | 450 | 450 | 450 | 450 | 450 | 450 | 450 | 450 |
| 3. Spare parts consumed | VI-4/2 | – | – | – | – | – | – | – | – | – | – | – |
| 4. Repair, maintenance, material | VI-4/2 | 193 | 263 | 315 | 350 | 350 | 350 | 350 | 350 | 350 | 350 | 350 |
| 5. Royalties | VI-4/2 | – | – | – | – | – | – | – | – | – | – | – |
| 6. Labour | VIII-2 | 687 | 937 | 1125 | 1250 | 1250 | 1250 | 1250 | 1250 | 1250 | 1250 | 1250 |
|     Skilled labour | | – | – | – | – | – | – | – | – | – | – | – |
|     Unskilled labour | | – | – | – | – | – | – | – | – | – | – | – |
| 7. Labour overheads (taxes etc.) | VIII-2 | – | – | – | – | – | – | – | – | – | – | – |
| 8. Factory overhead costs | VI-4/2 | – | – | – | – | – | – | – | – | – | – | – |
|     Salaries, wages | | – | – | – | – | – | – | – | – | – | – | – |
|     Social costs etc. (on salaries) | | – | – | – | – | – | – | – | – | – | – | – |
|     Materials and services | | – | – | – | – | – | – | – | – | – | – | – |
|     Rents, leasing costs (factory) | | – | – | – | – | – | – | – | – | – | – | – |
|     Insurance | | – | – | – | – | – | – | – | – | – | – | – |
| FACTORY COSTS | | 3575 | 4875 | 5850 | 6500 | 6500 | 6500 | 6500 | 6500 | 6500 | 6500 | 6500 |

| | | | | | | | | | | | | |
|---|---|---|---|---|---|---|---|---|---|---|---|---|
| 9. Administrative overhead costs | VII-2 | – | – | – | – | – | – | – | – | – | – | – |
|   Salaries, wages | | – | – | – | – | – | – | – | – | – | – | – |
|   Social costs etc. (on salaries) | | – | – | – | – | – | – | – | – | – | – | – |
|   Materials and services | | – | – | – | – | – | – | – | – | – | – | – |
|   Rents, leasing costs | | – | – | – | – | – | – | – | – | – | – | – |
|   Insurance | | – | – | – | – | – | – | – | – | – | – | – |
| OPERATING COSTS | | 3575 | 4875 | 5850 | 6500 | 6500 | 6500 | 6500 | 6500 | 6500 | 6500 | 6500 |
| 10. Depreciation | X-7/4 | – | – | – | – | – | – | – | – | – | – | – |
| 11. Financial costs | | | | | | | | | | | | |
|   Interests | | – | – | – | – | – | – | – | – | – | – | – |
|   Leasing costs | | – | – | – | – | – | – | – | – | – | – | – |
| TOTAL PRODUCTION COSTS | | 3575 | 4875 | 5850 | 6500 | 6500 | 6500 | 6500 | 6500 | 6500 | 6500 | 6500 |
| 12. Direct marketing costs | III-3 | – | – | – | – | – | – | – | – | – | – | – |
|   Salaries etc. | | – | – | – | – | – | – | – | – | – | – | – |
|   Rents, leasing costs | | – | – | – | – | – | – | – | – | – | – | – |
|   Other direct costs | | 83 | 112 | 135 | 150 | 150 | 150 | 150 | 150 | 150 | 150 | 150 |
| 13. Marketing overhead costs | III-3 | – | – | – | – | – | – | – | – | – | – | – |
|   Salaries etc. | | – | – | – | – | – | – | – | – | – | – | – |
|   Rents, leasing costs | | – | – | – | – | – | – | – | – | – | – | – |
|   Other indirect costs | | – | – | – | – | – | – | – | – | – | – | – |
| COSTS OF PRODUCT SOLD | | 3658 | 4987 | 5985 | 6650 | 6650 | 6650 | 6650 | 6650 | 6650 | 6650 | 6650 |
| Share of total (%) | | 50.0 | 57.6 | 62.6 | 65.7 | 66.4 | 67.1 | 67.3 | 67.6 | 67.6 | 70.1 | 73.0 |
| Foreign share (%) | | 34.6 | 34.6 | 34.6 | 34.6 | 34.6 | 34.6 | 34.6 | 34.6 | 34.6 | 34.6 | 34.6 |

Project/alternative: sample case, annex I.
Date: 19xx/xx/xx

## Schedule X–4/1. Total net working capital requirements

### TOTAL NET WORKING CAPITAL REQUIREMENTS (thousand NCU)

| Investment category | From schedule | Coefficient of turnover [a] | Construction 1991 | 1992 | Production 1993 | 1994 | 1995 | 1996 | 1997 | 1998 |
|---|---|---|---|---|---|---|---|---|---|---|
| Capacity utilization (%) | | | – | – | 55 | 75 | 90 | 100 | 100 | 100 |
| 1. Total inventory | | | | | | | | | | |
| Raw materials in stock | X-3/1 | – | – | 400 | 21 | 21 | – | – | – | – |
| Raw material A | X-3/1 | 4 | – | – | 316 | 432 | 518 | 575 | 575 | 575 |
| Raw material B | X-3/1 | 12 | – | – | 99 | 134 | 161 | 179 | 179 | 179 |
| Factory supplies in stock | X-3/1 | 12 | – | – | 21 | 28 | 34 | 37 | 37 | 37 |
| Spare parts in stock | X-3/1 | 2 | – | – | 125 | 125 | 125 | 125 | 125 | 125 |
| Work in progress | X-3/1 | 40 | – | – | 129 | 162 | 186 | 203 | 203 | 203 |
| Finished products | | 24 | – | – | 236 | 291 | 331 | 358 | 358 | 358 |
| 2. Accounts receivable | | 12 | – | – | 501 | 611 | 695 | 750 | 750 | 750 |
| 3. Cash-in-hand | | 24 | – | – | 123 | 136 | 146 | 153 | 153 | 153 |
| CURRENT ASSETS | | | – | 400 | 1571 | 1940 | 2196 | 2380 | 2380 | 2380 |
| 4. Current liabilities | | | | | | | | | | |
| Accounts payable | X-3/1 | 24 | – | – | 216 | 270 | 310 | 337 | 337 | 337 |
| TOTAL NET WORKING CAPITAL REQUIREMENTS | | | – | 400 | 1355 | 1670 | 1886 | 2043 | 2043 | 2043 |
| INCREASE IN NET WORKING CAPITAL | | | – | 400 | 955 | 315 | 216 | 157 | – | – |
| Foreign share (%) | | | – | 62.5 | 34.2 | 37.8 | 39.9 | 40.9 | 40.9 | 40.9 |

[a] The coefficient of turnover (CTO) is obtained as follows:
CTO = 360/MDC (minimum days of coverage).

Project/alternative: sample case, annex I.
Date: 19xx/xx/xx

*Schedule X–4/2. Total net working capital requirements: foreign or local components*

## TOTAL NET WORKING CAPITAL REQUIREMENTS (thousand NCU)     Foreign [X]     Local [ ]

| Investment category | From schedule | Coefficient of turnover[a] | Construction 1991 | 1992 | Production 1993 | 1994 | 1995 | 1996 | 1997 | 1998 |
|---|---|---|---|---|---|---|---|---|---|---|
| Capacity utilization (%) | | | — | — | 55 | 75 | 90 | 100 | 100 | 100 |
| 1. Total inventory | X-3/2 | | | | | | | | | |
| Raw materials in stock | X-3/2 | — | — | 250 | | | | | | |
| Raw material A | X-3/2 | 4 | — | — | 316 | 432 | 518 | 575 | 575 | 575 |
| Raw material B | X-3/2 | — | — | — | — | — | — | — | — | — |
| Factory supplies in stock | X-3/2 | — | — | — | — | — | — | — | — | — |
| Spare parts in stock | X-3/2 | — | — | — | — | — | — | — | — | — |
| Work in progress | | 40 | — | — | 32 | 44 | 52 | 58 | 58 | 58 |
| Finished products | | 24 | — | — | 54 | 73 | 87 | 97 | 97 | 97 |
| 2. Accounts receivable | | 12 | — | — | 116 | 155 | 183 | 203 | 203 | 203 |
| 3. Cash-in-hand | | — | — | — | — | — | — | — | — | — |
| CURRENT ASSETS | | | — | 250 | 518 | 704 | 841 | 933 | 933 | 933 |
| 4. Current liabilities | | | | | | | | | | |
| Accounts payable | X-3/2 | 24 | — | — | 54 | 73 | 88 | 97 | 97 | 97 |
| TOTAL NET WORKING CAPITAL REQUIREMENTS | | | — | 250 | 464 | 631 | 753 | 836 | 836 | 836 |
| INCREASE IN NET WORKING CAPITAL | | | — | 250 | 214 | 167 | 122 | 83 | — | — |
| Share of total (%) | | | — | 62.5 | 34.2 | 37.8 | 39.9 | 40.9 | 40.9 | 40.9 |

[a] The coefficient of turnover (CTO) is obtained as follows:
CTO = 360/MDC (minimum days of coverage).

Project/alternative: sample case, annex I.
Date: 19xx/xx/xx

321

## Schedule X-5/1. Calculation of working capital requirements according to seasonal fluctuations

Inventory/stock:

Inventory/stock:

Inventory/stock: raw material

| Month | STOCK b/f | IN | OUT | STOCK c/f | |
|-------|-----------|------|------|-----------|-----|
| I | 775 | 0 | 180 | 595 | |
| II | 595 | 500 | 190 | 905 | MAX |
| III | 905 | 0 | 220 | 685 | |
| IV | 685 | 0 | 260 | 425 | |
| V | 425 | 250 | 250 | 425 | |
| VI | 425 | 150 | 220 | 355 | MIN |
| VII | 355 | 0 | 0 | 355 | MIN |
| VIII | 355 | 600 | 200 | 755 | |
| IX | 755 | 400 | 260 | 895 | |
| X | 895 | 0 | 270 | 625 | |
| XI | 625 | 350 | 180 | 795 | |
| XII | 795 | 0 | 70 | 725 | |
| TOTAL | – | 2250 | 2300 | 7540 | |
| AVERAGE | – | – | – | 628 | |

### ACCOUNTS PAYABLE

| Month | balance b/f | IN | OUT | balance c/f |
|-------|-------------|----|-----|-------------|
| I | | | | |
| II | | | | |
| III | | | | |
| IV | | | | |
| V | | | | |
| VI | | | | |
| VII | | | | |
| VIII | | | | |
| IX | | | | |
| X | | | | |
| XI | | | | |
| XII | | | | |
| TOTAL | | | | |
| AVERAGE | | | | |

### TOTAL CURRENTS ASSETS
(value of materials in stock)

| Month | STOCK b/f | IN | OUT | STOCK c/f |
|-------|-----------|----|-----|-----------|
| I | | | | |
| II | | | | |
| III | | | | |
| IV | | | | |
| V | | | | |
| VI | | | | |
| VII | | | | |
| VIII | | | | |
| IX | | | | |
| X | | | | |
| XI | | | | |
| XII | | | | |
| TOTAL | | | | |
| AVERAGE | | | | |

### Distribution of NET WORKING CAPITAL requirements

| Month | balance b/f | IN | OUT | balance c/f |
|-------|-------------|----|-----|-------------|
| I | | | | |
| II | | | | |
| III | | | | |
| IV | | | | |
| V | | | | |
| VI | | | | |
| VII | | | | |
| VIII | | | | |
| IX | | | | |
| X | | | | |
| XI | | | | |
| XII | | | | |
| TOTAL | | | | |
| AVERAGE | | | | |

Note: b/f = brought forward.
c/f = carried forward.

### Schedule X-5/2. Calculation of the short-term liquidity
#### (Cash and bank overdraft requirements)

| Month | Receipts | Payments | Deficit | Surplus | Aggregated deficit | |
|---|---|---|---|---|---|---|
| I | 500 | 910 | 410 | – | 410 | |
| II | 840 | 710 | – | 130 | 280 | |
| III | 1340 | 1150 | – | 190 | 90 | MIN |
| IV | 1180 | 1560 | 380 | – | 470 | |
| V | – | 640 | 640 | – | 1110 | |
| VI | – | 580 | 580 | – | 1690 | |
| VII | – | 480 | 480 | – | 2170 | |
| VIII | – | 540 | 540 | – | 2710 | MAX |
| IX | 1720 | 1080 | – | 640 | 2070 | |
| X | 1960 | 1510 | – | 450 | 1620 | |
| XI | 2700 | 1210 | – | 1490 | 130 | |
| XII | 2260 | 720 | – | 1540 | – | |
| TOTAL | 12500 | 11090 | 3030 | 4440 | | |
| AVERAGE | 1042 | 924 | 253 | 370 | 1400 | (MEAN) |
| Peak of short-term requirements = (MAX deficit) - NWC = 2710 - 2040 = 670 | | | | | | |

Note : NWC = net working capital (rounded) from schedule X-4.

## Schedule X–6/1.  Total investment costs

**TOTAL INVESTMENT COSTS** (thousand NCU)

| Investment category | From schedule | Total[a] construction | Total[b] production | Construction | | Production | | | | | |
|---|---|---|---|---|---|---|---|---|---|---|---|
| | | | | 1991 | 1992 | 1993 | 1994 | 1995 | 1996 | 1997 | 1998 |
| 1. Total fixed investment | X-1/1 | 7710 | 1000 | 3000 | 4710 | – | – | – | – | – | 1000 |
| 2. Total pre-production expenditures | X-2/1 | 610 | – | 320 | 290 | – | – | – | – | – | – |
| Net of interest | X-2/1 | 308 | – | 291 | 17 | – | – | – | – | – | – |
| Interest accrued | X-7/4 | 302 | – | 29 | 273 | – | – | – | – | – | – |
| 3. Total net working capital (increase) | X-4/1 | 400 | 1643 | – | 400 | 955 | 315 | 216 | 157 | – | – |
| TOTAL INVESTMENT COSTS | | 8720 | 2643 | 3320 | 5400 | 955 | 315 | 216 | 157 | – | 1000 |
| Foreign share (%) | | 37.3 | 37.3 | 32.2 | 40.4 | 22.4 | 53.0 | 56.5 | 52.9 | – | 40,0 |

[a] Initial investment.
[b] Investment during plant operation.

Project/alternative: sample case, annex I.
Date: 19xx/xx/xx

Schedule X–6/2.  *Total investment costs: foreign or local components*

## TOTAL INVESTMENT COSTS (thousand NCU)    Foreign [X]    Local [ ]

| Investment category | From schedule | Total[a] construction | Total[b] production | Construction | | Production | | | | | |
|---|---|---|---|---|---|---|---|---|---|---|---|
| | | | | 1991 | 1992 | 1993 | 1994 | 1995 | 1996 | 1997 | 1998 |
| 1. Total fixed investment | X–1/2 | 2700 | 400 | 1000 | 1790 | – | – | – | – | – | 400 |
| 2. Total pre-production expenditures | X–2/2 | 210 | – | 70 | 140 | – | – | – | – | ! | – |
| Net of interest | X–2/2 | 48 | – | 41 | 7 | – | – | – | – | – | – |
| Interest accrued | X–7/5 | 162 | – | 29 | 133 | – | – | – | – | – | – |
| 3. Total net working capital (increase) | X–4/2 | 250 | 586 | – | 250 | 214 | 167 | 122 | 83 | – | – |
| TOTAL INVESTMENT COSTS | | 3250 | 986 | 1070 | 2180 | 214 | 167 | 122 | 83 | – | 400 |
| Share of total (%) | | 37.3 | 37.3 | 32.2 | 40.4 | 22.4 | 53.0 | 56.5 | 52.9 | – | 40.0 |

[a] Initial investment.
[b] Investment during plant operation.

Project/alternative: sample case, annex I.
Date: 19xx/xx/xx

## Schedule X-7/1. Sources of finance

| Source of finance | Amount(NCU) | Financial terms | |
|---|---|---|---|
| **EQUITY CAPITAL** | | | |
| 1. Equity, local investor | 2 800 000 | First payment starting (year) | 1991 |
| | | Payable in instalments | YES |
| | | Dividend payment conditions | |
| | |     After build-up of legal reserves | |
| | |     Up to 12% of equity share | |
| 2. Equity, foreign partner | 700 000 | First payment starting (year) | 1991 |
| | | Payable in instalments | YES |
| | | Dividend payment conditions | |
| | |     After build-up of legal reserves | |
| | |     Up to 12% of equity share | |
| **LOAN CAPITAL** | | | |
| 1. Supplier's credit | 2 600 000 | Disbursement starting (year) | 1991 |
| | | Repayment starting (year) | 1994 |
| | | Duration of loan (years) | 8 |
| | | Type of amortization | Constant principal |
| | | Interest rate | 8% p.a. |
| | | Other costs of finance | None |
| 2. Local loan | 3 000 000 | Disbursement starting (year) | 1992 |
| | | Repayment starting (year) | 1995 |
| | | Duration of loan (years) | 8 |
| | | Type of amortization | Constant principal |
| | | Interest rate | 10% p.a. |
| | | Other costs of finance | None |
| 3. Bank overdraft | 400 000 | Disbursement starting (year) | 1993 |
| | | Period of grace (years) | – |
| | | Duration of loan (years) | 3 |
| | | Type of amortization | – |
| | | Interest rate | 12% p.a. |
| | | Other costs of finance | None |
| Foreign currency exchange rates: | | NCU 120 = $ 100 | |

Project/alternative: sample case, annex I.
Date: 19xx/xx/xx

326

## Schedule X–7/2. Flow of financial resources
### (excluding cash generated internally)

**TOTAL FINANCIAL FLOW** (thousand NCU)

| Source | From schedule | Total disbursement | Construction | | Production | | | | | | |
|---|---|---|---|---|---|---|---|---|---|---|---|
| | | | 1991 | 1992 | 1993 | 1994 | 1995 | 1996 | 1997 | 1998 | 1999 |
| 1. Equity capital | X-7/1 | | | | | | | | | | |
| Ordinary capital | | 3500 | 2600 | 900 | — | — | — | — | — | — | — |
| Preference capital | | — | | — | — | — | — | — | — | — | — |
| Subsidies | | — | | — | — | — | — | — | — | — | — |
| 2. Long-term loan | X-7/4 | | | | | | | | | | |
| Supplier's credit | | 2600 | 720 | 1880 | — | (520) | (520) | (520) | (520) | (520) | — |
| Development finance institutions | | — | | — | — | — | — | — | — | — | — |
| Commercial banks | | 3000 | — | 2800 | 200 | — | (600) | (600) | (600) | (600) | (600) |
| Government loan | | — | | — | — | — | — | — | — | — | — |
| Others | | — | | — | — | — | — | — | — | — | — |
| **TOTAL LONG-TERM FINANCE** | | 9100 | 3320 | 5580 | 200 | (520) | (1120) | (1120) | (1120) | (1120) | (600) |
| 3. Short-term finance | | | | | | | | | | | |
| Bank overdraft | X-7/4 | 400 | — | — | 400 | (300) | (100) | — | — | — | — |
| Accounts payable | X-4/1 | 338 | — | — | 216 | 54 | 41 | 27 | — | — | — |
| **TOTAL FINANCIAL FLOW** | | 9838 | 3320 | 5580 | 816 | (746) | (1159) | (1093) | (1120) | (1120) | (600) |
| Foreign share (%) | | 34.5 | 32.2 | 40.0 | 7.2 | 67.2 | 43.7 | 46.7 | 46.4 | 46.4 | 0.0 |

*Note*: Figures in parentheses are negative.

Project/alternative: sample case, annex I.
Date: 19xx/xx/xx

327

*Schedule X–7/3. Flow of financial resources: foreign or local components*
*(excluding cash generated internally)*

**TOTAL FINANCIAL FLOW** (thousand NCU)

Foreign [X]     Local [ ]

| Source | From schedule | Total disbursement | Construction 1991 | 1992 | Production 1993 | 1994 | 1995 | 1996 | 1997 | 1998 | 1999 |
|---|---|---|---|---|---|---|---|---|---|---|---|
| 1. Equity capital | | | | | | | | | | | |
| Ordinary capital | X-7/1 | 700 | 350 | 350 | – | – | – | – | – | – | – |
| Preference capital | | – | – | – | – | – | – | – | – | – | – |
| Subsidies | | – | – | – | – | – | – | – | – | – | – |
| 2. Long-term loan | X-7/5 | | | | | | | | | | |
| Supplier's credit | | 2600 | 720 | 1880 | – | (520) | (520) | (520) | (520) | (520) | – |
| Development finance institutions | | – | – | – | – | – | – | – | – | – | – |
| Commercial banks | | – | – | – | – | – | – | – | – | – | – |
| Government loan | | – | – | – | – | – | – | – | – | – | – |
| Others | | – | – | – | – | – | – | – | – | – | – |
| TOTAL LONG-TERM FINANCE | | 3300 | 1070 | 2230 | – | (520) | (520) | (520) | (520) | (520) | – |
| 3. Short-term finance | | | | | | | | | | | |
| Bank overdraft | X-7/5 | – | – | – | – | – | – | – | – | – | – |
| Accounts payable | X-4/2 | 97 | – | – | 54 | 19 | 14 | 10 | – | – | – |
| TOTAL FINANCIAL FLOW | | 3397 | 1070 | 2230 | 54 | (501) | (506) | (510) | (520) | (520) | – |
| Share of total (%) | | 34.5 | 32.2 | 40.0 | 7.2 | 67.2 | 43.7 | 46.7 | 46.4 | 46.4 | 0.0 |

*Note :* Figures in parentheses are negative.

Project/alternative: sample case, annex I
Date: 19xx/xx/xx

328

*Schedule X–7/4. Total debt service*

## TOTAL DEBT SERVICE (thousand NCU)

| | From schedule | Total disbursement | Construction | | | | Production | | | | |
|---|---|---|---|---|---|---|---|---|---|---|---|
| | | | 1991 | 1992 | 1993 | 1994 | 1995 | 1996 | 1997 | 1998 | 1999 |
| **1. Total long-term loans** | X-7/5 | 5600 | | | | | | | | | |
| Disbursements | | | 720 | 4680 | 200 | – | – | – | – | – | – |
| Repayments | | | – | – | – | 520 | 1120 | 1120 | 1120 | 1120 | 600 |
| Debt balance end of year | | | 720 | 5400 | 5600 | 5080 | 3960 | 2840 | 1720 | 600 | – |
| Capitalized interest | | | – | – | – | – | – | – | – | – | – |
| Interest payable | | | 29 | 273 | 498 | 498 | 441 | 339 | 238 | 136 | 45 |
| Other financial costs | | | – | – | – | – | – | – | – | – | – |
| **2. Total short-term loans** | X-7/5 | 400 | | | | | | | | | |
| Disbursements | | | – | – | 400 | – | – | – | – | – | – |
| Repayments | | | – | – | – | 300 | 100 | – | – | – | – |
| Debt balance end of year | | | – | – | 400 | 100 | – | – | – | – | – |
| Capitalized interest | | | – | – | – | – | – | – | – | – | – |
| Interest payable | | | – | – | 24 | 48 | 12 | – | – | – | – |
| Other financial costs | | | – | – | – | – | – | – | – | – | – |
| **3. TOTAL DEBT SERVICE** | X-7/5 | 6000 | | | | | | | | | |
| Disbursements | | | 720 | 4680 | 600 | – | – | – | – | – | – |
| Repayments | | | – | – | – | 820 | 1220 | 1120 | 1120 | 1120 | 600 |
| Debt balance end of year | | | 720 | 5400 | 6000 | 5180 | 3960 | 2840 | 1720 | 600 | – |
| Capitalized interest | | | – | – | – | – | – | – | – | – | – |
| Interest payable | | | 29 | 273 | 522 | 546 | 453 | 339 | 238 | 136 | 45 |
| Other financial costs | | | – | – | – | – | – | – | – | – | – |

Project/alternative: sample case, annex I.
Date: 19xx/xx/xx

*Schedule X–7/5. Total debt service: foreign or local components*

**TOTAL DEBT SERVICE** (thousand NCU)  Foreign [X]  Local [ ]

| | From schedule | Total disbursement | Construction 1991 | 1992 | Production 1993 | 1994 | 1995 | 1996 | 1997 | 1998 | 1999 |
|---|---|---|---|---|---|---|---|---|---|---|---|
| **1. Total long-term loans** | X-7/6 | | | | | | | | | | |
| Disbursements | | 2600 | 720 | 1880 | – | – | – | – | – | – | – |
| Repayments | | – | – | – | – | 520 | 520 | 520 | 520 | 520 | – |
| Debt balance end of year | | – | 720 | 2600 | 2600 | 2080 | 1560 | 1040 | 520 | – | – |
| Capitalized interest | | – | – | – | – | – | – | – | – | – | – |
| Interest payable | | – | 29 | 133 | 208 | 198 | 156 | 114 | 73 | 31 | – |
| Other financial costs | | – | – | – | – | – | – | – | – | – | – |
| **2. Total short-term loans** | X-7/6 | | | | | | | | | | |
| Disbursements | | – | – | – | – | – | – | – | – | – | – |
| Repayments | | – | – | – | – | – | – | – | – | – | – |
| Debt balance end of year | | – | – | – | – | – | – | – | – | – | – |
| Capitalized interest | | – | – | – | – | – | – | – | – | – | – |
| Interest payable | | – | – | – | – | – | – | – | – | – | – |
| Other financial costs | | – | – | – | – | – | – | – | – | – | – |
| **3. TOTAL DEBT SERVICE** | X-7/6 | | | | | | | | | | |
| Disbursements | | 2600 | 720 | 1880 | – | – | – | – | – | – | – |
| Repayments | | – | – | – | – | 520 | 520 | 520 | 520 | 520 | – |
| Debt balance end of year | | – | 720 | 2600 | 2600 | 2080 | 1560 | 1040 | 520 | – | – |
| Capitalized interest | | – | – | – | – | – | – | – | – | – | – |
| Interest payable | | – | 29 | 133 | 208 | 198 | 156 | 114 | 73 | 31 | – |
| Other financial costs | | – | – | – | – | – | – | – | – | – | – |

Project/alternative: sample case, annex I.
Date: 19xx/xx/xx

*Schedule X–7/6. Debt service: foreign or local currency loans*

**DEBT SERVICE** (thousand NCU)     Foreign [X]    Local [ ]

| | From schedule | Total disbursement | Construction 1991 | 1992 | 1993 | Production 1994 | 1995 | 1996 | 1997 | 1998 | 1999 |
|---|---|---|---|---|---|---|---|---|---|---|---|
| **1. Loan A** | X-7/1 | | | | | | | | | | |
| Disbursement | | 2600 | 720 | 1880 | – | – | – | – | – | – | – |
| Repayment | | – | – | – | – | 520 | 520 | 520 | 520 | 520 | – |
| Debt balance end of year | | – | 720 | 2600 | 2600 | 2080 | 1560 | 1040 | 520 | – | – |
| Capitalized interest | | – | – | – | – | – | – | – | – | – | – |
| Interest payable | | – | 29 | 133 | 208 | 198 | 156 | 114 | 73 | 31 | – |
| Other financial costs | | – | – | – | – | – | – | – | – | – | – |
| **2. Loan B** | | | | | | | | | | | |
| Disbursement | | – | – | – | | | | | | | |
| Repayment | | – | – | – | | | | | | | |
| Debt balance end of year | | – | – | – | | | | | | | |
| Capitalized interest | | – | – | – | | | | | | | |
| Interest payable | | – | – | – | | | | | | | |
| Other financial costs | | – | – | – | | | | | | | |
| **3. TOTAL DEBT SERVICE** | | | | | | | | | | | |
| Disbursements | | 2600 | 720 | 1880 | – | – | – | – | – | – | – |
| Repayments | | – | – | – | – | 520 | 520 | 520 | 520 | 520 | – |
| Debt balance end of year | | – | 720 | 2600 | 2600 | 2080 | 1560 | 1040 | 520 | – | – |
| Capitalized interest | | – | – | – | – | – | – | – | – | – | – |
| Interest payable | | – | 29 | 133 | 208 | 198 | 156 | 114 | 73 | 31 | – |
| Other financial costs | | – | – | – | – | – | – | – | – | – | – |

*Note*: Disbursement of loan has been assumed to take place in the middle of the year. Interest payable on mean debt before start of repayment is computed as follows:[a]

$$(Debt_{j-1} + Debt_j)/2 \times i = interest_j \ (p.a.)$$

The loan is assumed to be repaid in 10 half-yearly installments.

[a] i = interest rate; j = year.

Project/alternative: sample case, annex I.
Date: 19xx/xx/xx

331

## CASH FLOW FOR FINANCIAL PLANNING (thousand NCU)

| | From schedule | Construction 1991 | Construction 1992 | Production 1993 | Production 1994 | Production 1995 | Production 1996 |
|---|---|---|---|---|---|---|---|
| **TOTAL CASH INFLOW** | | 3320 | 5580 | 7691 | 9429 | 11291 | 12527 |
| 1. Inflow funds | | | | | | | |
| Total equity | X-7/2 | 2600 | 900 | – | – | – | – |
| Total long-term loans | X-7/2 | 720 | 4680 | 200 | – | – | – |
| Total short-term finance | X-7/2 | – | – | 616 | 54 | 41 | 27 |
| 2. Inflow operation | | | | | | | |
| Sales revenue | III -1 | – | – | 6875 | 9375 | 11250 | 12500 |
| Interest on securities | | – | – | – | – | – | – |
| 3. Other income | | – | – | – | – | – | – |
| **TOTAL CASH OUTFLOW** | | 3320 | 5400 | 7700 | 9072 | 10894 | 11274 |
| 4. Increase in fixed assets | | | | | | | |
| Fixed investments | X-1/1 | 3000 | 4710 | – | – | – | – |
| Pre-production expenditures (net of interest paid) | X-2/1 | 291 | 17 | – | – | – | – |
| 5. Increase in current assets | X-4/1 | – | 400 | 1171 | 369 | 256 | 184 |
| 6. Operating costs | X-3/1 | – | – | 5675 | 6975 | 7950 | 8600 |
| 7. Marketing costs | X-3/1 | – | – | 333 | 362 | 385 | 400 |
| 8. Corporate tax paid | X-10 | – | – | – | – | – | – |
| 9. Interest paid | X-7/4 | 29 | 273 | 522 | 546 | 453 | 339 |
| 10. Loan repayments | X-7/4 | – | – | – | 820 | 1220 | 1120 |
| 11. Dividends paid | X-10 | – | – | – | – | 630 | 630 |
| SURPLUS (DEFICIT) | | – | 180 | (10) | 357 | 397 | 1253 |
| CUMULATIVE CASH BALANCE | | – | 180 | 170 | 527 | 924 | 2177 |
| Foreign surplus (deficit) | | – | 50 | 183 | 75 | 250 | 478 |
| Local surplus (deficit) | | – | 130 | (193) | 282 | 147 | 775 |
| Foreign cumulative cash balance | | – | 50 | 233 | 308 | 558 | 1036 |
| Local cumulative cash balance | | – | 130 | (63) | 219 | 366 | 1141 |

Project/alternative: sample case, annex I.
Date: 19xx/xx/xx

## table for financial planning

| | 1997 | 1998 | 1999 | 2000 | 2001 | Production 2002 | 2003 | 2004 | 2005 | 2006 | 2007 | Scrap value 2008 |
|---|---|---|---|---|---|---|---|---|---|---|---|---|
| | 12500 | 12500 | 12500 | 12500 | 12500 | 12500 | 12500 | 12500 | 12500 | 12500 | 12500 | 3123 |
| | – | – | – | – | – | – | – | – | – | – | – | – |
| | – | – | – | – | – | – | – | – | – | – | – | – |
| | – | – | – | – | – | – | – | – | – | – | – | – |
| | 12500 | 12500 | 12500 | 12500 | 12500 | 12500 | 12500 | 12500 | 12500 | 12500 | 12500 | – |
| | – | – | – | – | – | – | – | – | – | – | – | – |
| | – | – | – | – | – | – | – | – | – | – | – | 3123 |
| | 12229 | 13178 | 11583 | 10960 | 10960 | 11135 | 11325 | 11325 | 11325 | 11325 | 11325 | – |
| | – | 1000 | – | – | – | – | – | – | – | – | – | – |
| | – | – | – | – | – | – | – | – | – | – | – | – |
| | – | – | – | – | – | – | – | – | – | – | – | – |
| | 8600 | 8600 | 8600 | 8600 | 8600 | 8600 | 8600 | 8600 | 8600 | 8600 | 8600 | – |
| | 400 | 400 | 400 | 400 | 400 | 400 | 400 | 400 | 400 | 400 | 400 | – |
| | 1241 | 1292 | 1308 | 1330 | 1330 | 1505 | 1695 | 1695 | 1695 | 1695 | 1695 | – |
| | 238 | 136 | 45 | – | – | – | – | – | – | – | – | – |
| | 1120 | 1120 | 600 | – | – | – | – | – | – | – | – | – |
| | 630 | 630 | 630 | 630 | 630 | 630 | 630 | 630 | 630 | 630 | 630 | – |
| | 271 | (678) | 918 | 1540 | 1540 | 1365 | 1175 | 1175 | 1175 | 1175 | 1175 | 3123 |
| | 2448 | 1770 | 2688 | 4228 | 5768 | 7133 | 8308 | 9483 | 10658 | 11833 | 13008 | 16131 |
| | 601 | 243 | 1194 | 1194 | 1194 | 1194 | 1194 | 1194 | 1194 | 1194 | 1194 | 1486 |
| | (330) | (921) | (276) | 346 | 346 | 171 | (19) | (19) | (19) | (19) | (19) | 1637 |
| | 1637 | 1880 | 3074 | 4268 | 5462 | 6656 | 7850 | 9044 | 10238 | 11432 | 12626 | 14112 |
| | 811 | (110) | (386) | (40) | 306 | 477 | 458 | 439 | 420 | 401 | 382 | 2019 |

Note : Figures in parentheses are negative.

## Schedule X–8/2. Cash-flow table for financial planning:

| | From schedule | Construction 1991 | 1992 | Production 1993 | 1994 | 1995 | 1996 |
|---|---|---|---|---|---|---|---|
| **CASH FLOW FOR FINANCIAL PLANNING** (thousand NCU) | | | | | | | |
| TOTAL CASH INFLOW | | 1070 | 2230 | 2054 | 2834 | 3389 | 3760 |
| 1. Inflow funds | | | | | | | |
| Total equity | X-7/3 | 350 | 350 | – | – | – | – |
| Total long-term loans | X-7/3 | 720 | 1880 | – | – | – | – |
| Total short-term finance | X-7/3 | – | – | 54 | 19 | 14 | 10 |
| 2. Inflow operation | | | | | | | |
| Sales revenue | III -1 | – | – | 2000 | 2815 | 3375 | 3750 |
| Interest on securities | | – | – | – | – | – | – |
| 3. Other income | | – | – | – | – | – | – |
| TOTAL CASH OUTFLOW | | 1070 | 2180 | 1871 | 2759 | 3139 | 3282 |
| 4. Increase in fixed assets | | | | | | | |
| Fixed investments | X-1/2 | 1000 | 1790 | – | – | – | – |
| Pre-production expenditures (net of interest paid) | X-2/2 | 41 | 7 | – | – | – | – |
| 5. Increase in current assets | X-4/2 | – | 250 | 268 | 186 | 137 | 92 |
| 6. Operating costs | X-3/2 | – | – | 1295 | 1755 | 2100 | 2330 |
| 7. Marketing costs | X-3/2 | – | – | 100 | 100 | 100 | 100 |
| 8. Corporate tax paid | X-10 | – | – | – | – | – | – |
| 9. Interest paid | X-7/5 | 29 | 133 | 208 | 198 | 156 | 114 |
| 10. Loan repayments | X-7/5 | – | – | – | 520 | 520 | 520 |
| 11. Dividends paid | X-10 | – | – | – | – | 126 | 126 |
| SURPLUS (DEFICIT) | | – | 50 | 183 | 75 | 250 | 478 |
| CUMULATIVE CASH BALANCE | | – | 50 | 233 | 308 | 558 | 1036 |

Project/alternative: sample case, annex I.
Date: 19xx/xx/xx

*foreign or local components*

| Foreign [X]   Local [ ] | | | | | | | | | | | |
|---|---|---|---|---|---|---|---|---|---|---|---|
| | | | | | Production | | | | | | Scrap value |
| *1997* | *1998* | *1999* | *2000* | *2001* | *2002* | *2003* | *2004* | *2005* | *2006* | *2007* | *2008* |
| 3750 | 3750 | 3750 | 3750 | 3750 | 3750 | 3750 | 3750 | 3750 | 3750 | 3750 | 1486 |
| | | | | | | | | | | | |
| – | – | – | – | – | – | – | – | – | – | – | – |
| – | – | – | – | – | – | – | – | – | – | – | – |
| – | – | – | – | – | – | – | – | – | – | – | – |
| 3750 | 3750 | 3750 | 3750 | 3750 | 3750 | 3750 | 3750 | 3750 | 3750 | 3750 | – |
| – | – | – | – | – | – | – | – | – | – | – | – |
| – | – | – | – | – | – | – | – | – | – | – | 1486 |
| 3149 | 3507 | 2556 | 2556 | 2556 | 2556 | 2556 | 2556 | 2556 | 2556 | 2556 | – |
| | | | | | | | | | | | |
| – | 400 | – | – | – | – | – | – | – | – | – | – |
| | | | | | | | | | | | |
| – | – | – | – | – | – | – | – | – | – | – | – |
| – | – | – | – | – | – | – | – | – | – | – | – |
| 2330 | 2330 | 2330 | 2330 | 2330 | 2330 | 2330 | 2330 | 2330 | 2330 | 2330 | – |
| 100 | 100 | 100 | 100 | 100 | 100 | 100 | 100 | 100 | 100 | 100 | – |
| – | – | – | – | – | – | – | – | – | – | – | – |
| 73 | 31 | – | – | – | – | – | – | – | – | – | – |
| 520 | 520 | – | – | – | – | – | – | – | – | – | – |
| 126 | 126 | 126 | 126 | 126 | 126 | 126 | 126 | 126 | 126 | 126 | – |
| 601 | 243 | 1194 | 1194 | 1194 | 1194 | 1194 | 1194 | 1194 | 1194 | 1194 | 1486 |
| 1633 | 1876 | 3070 | 4264 | 5458 | 6652 | 7846 | 9040 | 10234 | 11428 | 12622 | 14108 |

335

## DISCOUNTED CASH FLOW – TOTAL CAPITAL INVESTED

| | From schedule | Construction 1991 | 1992 | Production 1993 | 1994 | 1995 | 1996 |
|---|---|---|---|---|---|---|---|
| TOTAL CASH INFLOW | | – | – | 6875 | 9375 | 11250 | 12500 |
| 1. Inflow operation | | | | | | | |
|     Sales revenue | III-1 | – | – | 6875 | 9375 | 11250 | 12500 |
|     Interest on securities | | – | – | – | – | – | – |
| 2. Other income | | – | – | – | – | – | – |
| TOTAL CASH OUTFLOW | | 3291 | 5127 | 6963 | 7652 | 8551 | 9157 |
| 3. Increase in fixed assets | | | | | | | |
|     Fixed investments | X-1/1 | 3000 | 4710 | – | – | – | – |
|     Pre-production expenditures | | | | | | | |
|     (net of interest paid) | X-2/1 | 291 | 17 | – | – | – | – |
| 4. Increase in net working capital | X-4/1 | – | 400 | 955 | 315 | 216 | 157 |
| 5. Operating costs | X-3/1 | – | – | 5675 | 6975 | 7950 | 8600 |
| 6. Marketing costs | X-3/1 | – | – | 333 | 362 | 385 | 400 |
| 7. Corporate tax paid | X-10 | – | – | – | – | – | – |
| NET CASH FLOW | | (3291) | (5127) | (88) | 1723 | 2699 | 3343 |
| CUMULATIVE NET CASH FLOW | | (3291) | (8418) | (8506) | (6783) | (4084) | (741) |
| Net present value (at 12%) | | (3291) | (4578) | (70) | 1226 | 1716 | 1897 |
| Cumulative net present value | | (3291) | (7869) | (7939) | (6713) | (4997) | (3100) |
| NET PRESENT VALUE (at 12%) | | **3856** | | | | | |
| INTERNAL RATE OF RETURN | | **18.8%** | | | | | |

Project/alternative: sample case, annex I.
Date: 19xx/xx/xx

## cash flow – total capital invested

(thousand NCU)

| | | | | | Production | | | | | | Scrap value |
|---|---|---|---|---|---|---|---|---|---|---|---|
| 1997 | 1998 | 1999 | 2000 | 2001 | 2002 | 2003 | 2004 | 2005 | 2006 | 2007 | 2008 |
| 12500 | 12500 | 12500 | 12500 | 12500 | 12500 | 12500 | 12500 | 12500 | 12500 | 12500 | 3123 |
| 12500 | 12500 | 12500 | 12500 | 12500 | 12500 | 12500 | 12500 | 12500 | 12500 | 12500 | – |
| – | – | – | – | – | – | – | – | – | – | – | – |
| – | – | – | – | – | – | – | – | – | – | – | 3123 |
| 10241 | 11292 | 10308 | 10330 | 10330 | 10505 | 10695 | 10695 | 10695 | 10695 | 10695 | – |
| – | 1000 | – | – | – | – | – | – | – | – | – | – |
| – | – | – | – | – | – | – | – | – | – | – | – |
| – | – | – | – | – | – | – | – | – | – | – | – |
| 8600 | 8600 | 8600 | 8600 | 8600 | 8600 | 8600 | 8600 | 8600 | 8600 | 8600 | – |
| 400 | 400 | 400 | 400 | 400 | 400 | 400 | 400 | 400 | 400 | 400 | – |
| 1241 | 1292 | 1308 | 1330 | 1330 | 1505 | 1695 | 1695 | 1695 | 1695 | 1695 | – |
| 2259 | 1208 | 2192 | 2170 | 2170 | 1995 | 1805 | 1805 | 1805 | 1805 | 1805 | 3123 |
| 1518 | 2726 | 4918 | 7088 | 9258 | 11253 | 13058 | 14863 | 16668 | 18473 | 20278 | 23401 |
| 1144 | 546 | 885 | 783 | 699 | 574 | 463 | 414 | 369 | 330 | 294 | 455 |
| (1956) | (1410) | (525) | 258 | 957 | 1531 | 1994 | 2408 | 2777 | 3107 | 3401 | 3856 |

Note : Figures in parentheses are negative.

| DISCOUNTED RETURN ON EQUITY CAPITAL INVESTED | | | | | | | |
|---|---|---|---|---|---|---|---|
| | *From schedule* | *Construction* | | *Production* | | | |
| | | *1991* | *1992* | *1993* | *1994* | *1995* | *1996* |
| TOTAL CASH INFLOW | | – | 180 | (10) | 357 | 1027 | 1883 |
| 1. Cash surplus (deficit) | X-8/1 | – | 180 | (10) | 357 | 397 | 1253 |
| 2. Dividends paid | X-8/1 | – | – | – | – | 630 | 630 |
| TOTAL CASH OUTFLOW | | 2600 | 900 | – | – | – | – |
| 3. Equity capital paid (net of subsidies) | X-7/2 | 2600 | 900 | – | – | – | – |
| NET CASH RETURN | | (2600) | (720) | (10) | 357 | 1027 | 1883 |
| CUMULATIVE NET CASH RETURN | | (2600) | (3320) | (3330) | (2973) | (1946) | (63) |
| Net present value (at 12%) | | (2600) | (643) | (8) | 254 | 653 | 1068 |
| Cumulative net present value | | (2600) | (3243) | (3251) | (2997) | (2344) | (1276) |
| NET PRESENT VALUE (at 12%) | | **4164** | | | | | |
| INTERNAL RATE OF RETURN ON EQUITY | | **23.4%** | | | | | |

Project/alternative: sample case, annex I.
Date: 19xx/xx/xx

*on equity capital invested*

| (thousand NCU) | | | | | | | | | | | |
|---|---|---|---|---|---|---|---|---|---|---|---|
| | | | | | Production | | | | | | Scrap value |
| 1997 | 1998 | 1999 | 2000 | 2001 | 2002 | 2003 | 2004 | 2005 | 2006 | 2007 | 2008 |
| 901 | (48) | 1548 | 2170 | 2170 | 1995 | 1805 | 1805 | 1805 | 1805 | 1805 | 3123 |
| 271 | (678) | 918 | 1540 | 1540 | 1365 | 1175 | 1175 | 1175 | 1175 | 1175 | 3123 |
| 630 | 630 | 630 | 630 | 630 | 630 | 630 | 630 | 630 | 630 | 630 | – |
| – | – | – | – | – | – | – | – | – | – | – | – |
| – | – | – | – | – | – | – | – | – | – | – | – |
| 901 | (48) | 1548 | 2170 | 2170 | 1995 | 1805 | 1805 | 1805 | 1805 | 1805 | 3123 |
| 838 | 790 | 2338 | 4508 | 6678 | 8673 | 10478 | 12283 | 14088 | 15893 | 17698 | 20821 |
| 456 | (22) | 625 | 783 | 699 | 574 | 463 | 414 | 369 | 330 | 294 | 455 |
| (820) | (842) | (217) | 566 | 1265 | 1839 | 2302 | 2716 | 3085 | 3415 | 3709 | 4164 |

*Note* : Figures in parentheses are negative.

## NET INCOME STATEMENT (thousand NCU)

| | From schedule | 1993 | 1994 | 1995 | 1996 | 1997 | 1998 |
|---|---|---|---|---|---|---|---|
| | | | | Production | | | |
| Capacity utilization (%) | | 55 | 75 | 90 | 100 | 100 | 100 |
| 1. Total income | | 6875 | 9375 | 11250 | 12500 | 12500 | 12500 |
| Sales revenue | III -1 | 6875 | 9375 | 11250 | 12500 | 12500 | 12500 |
| Interest on securities | X-8/1 | – | – | – | – | – | – |
| Other income | X-8/2 | – | – | – | – | – | – |
| 2. Less variable costs | X-3/3 | 3658 | 4987 | 5985 | 6650 | 6650 | 6650 |
| Material | | – | – | – | – | – | – |
| Personnel (salaries, wages) | | – | – | – | – | – | – |
| Marketing (except personnel) | | – | – | – | – | – | – |
| Other variable costs | | – | – | – | – | – | – |
| VARIABLE MARGIN | | 3217 | 4388 | 5265 | 5850 | 5850 | 5850 |
| (in % of total income) | | 46.8 | 46.8 | 46.8 | 46.8 | 46.8 | 46.8 |
| 3. Less fixed costs | X-3/3 | 3130 | 3130 | 3130 | 3130 | 3130 | 3130 |
| Material | | – | – | – | – | – | – |
| Personnel (salaries, wages) | | – | – | – | – | – | – |
| Marketing (except personnel) | | – | – | – | – | – | – |
| Depreciation | | – | – | – | – | – | – |
| Other fixed costs | | – | – | – | – | – | – |
| OPERATIONAL MARGIN | | 87 | 1258 | 2135 | 2720 | 2720 | 2720 |
| (in % of total income) | | 1.3 | 13.4 | 19.0 | 21.8 | 21.8 | 21.8 |
| 4. Less costs of finance | X-7/4 | 522 | 546 | 453 | 339 | 238 | 136 |
| GROSS PROFIT | | (435) | 712 | 1682 | 2381 | 2482 | 2584 |
| 5. Less allowances | | – | – | – | – | – | – |
| TAXABLE PROFIT | | (435) | 712 | 1682 | 2381 | 2482 | 2584 |
| 6. Income (corporate) tax | | – | – | – | – | 1241 | 1292 |
| NET PROFIT | | (435) | 712 | 1682 | 2381 | 1241 | 1292 |
| 7. Dividends payable | | – | – | 630 | 630 | 630 | 630 |
| RETAINED PROFIT | | (435) | 712 | 1052 | 1751 | 611 | 662 |
| RATIOS (%) | | | | | | | |
| Gross profit / sales | | (6.3) | 7.6 | 15.0 | 19.0 | 19.9 | 20.7 |
| Net profit after tax / sales | | (6.3) | 7.6 | 15.0 | 19.0 | 9.9 | 10.3 |
| Net profit / equity capital | | (12.4) | 20.3 | 48.1 | 68.0 | 35.5 | 36.9 |
| Net profit + interest / investment | | 0.9 | 13.0 | 21.6 | 27.0 | 14.7 | 12.9 |

Project/alternative: sample case, annex I.
Date: 19xx/xx/xx

*statement from operations*

| | | | | Production | | | | |
|---|---|---|---|---|---|---|---|---|
| 1999 | 2000 | 2001 | 2002 | 2003 | 2004 | 2005 | 2006 | 2007 |
| 100 | 100 | 100 | 100 | 100 | 100 | 100 | 100 | 100 |
| 12500 | 12500 | 12500 | 12500 | 12500 | 12500 | 12500 | 12500 | 12500 |
| 12500 | 12500 | 12500 | 12500 | 12500 | 12500 | 12500 | 12500 | 12500 |
| – | – | – | – | – | – | – | – | – |
| – | – | – | – | – | – | – | – | – |
| 6650 | 6650 | 6650 | 6650 | 6650 | 6650 | 6650 | 6650 | 6650 |
| – | – | – | – | – | – | – | – | – |
| – | – | – | – | – | – | – | – | – |
| – | – | – | – | – | – | – | – | – |
| – | – | – | – | – | – | – | – | – |
| 5850 | 5850 | 5850 | 5850 | 5850 | 5850 | 5850 | 5850 | 5850 |
| 46.8 | 46.8 | 46.8 | 46.8 | 46.8 | 46.8 | 46.8 | 46.8 | 46.8 |
| 3190 | 3190 | 3190 | 2840 | 2460 | 2460 | 2460 | 2460 | 2460 |
| – | – | – | – | – | – | – | – | – |
| – | – | – | – | – | – | – | – | – |
| – | – | – | – | – | – | – | – | – |
| – | – | – | – | – | – | – | – | – |
| – | – | – | – | – | – | – | – | – |
| 2660 | 2660 | 2660 | 3010 | 3390 | 3390 | 3390 | 3390 | 3390 |
| 21.3 | 21.3 | 21.3 | 24.1 | 27.1 | 27.1 | 27.1 | 27.1 | 27.1 |
| 45 | – | – | – | – | – | – | – | – |
| 2615 | 2660 | 2660 | 3010 | 3390 | 3390 | 3390 | 3390 | 3390 |
| – | – | – | – | – | – | – | – | – |
| 2615 | 2660 | 2660 | 3010 | 3390 | 3390 | 3390 | 3390 | 3390 |
| 1307 | 1330 | 1330 | 1505 | 1695 | 1695 | 1695 | 1695 | 1695 |
| 1308 | 1330 | 1330 | 1505 | 1695 | 1695 | 1695 | 1695 | 1695 |
| 630 | 630 | 630 | 630 | 630 | 630 | 630 | 630 | 630 |
| 678 | 700 | 700 | 875 | 1065 | 1065 | 1065 | 1065 | 1065 |
| 20.9 | 21.3 | 21.3 | 24.1 | 27.1 | 27.1 | 27.1 | 27.1 | 27.1 |
| 10.5 | 10.6 | 10.6 | 12.0 | 13.6 | 13.6 | 13.6 | 13.6 | 13.6 |
| 37.4 | 38.0 | 38.0 | 43.0 | 48.4 | 48.4 | 48.4 | 48.4 | 48.4 |
| 12.2 | 12.0 | 12.0 | 13.6 | 15.3 | 15.3 | 15.3 | 15.3 | 15.3 |

*Note* : Figures in parentheses are negative.

## PROJECTED BALANCE SHEET (thousand NCU)

| | From schedule | Construction 1991 | Construction 1992 | Production 1993 | Production 1994 | Production 1995 | Production 1996 |
|---|---|---|---|---|---|---|---|
| TOTAL ASSETS | | 3320 | 8900 | 9716 | 9662 | 9729 | 10387 |
| 1. Total current assets | | – | 580 | 1741 | 2467 | 3750 | 5187 |
|    Inventory on materials & supplies | X-4/1 | – | 400 | 582 | 740 | 838 | 916 |
|    Work in progress | X-4/1 | – | – | 129 | 162 | 186 | 203 |
|    Finished products in stock | X-4/1 | – | – | 236 | 291 | 331 | 358 |
|    Accounts receivable | X-4/1 | – | – | 501 | 611 | 695 | 750 |
|    Cash-in-hand | X-4/1 | – | – | 123 | 136 | 146 | 153 |
|    Cash surplus, finance available | X-8/1 | – | 180 | 170 | 527 | 1553[a] | 2807 |
|    Securities | | – | – | – | – | – | – |
| 2. Total fixed assets, net of depreciation | | – | 8320 | 7540 | 6760 | 5980 | 5200 |
|    Fixed investment | X-6/1 | – | 3000 | 7710 | 7710 | 7710 | 7710 |
|    Construction in progress | X-6/2 | 3000 | 4710 | – | – | – | – |
|    Pre-production expenditures | X-6/1 | 320 | 610 | 610 | 610 | 610 | 610 |
|    Less accumulated depreciation | X-3/1 | – | – | 780 | 1560 | 2340 | 3120 |
| 3. Accumulated losses brought forward | | – | – | – | 435 | – | – |
| 4. Loss in current year | | – | – | 435 | – | – | – |
| TOTAL LIABILITIES | | 3320 | 8900 | 9716 | 9662 | 9729 | 10387 |
| 5. Total current liabilities | | – | – | 616 | 370 | 310 | 337 |
|    Accounts payable | X-4/1 | – | – | 216 | 270 | 310 | 337 |
|    Bank overdraft | X-7/2 | – | – | 400 | 100 | – | – |
| 6. Total long-term debt | X-7/4 | 720 | 5400 | 5600 | 5080 | 3960 | 2840 |
|    Loan A | | 720 | 2600 | 2600 | 2080 | 1560 | 1040 |
|    Loan B | | | 2800 | 3000 | 3000 | 2400 | 1800 |
| 7. Total equity capital | X-7/2 | 2600 | 3500 | 3500 | 3500 | 3500 | 3500 |
|    Ordinary capital | | 2600 | 3500 | 3500 | 3500 | 3500 | 3500 |
|    Preference capital | | – | – | – | – | – | – |
|    Subsidies | | – | – | – | – | – | – |
| 8. Reserves, retained profit brought forward | | – | – | – | – | 277 | 1329 |
| 9. Net profit after tax | X-10 | – | – | – | 712 | 1682 | 2381 |
|    Dividends payable | X-10 | – | – | – | – | 630 | 630 |
|    Retained profit | X-10 | – | – | – | 712 | 1052 | 1751 |
| RATIOS (%) | | | | | | | |
| Equity / total liabilities | | 78.3 | 39.3 | 36.0 | 36.2 | 36.0 | 33.7 |
| Long-term debt / net worth | | 0.3 | 1.5 | 1.6 | 1.5 | 1.0 | 0.6 |
| Current assets / current liabilities | | – | – | 2.8 | 6.7 | 12.1 | 15.4 |

Project/alternative: sample case, annex I.
Date: 19xx/xx/xx

[a] Rounded figure.

## balance sheet

| | Production | | | | | | | | | | |
|---|---|---|---|---|---|---|---|---|---|---|---|
| | 1997 | 1998 | 1999 | 2000 | 2001 | 2002 | 2003 | 2004 | 2005 | 2006 | 2007 |
| | 9978 | 9420 | 9498 | 10198 | 10898 | 11773 | 12838 | 13903 | 14968 | 16033 | 17098 |
| | 5458 | 4780 | 5698 | 7238 | 8778 | 10143 | 11318 | 12493 | 13668 | 14843 | 16018 |
| | 916 | 916 | 916 | 916 | 916 | 916 | 916 | 916 | 916 | 916 | 916 |
| | 203 | 203 | 203 | 203 | 203 | 203 | 203 | 203 | 203 | 203 | 203 |
| | 358 | 358 | 358 | 358 | 358 | 358 | 358 | 358 | 358 | 358 | 358 |
| | 750 | 750 | 750 | 750 | 750 | 750 | 750 | 750 | 750 | 750 | 750 |
| | 153 | 153 | 153 | 153 | 153 | 153 | 153 | 153 | 153 | 153 | 153 |
| | 3078 | 2400 | 3318 | 4858 | 6398 | 7763 | 8938 | 10113 | 11288 | 12463 | 13638 |
| | – | – | – | – | – | – | – | – | – | – | – |
| | 4420 | 4640 | 3800 | 2960 | 2120 | 1630 | 1520 | 1410 | 1300 | 1190 | 1080 |
| | 7710 | 7710 | 8710 | 8710 | 8710 | 8710 | 8710 | 8710 | 8710 | 8710 | 8710 |
| | – | 1000 | – | – | – | – | – | – | – | – | – |
| | 610 | 610 | 610 | 610 | 610 | 610 | 610 | 610 | 610 | 610 | 610 |
| | 3900 | 4680 | 5520 | 6360 | 7200 | 7690 | 7800 | 7910 | 8020 | 8130 | 8240 |
| | – | – | – | – | – | – | – | – | – | – | – |
| | – | – | – | – | – | – | – | – | – | – | – |
| | 9978 | 9420 | 9498 | 10198 | 10898 | 11773 | 12838 | 13903 | 14968 | 16033 | 17098 |
| | 337 | 337 | 337 | 337 | 337 | 337 | 337 | 337 | 337 | 337 | 337 |
| | 337 | 337 | 337 | 337 | 337 | 337 | 337 | 337 | 337 | 337 | 337 |
| | – | – | – | – | – | – | – | – | – | – | – |
| | 1720 | 600 | – | – | – | – | – | – | – | – | – |
| | 520 | – | – | – | – | – | – | – | – | – | – |
| | 1200 | 600 | – | – | – | – | – | – | – | – | – |
| | 3500 | 3500 | 3500 | 3500 | 3500 | 3500 | 3500 | 3500 | 3500 | 3500 | 3500 |
| | 3500 | 3500 | 3500 | 3500 | 3500 | 3500 | 3500 | 3500 | 3500 | 3500 | 3500 |
| | – | – | – | – | – | – | – | – | – | – | – |
| | – | – | – | – | – | – | – | – | – | – | – |
| | 3080 | 3691 | 4353 | 5031 | 5731 | 6431 | 7306 | 8371 | 9436 | 10501 | 11566 |
| | 1241 | 1292 | 1308 | 1330 | 1330 | 1505 | 1695 | 1695 | 1695 | 1695 | 1695 |
| | 630 | 630 | 630 | 630 | 630 | 630 | 630 | 630 | 630 | 630 | 630 |
| | 611 | 662 | 678 | 700 | 700 | 875 | 1065 | 1065 | 1065 | 1065 | 1065 |
| | 35.1 | 37.2 | 36.8 | 34.3 | 32.1 | 29.7 | 27.3 | 25.2 | 23.4 | 21.8 | 20.5 |
| | 0.3 | 0.1 | – | – | – | – | – | – | – | – | – |
| | 16.2 | 14.2 | 16.9 | 21.5 | 26.3 | 30.1 | 33.6 | 37.1 | 40.6 | 44.0 | 47.5 |

*Annex I*

# CASE-STUDY

The case-study presented in this annex has been worked out to facilitate the application of the concepts dealt with in this *Manual*, particularly when calculating fixed and working capital and when preparing cash flow tables for financial planning and evaluation. All schedules and calculations discussed in chapter X contain data taken from this case. However, to minimize statistics, no data were put into the schedules attached to chapters II through IX, and, for the same reason, inflationary impacts were not considered.

## 1. Project idea and basic strategy

The textile and garment industry is a high-employment activity that has contributed considerably to industrial development in various developing countries. In a number of newly industrializing countries[148] foreign exchange earnings from textile exports have reached a share of from 20 to 40 per cent of total earnings from exports of manufactured goods.

The selected project strategy is to produce textile products such as shirts, blouses and other garments for selected export markets, employing skilled local labour available at comparatively low costs. Considerable local demand for foreign trade marks is taken into account, with foreign (joint-venture) partner being interested in granting the use of its trade mark on the domestic market and in undertaking the export marketing.

*The basic project strategy is characterized by:*

- Focusing on main points: high-quality products (foreign trade mark) on the national market and selected export markets (see chapter III, figure XVIII);

- A market development strategy (see chapter III, figure XXI) using production and marketing know-how of a foreign joint-venture partner (cooperation strategy) to enter an expanding national market as well as to penetrate growing markets in selected foreign countries.

## 2. Market, products and marketing budget

The total value of annual product sales is projected at NCU 12,500,000, 30 per cent of which will be exported. The value of outputs has been estimated at prices 10 per cent lower than the average market prices[149] valid over the last five years. This assumption

---

[148]The term newly industrializing country is used extensively to describe developing economies, be they countries, provinces or areas, where there has been particularly rapid industrial growth. It does not imply any political division within the ranks of developing countries and is not officially endorsed by UNIDO.

[149]With f.o.b. price basis and transport to clients through forwarding companies that will invoice the client.

has been made in spite of a growing market, because the potential investors expect their competitors to change their prices with the market entry of the newcomer. In the case of exports, a 6 per cent export charge has to be paid to the State Trading Organization through which all exports have to be made.

Projected sales programme (schedule III-1)*

Estimate of total marketing costs (schedule III-2)**

## 3. Raw materials and factory supplies

Fabrics that depend mainly on synthetic raw materials are not available to the project from domestic resources and have to be imported. At full capacity utilization the annual costs for imported raw materials are projected at NCU 2,300,000. Fabrics made of natural fibres (cotton) are available from domestic suppliers in sufficient quality and quantity. The total annual consumption of domestic raw materials is projected at NCU 2,150,000.

Raw material and factory supplies (annual costs at full capacity utilization), are listed in the following schedule:

Estimate of total factory costs (schedule VI-4)

## 4. Initial total investment costs

The initial fixed investment costs are shown in chapter X, schedule X-1, the pre-production expenditures in schedule X-2, and the total initial investment in schedule X-6/1.

## 5. Investment during plant operation (replacement)

Replacement of equipment will be necessary in the sixth year of production; the total costs are projected at NCU 1,000,000 (40 per cent thereof for imported equipment) in schedule X-1.

## 6. Computation of depreciation

The following depreciation rates are used for the computation of the annual depreciation charges:

- At 10 per cent per annum for all fixed investment items, except for a part of locally supplied civil works (NCU 1,000,000) depreciated at 5 per cent per annum;

- For plant machinery and equipment, the end-of-life (salvage) value has been assumed at 10 per cent of the price of the new equipment.

---

*Excluding 6 per cent export charge of the State Trading Organization. During the first three years the volume of production is assumed to be 55 per cent, 75 per cent and 90 per cent of the installed production capacity.

**Excluding 6 per cent export charge of the state Trading Organization, but including royalties payable to the foreign joint venture partner who will market the exports.

## 7. Operating costs

The following standard costs have been projected for full capacity utilization (fourth year of operation); the detailed figures are shown in schedule X-3/1.

| Item | Thousands of NCU |
|---|---|
| Factory costs | 8 100 |
| Administrative overhead costs | 500 |

## 8. Net working capital requirement

The minimum days of coverage assumed are shown in table 9.

**Table 9. Minimum days of coverage for computation of net working capital**

| Item | Minimum days of coverage | |
|---|---|---|
| | Foreign components | Local components |
| Accounts receivable | 30 | 30 |
| Raw materials | 90 | 30 |
| Factory supplies | 30 | 30 |
| Spare parts | 180 | 180 |
| Production in progress | 9 | 9 |
| Finished products | 15 | 15 |
| Cash-in-hand | — | 15 |
| Accounts payable | 15 | 15 |

## 9. Project financing

The investors intend to finance 40 per cent of the total initial investment by equity capital and 60 per cent by long-term loans. Of the equity capital, 20 per cent will be paid by the foreign joint-venture partner and 80 per cent by the local investors.

For the imported goods and services a supplier credit of NCU 2.6 million will be available, subject to the following conditions:

- Disbursement during the construction phase (two years);
- The duration of the loan is eight years, with repayment in 10 equal instalments (principals) payable half-yearly, starting three years (36 months) after the first disbursement (two years after the last disbursement);
- The interest rate will be 8 per cent per annum payable on the outstanding debt balance.

In addition, a commercial loan is available to cover local investment costs (NCU 3 million):

- Disbursement will start in the second year of construction, and continue into the first year of operation (start-up phase);
- The duration of the local loan is eight years, with repayment in 10 equal instalments payable half-yearly, starting three years after the first disbursement. The interest rate will be 10 per cent per annum payable on the outstanding debt balance.

It is estimated that short-term finance will be required during start-up, amounting to NCU 400,000 in the first year and NCU 100,000 in the second year of plant operation. The interest will be 12 per cent per annum.

## 10.  Income (corporate) tax

The tax on corporate income is 50 per cent of taxable profits. The first four years after starting production are exempt from tax (tax holidays), and losses may be carried forward for up to three years.

## 11.  Return on equity capital (dividends)

The shareholders will be paid a dividend of 12 per cent per annum (before tax) on paid-in equity capital. However, payments will be made only after covering any previous losses carried forward and after the build-up of legal reserves.

The mean value of the annual rate of return on equity capital is 31 per cent ($-12$, 20, 48, 68) during the first four years of operations; for the same period the project would be exempt from the corporate tax. After this period the annual rate of return on equity after corporate tax is 35 per cent, increasing to 38 per cent over a five-year period (schedule X-10). The IRR on equity (that is, the discounted net cash return) is 22.7 per cent (schedule X-9/2). The profitability of equity capital is higher than that of the total capital invested, which is due to the leverage effect resulting from loan costs lower than the IRR of the overall investment.

The NPV of the annual net cash returns on equity generated during nine years from the start of construction (that is, the seventh year of operations) and discounted at a rate of 12 per cent, equals the paid-in equity, meaning that the equity capital can be repaid (before income tax paid on dividends) by the project in approximately nine years including an interest payment of 12 per cent per annum (see also schedule X-9/2).

## 12.  Break-even analysis

The break-even point is defined as the equilibrium point at which the variable margin (see also schedule X-10) equals the fixed costs. At this point the fixed-cost-coverage ratio equals 1.00. Table 10 shows that the project would not break even in the first year of production.

**Table 10.  Coverage of fixed costs**

| Item | Year | | | | |
|---|---|---|---|---|---|
| | 1 | 2 | 3 | 4 | 5 |
| | *(thousand national currency units)* | | | | |
| Sales revenues | 6 875 | 9 375 | 11 250 | 12 500 | 12 500 |
| Variable costs | 3 658 | 4 957 | 5 985 | 6 650 | 6 650 |
| Variable margin | 3 217 | 4 388 | 5 265 | 5 850 | 5 850 |
| Total fixed costs | 3 652 | 3 676 | 3 583 | 3 469 | 3 368 |
| Ratio[a] | 0.88 | 1.19 | 1.47 | 1.69 | 1.74 |

[a]Ratio of variable margin to fixed costs.

Before costs of finance but including depreciation, the ratio given in table 10 would be 1.03 for the first production year and increase during the following years from 1.40 to 1.87. The planned capacity utilization and break-even capacities are given in table 11.

## Table 11. Production cost factors

| Item | Year | | | | |
|---|---|---|---|---|---|
| | 1 | 2 | 3 | 4 | 5 |
| Capacity utilization (per cent) | 55 | 75 | 90 | 100 | 100 |
| Break-even production (thousand national currency units) | 63 | 63 | 62 | 59 | 54 |

# Annex II

# OUTLINES OF GENERAL OPPORTUNITY STUDIES

### A.    Outline of an area study

1.  Basic features of the area: area size and leading physical features, with maps showing the main characteristics

2.  Population, occupational pattern, per capita income and socio-economic background of the area, all set in the context of the socio-economic structure of the country concerned, highlighting differences in the area considered

3.  Leading exports from and imports to the area

4.  Basic exploited and potentially exploitable production factors

5.  Structure of any existing manufacturing industry utilizing local resources

6.  Infrastructural facilities, especially in the field of transport and power, conducive to development of industries

7.  A comprehensive check-list of industries that can be developed on the basis of the available resources and infrastructural facilities

8.  A check-list revising the one mentioned in item 7 by a process of elimination, excluding the following industries:

    ● Those for which present local demand is too small and transport costs are too high

    ● Those which face too severe competition from adjoining areas

    ● Those which can be more favourably located in other areas

    ● Those which would have unacceptable environmental impacts

    ● Those which require feeder industries not available in the area

    ● Those requiring substantial export markets, if the area is located in the interior and transport to the port is difficult or freight costs are high

    ● Those for which markets are distantly located

    ● Those which are geographically not suited to the area

    ● Those which do not fit in with national plan priorities and allocations

9.  Estimation of present demand and identification of opportunity for development based on other studies or secondary data, such as trade statistics, for the list of industries left after the revision referred to in item 8

349

10. Identification of recommendable project objectives and suitable strategies determining the type and scope of the project, including approximate capacities of new or expanded units that could be developed

11. Estimated capital costs of selected projects (lump sum), taking into account the following:
    - Land
    - Technology
    - Equipment
        Production equipment
        Auxiliary equipment
        Service equipment
        Spare parts, wear-and-tear parts, tools
    - Civil engineering works
        Site preparation and development
        Buildings
        Outdoor works
    - Project implementation
    - Pre-investment capital expenditures, including expenditures for preparatory investigations
    - Working capital requirements

*Major input requirements*

12. For each project approximate quantities of essential inputs should be estimated, so as to obtain the total input requirements. Sources of inputs should be stated and classified (local, shipped from other areas of the country, or imported). Inputs should be classified as follows:
    - Raw materials
    - Processed industrial materials and components
    - Factory supplies, such as auxiliary materials and utilities;
    - Labour

*Further project requirements*

13. Estimated production costs to be derived from item 12

14. Estimated annual sales revenues

15. Organizational and management aspects typical for the industry

16. An indicative time schedule for project implementation

17. Estimated level of total investment contemplated in projects and peripheral activities, such as development of infrastructure

18. Projected and recommended sources of finance (estimated)

19. Estimated foreign exchange requirements and earnings (including savings)

20. Financial evaluation: approximate pay-off period, approximate rate of return. Assessment of possible enlargement of product-mix, increased profitability and other advantages of diversification (if applicable)

21. A tentative analysis of overall economic benefits, and especially those related to national economic objectives, such as balanced dispersal of economic activity, estimated saving of foreign exchange, estimated generation of employment opportunities, and economic diversification. Indicative figures based on reference programming data, such as surveys and related studies, secondary data and data on the performance of other similar industrial establishments should be sufficient for this purpose

## B. Outline of a subsector opportunity study

1. Place and role of the subsector in industry

2. Size, structure and growth rate of the subsector

3. Present size and growth rates of demand for items that are not imported and for those which are wholly or partially imported

4. Rough projections of demand for each item

5. Identification of the items in short supply that have growth or export potential

6. A broad survey of the raw materials indigenously available

7. Identification of opportunities for development based on headings items 2, 5 and 6, and on other important factors such as transport costs and available or potentially available infrastructure

The items numbered from 10 to 21 in section A of this appendix follow item 7 of the subsector opportunity studies, since the structural requirements of the studies are the same once the investment opportunities have been identified.

## C. Outline of resource-based opportunity studies

1. Characteristics of the resource, prospective and proven reserves, past rate of growth and potential for future growth

2. Role of the resource in the national economy, its utilization, demand in the country and exports

3. Industries currently based on the resources, their structure and growth, capital employed and labour engaged, productivity and performance criteria, future plans and growth prospects

4. Major constraints and conditions in the growth of industries based on the resource

5. Estimated growth in demand and prospects of export of items that could utilize the resource

6. Identification of investment opportunities based on items 3, 4 and 5

The items numbered from 11 to 21 from section A of this appendix follow item 6 of the resource-based opportunity studies, since the structural requirements of the studies are the same once the investment opportunities have been identified.

351

# Annex III

# OUTLINE OF PRE-FEASIBILITY STUDY

1.  Executive summary—a synoptic review of all the essential findings of each chapter

2.  Project background and history:
    - Project sponsors
    - Project history
    - Cost of studies and investigations already performed

3.  Market analysis and marketing concept:
    - Definition of the basic idea of the project, objectives and strategy
    - Demand and market
        Structure and characteristics of the market
        The estimated existing size and capacities of the industry (specifying market leaders), its past growth, estimated future growth (specifying major programmes of development), local dispersal of industry, major problems and prospects, general quality of goods
        Past imports and their future trends, volume and prices
        Role of the industry in the national economy and the national policies, priorities and targets related or assigned to the industry
        Approximate present size of demand, its past growth, major determinants and indicators
    - Marketing concept, sales forecast and marketing budget
        Description of the marketing concept, selected targets and strategies
        Anticipated competition for the project from existing and potential local and foreign producers and supplies
        Localization of markets and product target group
        Sales programme
        Estimated annual sales revenues from products and by-products (local and foreign)
        Estimated annual costs of sales promotion and marketing
    - Production programme required
        Products
        By-products
        Wastes (estimated annual cost of waste disposal)

4.  Material inputs (approximate input requirements, their present and potential supply positions, and a rough estimate of annual costs of local and foreign material inputs):
    - Raw materials

- Processed industrial materials
- Components
- Factory supplies
  Auxiliary materials, utilities (especially power and energy requirements)

5. Location, site and environment:
   - Pre-selection, including, if appropriate, an estimate of the cost of land
   - Preliminary environmental impact assessment

6. Project engineering:
   - Determination of plant capacity
     Feasible normal plant capacity
   - Quantitative relationship between sales, plant capacity and material inputs
   - Preliminary determination of scope of project
   - Technology and equipment
     Technologies and processes that can be adopted, given in relation to capacity
     Technology description and forecast
     Environmental impacts of technologies
     Rough estimate of costs of local and foreign technology
     Rough layout of proposed equipment (major components)
       Production equipment
       Auxiliary equipment
       Service equipment
       Spare parts, wear and tear parts, tools
     Rough estimate of investment cost of equipment (local and foreign), classified as above
   - Civil engineering works
     Rough layout of civil engineering works, arrangement of buildings, short description of construction materials to be used
       Site preparation and development
       Buildings and special civil works
       Outdoor works
     Rough estimate of investment cost of civil engineering works (local and foreign), classified as above

7. Organization and overhead costs:
   - Rough organizational layout
     General management
     Production
     Sales
     Administration
   - Estimated overhead costs
     Factory
     Administrative
     Financial

8. Human resources:
   - Estimated human resource requirements, broken down into labour and staff and into major categories of skills (local/foreign)

- Estimated annual human resource costs, classified as above, including overheads on wages and salaries

9. Implementation scheduling:
   - Proposed approximate implementation time schedule
   - Estimated implementation costs

10. Financial analysis and investment:
    - Total investment costs
      Rough estimate of working capital requirements
      Estimated fixed assets
    - Project financing
      Proposed capital structure and proposed financing (local and foreign)
      Cost of finance
    - Production cost (significantly large cost items to be classified by materials, personnel and overhead costs, as well as by fixed and variable costs)
    - Financial evaluation based on the above-mentioned estimated values
      Payback period
      Simple rate of return
      Break-even point
      Internal rate of return
      Sensitivity analysis
    - National economic evaluation (economic cost-benefit analysis)
      Preliminary tests, for example, of
         Foreign exchange effects
         Value-added generated
         Absolute efficiency
         Effective protection
         Employment effects
      Determination of significant distortions of market prices (foreign exchange, labour, capital)
         Economic industrial diversification; estimate of employment-creation effect

*Note:* Additional information may be taken from the detailed check-lists and schedules given in each chapter of the *Manual.*

354

## *Annex IV*

# TYPES OF DECISIONS TO BE TAKEN DURING DIFFERENT PRE-INVESTMENT STAGES

| *Decision* | *Type of study* | *Decision Goal* |
|---|---|---|
| Identification | General or project opportunity studies | Identify opportunity |
| | | Determine critical areas for support studies |
| | | Determine area for pre-feasibility or feasibility study |
| Pre-selection and preliminary analysis | Support studies | Determine which of the possible choices is the most viable |
| | | Identify the choice of project criteria |
| | Pre-feasibility study | Determine provisional viability of project |
| | | Appraise whether the feasibility study should be launched |
| Final analysis | Support studies | Investigate in detail selected criteria requiring in-depth study |
| | Feasibility study | Make the final choices of project characteristics |
| | | Determine the feasibility of the project and selected criteria |
| Project evaluation[150] | Evaluation study | Make final investment decision |
| Project appraisal | Appraisal report | |

---

[150]The term evaluation is used by the World Bank for the ex-post evaluation of a project, which is carried out when a project is completed. Analysis and evaluation ex-ante is then called project appraisal.

## Annex V

# STATUS OF AN EXISTING INDUSTRIAL ENTERPRISE[151]

In order to facilitate their eventual merger, the structure of the check-list given below is the same as that of a feasibility study as outlined in the *Manual*.

1. Executive summary (gives a brief summary of the findings of the inquiries performed):
   - The enterprise: its principal position in and interrelations with the business environment (see chapter III and check-list III-5)
   - General indicators: business objectives and corporate strategies; general strengths and weaknesses
   - Marketing concept (chapter III) and plant capacity (chapter VI)
   - Raw material inputs and factory supplies (chapter IV)
   - Location, site and environment (chapter V)
   - Engineering situation and technology (chapter VI)
   - Administration and overhead costs (chapter VII)
   - Human resources (chapter VIII)
   - Plant implementation, for example, ex-post evaluation (chapter IX)
   - Financial analysis and standing (evaluation) of the firm (chapter X)

2. Background and history:
   - Background
     Describe task of the enterprise in the context of the economic, industrial, financial, and social policies applied in the private and public sector
     Describe international, regional, national, area and local relationships
   - The enterprise
     State the name, address, date of incorporation, ownership, and control of the enterprise
     Corporate set-up
     Affiliation to other companies, groups or individuals
     Competitors (firms, status, management assessment, plant and machinery, efficiency etc.)
   - History
     Investigations made before foundation (studies performed)
     Historical development, year of foundation, major events etc.

---

[151]See also the discussion of corporate or internal analysis in chap. III, sect. B.

3. Market analysis and marketing concept:

- Market structure and characteristics (see chapter III, check-lists III-1, III-3, III-4 and III-6)

    Describe existing market for products and by-products, and show its location on maps

    Describe its historic development

- Sales of products and by-products

    Existing sales volume, domestic and export markets, historical development

    Seasonal variations of sales

    Estimate of market share (percentage of total market)

- Sales organization

    Channels (own sales force, brokers, agents, direct to consumer)

    Sales organization, staff

    Marketing, advertising etc.

    Competitors, capacity

    Prices, discounts, commissions

    Annual sales revenues

- Value of stock of semi-finished and finished products

- Analysis of marketing costs (direct and overhead costs)

- Analysis of the main competitors

- Analysis of strengths and weaknesses of the firm

- Evaluation of the marketing concept; conclusions and recommendations

4. Raw materials and factory supplies:

- Characteristics of raw materials and factory supplies (specify and list sources of materials and inputs, classified into raw materials, processed industrial materials, components, auxiliary materials, factory supplies and utilities)

- Supply programme

    Quantitative supply programme, seasonal variations, subdivided into a programme for the entire plant, project components, and cost centres

    Development of supplies, seasonal restrictions

    Possible substitutes

    Organization of supplies (purchase, transport etc.)

    Prices

    Annual cost of supplies, seasonal variations

    Inventory of materials and inputs in terms of quantities and seasonal variations, as well as book and market value of inventories

5. Location, site and environment:

- Location

    Describe the location of the plant and show it on appropriate maps

    Give country, district, town

    Show connections to existing infrastructure (traffic, electricity, water, population etc.)

    Describe socio-economic environment, nearness to market etc.

- Site

    State town, street, number

Show situation and size on geodetic maps

Existing rights of way, easements etc.

Value of land

Annual costs of rights of way, rents, taxes, payments to neighbours etc.

- Local conditions

  Describe impacts of project on population, infrastructure, ecology, landscape etc.

  Evaluate the tendency of impacts (positive or negative)

- Assessment of environmental impacts, public and corporate policies, conflicts, costs and environmental forecast

6. Engineering and technology:

- Production programme

  Production programme of products and by-products: quality specifications, quantities produced, time schedule of production (seasonal variations), percentage of spoilage and waste

  Emissions: specifications, quantities, time schedule means of treating emissions and waste disposal

  Cost of emissions disposal

- Plant capacity

  Installed nominal maximum capacity

- Feasible nominal plant capacity of entire plant, main departments, major equipment units

- Plant layouts and charts (show existing structure of plant on physical layouts and on functional charts and layouts)

- Scope of enterprise (show scope of enterprise on layout drawings, and divide it into project components and cost centres)

- Technology

  List and describe technologies used, historic development

  Sources of technology

  Type of acquisition: licensing, purchase, joint venture

  Experiences (positive or negative)

  Technology forecast

  Annual costs of technologies (royalties, fixed payments)

- Equipment

  List and specify equipment, classify into production, auxiliary and service equipment

  Show equipment on plant layouts

  Describe sources, age, type (automatic, semi-automatic etc.)

  State capacity, condition (up-to-date, obsolete etc.)

  Value of installed equipment

  Annual depreciation and repair costs

  Estimated life and replacement costs

- Civil engineering works

  List and specify civil engineering works, classify into works for site preparation and development, buildings and special civil works, outdoor works

  Show situation and dimensions on maps and drawings

358

Describe construction and status (up-to-date, obsolete etc.)
Value of civil works and buildings
Annual depreciation and repair costs
Estimated life and replacement costs

7. Plant organization and overhead costs:

   - Cost centres
     List cost centres, classify them into production cost centres, service cost centres, administration and finance
     Show structure on charts and layouts
   - Overhead costs (list overhead costs and classify into factory overheads, administrative and marketing overheads, depreciation charges and financial overheads)

8. Human resources:

   - Labour
     List and describe labour force
     Describe skill and availability
     State annual cost of labour at nominal feasible capacity, subdivide into production labour (variable) and non-production labour (fixed)
   - Staff
     List and describe staff, show structure on manning tables
     State annual staff cost

9. Financial standing of the enterprise:

   - Reputation with reference to
     Bankers: credit standing, balances carried, type and length of loans, guarantees, general performance
     Major creditors: buying policies, special terms, payment record, general performance
     Customers: standing of the enterprise and its products in the trade, and its advantages or disadvantages over other companies in the same trade
   - Capital structure
     Capital stock

     Distribution into shares shown as follows:

     |  | No. issued | Total nominal amount | Total paid-up amount | No. of votes per share |
     |---|---|---|---|---|
     | Ordinary |  |  |  |  |
     | Preference |  |  |  |  |
     | Deferred |  |  |  |  |

     Unissued stock held for special purposes
     Voting, pre-emptive rights, liability to further calls, stock issue in recent years
     Securities listed on stock exchange: annual price range in recent years, ratio of current security prices to earnings

Bonds and mortgages
  Security provisions (secured and unsecured)
  Type and priority of mortgages or other liens
  Redemption provisions
  Convertibility

- Marketing costs (direct and indirect costs of sales and distribution)

- Production costs
  Direct materials and inputs
  Direct labour and staff
  Factory overhead costs (labour and materials)
  Depreciation
  Administrative overheads
  Financial overheads
  Fixed and variable costs as percentage of production costs
  Maintenance expenditures for recent years
  Cost accounting (costing) system (inventory control, burden determination and charge, labour and material charge, check of costing system with operating figures)

- Accounts and statements
  Copies of the last four (or more) annual reports, income statements, cash flow tables and balance sheets
  Auditors' report and certificate

- Analysis of financial statements
  Prepare a summary of comparative balance sheets, cash flow tables and income statements
  Analyse background of important changes during the period under review in assets, liabilities, income or cost items
  When a parent-company-subsidiary relationship exists, a thorough investigation of inter-company relations is necessary

- Detailed analysis of balance sheets (analyse major balance sheets, identify significant items, note variations in accounting methods)
  Receivables: financing by discounting or other methods, terms, amount of claims overdue, amount of debt written off
  Inventory: method of evaluation, unsaleable or obsolete stock
  Fixed assets: changes on fixed assets, depreciation rates, accelerated or extraordinary depreciation
  Investments: itemized list of investments at book value
  Short-term debt: original amount, outstanding amount, interest
  Notes payable
  Long-term debt: list of outstanding issues (date, amount, interest rate, maturity)
  Deficiencies: amount, period, debt interest or principal in arrears, preferred dividends in arrears
  Capital: share capital (authorized, issued, subscribed, paid-up), capital account (balance, plus net profit and deposits, minus losses, withdrawals and tax)
  Owners' account: amounts outstanding from or due to partners
  Surplus: earned, unearned (appreciation of assets, premium on bonds or stocks)
  Reserves: bad debts, depreciation, inventory, tax, hidden reserves

Contingencies: notes and receivables discounted, guarantees, endorsements, contingent liabilities with regard to subsidiaries

Bad debt: average annual amount written off

- Tax position

    Tax legislation applicable to company

    Production or turnover tax

    Income tax

    Property tax

    Others

- Insurance (coverage of fixed assets, inventories etc.)

    Pending litigations by or against the company

## Annex VI

# DEMAND FORECASTING TECHNIQUES

### A. Employment of demand forecasting techniques

The utmost caution should be exercised in the use of demand forecasting techniques, in order to avoid highly misleading results that could be derived from existing data. The following points must be noted:

- Characteristics should be precisely defined and scrupulously adhered to. For example, distinctions between different gases (oxygen, carbon dioxide) must be strictly maintained in the analysis of demand for industrial gases, because the process of production differs for each, and break-even points can vary widely;

- When identifying averages, norms, standards, trends and coefficients, account should be taken of a fairly large number of observations amenable to statistical tests of significance. A trend established, for example, over a four-year period, however marked, is not valid for a long-term forecast;

- Data and coefficients associated with one market or segment cannot be transplanted to others. For example, the income elasticity of demand for low-income groups is not the same as that for high-income groups;

- Assumptions made in the analysis and application of data, the formulation of coefficients and correlations must be distincly expressed without reservation;

- The selection of statistical techniques for estimating, analysis and forecasting should be appropriate to the nature of the product, market and data patterns;

- Reference data should be used with the necessary adjustment. For instance, the salary and wage levels of a small sugar refinery cannot be transplanted to a steel mill;

- The dynamics of data and coefficients have to be recognized. A price elasticity coefficient at $10 per unit cannot be used if the price rises to $20 per unit. The price elasticity may have been 1.2 in accounting for the demand for printing paper in 1985; it may be 0.8 in 1990;

- In the identification of trends, coefficients and relationships, only the aberrant case ought to be eliminated;

- Simple averages should be avoided, in preference to weighted averages;

- When data are not available, it is sometimes advocated that the analyst be content with a few rough estimates. The purpose of demand studies is to generate statistical information when it does not already exist and to analyse and process what does exist. Hence there is no justification for making rough estimates unsupported by dependable data, especially since these may mislead the investor.

### Consideration of competition from domestic and foreign suppliers

As opposed to alternative techniques or combinations of techniques that can be used to forecast demand, projections of the supply of a product are a matter of judgement, since they depend on the availability of a product through increased domestic production or imports. New domestic production can take the form of expansion of existing enterprises or the establishment of new industrial units in the same line of production. Existing domestic enterprises have an obvious advantage in that their production capacity can be increased with less capital outlay than is needed for a new unit. In countries where a formal or informal system of industrial licensing or governmental approval operates, it is possible to project estimates of manufacturing capacity to a reasonable degree. In other cases, however, an independent assessment of domestic manufacture of a particular product has to be made. The availability of a product in a particular market is also determined by government policies relating to imports.

## Projection of exports

The possibility of extending the market to other countries should be explored for most projects of any size, as export sales have to be taken into consideration in determining plant capacity. It may be possible, through expansion of plant capacity, to cater for a much larger market than the home country. Though a project may be conceived primarily as an import-substitution measure, nevertheless it may have export capability either immediately on commencement of production or within a reasonable period during which productive skills can be developed in order to be able to offer a product of international quality standard at a competitive price. For example, a petrochemical or fertilizer plant can enter export markets much easier after commencement of production than a plant producing heavy electrical equipment, which takes some years until plant capability is adequately established and products are fully proven. In all such cases, export capability needs to be assessed, and therefore the determination of possible export markets is an essential feature of demand forecasts.

The evelution of export markets has a somewhat different emphasis from that of domestic markets. For products that have been, or are currently being, exported, the starting-point is the collection and evaluation of data relating to the quantities exported, units, unit prices for exports, countries to which exports have been or are being made, and any special characteristics of the products exported, such as quality specifications or use of a particular brand name, either foreign or domestic, or use of a particular foreign selling agency. In certain countries, particular specifications are enforced for engineering goods and other products, and these need to be identified for particular products. Such information can generally be obtained either from the exporter or from the importing country, and should then be related to the products to be manufactured and to the nature of the proposed enterprise. A further survey then has to be undertaken of the size of the market in countries already importing the proposed product and in other countries that are similar in terms of development, import policies, shipping costs etc.

In the case of products that developing countries are contemplating, or have just started, manufacturing—and these would be the majority of goods and services from developing countries—the starting-point should be an analysis of past imports into the home country, the unit cost of such imports, the exporting countries and the characteristics of the imported product. Such information is necessary, even from the point of view of domestic production.[152] The price and quality of the product in the

---

[152]Except for small projects designed solely for local markets, there is a close relationship and interaction between the domestic and foreign manufacture of a product. Domestic products are frequently in competition with imported products except in countries imposing severe import controls. But even then, the price, quality and delivery of equivalent imported products has a considerable impact on the price and quality of domestic products. In some countries, a direct relationship is established in the matter of pricing, and domestically manufactured products have to sell at a certain percentage (approximately 20-25 per cent) below equivalent imported products. Even in the case of public sector products, an attempt is made to relate product pricing of comparable imported products.

international market should first be defined, which is not difficult. When related to export incentives and facilities provided by the home country, the pricing factors can be identified. Secondly, the geographical divisions of possible export markets should be defined in the context of a particular product. While there is an international market for most products, some are less popular than others, and various obvious constraints have to be taken into account. The market for consumer products such as cameras, colour television sets, stereo equipment and electronic calculators is international but highly competitive. However, if a proposed product is considered to be internationally competitive in terms of quality and technological input, the global market should be tackled step by step. There is no reason why such products, if produced in Latin America, should not be able to enter markets in Asia, provided the products are competitive in terms of technology, quality and price. In such cases, no detailed survey of all countries is necessary, and the export market survey can start with certain principal markets to be penetrated initially and gradually extended to other countries as plant capacity is expanded to meet increased market demand.

For some products, economies of scale may prove a determining factor in defining export markets. A plant contemplating an annual production of from 30,000 to 50,000 motor cars in an Asian country cannot expect to compete effectively in external markets with other manufacturers producing more than 300,000 motor cars annually. However, the possibility of exporting trucks is much greater, as economies of scale may allow operation at a much lower level of production, and an export market survey could be undertaken starting with neighbouring markets and gradually penetrating other markets.

In the case of intermediate products and the products of process industries, their export could be determined by transport costs, assuming that such products are comparable in quality, which is usually the case. For capital goods, export markets have to be gauged in terms of the possible acceptability of particular products by principal users. The number of such users is much smaller than in the case of consumer goods, and greater stress is normally placed on quality and reliability as related to prices, together with such aspects as availability of spares and after-sales services. Machine tools produced in India are currently being exported to the United States of America in small quantities, but to set up a full-scale machine-tool assembly plant oriented solely to such exports may not prove feasible, despite the fact that the United States market for machine tools is very large. Projections of exports have to be related to the degree of penetration considered practicable in any particular market.

After delineation of the geographical divisions of possible export markets on the basis of reasonable projections as to the degree of penetration, a market survey may need to be undertaken in selected countries. The scope of such a survey would vary depending on the degree of export orientation contemplated for a project. Thus, export surveys could range from projections of past imports in an external market with general projections for the future, to a detailed demand forecast in any particular external market using the forecasting techniques described earlier. The latter should, however, be undertaken rarely and only when export prospects of a particular product justify such an expensive course.

Information on imports and sources of imports into developed countries can generally be obtained without too much difficulty. In the case of developing countries, such information may be more difficult to obtain from published sources, and visits to selected countries may be necessary. Most developed countries have agencies to collect and collate economic data on possible export markets, and similar agencies may have to be established by developing countries contemplating exports of new and non-traditional products.

While an assessment of potential exports is essential to demand forecasts, a word of caution is necessary on the scope of such studies and on their reliability over a period. Because of rapid technological development, market prospects in developed and developing countries tend to alter within a few years, and it is far more difficult accurately to foretell such developments in foreign markets than in domestic ones.

364

## Types of surveys

Whereas overall quantitative estimates are based entirely or mainly on the results of desk research, more detailed quantitative findings and those of a qualitative nature emerge typically from the other principal form of market research: the field survey. Overlap between these two types of survey occurs because, in estimating total market size, written sources will quite commonly have to be supplemented by interviewing, while the necessity for some such field work for more detailed and qualitative answers will be obviated if appropriate written sources are accessible.

All relevant written material from within and outside the enterprise must be collected and analysed, in order to minimize both the various financial costs incurred in field surveys and the possibility of straining the tolerance of respondents by undue consumption of time at interviews. Furthermore, the results of desk research should impart perspective and extra definition to a questionnaire. No field survey should be undertaken before the full potential of desk research has been exhausted.

On the basis of sampling principles explained in annex VII, the field survey will fall within one of two categories, namely consumer or industrial, which includes trade research.

Both categories are described in annex VIII. Independent specialists in market research are commissioned to ensure objectivity, the application of experience and expertise, and observation of the rule that confidentiality will attach to the answers and comments of individual respondents unless they are informed otherwise beforehand. Owing to the large number of interviews involved in consumer research, a market research agency or company operating within the country concerned must be engaged. In industrial research the number of interviews is typically between 50 and 100, but frequently less. Thus one experienced specialist in industrial surveys may be commissioned, and, if necessary, he can be imported for the assignment. Sometimes in developing countries the prospective respondents for industrial surveys, traders perhaps, constitute the only viable source of information in the field.

Many manufacturing executives tend to regard their own industries as being uniquely complex. The intensity of such an attitude may be correlated with the number of years served and, to a lesser degree, with seniority of organizational position. The attitude becomes a problem when the skills needed for useful and valid results from market research are not understood, causing personnel to be engaged primarily for their knowledge of the industry. That knowledge must never be more than a secondary consideration, though the prospective client should be satisfied, before commissioning, about the suitability of the individual or individuals who will direct and supervise the research. Experience of the manufacturing industry concerned, or of a related one, is advantageous, but advantage may also accrue from opposite conceptual cross-fertilization.

The brief for a field survey must be carefully prepared in terms of objectives, scope and time scale. Typically the proposals of the research house or expert on industrial research will not be approved without modification or addition, the desirability of which will have become evident in discussions. As a general rule, the researcher should be required, by his terms of reference, to interpret the results in a written report; this will include a succinct presentation of the conclusions and, probably, his recommendations.

## Total demand

Total demand, present and projected, should therefore cover both the domestic and export markets and relate to the phasing of market penetration for a particular product. The demand or market study should also highlight the broad requirements of such markets in terms of product pricing, quality, technology and special characteristics such as consumer preference for particular brands. Any marketing strategy necessary for these markets should also be broadly defined. It is only then that the demand study can serve an effective purpose in determining plant capacity and the strategy to be followed in project formulation and implementation.

*Market penetration*

An essential feature of demand projections is an estimate of the market penetration that is possible for a particular product. This would be related to: the degree of competitiveness, either domestic or foreign; consumer response; and the amount of substitution that would be possible. These aspects have to be considered for the product to be manufactured, and an assessment made of which share of the market can be assumed. Also, the conditions of market penetration, such as product quality, packaging, marketing and distribution arrangements and after-sales services for machinery and other products, must be defined as part of the overall marketing strategy to achieve a sales and income target. Where a particular product is to be manufactured in a country for the first time and a system of licensing and import controls is operating, consumer reaction and the possibility of product substitution would be the determinant factors. For instance, the market penetration of the first synthetic fabrics produced in a country would depend on the substitution of such fabrics for natural fibres. As successive units are established, however, the competitive element would be the principal determinant factor and price considerations would be dominant, although other aspects, such as quality and brand name would still operate to a lesser extent.

## B. Trend (extrapolation) method

The trend method, a quite common technique is based on the extrapolation of past data, and involves the determination of a trend and the identification of its parameters. Two of the alternative trend curves for forecasting are indicated below.

*Arithmetic (linear) trend.* The equation is:

$Y = a + bT$

where $Y$ is the variable being forecast, and $T$ is to be estimated.

*Exponential (semi-log) trend.* The equation is:

$Y = ae^{bT}$

or $\ln Y = \ln a + bT$

This trend assumes a constant growth rate $b$ within each period.

The first step in measuring a trend is to take a moving average of two to three years, in order to correct for major annual fluctuations. Where such a moving average results in a smooth curve, a growth pattern will be discernible. It is, however, possible that fluctuations will cover a period longer than a year (for example, the demand for power-generating equipment when attributable to an intensified programme for expanding capacity). Correction should be made for such fluctuations. Figures for one year are sometimes missing, in which case statistical interpolation may be necessary.

## C. Consumption-level method

The consumption-level method considers the level of consumption, using standard and defined coefficients, and can be usefully adopted for consumer products. Thus the demand for cars can be estimated by determining the ratio of cars per 1,000 inhabitants, or the coefficients of car ownership among identified income levels, industrial units and Government. Once the total requirements are known, the actual car population is subtracted from the total to arrive at the new demand. Replacement requirements can be added to this forecast.

A major determinant of consumption levels is consumer income, influencing, *inter alia*, the household budget allocations which consumers are willing to make for a given product. With few exceptions, product consumption levels demonstrate a high degree of positive correlation with the income levels of consumers. However, the degrees of correlation differ between products. An example of products being negatively correlated with income levels is the consumption of such items as cheaper varieties of cloth and paper by the poor.

### Income elasticity of demand

The extent to which demand changes in response to variations in income is measured by the income elasticity of demand. Income elasticities differ not only between products but also, for a given product, between different income groups and different regions. Therefore, whenever it is possible to determine variations in per capita income by income groups and regions, the analysis should not be limited to the average per capita income in the whole national economy, but should be extended to occupational, socio-economic and geographical areas.

Some authors of demand studies overlook the fact that income elasticity changes from one income level to another. Products commonly supposed to have a negative correlation with incomes can show positive up to certain levels of income. The high income-elasticity evident at lower income levels declines as high income thresholds are crossed. This is true of most products. In developing countries, these thresholds are not crossed quite so often over the life span of industrial projects. None the less, the tendency for lower income elasticities with increased incomes is repeatedly found within lower income brackets. The aggregate result will therefore depend on the income structure. The demand for refrigerators is low up to a fairly high level of income. Above these levels the income elasticity rises and then reaches a plateau. The demand for radios shows a similar pattern.

When comparatively small changes in demand are involved, a coefficient may be developed and applied to changes in per capita incomes. Thus, if it were found that an increase in per capita income by 1 per cent led to an increase in consumption of paper by 2 per cent, the demand for paper in future years could be estimated by applying the income elasticity coefficient. This is illustrated n the example given in table 12.

#### Table 12.   Income and demand projections

| Year | Per capita income (dollars) | Increase in per capita income (relative to base year) | Increase in demand for paper (per cent) | Per capita demand for paper (kilograms) | Population (millions) | Demand for paper (thousand tonnes) |
|---|---|---|---|---|---|---|
| 1975 (base year) | 90.0 | | | 2.00 | 540 | 1 080 |
| *Projections* | | | | | | |
| 1976 | 91.0 | 2 | 4 | 2.08 | 557 | 1 158 |
| 1977 | 94.5 | 5 | 10 | 2.20 | 571 | 1 256 |
| 1978 | 94.5 | 5 | 10 | 2.20 | 585 | 1 280 |
| 1979 | 99.1 | 10 | 20 | 2.40 | 601 | 1 442 |
| 1980 | 104.4 | 16 | 32 | 2.64 | 616 | 1 636 |

The following formula gives the income elasticity coefficient

$$E_Y = \frac{Q_2 - Q_1}{Y_{P_2} = Y_{P_1}} \times \frac{Y_{P_1} + Y_{P_2}}{Q_1 + Q_2}$$

where $E_Y$ is the income elasticity coefficient of the product, $Q_1$ is the quantity demanded in the base year, $Q_2$ is the quantity demanded in the subsequent

367

observation year, $Y_{P_1}$ is the per capita income in the base year, and $Y_{P_2}$ is the per capita income in the subsequent observation year.

Values of $E_Y$ above 1.0 imply elasticity; values below 1.0 imply inelastic demand.

Using the data from table 12 as an example of per capita income and per capita demand for paper in 1975 and 1978, the income elasticity of paper in the case cited would be:

$$E_Y = \frac{2.20 - 2.00}{94.5 - 90\ 0} \times \frac{90.0 + 94.5}{2.00 + 2.20} = 1.952$$

The income elasticity of demand for paper is therefore elastic to income. Once determined, the coefficient of income elasticity can be applied to any future year to obtain the (unadjusted) per capita consumption of paper in that year. Thus, if per capita income in 1990 is 15 per cent higher than in 1985, per capita consumption of paper in 1990 would be 30 per cent higher than in 1985. The figure for projected per capita consumption may then be multiplied by the consumer population to arrive at the absolute size of demand.

## Price elasticity of demand

The determination of the price elasticity coefficient of demand for a product is a valuable adjunct to demand projections. The price elasticity of demand, that is, the ratio of relative variations in the volume of demand to the relative variation in price, may be expressed as a coefficient:

$$E_P = \frac{Q_1 - Q_0}{Q_1 + Q_0} \bigg/ \frac{P_1 - P_0}{P_1 + P_0} = \frac{Q_1 - Q_0}{P_1 - P_0} \times \frac{P_1 + P_0}{Q_1 + Q_0}$$

where $E_p$ is the price elasticity coefficient, $Q_1$ is the new demand, $Q_0$ is the existing demand at the present price $P_0$ and $P_1$ is the new price.

Application of the formula may be demonstrated by a simple example. If 500,000 and 400,000 refrigerators sell at \$500 and \$600 respectively, the price elasticity of demand is:

$$\frac{500,000 - 400,000}{500,000 + 400,000} \bigg/ \frac{500 - 600}{500 + 600} \text{ or}$$

$$\frac{100,000}{900,000} \times \frac{1,100}{-100} = -1.22$$

This coefficient can be very useful for studying sensitivities in the economics of a project, by enabling consideration of the price levels that may prevail in future. Variations in price clearly affect sales, and consequently production levels and the unit costs of production. The coefficient assumes, however, that other market conditions and behaviour remain constant. Furthermore, the coefficient is applicable only to quite small variations in price, since it does not remain constant over a wide range of price variations.

## Cross elasticity

The demand for a product is determined not only by its own price, but also by the price of complementary or substitute products. It is often necessary to identify the products with price variations that may affect demand for the product under consideration. That is determined by cross elasticity.

The cross elasticity of product $A$ to product $B$ is determined by the following formula:

$$C_{AB} = \frac{Q_{2A} - Q_{1A}}{Q_{2A} + Q_{1A}} \bigg/ \frac{P_{2B} - P_{1B}}{P_{2B} + P_{1B}}$$

This cross elasticity of product $A$ to product $B$, $C_{AB}$, is therefore the ratio of the proportionate change in the demand of product $B$ to the proportionate change in the price of product $B$. The value of $C_{AB}$ is interpreted as follows:

If $C_{AB} > 0$, the product is a substitute for $A$;

If $C_{AB} < 0$, the product is complementary to $A$;

If $C_{AB} = 0$, no cross elasticity exists between $A$ and $B$.

Three examples may be taken to demonstrate the application of the cross-elasticity ratio.

|  |  | Value 1 | Value 2 |
|---|---|---|---|
| (X) | Price of petrol (dollars per litre) | 0.40 | 0.50 |
|  | Demand for cars (thousands) | 200 | 160 |
| (Y) | Average price of electric shavers (dollars) | 25 | 30 |
|  | Demand for safety razors (thousands) | 6 | 9 |
| (Z) | Price of milk (dollars per litre) | 0.20 | 0.25 |
|  | Quantity (length) of cloth (million metres) | 100 | 100 |

The value of $C_{AB}$ in each case is calculated as follows:

Case X: $\dfrac{-40 \times 0.90}{360 \times 0.10} = -1.0$

Case Y: $\dfrac{3 \times 55}{15 \times 5} = 2.2$

Case Z: $\dfrac{0 \times 0.45}{200 \times 0.50} = 0$

Since $C_{AB}$ is less than zero in case $X$, the demand for cars is complementary to, or correlates positively with, the price of petrol. Since $C_{AB}$ is greater than zero and as high as 2.2 in case $Y$, safety razors are a sensitive substitute for electric shavers. As may be expected, since $C_{AB}$ is zero in case $Z$, there is no cross elasticity between milk and cloth. When complementarity or substitutability of products is established, demand forecasts should be amended to provide for the impact of expected price changes in a complementary or substitute product.

### D.  End-use or consumption coefficient method

The end-use or consumption coefficient method is particularly suitable for assessing intermediate products. It involves the following:

● All possible uses of a product are identified, including, for example, input to other industries, direct consumption demand, imports and exports;

● The input-output coefficient of the product and the industries using the product are obtained or estimated. It is then possible to derive the demand for a product, that is, for consumption plus its exports and net of imports, from the projected output levels of the consuming industries.

In order to forecast the demand for methanol, for instance, industries using methanol would initially be identified. These would include the formaldehyde, fertilizer and pharmaceutical industries. The planned manufacturing programmes of these three industries would define the future requirements of methanol, after allowing for demand from other users (who would be grouped together).

A similar approach could be adopted for some items of machinery, such as compressors or industrial turbines. The technique can also be used for consumer products and for mixed types of product. For example, the demand for cement can be assessed by estimating the requirements of cement for various construction activities, such as private and public housing, dams, public works and other types of construction.

The end-use method utilizes consumption coefficients, and is therefore also called the consumption coefficient method. When identified, the coefficient appropriate for a consumption goal is multiplied by the size of the activity to arrive at the forecast consumption level. The following example demonstrates the application of the method.

| Vehicle | Annual petrol consumption per vehicle (thousand litres) |
|---|---|
| Private cars | 3.20 |
| Taxis | 8.60 |
| Commercial vehicles using petrol | 11.20 |
| Scooters, motor cycles, three-wheelers | 0.12 |
| Other uses (10 per cent of figure for private cars) | 0.32 |

Forecasts of demand for petrol based on the above consumption coefficients are given in table 13.

**Table 13.  Forecast of petrol consumption**

| Vehicle | 1985 | | 1990 | | 1995 | |
|---|---|---|---|---|---|---|
| | Thousand cars | Million litres | Thousand cars | Million litres | Thousand cars | Million litres |
| Private cars | 110 | 352 | 150 | 480 | 210 | 672 |
| Taxis | 40 | 344 | 60 | 546 | 90 | 774 |
| Commercial vehicles | 80 | 996 | 110 | 1 232 | 140 | 1 568 |
| Two-wheeled vehicles (scooters etc.) | 280 | 37 | 410 | 49 | 700 | 84 |
| Others | .. | 35 | .. | 48 | .. | 67 |
| Total | 510 | 1 764 | 730 | 2 355 | 1 140 | 3 165 |

Consumption coefficients vary over time from one market to another, in size of producing units and as a function of technological change. For petrol consumption, the consumption coefficients differ between the types of vehicle, but each coefficient can vary from one period to another. Therefore, extreme caution must be exercised in the determination of past, and especially in the projection of future, coefficients.

In the case of intermediate products, coefficients can vary with the size of the consuming unit and with technological changes. In steel-plate production, for example, consumption of steel might be reduced by reducing the thickness of plates, while still conforming to prescribed standards.

As a result of the divergences in consumption coefficients, a considerable amount of skill is required in projecting the coefficients (and hence demand), even though the data may be precise and reliable. This forecasting technique can be applied fairly effectively, if adequate projections of change in the consuming industries are available, which is frequently not the case. To some extent, such projections can be obtained from national plans.

## Regression models

In the regression technique, forecasts are made on the basis of a relationship estimated between the forecast (or dependent) variable and the explanatory (or independent) variables. Different combinations of independent variables can be tested with data, until an accurate forecasting equation is derived. Unfortunately, projection of the independent variables is difficult.

## Leading indicator method

The leading indicator method is a variant of the consumption-coefficient and regression methods. Leading indicators are variables that react to change before, and which can be used to predict, other variables. Thus the demand for electric fans might be found to lag, for instance, two years behind the housing investment of various agencies. To use these indicators for forecasting purposes, at first the appropriate leading indicators would have to be identified, and then the relationship between them and the variable being forecast is determined.

This method obviates the need for projecting an explanatory variable, but it is not always possible to determine the leading indicator, and the lead time may not be stable. The relationship itself may also change with time. The method is used to only a limited extent.

## Bibliography

Makridakis, S., S. C. Wheelright *and* V. E. McGee. Forecasting: methods and application. 2. ed. New York, John Wiley, 1983.

Lucey, T. Quantitative techniques. 3. ed. London, DP Publications, 1988.

*Annex VII*

# SAMPLING PRINCIPLES

The purpose of sampling is to estimate the true (unknown) values of population characteristics. It is possible to do this because, for most practical purposes, the analysis of a small, carefully selected section of a population will yield information about that population which is nearly as accurate as if the whole population had been studied. This finding is based on the following two premises:

- The similarity existing among large numbers of a population is great enough for a few to be representative of the entire group.

- The sample taken is large enough to be likely to compensate for errors.

## A.   Selection of the sample

The selection of the sample is obviously very important. The basic requirement is that the selection should be random, or, in other words, that every member of the population should have an equal chance of being selected. This ideal is in fact seldom achieved; most samples are biased to some extent. Finding out as much as possible about the population before designing a sample is one way of eliminating bias. There are many different types of sample design, but all are based on the assumption of random selection. The simplest is unrestricted random sampling.

More valid results are usually obtained from a stratified sample, where the population is divided into groups according to some characteristic such as income levels or geographical regions. Random samples are then taken within each group and the results are weighted according to the proportions of each group within the population and combined. The size of the sample in each stratum should be determined not by the relative size of the population stratum, but by, the amount of variation within each stratum.

## B.   Results

A sample will never provide a perfect representation of the population, because of random errors inherent in sampling. A sample provides not a point estimate but a range of values within which the true value is reasonably sure to lie. This range of random variation can be measured statistically, for it is known that if a large number of samples are taken from the same population, their mean values will form a normal distribution around the mean value of the population, so that 68 per cent of them will lie between the population mean ($\mu$) plus or minus one standard deviation. Thus there is a 68 per cent chance that the mean of one sample lies within this interval. The estimated value of the (unknown) standard deviation of the sample means from the population mean is called the standard error of estimate or standard error of the mean value ($S\mu$).

The formula is:

$$S_\mu = \frac{\sigma}{\sqrt{n}}$$

where $\sigma$ is the standard deviation of the sample mean ($\bar{x}$), and $n$ is the size of the sample.

There is a 68 per cent chance that the true mean lies within the sample mean plus or minus one standard error, and a 95 per cent chance that the true mean lies between the sample mean plus or minus two standard errors. The results of each sample survey of consumers (except in motivation or psychological research) ought to be expressed in terms of the mean and the standard error.

## C.   Statistical techniques

Some of the statistical techniques of basic importance are outlined below.

*Frequency distributions.* When a large amount of numerical data has been collected, it is condensed and presented in tabular form. One development of this form is a frequency distribution in which a set of items, for instance households, is classified according to the values of one or more variable characteristics, such as income. A frequency distribution is shown graphically in a histogram; the number of households in each income group might be represented by the area of one of a number of rectangles.

*Averages.* The next step in analysing figures is to derive statistics that describe them. Averages are the most commonly used and misused of such statistics. An average can be defined as a measure of central tendency, representative of the data that it describes. There are several different kinds of averages, and it is important to choose the best one for any data. The averages most commonly used are the arithmetic mean, the median and the mode, which are illustrated in the following example.

Values: 10,000, 1,800, 1,600, 1,000, 800 (= median), 700, 700, 700, 700;

The median is here the fifth value out of nine (mid-point);

The mode is the most frequently occurring number (i.e. 700)

$$\bar{x} = \frac{\Sigma_x}{n} = \frac{18,000}{9} = 2,000$$

where $\Sigma_x$ is the sum of all values (observations) and $n$ the number of observations and $\bar{x}$ is the arithmetic mean of the variable $x$

*Measures of dispersion.* An average is of limited value in describing numerical data unless it is accompanied by some measure of dispersion of the data around the average. The simplest of these measures is the range; in the above example the range is 700 to 10,000. Another measure of dispersion is the mean deviation, which is simply the arithmetic mean of the sum of the deviation of each item from the mean. In the example the mean deviation is:

$$\frac{\Sigma |x - \bar{x}|}{n} = 1,778$$

The signs $||$ indicate that signs are ignored.

A more useful measure of dispersion is the standard deviation. The standard deviation of the arithmetic mean is designated by the Greek letter $\sigma$ and the formula is

$$\sigma = \sqrt{\frac{\Sigma(x - \bar{x})^2}{n}}$$

The deviations from the mean are squared and averaged, and the square root is taken. This measure of dispersion is extremely important in sampling.

*Normal distribution.* When data are dispersed symmetrically around their mean, so that the arithmetic mean equals the median and the mode as well, a normal distribution is attained. This is a basic concept for all sampling. In such a distribution, 68 per cent of all items occur within the range of the mean plus or minus one standard deviation, and 95 per cent of all items occur within the range of the mean plus or minus two standard deviations. Thus a normal distribution is described by the arithmetic mean and the standard deviation. The normal distribution can be represented by the "normal curve". The value of the normal distribution is that many distributions approach it, and that the characteristics of the normal distribution are valid for reasonably normal distributions.

# Annex VIII

# FIELD SURVEYS

The five principal functions involved in field surveys are as follows: sampling; questionnaire design; interviewing; data processing; and interpretation and report writing.

A market survey is an expensive and time-consuming way to forecast demand for a particular product. It also involves extensive field work, the extent depending upon how detailed the survey needs to be. Market surveys can either cover a broad field of inquiry or be related to a specific product. The procedure followed in both cases is fairly similar, though it differs widely in detail. Usually limited market surveys are undertaken as part of a demand and market analysis, in so far as specific products are concerned, to cross-check the results of forecasts made on the basis of one of the forecasting techniques described earlier. Thus, if by use of the trend or end-use technique the market for electrical motors in the higher ranges is defined over a period, the results can be cross-checked through a survey of the principal industrial sectors that would be purchasing such motors.

## A. Consumer surveys

The procedure in the face-to-face interviewing of consumers, for obtaining quantitative or qualitative answers, is presented below.

- Identify the problems and draw up the terms of reference, in consultation with the other interested parties;

- Define the statistical population, or universe, as the foundation of the sampling frame;

- Design the sample, stratified if necessary;

- Decide how many interviews will be needed and select at least the nucleus of the (trained) interviewing team;

- Draft a questionnaire in such a way as to make it as unambiguous as possible to both interviewer and respondent, brief the interviewers, and run a short pilot survey;

- On the basis of the results from the pilot study, formulate the final questionnaire (with coding to facilitate processing of the results);

- Finalize the sampling plan;

- Instruct the interviewers (having selected more if needed) and start interviewing.

- Check the completed questionnaires, as they are returned, for such factors as "interviewer bias";

- Complete the interviewing;

- Collate, make a preliminary analysis of and tabulate the results, applying data-processing operations as required;

- Interpret the results in a written report and present it, perhaps with recommendations.

Success depends, to a large extent, upon the preliminary work and the selection of trained interviewers who must be properly briefed and supervised. The quality of the fieldwork and the variations in and overall nature of the results need constant attention. Special care must be taken in interpreting the results, in which task the report writer should at the very least participate. Additional tabulations and cross-tabulations are nearly always necessary or desirable.

## B.  Industrial surveys

There are nine broad categories of respondent:

- Manufacturers, processors, assemblers or finishers
- Mining and other extractive enterprises
- Construction and civil engineering companies
- Utilities, notably the generation and distribution of electricity
- Transporters of people, livestock or things
- Re-sellers or traders, agents such as manufacturers' agents
- Government, including senior representatives of foreign Governments
- International agencies, for instance, the Asian Development Bank, the United Nations Children's Fund and the World Bank
- Expert or professional advisers and consultants, for example, architects and engineering consultants

The number of possible customers, compared with that in most consumer markets, is very small. In fact, the universe is occasionally so small that a census must be the preferred method of field research, especially as patterns of purchase tend to be more varied than among consumers. An experienced face-to-face interviewer will sometimes achieve a response rate of 100 per cent in a census or sample survey. A flexible empiricism, rather than theoretical orthodoxy, distinguishes this kind of field survey.

*Sampling.* The procedure typically involves setting approximate quotas geographically, by category of distributor (for example, wholesale or retail), or simply by respondents who represent most of the market, including those within growth sectors (as revealed through the fieldwork).

*Questionnaire.* The questionnaire is characterized by a high incidence of open-ended questions. Occasionally, if there is only one interviewer, a check-list alone is used.

*Interviewers.* Industrial interviewers almost invariably have more formal education than the consumer interviewer. They must be flexible thinkers, but the "gentleman-amateur" can pose a grave threat to the validity of results. The interview must be structured as far as is practicable.

*Calling back.* For some respondents, further inquiries are commonly necessary to establish a basis of comparability regarding important points that emerged during the fieldwork but not in the pilot survey. In that way, pilot interviews can also be "completed" for inclusion in the final results. Where available, the telephone can normally be used for these purposes.

*Collation and analysis.* Processing is frequently manual. Some especially useful data or ideas may have been contributed by one respondent, to whom allocation of a significant amount of space in the written report may be warranted.

*Report.* The report is usually of a somewhat creative character, going beyond market facts to touch on promotional policies and production. The first section is likely to be quantitative, based mainly on the findings of desk research.

# Index

378